Corruption and Reform

A National Bureau
of Economic Research
Conference Report

Corruption and Reform

Lessons from America's
Economic History

Edited by **Edward L. Glaeser and
Claudia Goldin**

The University of Chicago Press

Chicago and London

EDWARD L. GLAESER is professor of economics at Harvard University and director of the John F. Kennedy School of Government's Taubman Center for State and Local Government. He is a research associate of the NBER and the editor of *The Governance of Not-for-Profit Organizations.* CLAUDIA GOLDIN is the Henry Lee Professor of Economics at Harvard University and director of the Development of the American Program and research associate of the NBER. She has written or coedited several books, most recently *The Defining Moment: The Great Depression and the American Economy in the Twentieth Century.*

The University of Chicago Press, Chicago 60637
The University of Chicago Press, Ltd., London
© 2006 by the National Bureau of Economic Research
All rights reserved. Published 2006
Printed in the United States of America
14 13 12 11 10 09 08 07 06   1 2 3 4 5
ISBN: 0-226-29957-0 (cloth)

Library of Congress Cataloging-in-Publication Data

Corruption and reform : lessons from America's economic history /
    edited by Edward L. Glaeser and Claudia Goldin.
        p.   cm. — (A National Bureau of Economic Research
    conference report)
    Includes bibliographical references and index.
    ISBN 0-226-29957-0 (cloth : alk. paper)
        1. Corruption—United States—History. 2. Political corruption—
    United States—History. 3. Corporations—Corrupt practices—
    United States—History. 4. Corruption—United States—Preven-
    tion—History. I. Glaeser, Edward L. (Edward Ludwig), 1967–
    II. Goldin, Claudia Dale. III. Series.

    HV6783 .C784 2006
    364.1′323′9863—dc22

                                                        2005022496

Relation of the Directors to the
Work and Publications of the
National Bureau of Economic Research

1. The object of the NBER is to ascertain and present to the economics profession, and to the public more generally, important economic facts and their interpretation in a scientific manner without policy recommendations. The Board of Directors is charged with the responsibility of ensuring that the work of the NBER is carried on in strict conformity with this object.

2. The President shall establish an internal review process to ensure that book manuscripts proposed for publication DO NOT contain policy recommendations. This shall apply both to the proceedings of conferences and to manuscripts by a single author or by one or more co-authors but shall not apply to authors of comments at NBER conferences who are not NBER affiliates.

3. No book manuscript reporting research shall be published by the NBER until the President has sent to each member of the Board a notice that a manuscript is recommended for publication and that in the President's opinion it is suitable for publication in accordance with the above principles of the NBER. Such notification will include a table of contents and an abstract or summary of the manuscript's content, a list of contributors if applicable, and a response form for use by Directors who desire a copy of the manuscript for review. Each manuscript shall contain a summary drawing attention to the nature and treatment of the problem studied and the main conclusions reached.

4. No volume shall be published until forty-five days have elapsed from the above notification of intention to publish it. During this period a copy shall be sent to any Director requesting it, and if any Director objects to publication on the grounds that the manuscript contains policy recommendations, the objection will be presented to the author(s) or editor(s). In case of dispute, all members of the Board shall be notified, and the President shall appoint an ad hoc committee of the Board to decide the matter; thirty days additional shall be granted for this purpose.

5. The President shall present annually to the Board a report describing the internal manuscript review process, any objections made by Directors before publication or by anyone after publication, any disputes about such matters, and how they were handled.

6. Publications of the NBER issued for informational purposes concerning the work of the Bureau, or issued to inform the public of the activities at the Bureau, including but not limited to the NBER Digest and Reporter, shall be consistent with the object stated in paragraph 1. They shall contain a specific disclaimer noting that they have not passed through the review procedures required in this resolution. The Executive Committee of the Board is charged with the review of all such publications from time to time.

7. NBER working papers and manuscripts distributed on the Bureau's web site are not deemed to be publications for the purpose of this resolution, but they shall be consistent with the object stated in paragraph 1. Working papers shall contain a specific disclaimer noting that they have not passed through the review procedures required in this resolution. The NBER's web site shall contain a similar disclaimer. The President shall establish an internal review process to ensure that the working papers and the web site do not contain policy recommendations, and shall report annually to the Board on this process and any concerns raised in connection with it.

8. Unless otherwise determined by the Board or exempted by the terms of paragraphs 6 and 7, a copy of this resolution shall be printed in each NBER publication as described in paragraph 2 above.

Contents

Acknowledgments

The chapters in this volume were presented on July 30–31, 2004, at the "Corruption and Reform" conference held at the Hawthorne Hotel in Salem, MA. The conference was preceded by a planning session (July 2002) and a preconference (July 2003) at the NBER, Cambridge, MA. We gratefully acknowledge the support of the Center for American Political Studies (CAPS) at Harvard University for the funding of the conference and the NBER for holding the two sessions that preceded the conference. Abigail Peck of CAPS helped with the arrangements in Salem. The discussants at the conference were: Lee Alston, Judith Chevalier, Lawrence F. Katz, Jason Kaufman, Morton Keller, Robert A. Margo (who did double duty as referee for the entire volume), Tomas Nonnenmacher, Paul Rhode, and Susan Rose-Ackerman. We are grateful to all these individuals for improving both the conference and the volume.

I

Corruption and Reform
Definitions and Historical Trends

Corruption and Reform: Introduction

Edward L. Glaeser and Claudia Goldin

Political Corruption: Today and Yesterday

International measures of corruption rank the United States today among the lowest 10 percent of countries worldwide. To most Americans, corruption is something that happens to less fortunate people in poor nations and transition economies.[1] But America's reputation as an untarnished republic is a modern phenomenon.

Conventional histories of nineteenth- and early twentieth-century America portray its corrupt elements as similar, and at times equal, to those found in many of today's modern transition economies and developing regions. Nineteenth-century American urban governments vastly overpaid for basic services, such as street cleaning and construction, in exchange for kickbacks garnered by elected officials. Governments gave away public services for nominal official fees and healthy bribes.[2] As late as the 1950s, reports Robert A. Caro (2002, pp. 403–13), cash-filled envelopes floated in the hallowed halls of the U.S. Senate. Harry Truman made it into

Edward L. Glaeser is a professor of economics at Harvard University and a research associate of the National Bureau of Economic Research. Claudia Goldin is the Henry Lee Professor of Economics at Harvard University and director of the Development of the American Economy program and a research associate of the National Bureau of Economic Research.

1. A growing literature in economic development has documented the extent of corruption in transition economies and poorer nations and its role in reducing economic growth. The literature begins with Mauro (1995) and includes, for example, Hellman, Jones, and Kaufman (2003) and Leite and Weidmann (2002). On the extent and consequences of corruption within a country, see, for example, Di Tella and Schargrodsky (2003), Gaviria (2002), McMillan and Zoido (2004), and Svensson (2003). These empirical papers give support to a theoretical literature (e.g., Rose-Ackerman 1975; Shleifer and Vishny 1993) about the negative consequences of corruption.

2. See, for example, Glaeser (2003), Menes (this volume), and Steffens (1904).

the Senate as an agent of the notoriously corrupt Pendergast machine (McCullough 1992). Some of the greatest U.S. universities were funded by individuals infamous for their roles in extracting public resources through allegedly corrupt political influence—Leland Stanford and George D. Widener, whose surname adorns Harvard's largest library, come to mind. The presidential legacies of Ulysses Grant and Warren Harding were forever marred by the Crédit Mobilier and Teapot Dome scandals, respectively. The list could go on and on.

If the United States was once more corrupt than it is today, then America's history should offer lessons about how to reduce corruption. After all, the dominant political movement of the early twentieth century—Progressivism—was dedicated to the elimination of corruption. From 1901 to 1917, under Presidents T. Roosevelt, Taft, and Wilson, a national legislative and administrative agenda was justified in part by a perceived need to reduce corruption. Municipalities and states throughout the twentieth century regularly elected reform slates that promised to exercise a strong hand to root out corruption. Crusading journalists and ambitious prosecutors have frequently taken aim at corruption. While scholars can debate the impact of these various forces, there is no doubt that U.S. history offers many examples of reform movements that claimed as a primary goal to reduce corruption, similar to the stated goals of reformers in developing countries today.

In this volume we take stock of corruption and reform in American history. Because conceptual clarity is a precondition for measuring the level of and temporal change in corruption, the first three chapters—this introduction, the essay by John Joseph Wallis, and that by Rebecca Menes—each squarely confront what is meant by corruption.

Because corruption is generally illegal, or at least embarrassing, it tends to be hidden and, understandably, as the modern cross-national empirical literature has found, difficult to measure. Time series measurement is yet more difficult. Despite these problems there is great value in searching U.S. history for evidence on corruption and its time trend. Several of the chapters address the measurement of corruption over time. The Menes essay uses information on the number of corrupt mayors and municipal administrations. That by Stanley L. Engerman and Kenneth L. Sokoloff uses evidence on cost overruns for major governmental projects. This introductory essay uses data on the reporting of corruption by hundreds of newspapers for the 160-year period from 1815 to 1975. The contributions by Howard Bodenhorn and Wallis, Price V. Fishback, and Shawn Kantor add evidence on the time path but focus on shorter time periods.

After the discussion of the meaning and measurement of corruption, two of the essays in this volume address the consequences of corruption or of weak legal regimes more generally. Naomi R. Lamoreaux and Jean-Laurent Rosenthal discuss the rise of corporations during the late nineteenth century and how their emergence was accompanied by decreased protection of minority shareholder rights. David Cutler and Grant Miller examine the diffusion of plentiful water in America's cities during an era of legendary municipal corruption. Clearly corruption does not alone determine the extent of public good formation.

According to Lamoreaux and Rosenthal, the number of corporations in the late nineteenth century exploded, despite inadequate protection of minority shareholders, because returns to scale in production increased. Cutler and Miller argue, in a somewhat similar manner, that despite the corruption of municipal governments the increasing availability of municipal credit during the Gilded Age made large-scale water projects feasible. Of course, the increase in municipal credit availability must have had something to do with improvements in accountability, suggesting that some forms of corruption had been curtailed. Both essays suggest that despite substantial corruption in government and fraud in private dealings economic growth was curtailed far less in America than in today's developing economies.

The volume then turns to the causes and consequences of reform. Reform and regulation were often rationalized as tools to protect consumers and workers, but as three of the essays—by Fishback, Bodenhorn, and Marc T. Law and Gary D. Libecap—note, the actual situation was often more complex. Fishback suggests the importance of a Stiglerian view of workplace safety regulation. Workplace safety regulations in the manufacturing and mining industries, he finds, were supported by unions and opposed by certain manufacturers. Because workplace safety laws in manufacturing disproportionately raised costs for small firms, the laws were championed by large firms. Because they were perceived as protecting workers, the laws were supported by unions.

Bodenhorn's essay emphasizes that reform can be the result of self-interested, competing politicians. He analyzes one of the first episodes of anticorruption reform in U.S. history—the fight against corruption in the chartering of New York State banks during the late 1830s. Bodenhorn argues that reform emerged from the Whigs' desire to deprive their opponents—Van Buren's Democratic Regency—of the rents of patronage. Deregulation was the weapon of choice against corruption since reducing chartering requirements limited the ability of government to manage their monopoly in a corrupt manner.

Law and Libecap analyze the origins of today's Food and Drug Administration (FDA) and also emphasize the political roots of reform. Passage of the Pure Food and Drugs Act (1906), which gave rise to the FDA, was driven by a combination of producer interests and consumer concerns about food quality. But concerns about food quality were based more on stories promulgated by political entrepreneurs and the press than on any objective reality. Moreover, political entrepreneurs appear to have manipulated consumer outrage to produce institutions that were, at least in the short run, only moderately aimed at protecting consumer interests.

Corruption is often kept in check by the media, and the role of the press is directly confronted in the chapter by Matthew Gentzkow, Glaeser, and Goldin. In 1870, the press was partisan, histrionic, and prone to omit facts that went against acknowledged political biases. But by 1920, most newspapers eschewed party affiliations, used more moderate and civil language, and made at least a pretense of reporting the facts of the day without spin. The chapter argues that the rise of the independent press and the remarkable transformation in U.S. newspapers between 1870 and 1920 was fundamentally the result of the increasing financial returns to selling newspapers rather than placating politicians for patronage and other reasons. While the essay does not document the impact that the press may have had on corruption, it does discuss circumstantial evidence suggesting that the rise of the independent press was an important factor in movements to reform American political corruption.

A particular outcome of these reform movements—the public ownership of utilities, specifically water provision—is examined by Werner Troesken. Troesken's evidence suggests, paradoxically, that the move to public ownership in the early twentieth century *and* the move away from public ownership seventy-five years later were both associated with gains in service quality. As Troesken notes, the evidence is consistent either with the view that ownership was productive during the earlier corruption but less productive today, or with Mancur Olson's (1982) view that change in any direction reduces corruption, at least in the short run, because of the ossification that all bureaucracies incur after some time.[3]

Wallis, Fishback, and Kantor, in the last chapter of the volume, look specifically at the presence of corruption in the provision of public relief, such as welfare and unemployment insurance. The move to federal provision in public relief, they argue, played a major role in reducing corruption in the welfare system. The institutional change occurred because the effectiveness and credibility of the Roosevelt administration would have been seriously hampered by allegations of corruption. While those in the Roosevelt administration would not have enjoyed the benefits that local leaders would from a corrupt welfare system, they would have incurred most of the costs. Because of the separation between national and local authority, Franklin Roosevelt had a strong incentive to place checks on corruption. These checks, it appears, substantially reduced the amount of corruption that developed. This chapter, and that by Bodenhorn, suggest the roles that separation of powers and intergovernmental competition can play in bringing about effective reform.

---

3. Thomas Jefferson's often-cited quotation makes a similar point: "The tree of liberty must be refreshed from time to time with the blood of patriots and tyrants."

Corruption: Definitions and Theory

As Wallis's essay makes clear, the term *corruption* has its origins in an analogy between the state and the human body. In its first incarnation, corruption referred to the process by which a well-functioning system of government decays into one that fails to deliver and maltreats its citizens. According to the Greek historian Polybius (c. 200–120 BCE), monarchy corrupts into tyranny, aristocracy into oligarchy, and democracy into mob rule.

During the nineteenth century, the definition of corruption morphed into one specifically related to the bribery of public officials by private agents. Bribery was generally an illicit payment in exchange for some government controlled resource, such as a service, a public property, or an exemption from government regulation. These forms of bribery, detailed in the chapter by Menes, form the lion's share of what is known about nineteenth-century municipal corruption. City governments were corrupt in the purchase of inputs, such as street cleaning or construction services, and bribes were routinely given in exchange for overpayment for these inputs. City governments were corrupt in the distribution of publicly owned property—land or access to a port—that was sold, not to the highest bidder for the good of the citizens, but to the most generous briber for the benefit of the few. Finally, city governments were corrupt in the administration of rules, such as prohibitions on gambling and prostitution, and officials accepted bribes for leniency in the administration of such regulations.

In this volume we will use the word *corruption* to refer to what Wallis terms "venal corruption." We view corruption to have three central elements: (a) payments to public officials beyond their salaries; (b) an action associated with these payments that violates either explicit laws or implicit social norms; and (c) losses to the public either from that action or from a system that renders it necessary for actions to arise only from such payment. Two examples from the volume illustrate how these elements describe corruption.

Engerman and Sokoloff discuss overpayment in the construction of antebellum U.S. canals. Corruption, if it occurred, would take the form of excessively large government payments for inputs that would be accompanied by bribes to legislators and a waste of government funding. Notably, if government pays too much for a project relative to a private purchaser but the overpayment was not accompanied by payments to government officials, corruption (according to the definition) has not occurred. Government inefficiency and bureaucratic stupidity are not equivalent to corruption. We believe this definition of corruption accords well with common usage.

The Bodenhorn essay discusses how state banks received charters in the 1830s after paying bribes to the New York Regency machine. In this case, payments were made to public officials. Although the actions taken did not violate any existing law, they did, it appears, infringe upon a social norm concerning quid pro quo exchanges of cash for licenses. The social losses did not, it appears, come from the act of chartering, which was probably beneficial, but from the system that made charters valuable by limiting entry into the banking sector.

Within this broad definition are a number of different types of corruption. Most modern corruption is illegal, but there are forms of legal corruption. One prominent example of the latter is given by George Washington Plunkitt's description of honest graft (see Riordon 1905). Honest graft, in Plunkitt's terminology, is the gain of wealth by public officials through private information, such as the proposed route of a new highway. The expropriation of this information involved a loss of wealth to the public, but it was not necessarily illegal. However, as shown by Plunkitt's need to defend his actions and by Progressive Era outrage at actions of this nature, Plunkitt's dealings were in conflict with social norms. Plunkitt's form of corruption involved payments to public officials, losses to the general public (if Plunkitt had not bought the property, its prior owner would have benefited from the public purchase), and a violation of a social norm. In general, as societies develop and as social norms get transformed into formal rules, we expect the share of corruption that is illegal to rise.

While the three-part characterization—excessive payments, violation of a law or social convention, and social losses—may serve as a reasonable definition of corruption, it is only a beginning in helping us measure corruption. The definition suggests ways of measuring the extent of corruption. First, in principle, one can measure corruption by the payments to public officials, perhaps relative to the formal payments received by the same officials. McMillan and Zoido (2004) use this type of methodology in their study of corruption in Peru. This measure would provide some sense about the importance of corruption in the public sector, but it might correlate only weakly with the social costs of corruption.

A second method of measuring corruption would focus on the frequency with which laws are violated. Studies that focus on corruption convictions (such as Glaeser and Saks 2004) attempt to measure corruption by counting the number of times a court finds that corruption laws have been violated. Since we have no natural measure of the number of possible opportunities to be corrupt, the measure lacks a natural denominator, although the size of government might be used.

A third approach is to focus on the social costs of corruption. Even though the social costs from corruption are potentially quite large, measuring them is near impossible. In the developing world, for example, corruption in the education sector may retard long-run economic growth (Reinikka and Svensson 2004). Corruption of the political system may lead to a breakdown in property rights enforcement causing enormous social losses. Payments to officials may be measurable, but those payments are generally transfers, not social costs, and losses to the public coffers may be offset by the payment of lower salaries to officials (as in Becker and Stigler 1974). And even if the social costs of corruption could be measured, one must decide whether to deflate by the size of the economy, the potential size of the economy, or the size of the government, among other reasonable deflators.

A difficult question that reappears throughout this volume, but which is still inadequately answered in the literature, is what the full cost was of corruption in U.S. history. The irony may be that corruption was large as a fraction of government, particularly in the late nineteenth century, but that the economy prospered nationally and locally.

The Determinants of Corruption

The economic approach to corruption (as in Rose-Ackerman 1975) starts with the costs and benefits facing potentially corrupt public officials. Since economics predicts that we should expect to see corruption when the benefits are high and costs are low, it is worth analyzing what factors should impact the benefits and costs of corrupt behavior by a government official. The benefits from being corrupt are determined by the ability of a government official to increase someone's private wealth; the costs come from the expected penalties from being caught.

What determines the ability of a government official to increase someone's private wealth? The most obvious means is to pay the person out of the public purse. In extreme circumstances, the person can just be the official himself; embezzlement is one example of corrupt behavior. More usually, paying someone out of the public purse occurs in exchange for services of some form, either labor or subcontracting. If fees are close to the costs of contracting firms or the opportunity costs of workers, then the opportunities for corruption are limited. If fees are significantly above free market prices, then there is opportunity for corruption in the assignment of work. High public-sector wages and discretion over hiring have traditionally created some of the best opportunities for corrupt earnings.

This simple analysis helps us to understand some of the most popular reforms attempted to arrest corruption. Civil service reform that would take patronage out of the hands of politicians and replace discretion with test-based rules would naturally serve limit the opportunity for corruption, especially when combined with a rigid pay scale for civil servants.[4] Rules concerning procurement fees have also tended to be a popular tool against corruption. Competitive bids for public projects linked to the requirement that the government accept the low cost bid is one of the sim-

4. See, for example, Johnson and Libecap (1994).

plest means of limiting corruption in administration of government projects. The approach relies on the existence of a competitive supply of contractors.

The second means that public officials have to create private wealth is to transfer government property to private individuals for their own profit. The transfer of government land to traction companies was a popular form of corruption in the nineteenth century. Information about future government actions is a more subtle form of in-kind transfer. The returns to corruption in these cases depend on the size of the assets at the government's disposal and the discretion that individuals have in the distribution of these assets.

The third primary means that governments have to create private wealth is the manipulation of legal rulings or the enforcement of rules, such as regulations. Rules banning gambling and prostitution, for example, create the opportunity to extract bribes from potential providers. These bribes can be extracted by any and all members in the chain of enforcement. As the amount of regulation increases, the opportunity to extract bribes also rises and leads reformers to fight against regulation and government monopoly (as in Bodenhorn's essay). Conversely, the connection between the intrusiveness of regulation and the ability to extract bribes creates an incentive for politicians to push for further regulation.

Even in a libertarian's dream world where government is restricted to resolving disputes over property rights, there would still be considerable scope for corruption in the arbitration of these disputes. Every dispute over ownership creates the possibility for a corrupt ruling. After all, a corrupt judge can extract bribes even when he rules in favor of the rightful owner. As the legal system has the ability to redistribute all of the wealth in society, the opportunities for corruption within the system are enormous. As corruption within the courts destroys the clear definition of property rights, this corruption has the potential to turn the libertarian dream into a Hobbesian nightmare. In practice, this ability may be limited by the ability of private litigants to rely on private arbitration and avoid a corrupt legal system.

Together these factors suggest that the benefits from corrupt practices for bribe-taking politicians or bribe-giving businessmen will rise with the size and discretion of the government and the amount of social and economic regulation. Benefits from corruption will also rise when the size of assets or damages involved in property rights disputes increases (Glaeser and Shleifer 2003). The late nineteenth century was a period of increasingly larger governments, more valuable public assets, more aggressive regulation, and bigger-stakes litigation. The potential benefits from corruption rose along almost every conceivable dimension. The prediction is an absolute increase in the total amount of corruption (measured in either bribes given or in social losses). But the increase in corruption might not translate into an increase relative to the size of government or the size of the economy.

The limits on corruption have customarily come from three sources: legal penalties, career or social costs, and internal psychic pain. Thus, the overall costs of corruption come from the size of the potential penalties and the probability that these costs are imposed that are in turn a function of information flows, social opprobrium, and the legal system.

The most obvious parameter influencing the cost of illegal corruption is the stated legal penalty for corrupt practices (the cost of corruption that violates social norms, but not laws, will not be connected to legal penalties). While this is certainly obvious, it is also important to remember that these penalties have changed significantly over time. For example, while Plunkitt's honest graft—the use of insider information by politicians to enrich themselves—was surely corruption, at least by our definition, it was fully legal during Plunkitt's time. Even the gifts of railway stock given to congressmen and others during the Crédit Mobilier scandal were perfectly legal at the time. In the 1790s, the number of laws regarding corruption was so modest that legal penalties against corruption were often negligible. Since that time, there has been a steady increase in the range of behaviors by public officials that are punishable by law and a steady increase in the attempt to craft laws, such as the RICO statute, that render illegal as yet unspecified forms of corrupt behavior.[5]

Although the number of political activities proscribed by law has generally increased with time, the trend of enforcement is less clear. We do not know the probability of being convicted for a corrupt practice in the past as well as today. Even when we know the number of convictions, we do not know the number of corrupt actions that could have led to a conviction. Enforcement requires both an initial report informing the police or the public about the corrupt action and a legal proceeding that responds to the report. Initial reports informing the public about corruption have been made mainly by third parties or by investigators from some branch of government separated from the actual corruption. As the Gentzkow, Glaeser, and Goldin chapter reminds us, the press played a major role in exposing scandals like Crédit Mobilier and Teapot Dome. However, in some cases, such as the famous exposure of the Tweed Ring's corruption by the press, exposure was initiated by a rival politician. In the more modern era, journalistic careers, such as those of investigative reporters Robert Woodward and Carl Bernstein, writing for the *Washington Post,* have been made through intrepid uncovering of governmental malfeasance.

Government does, however, occasionally police itself. Today there are hundreds of prosecutions of state and local officials by federal investiga-

---

5. RICO is the acronym for the Racketeer Influenced and Corrupt Organizations Act, passed by Congress in 1970.

tors under the national Corrupt Practices Act. The Tweed Ring faced legal prosecution not by local city police, who were often part of the ring, but rather through prosecution by officials of New York State. Today, perhaps 80 percent of public corruption prosecutions are brought by federal officials (Corporate Crime Reporter 2004). Separation of powers and federalism create rivalries between different government actors, and these rivalries create incentives to uncover and prosecute corruption. Of course, the true importance of self-policing is understated because in cases where internal monitoring functions well, corruption is unlikely to occur.

To generate legal penalties, the uncovering of corruption must be followed by successful legal prosecution, which in turn requires an independent judiciary and judges who are willing to convict officials found guilty of corruption. Conviction will occur if the legal system is itself free from corruption. But even if judges are themselves corrupt, they may still be willing to convict corrupt politicians if their political interests conflict with those of the accused politicians. Judges appointed by a Republican machine, even if they were completely complicit in that machine's corruption, would still be willing to convict a corrupt representative of an urban Democratic machine. The rise of professionalism in the judiciary has meant that it is increasingly less likely that a corrupt politician can count on a friendly judge to be lenient.

Even if the judicial system is dormant, the revelation of corruption can still create costs if the exposure damages a politician's career or social standing. For a politician, career costs typically depend on the willingness of voters to oust corrupt officials. The track record of the electorate is mixed in this area. Many notoriously corrupt officials have been re-elected, perhaps because the corruption is funneled back to voters or because voters are sufficiently cynical (or realistic) that they think that political challengers are likely to be no less corrupt than the incumbent. The political career of James Michael Curley, whose corrupt actions eventually landed him in jail, was in real danger only when he faced political challengers who combined a clean image with the same aggressive Hibernianism—Irish-Catholic jingoism—that Curley championed. Naturally, the role of career concerns suggests that corruption will be more costly in areas with robust competition between two or more political parties.

The Time Path of Corruption in the United States

Because it is important to have a sense of the time trend, we offer our assessment of the relative magnitude of corruption across U.S. history. We know that the evidence we employ is open to discussion and will be subject to debate. But we will argue from several sources that there is reason to believe that corruption increased during the first three-quarters of the nineteenth century or was at a high level in the antebellum era with much temporal variance. The most important of our findings is the decline in American corruption from the mid-1870s to the 1920s.

Our measure uses public documents—newspapers—to proxy for reported crimes. Although there are no historical victimization surveys or crime reports, corruption was reported in the press. There are reasons to question newspaper reporting as an indicator of the underlying facts (the Gentzkow, Glaeser, and Goldin chapter emphasizes the changing bias of the media), but given the absence of other measures, media coverage of corruption offers one possible means of assessing the amount of *reported* corruption.

With the advent of optical scanning technology, there are now a large number of digitally searchable newspapers published in the United States, some going back to the late eighteenth century. The drawback of using newspapers is that reporting often differs from the underlying reality. Changes in reporting can reflect changes in the newspaper market rather than actual changes in corrupt activity.

Our approach is to search for the words "corruption" and "fraud" (and their variants, such as "corrupt" and "fraudulent") and to count the appearance of articles (or pages) containing these words. This count gives us a measure of the amount of space newspapers gave to stories about corruption and fraud. We then deflate these counts by the number of articles (or pages) containing the words "January" or "political" (and its variants). This count gives us a measure of the overall size of the newspaper (in the case of "January") or the overall amount of attention given to politically relevant stories (in the case of "political"). Our results are not particularly sensitive to the exact choice of deflator words.[6] Deflating by the word "political" might be seen as a word count equivalent of trying to measure corruption divided by the size of government. Deflating by the word "January" might be seen as a word count analogy of trying to measure corruption divided by the size of the overall economy.

We use two sources that are available electronically online in fully searchable editions: the *New York Times* (available from Proquest) and a large group of small-town newspapers (available from Ancestry.com).[7] The *New York Times* has several advantages. Because it is a single newspaper, the series does not have a changing composition of papers. The *Times* is among the most serious American papers historically, and by the late nine-

---

6. The difference between the "January" and "political" deflators is most pronounced in the early, pre-1860 era because the majority of newspaper stories in the antebellum period were political. As newsprint prices plummeted, more attention was devoted to other types of stories and features.

7. By "small-town newspapers" we mean papers such as the *Bangor Daily Whig and Courier* (Bangor, ME), the *Lorain Standard* (Elyria, OH), the *Adams Sentinel* (Gettysburg, PA), the *Janesville Gazette* (Janesville, WI), the *Morning Oregonian* (Portland, OR), and the *Statesville Landmark* (Statesville, NC).

teenth century it was unlikely to have made unsubstantiated claims about corruption or knowingly omitted major stories on corruption.

Relying on the *Times* has the disadvantages that it affords us primarily a picture of New York City. Furthermore, its reporting begins in 1851 with the establishment of the paper. To supplement the evidence from the *Times,* we use a large collection of newspapers available from www.ancestry.com, a website containing sources including the U.S. population censuses and immigration records of particular value to genealogists.[8] The papers are geographically spread throughout the United States mainly from small cities and towns and have fairly good coverage by the early nineteenth century. The disadvantage is that the composition of papers changes over time. Although neither series is perfect, they yield a remarkably similar picture for the century of overlap.

We have presented in figure 1 three series given as three-year centered moving averages to smooth the data. The series that are deflated by "political" are remarkably close in the period of overlap (the correlation coefficient between the two series is 0.943 for the period 1852 to 1960).[9] If the variation in corruption reporting were caused by reporting fads or changes in the market for news, these fads and market changes must have had a remarkable consistency between New York City and small-town America.

One check on the series is to see whether the reporting corresponds well with known facts about corruption. Do peaks in the series occur during periods known to have contained considerable corruption? Table 1 gives thumbnail sketches of the stories during the local peaks in "corruption" and "fraud" in figure 1.

The first great boom in corruption reporting occurred around the 1840 election. Stories of corruption during this period focused on Tammany Hall and also Martin Van Buren, the first president who owed his success to a political machine (for a description of Van Buren's activities in the banking sector, see the Bodenhorn essay).[10] The next peak in corruption reporting occurred between 1857 and 1861 and focused on voting irregularities in Kansas. There is a global peak in the 1870s during the Grant administration. Top stories concerned Crédit Mobilier, the Whiskey Ring, and southern Reconstruction and the Ku Klux Klan. Finally, there is a small local peak in the late 1920s during the era of prohibition and the Teapot Dome scandal. The *New York Times* series is similar and shows basic patterns that conform to our notions about periods of major corruption in U.S. history.

Both series reveal one major trend: reporting on corruption declined be-

---

8. Because the Ancestry.com site is updated almost daily, we did the counts during a short interval.

9. The correlation is likely enhanced by the copying by small-town newspapers from the larger city papers and also by the use of wire services.

10. There was also a brief advertising craze concerning remedies for "corrupted livers."

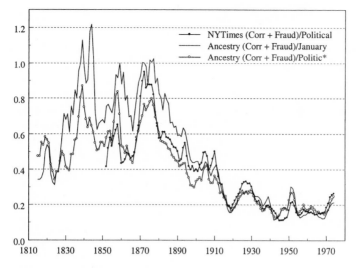

Fig. 1   Indexes of corruption and fraud: 1815–1975

Sources: NYTimes: online, fully searchable edition of the *New York Times* from ProQuest Information and Learning Company, Ann Arbor, Michigan. Ancestry: Ancestry.com, part of MyFamily.com, Inc., Provo, Utah.

Notes: The series for the *New York Times* gives counts of the words "corrupt*" and "fraud*" divided by counts of the word "political," where an asterisk (*) indicates that all variants are selected. The search engine (Proquest) gives the number of separate *articles* containing at least one "hit." The series for Ancestry gives counts of the words "corrupt*" and "fraud*" divided by counts of the word "politic*." The search engine (Ancestry.com) gives the number of newspaper *pages* containing at least one hit. The number of separate newspapers changes over time, as does the mix of papers. For example, the numbers at five-year intervals from 1820 to 1935 are

1820	3	1850	10	1880	42	1910	48
1825	3	1855	16	1885	46	1915	51
1830	10	1860	18	1890	53	1920	47
1835	4	1865	18	1895	53	1925	41
1840	6	1870	19	1900	45	1930	37
1845	8	1875	33	1905	50	1935	33

Because newspapers are constantly added at Ancestry.com, the numbers apply to those as of July 2004. All series in figure 1 are expressed as three-year centered moving averages.

tween 1870s and the 1920s. The decline, moreover, is concentrated in both series from the mid-1870s to 1890 and in the 1910s. In the 1870s our index (deflated by "political") was greater than 0.8, but ever since 1930, the index has hovered around 0.2. If these series reflect anything about reality then it is hard not to conclude that there was a significant secular decline in corruption.

The earliest period of a sustained decline in reporting on corruption and fraud occurred from the mid-1870s to 1890. At the national level, the period begins at the end of the scandal-ridden Grant administration. At the local level, the period was one of reform in New York city under "Honest"

Time period	Index	Corruption and fraud events
1820	0.567	Impeachment proceedings against the governor of Pennsylvania (most of the available newspapers in Ancestry.com were from PA).
1837–45	0.611 to 0.870	Whig accusations of corruption by the Van Buren administration, particularly in 1840 (election year). After Harrison died in office, the Tyler assumption of the presidency brought charges of corruption by those who thought he should be an interim president. Tammany Hall corruption scandals also dotted the news.
1857–59	0.711 to 0.837	Voting irregularities after the Kansas-Nebraska Act. The pro-slave voting by Missourians in the Kansas elections and the "Lecompton Constitution" were deemed fraudulent and corrupt.
1870–79	0.876 to 1.03	Voter intimidation in the South by the Ku Klux Klan. Various aspects of Reconstruction (including carpetbaggers, use of federal money by the Radicals, and the Freedmen's Bureau) were deemed corrupt. The 1872 election, Greeley's alleged connections to Tammany Hall. The Crédit Mobilier corruption scandal and various criticisms of the Union Pacific Railroad. Other corruption during the Grant administration, including the Whiskey Ring. The 1876 Democratic candidate, Tilden, was known for breaking the Tweed Ring and the Canal Ring, and this made corruption a major issue in the presidential election. The election was heavily contested, and although Tilden appears to have won the popular vote a senatorial committee awarded the disputed electoral votes to Hayes.
1893	0.635	No single or major issue. Financial panic appears to have led people to place blame. Three major railroads collapsed, and stock fraud was discussed. Land grant fraud in the Northern Great Plains was alleged. Corrupt appointments in the Cleveland administration were discussed, as were claims that continued exclusion of southern Democrats from Congress would lead to corruption.
1925–28	0.264 to 0.274	The Teapot Dome scandal of the early 1920s was raised during the 1928 presidential election as an indication of Coolidge's corruption. Albert Fall was tried for his involvement in Teapot Dome. Andrew Mellon, treasury secretary, was investigated. Also the barring and subsequent reinstatement of Alfred Smith from his Senate seat for corrupt fundraising. Speakeasies and other "corrupt" ways to get around Prohibition and the power of organized crime. Congress passed the Corrupt Practices Act in 1925 governing campaign expenditures.
1951–52	0.269	Scandal in the Internal Revenue Service (IRS) led to the dismissal of many people and the discovery of misuse of funds in the Reconstruction Finance Corporation. Kefauver headed Senate committee to examine influence of organized crime in the government and exposed many.

John Kelly, whose administration was far cleaner than that of Boss Tweed. It seems reasonable that the decline in our index reflects a cleansing of politics, even though the decline occurred during the heart of the Gilded Age.

The first period of decline in our index is followed by one of stability from about 1895 to 1908. The period—a high point of the Progressive Era—does not seem likely to have been a moment when reform stood still. Instead, a more reasonable reading of the evidence is that even if reform continued, the vast attention paid to corruption by muckraking journalists meant that our series is stable despite continuing reductions in corruption. Perhaps it is worthwhile noting that, contrary to the view that Progressive Era muckrakers brought to the media a new awareness of corruption, our series suggests that such attention was much higher before. Our series, however, cannot reveal whether the informational content of the Progressive Era muckrakers was substantially higher than the more histrionic reporting of the earlier era.

The second period of decline occurs between 1908 and 1917. This period was legitimately one of significant reform, and it is certainly possible that corruption dropped greatly during this era. It is also conceivable that increasing coverage of the Great War may well have pushed corruption off of the front pages. After this period, there is a rise in the late 1920s, but even during that period, reporting on corruption never approaches the levels of the middle nineteenth century. By the 1930s corruption in the United States was far lower than in the nineteenth century, if the content of the press is any indication.

The time path shown by these series is compatible with mainstream histories of the period. The traditional view of much of the nineteenth century is that it was replete with great corruption, and the traditional view of the early twentieth century (see, for example, Hofstadter 1955) is that Progressive Era reforms were effective and that corruption actually fell. Furthermore, scattered evidence on conviction in high places also supports the downward trend observed in the index. For example, while charges of venal corruption were regularly leveled against nineteenth-century New York City mayors like Fernando Wood, Oakey Hall (a member of the Tweed Ring), and Robert Van Wyck, no New York City mayor since William O'Dwyer, fifty years ago, has been seriously accused of corrupt activity. Indeed, since Van Wyck more than 100 years ago, only O'Dwyer and James Walker seem to have been notably corrupt.

The time series gives clear evidence for a decline in corruption since the mid-1870s, but the evidence on the early part of the nineteenth century is more mixed. Our point estimates for the antebellum and immediate postbellum era indicate a steady rise in reporting about corruption between 1815 and 1850 and no change from about 1850 to 1870. The pattern is consistent with the rise in government budgets and the scale of the economy (as argued by Glaeser and Shleifer 2003). Although the data are consistent with the view that corruption followed an arc, first rising between 1815 and 1850 and then falling after 1870, the evidence for the early rise is weaker than that supporting the subsequent fall.

The findings on the time path of corruption gleaned from newspaper reporting are corroborated both by the Menes essay and the Engerman and Sokoloff essay in this volume. Menes argues that the history of corruption in urban machines follows roughly the time pattern given in figure 1—first rising and then falling. Engerman and Sokoloff argue that despite widespread accusations of corruption, early canal construction was relatively honest, although later canal construction was probably highly corrupt. Because canals were a large fraction of public projects in the antebellum era, corruption may have been high. Their evidence for the latter period is mixed. Although large public projects in the twentieth century had vast cost overruns, Engerman and Sokoloff find limited evidence of corruption.

Reform and the Fight against Corruption

To understand changes in corruption and its prosecution over time, it is vital to have a theory of reform in addition to one of corruption. Reform is probably the more difficult of the two tasks because it is rarely a unilateral decision.[11]

The essays in this volume deal with three main theories about the rise of reform. The first theory views institutional change as welfare maximizing and argues that institutional reform is more likely to succeed the higher are the social benefits of reform. This view dominated mid-twentieth-century historical writings on reform including the oft-cited volume by Hofstadter (1955). A second, revisionist theory follows Stigler (1971) and emphasizes the power of certain producers in shaping regulation. According to this view, regulation and reform fit the needs of big producers who want to increase their generally smaller rivals' costs. Finally, a third theory (suggested by Law and Libecap in this volume) argues that reform is driven by political entrepreneurs who sometimes gain support through the manipulation of popular opinion and the tools of government.

The welfare-maximizing view of reform was that espoused by reformers, such as Theodore Roosevelt, Woodrow Wilson, Herbert Croly, and John Landis. This optimistic view implies that reform movements should arise when the net social benefits of reform outweigh the costs. If this is correct, we should see corruption-reducing federal control over welfare programs whenever the benefits exceed the costs of central control, such as a lesser ability to target welfare most accurately or a weighty bureaucracy or the

---

11. For example, reform has seldom been credited to a particular political leader. Although there have been exceptions, as in the cases of the two Roosevelts and Woodrow Wilson, even their efforts are best seen as culminations of lengthy reform movements.

fixed costs of reform itself. According to Wallis, Fishback, and Kantor, federal oversight of New Deal relief eliminated corruption that had been endemic to transfer programs at the state and local levels. We should expect to see more reform when corruption is high, possibly resulting from an ossified system as in Olson (1965; see also the Troesken essay), or because exogenous variables have increased the returns to corruption. This view also predicts that reform will occur when the cost of introducing reformed institutions decreases, perhaps due to more-educated and better-informed elites with greater abilities to monitor such institutions.

The second, revisionist, view of reform argues that reform is controlled by well-organized special interest groups. In the case of regulation of industry, the relevant interest groups are big firms. According to this view we should see more reform when the benefits it provides to big firms are greater or when their political clout is greater. One somewhat surprising implication of this Stiglerian view is that it suggests that Progressive Era reform and regulation may not have signaled the triumph of popular sovereignty over business interests but rather the triumph of particular businesses over the state.

The third view of reform looks neither to special interest groups nor to public welfare as a whole, but to political entrepreneurs. According to this view, reforms are put forward by political entrepreneurs who seek either to get elected on a reforming ticket or be appointed to some new administrative body created as a result of reform. In the case of a perfectly informed electorate, this view and the first, welfare-maximizing, view of reform become identical. But in cases where the electorate is less than perfectly informed and its opinions can be shaped by entrepreneurs (as in the Law and Libecap essay), this view of reform yields different positive predictions about when we should expect to see reform. It also yields different predictions about the welfare benefits of reform and implies that reform may be socially costly.

One variant on this theory is that the "cry of reform" is basically the natural complement to accusing one's opponent of being corrupt, and any challenger, unless the opponent is known to be squeaky clean, will be tempted to make the accusation. A natural impediment to the cry of reform occurs when the challenger has been part of the system, and another is that reforms generally reduce rents to politicians when they get elected. Thus, reform is most likely to be championed by political entrepreneurs who have not been part of the system and who are unlikely to be able to take advantage of corruption (as in the Bodenhorn essay).

There is no question that each of these theories has been important during certain epochs of reform, and each of these theories can potentially explain the time path of reform over the last 150 years. Glaeser and Shleifer (2003) argue that Progressive Era reforms were necessary because an increasing scale of enterprise made old institutions unable to handle increasing incentives for corruption. As such, early twentieth-century reform was a response to the increased corruption created by increased scale. A Stiglerian view is that increased scale and business power naturally led to business-friendly reforms. Finally, changes in public literacy and sophistication, the media, the size of government, and the returns to offices might have all acted together to give political entrepreneurs greater ability and desire to sell reform to the public. Therefore, it is difficult to disentangle the relative importance of the three theories of reform. They are touched on by many of the essays in this volume.

Conclusion

Corruption within the United States appears to have followed something of an arc, beginning at a high level with a small increase and ending with a spectacular decrease.[12] The early period in U.S. history was probably a bit less corrupt than the Gilded Age that followed. But rule breaking in the modern era is far more circumspect than in the early twentieth century. If there was a rise in corruption across the nineteenth century, the rise can be easily explained by the increasing scale of both government and the economy. Vast increases in the budgets of local governments greatly increased the potential benefits of corruption. It would be surprising if corruption had not increased between 1800 and 1870.

But the decline in corruption between the mid-1870s and 1920 was not associated with declining returns to corruption. The size of the government continued to rise, and the returns from corruption in the judiciary increased as well. The big change over the twentieth century has been in the costs facing corrupt politicians. In 1900, many actions we would now prosecute were legal. Governments rarely prosecuted themselves, and the higher levels of government were sufficiently weak that they could not provide a check on local corruption. Newspapers had long provided exposure of corrupt practices, but in many smaller cities the news media were sufficiently tied to the political establishment that it was unlikely to trumpet information unfavorable to that establishment.

By the early twentieth century, the full apparatus of modern checks on corruption was in place. Rules had generally replaced discretion in many areas, such as patronage. Different levels of government more effectively patrolled each other. Greater competition and political independence in the news media meant that corrupt activities and charges of corruption were more likely to be reported everywhere in America, not just in the big cities. Finally, voter expectations about corrupt behavior had changed, and revealed corruption was more likely to lead to political defeat.

---

12. By "corruption" we mean a measure that is deflated by the size of the economy or government.

Because the costs of corruption rose along so many margins, it is hard to determine what particular factor or set of factors was most important. Still, American history does provide a striking story of a country that changed from a place where political bribery was a routine event infecting politics at all levels to a nation that now ranks among the least corrupt in the world.

References

Becker, Gary S., and George Stigler, J. 1974. Law enforcement, malfeasance, and compensation of enforcers. *Journal of Legal Studies* 3 (January): 1–18.

Caro, Robert A. 2002. *The years of Lyndon Johnson*. Vol. 3, *Master of the Senate*. New York: Alfred A. Knopf.

Corporate Crime Reporter. 2004. Public corruption in the United States. Report. http://www.corporatecrimereporter.com/corruptreport.pdf

Di Tella, Rafael, and Ernesto Schargrodsky. 2003. The role of wages and auditing during a crackdown on corruption in the city of Buenos Aires. *Journal of Law and Economics* 46 (April): 269–92.

Gaviria, Alejandro. 2002. Assessing the effects of corruption and crime on firm performance: Evidence from Latin America. *Emerging Markets Review* 3 (3): 245–68.

Glaeser, Edward. 2003. Public ownership in the American city. In *Urban issues and public finance: Essays in honor of Dick Netzer,* ed. Amy E. Schwartz, 130–62. Northhampton, MA: Edward Elgar.

Glaeser, Edward, and Raven Saks. 2004. Corruption in America. NBER Working Paper no. 10821. Cambridge, MA: National Bureau of Economic Research, October.

Glaeser, Edward, and Andrei Shleifer. 2003. The rise of the regulatory state. *Journal of Economic Literature* 41 (June): 401–25.

Hellman, Joel, Geraint Jones, and Daniel Kaufmann. 2003. Seize the state, seize the day: State capture and influence in transition economics. *Journal of Comparative Economics* 31 (December): 751–73.

Hofstadter, Richard. 1955. *The age of reform*. New York: Vintage Books.

Johnson, Ronald N., and Gary Libecap. 1994. *The federal civil service system and the problem of bureaucracy: The economics and politics of institutional change.* Chicago: University of Chicago Press.

Leite, Carlos, and Jens Weidmann. 2002. Does Mother Nature corrupt? Natural resources, corruption, and economic growth. In *Governance, corruption, and economic performance,* ed. George T. Abed and Sanjeev Gupta, 159–96. Washington, DC: International Monetary Fund.

Mauro, Paulo. 1995. Corruption and growth. *Quarterly Journal of Economics* 110 (August): 681–712.

McCullough, David D. 1992. *Truman.* New York: Simon and Schuster.

McMillan, John, and Pablo Zoido. 2004. How to subvert democracy: Montesinos in Peru. CEPR Discussion Paper no. 4361. London: Centre for Economic Policy Research, April.

Olson, Mancur. 1965. *The logic of collective action: Public goods and the theory of groups.* Cambridge, MA: Harvard University Press.

————. 1982. *The rise and decline of nations: Economic growth, stagflation, and economic rigidities.* New Haven, CT: Yale University Press.

Reinikka, Ritva, and Jakob Svensson. 2004. Local capture: Evidence from a central government transfer program in Uganda. *Quarterly Journal of Economics* 119 (May): 679–706.

Riordon, William L. 1905. Plunkitt of Tammany Hall: A series of very plain talks on very practical politics delivered by George Washington Plunkitt the ex-senator, the Tammany philosopher. Repr., New York: Knopf Press, 1948.

Rose-Ackerman, Susan. 1975. The economics of corruption. *Journal of Public Economics* 4 (February): 187–203.

Shleifer, Andrei, and Robert Vishny. 1993. Corruption. *Quarterly Journal of Economics* 108 (August): 599–617.

Steffens, Lincoln. 1904. *The shame of the cities.* Repr., New York: Amereon, 1957.

Stigler, George J. 1971. The theory of economic regulation. *Bell Journal of Economics and Management Science* 2 (Spring): 3–21.

Svensson, Jakob. 2003. Who must pay bribes and how much? Evidence from a cross section of firms. *Quarterly Journal of Economics* 118 (February): 207–30.

1

The Concept of Systematic Corruption in American History

John Joseph Wallis

> What is really educational and beneficial to students of history
> is the clear view of the causes of events, and the consequent
> power of choosing the better policy in a particular case. Now
> in every practical undertaking by a state we must regard as the
> most powerful agent for success or failure the form of its con-
> stitution; for from this as from a fountainhead all conceptions
> and plans of action not only proceed, but attain their consum-
> mation.
> —*The Histories of Polybius,* Book VI

Ever since Aristotle identified that the "true forms of government, therefore, are those in which the one, the few, or the many govern with a view to
the common interests," political philosophers and practitioners have been
concerned about corrupt governments: those perverted forms that "rule
with a view to the private interest" (1996, book III, 1279ᵃ, pp. 29–33). Aristotle, Polybius, Machiavelli and the sixteenth-century Italians, Harrington
and the seventeenth- and eighteenth-century English writers who became
known as Whigs or commonwealthmen, and Madison, Hamilton, and
other American founders all grappled with the problem of corruption.
Their search for an incorruptible form of true government required that
they understand how corruption perverted government. Their ideas about
corruption ranged from the moral and ethical values of princes and people
to features of legal systems and political institutions. In the late seven-

John Joseph Wallis is a professor of economics at the University of Maryland and a research associate of the National Bureau of Economic Research.

This paper originated in a series of conversations with Claudia Goldin, whom I gratefully acknowledge. Without her support and encouragement it never would have been written. Ed
Glaeser challenged me to extend the paper further back in time, a license I took advantage of.
Conversations with Naomi Lamoreaux, Lee Alston, Steve Webb, and William Novak, as well
as the discussion of Morton Keller at the first preconference, while not specifically on the topic
of this paper, were nonetheless extremely helpful, as were Professor Keller's comments at the final conference. At a critical time, Jeff Smith, Sally Snyder, and Barbara Gill forced me to be
more precise about the concept of systematic corruption. The seminar in Early American History at the University of Maryland gave me a valuable opportunity to present the paper to historians, and their comments were invaluable. Seminars at the Mercatus Center at George Mason University, the economics departments at the University of Maryland, Stanford University,
and the University of California at Irvine, the World Bank, and Universidad Carlos III provided stimulating discussion. This research was supported by National Science Foundation
grants SBR-9709490, SES-0078849, and SES-0241699 Finally, the central idea in the paper developed in conjunction with my ongoing conversations with Barry Weingast and Doug North.

teenth and early eighteenth century a specific concept of corruption, which I call "systematic corruption," crystallized in Britain and spread to the American colonies and France. Having identified the disease, all three societies spent a century or more designing and implementing constitutional reforms to protect their political systems against systematic corruption. Balanced or mixed government was the cure. Modern economic development was the result.

The reawakening of interest among economists about the role that political institutions play in determining economic performance has stimulated a renewed interest in the quality of governance and corruption. While corruption did not disappear from twentieth-century American politics, it has ceased to be a major concern. Concerns over corruption disappeared from American politics because Americans figured out how to control it. This suggests that a longer view of American history may offer insights into how economic and political institutions curb corruption.

The original idea behind this volume was to examine only the Progressive Era, but Americans began grappling with corruption long before the 1890s. As it turns out, Progressive Era reformers and twenty-first-century economists think about corruption in a way that is, in one critical dimension, 180 degrees removed from the concept of corruption that prevailed until the mid-nineteenth century. The title of McCormick's essay, "The Discovery that Business Corrupts Politics," captures the essence of the modern concept of corruption, or, as Shleifer and Vishny define corruption, "the sale by government officials of government property for personal gain" (1993, p. 599).[1]

In contrast, eighteenth-century British—English, Scotch, Irish, and American—political thinkers worried much more that the king and his ministers were manipulating grants of economic privileges to secure political support for a corrupt and unconstitutional usurpation of government powers. The commonwealth indictment of corruption in British government accused the Executive of subordinating parliamentary independence by granting economic privilege in a way that eroded balanced government and, with it, checks on the crown.

Commonwealth thinking shaped American colonial political thought and prepared the colonists to interpret the actions of Crown and Parliament after 1763 as unconstitutional threats to their fundamental liberties as British citizens. Once independent, Americans worried continuously about their governments and how to design their political institutions to limit corruption.[2]

---

1. For other treatments of corruption see Klitgaard (1988); Rose-Ackerman (1978); and Clague (2003).

2. "In the process, the rhetoric of corruption emerged as the common grammar of politics, so overwhelming that it became difficult to discuss public questions in any other language. The age of Jefferson bequeathed to the United States an obsession with corruption that still deeply colors the way we think about politics" (Murrin 1994, p. 104).

What I define as systematic corruption is both a concrete form of political behavior and an idea. In polities plagued with systematic corruption, a group of politicians deliberately create rents by limiting entry into valuable economic activities, through grants of monopoly, restrictive corporate charters, tariffs, quotas, regulations, and the like. These rents bind the interests of the recipients to the politicians who create them. The purpose is to build a coalition that can dominate the government. Manipulating the economy for political ends is systematic corruption. Systematic corruption occurs when politics corrupts economics.

In contrast, venal corruption denotes the pursuit of private economic interests through the political process. Venal corruption occurs when economics corrupts politics. Classical thinkers worried about venal corruption, too. They talked at great length about the moral and ethical corruption of entire peoples and societies, as well as governments. They realized, however, that venal corruption is an inevitable result of human nature. So they focused their intellectual enterprise on designing and then protecting a form of government that could resist systematic corruption. By eliminating systematic corruption, they hoped to mitigate the problems of venal corruption as well.

The economic consequences of systematic corruption are enormous. Venal corruption, by comparison, is small potatoes in terms of social welfare and economic growth. Systematically corrupt governments are rent creating, not rent seeking, governments. The survival of a systematically corrupt government depends on limiting access to markets and resources in order to create rents that bind the interests of the ruling coalition together. Systematic corruption prevents development because it cripples markets. No matter what advice the International Monetary Fund or the World Bank gives to developing countries, it won't work if a country's government remains systematically corrupt.[3]

American history provides an important lesson for modern developing countries about how to eliminate systematic corruption. Not only did some American governments exhibit clear evidence of systematic corruption, but Americans consciously tried to eliminate systematic corruption through changes in their constitutions. The American lesson, however, is not just hard to learn, it is hard to understand in the first place. This is largely the result of changes in language. "Corruption" is an anachronism: it is a word with a meaning two centuries ago that it no longer has today. In the late eighteenth and early nineteenth centuries Americans were fixated on systematic corruption as the nation's primary political problem. They

3. North, Wallis, and Weingast, in "The Natural State," generalize the idea of systematically corrupt governments to include a broad class of political economy organizations that limit economic entry to create rents that are then used to solidify the political systems. Such "natural states" appear to have been dominant for the last 5,000 years of human history, and continue to exist in most countries of the world today.

feared systematic corruption and worried about venal corruption, but they indiscriminately used the same word to identify both.

Corruption is not the only word that poses a problem. British common-wealthmen and the American founders used language about the dangers of slavery, tyranny, conspiracy, and corruption that seem to us so highly exaggerated that it must have been purely rhetorical, or even propagandistic. The great contribution of Bernard Bailyn was to demonstrate that Whigs and American revolutionaries, in fact, believed exactly what they were saying.[4] Fears that corruption would lead to tyranny and slavery don't make sense to us today—after all, we know how the American Revolution turned out. But at the end of the eighteenth century, Americans were surrounded by countries ruled by tyrants and populated by citizens who did not possess a full measure of liberty and self-determination, the eighteenth-century definition of slavery.[5]

Paradoxically, British and American citizens believed they lived under the best system of constitutional government ever devised, one where a mixed and balanced constitution of government protected individual liberties and freedoms. Americans had a deep and abiding fear that if they were not vigilant in protecting their liberties today, their governments would become corrupt and quickly evolve into tyrannies tomorrow. In other words, they worried about what was going to happen next.

The final difficulty in understanding how Americans eliminated systematic corruption in their government is that they did not get it right on the first try. Every American constitution embodied some form of balanced government by 1787, but balanced government alone was not enough to withstand systematic corruption. Americans had more to learn than their British ancestors taught them. Systematic corruption was an inherently constitutional problem that required a constitutional solution. In the 1840s, the states finally understood that mandating open economic entry

4. "I began to see a new meaning in phrases that I, like most historians, had readily dismissed as mere rhetoric and propaganda: 'slavery,' 'corruption,' 'conspiracy'. . . . I began to suspect that they meant something very real to both the writers and their readers: that there were real fears, real anxieties, a sense of real danger behind these phrases, and not merely the desire to influence by rhetoric and propaganda the inert minds of an otherwise passive populace" (Bailyn 1967, p. ix).

5. One of the clearest and most enlightening discussions of what British Whigs and Americans meant when they said "tyranny and slavery" is Quentin Skinner's short essay *Liberty before Liberalism.* "These writers are no less insistent, however, that a state or nation will be deprived of its liberty if it is merely subject or liable to having its actions determined by the will of anyone other than the representatives of the body politic as a whole. It may be that the community is not as a matter of fact governed tyrannically; its rulers may choose to follow the dictates of the law, so that the body politic may not in practice be deprived of any of its constitutional rights. Such a state will nevertheless be counted as living in slavery if its capacity for action is in any way dependent on the will of anyone other than the body of its own citizens" (Skinner 1998, p. 49).

undercut the ability of political factions to create rents and so to manipulate the economic system.[6]

The first section of this paper follows the concept of corruption as it developed in the philosophy of Aristotle, Polybius, Machiavelli, Harrington, through to the eighteenth-century British Whigs. Subsequent sections are devoted to Americans during the Revolution, in the 1790s, the 1830s, and finally the Progressive Era. The paper's fundamental conclusion is that the most basic economic institution in a modern, thriving, developed economy—unlimited free entry and competition unrestricted by government—developed as a solution to systematic corruption: a solution to the political problem of preventing narrow political groups from obtaining uncontested control of governments. The real lesson developing countries can learn from American history is how the United States eliminated systematic corruption. Eliminating systematic corruption required an economic solution to a political problem. Between the 1790s and 1840s, the United States developed a constitutional structure of state governments that mandated free economic entry and competition. It took seventy years, but the round of American state constitutional changes in the 1840s are the heart of what eliminated systematic corruption. American governments were so successful at eliminating systematic corruption that we no longer understand what the term corruption meant in the 1800s, nor do we worry about systematic corruption in our current political system.

1.1   From Aristotle to the British Whigs

> The King's ministers were not attacked for sitting in Parliament, but they were attacked for allegedly filling Parliament with the recipients of government patronage. For what was universally acknowledged was that if the members of the legislatures became dependent on patronage, the legislature would cease to be independent and the balance of the constitution would become corrupt. Corruption on an eighteenth-century tongue—where it was an exceedingly common term—meant not only venality, but disturbance of the political conditions necessary to human virtue and freedom.
> —J. G. A. Pocock (1985, p. 78)[7]

Aristotle was the first western philosopher to talk about mixed government: "But they are nearer the truth who combine many forms: for the con-

---

6. Between 1776 and 1850, the national government wrote two constitutions, and the original thirteen states wrote their first constitutions and an additional sixteen new constitutions. For the importance of opening entry as a deterrent to corruption in the 1840s state constitution see Wallis (2005).

7. Pocock's work is fundamental for understanding the evolution of ideas about balanced government. The argument is completely developed in *The Machiavellian Mo-*

stitution is better which is made up of more numerous elements" (1996, book III, 1255[a] 4). Polybius explicitly tied corruption to the idea of constitutional balance and the changing distribution of power within governments. From then, the nature of both balanced government and corruption evolved together until, by 1776, corruption became synonymous with a failure to maintain balance in the constitutional structure of government.

Aristotle defined pure forms of government as those that "govern with a view to the common interest." The pure and corrupt forms "are as follows: —of kingship, tyranny; of aristocracy, oligarchy; and of constitutional government, democracy." (1996, book III, 1279[a] 30 and 1279[b] 4). Aristotle's task in the *Politics* was to understand how constitutions affected the behavior of governments, with the purpose of discerning how good governments might be instituted in human society. Constitutions were originally thought of as literally the body politic, not as written documents or theoretical constructs.[8] All physical bodies exhibit a cycle of growth, maturity, and decay: corruption. Corruption happened to constitutions, just as certainly as decay and death happened to individuals. The central question of political philosophy asked whether a political constitution could possibly be devised that did not inevitably end in corruption.

Polybius extended Aristotle's categories of pure and corrupt forms of government into an explicit cyclical theory of constitutional development:

> So then we enumerate six forms of government,—the three commonly spoken of which I have just mentioned, [the pure forms of kingship, aristocracy, and democracy] and three more allied forms, I mean *despotism,*

---

ment. The intellectual history developed in this and the following sections is based on the work of Pocock (1972, 1973, 1975, 1977, 1985, 1987), Bailyn, Wood, Skinner (1978a,b), and many others. This literature is truly remarkable. What no one seems to have seen, however, is how the concept of corruption developed in western political thought ties economic and political institutions together so closely and directly. That is the contribution of this paper.

8. We speak of a person with a hearty constitution or with a fragile constitution. Constitutions were like bodies. "Like their contemporaries in England and like their predecessors for centuries before, the colonists at the beginning of the Revolutionary controversy understood by the word 'constitution' not, as we would have it, a written document or even an unwritten but deliberately contrived design of government and specification of rights beyond the power of ordinary legislation to alter; they thought of it, rather as the constituted—that is, existing— arrangement of governmental institutions, laws, and customs together with the principles and goals that animated them. So John Adams wrote that a political constitution is like 'the constitution of the human body'; 'certain contextures of the nerves, fibres, and muscles, or certain qualities of the blood and juices' some of which 'may be properly called *stamina vitae,* or essentials and fundamentals of the constitution; parts without which life itself cannot be preserved a moment" (Bailyn 1967, p. 68, citing Adams *Works,* III, pp. 478–79).

"By constitution we mean, whenever we speak with propriety and exactness, that assemblage of laws, institutions, and customs, derived from certain fixed principles of reason, directed to certain fixed objects of public good, that compose the general system, according to which the community hath agreed to be governed" (Bolingbroke 1997, p. 88). Bolingbroke was a leading Tory politician in the early eighteenth century and an articulate proponent of Commonwealth ideas.

oligarchy and *mob-rule.* The first of these arises without artificial aid and in the natural order of events. Next to this, and produced from it by the aid of art and adjustment, comes kingship; which degenerating into the evil form allied to it, by which I mean tyranny, both are once more destroyed and aristocracy produced. Again the latter being in the course of nature perverted to oligarchy, and the people passionately avenging the unjust acts of their rulers, democracy comes into existence; which again by its violence and contempt of law becomes sheer mob-rule. No clearer proof of the truth of what I say could be obtained than by a careful observation of the natural origin, genesis, and decadence of these several forms of government. For it is only by seeing distinctly how each of them is produced that a distinct view can also be obtained of its growth, zenith, and decadence, and the time, circumstance, and place in which each of these may be expected to recur. (Polybius 1962, book 6, 4, p. 460)

Polybius developed a theory of "the regular cycle of constitutional revolutions, in which and the natural order in which constitutions change, are transformed, and return again to their original stage" (book 6, 10, p. 466). Any society with governments of the pure forms inevitably cycled from kingship through tyranny, aristocracy, oligarchy, democracy, and mob-rule. The mob is subdued by the noble and pure king, setting the cycle in motion again. For Polybius, corruption was the process by which one form of government evolved into another form. It was a force beyond the individual, and so beyond individual moral or ethical behavior. Corruption was an "undeviating law of nature" in unmixed governments.

Polybius believed that it was possible to prevent corruption by resorting to mixed and balanced governments that combined elements of all three pure types, which he saw in the historical example of Lycurgus, who

accordingly combined together all the excellences and distinctive features of the best constitutions, that no part should become unduly predominant, and be perverted into its kindred vice; and that, each power being checked by the others, no one part should turn the scale or decisively out balance the others; but that, by being accurately adjusted and in exact equilibrium, the whole might remain long steady like a ship sailing close to the wind. The royal power was prevented from growing insolent by fear of the people, which had also assigned to it an adequate share in the constitution. The people in their turn were restrained from a bold contempt of the kings by fear of the Gerusia: the members of which, being selected on grounds of merit, were certain to throw their influence on the side of justice in every question that arose; and thus the party placed at a disadvantage by its conservative tendency was always strengthened and supported by the weight and influence of the Gerusia. The result of this combination has been that the Lacedaemonians retained their freedom for the longest period of any people with which we are acquainted. (book 6, 10, pp. 466–67).

Machiavelli took up Polybius. Machiavelli was concerned with stability and the process of political change.[9] Anything that disrupted the balance of the constitution was technically corruption, whether it resulted from morally corrupt individual behavior or not. Corruption resulted from inherent tendencies in the structure of societies.

The very term *balance* suggests the modern concept of an equilibrium, but constitutional balance was not thought to be a stable or self-enforcing equilibrium. Small changes in the relative balance of power between the groups that made up the political and social order could disrupt the system. A balanced constitution could ward off corruption, but it had to be maintained by the eternal vigilance of fallible human care and attention. Maintaining a balance required politicians and philosophers to define exactly what constituted the balance, that is, to define exactly what behavior was unconstitutional or corrupt. This way of thinking produced two important consequences:

First, articulating the concept of corruption was fundamental to the evolution of constitutions as fundamental law, captured in a written document, and realized in the lives of men and women through custom, practice, conflict, and adjudication. Implementing the idea that societies should be governed by laws, not men, required that society at large agree on a way to identify when it was corrupted.

Second, the balanced constitution was a theoretical construct similar to a unique and universal maximum.[10] Any movement away from the balance was a movement toward tyranny and slavery. This was true whether the movement was toward tyranny of the one, the many, or the few. The balanced constitution was a perfect equipoise from which a slippery slope led downward in all directions. Any change in the balance was inherently corrupt. Systematic corruption was not about specific behaviors; it was not like moral and ethical corruption. It was change that destabilized the political order.

The conflict between the Stuart kings and the British Parliament generated a wealth of thinking about the nature of political constitutions, including Hobbes, Harrington, and Locke. A defining moment in the history of the English constitution occurred when, on June 21, 1642, shortly before the Civil War began, two of Charles I's advisors drafted and persuaded the king to issue a document, *His Majesty's Answer to the Nineteen Propositions of Both Houses of Parliament,* in which the king declared that England was a mixed government and not a condescending monarchy. The *Answer* was a critical turning point in constitutional history because in it the king

---

9. See Machiavelli (1996, book I, pp. 10–23) and Pocock (1973, p. 129; 1975, pp. 83–219).

10. Harrington concluded his "Epistle to the Reader," which opens *Oceana,* with a theoretical bent: "I dare promise you that if I have not made you a good flight, I have sprung you the best quarry; for though the discourses be full of crudities, the model hath had perfect concoction" (1992, p. 2).

admitted that England possessed a balanced government, not an absolute monarchy. It quickly became part of the English constitutional canon.[11] The *Answer* did not concede sovereignty to Parliament nor was it a concession of royal prerogatives. It cemented the constitutionality of the monarchy and enshrined the idea of balanced government.

If the *Answer* guaranteed a balanced constitution, it did very little to indicate exactly how the balance was to be defined, maintained, and allowed to change. During the interregnum, the writings of James Harrington helped define the constitutional balance and move it from a static to a dynamic basis. Harrington made two fundamental contributions. First, he delineated how the distribution of military power in a society was a function of the distribution of land tenure, and thus how every government rested on a particular set of property rights in land. Second, he showed how the constitutional balance within government must correspond to the balance of military power between social orders implied by the distribution of land tenure. Harrington's model contained two balances, one of government and one of military power. His genius was to see that these two balances must correspond. A constitutional system that gave more power to an element of society (king, aristocracy, the people) than the relevant share of land possessed by that element of the population was inevitably unstable. Either the constitution or the underlying balance of military power must change and, in classic Polybian terms, Harrington defined corruption as change: "corruption in this sense signifieth no more than that the corruption of one government (as in natural bodies) is the generation of another . . ." (1992, pp. 60–61). Harrington saw balanced government as a way to provide political stability and prevent the endless struggles of the one, the few, and the many to control the government, and the warfare, disruption, and occasional tyranny that ensued.

The *Answers* and Harrington's *Oceana* defined a constitutional balance, but it was not yet in place. Between the restoration of Charles II in 1660 and the installation of William and Mary in 1688, "commonwealthmen" or "True Whigs" or "Real Whigs" articulated a version of the balanced constitution and its associated corruptions.[12] By 1675, they had developed

---

11. The text of the *Answer* is printed in Weston (1965), along with the *Political Catechism,* a popular document that interpreted the *Answer* in terms that would become a central part of Whig theory. The *Answer* is discussed in Pocock (1975, p. 361).

12. This group included Neville, Shaftesbury, Locke, Marvell, and Sidney. These men were contemporaries of Harrington, who died enfeebled and in poor health in 1677. The prominence of Harrington in this section is a matter of exposition. Harrington ultimately had the most influence, but he was only one of several important commonwealth thinkers. See Robbins (1959) for an in-depth treatment of the men and their ideas.

In the nineteenth century a "Whig" party developed, which was not identical with Whig theorists. Bolingbroke, for example, was a leading Whig thinker and a Tory politician. In the discussion that follows I use the term commonwealth thinkers or theorists to avoid confusion.

a coherent position containing the basic themes of opposition ideology.[13] Balanced government required that political actors, in Britain the king, the Lords, and the Commons, be truly independent of one another. If one branch of the government gained ascendancy over, or influence in, another branch the checks built into the system would be compromised. If, for example, the king gained control of the Commons, the Commons could no longer prevent the king from tyrannizing over the government.

The starting point of the commonwealth critique of the Stuart government was the creation of a standing army. This was not because a standing army was a direct physical threat to liberty. Instead, a professional standing army threatened the independence of Parliament, by filling the Commons with professional soldiers and other officeholders who careers and livelihood depended on the good will and patronage of the executive. "The standing army appears in this context as an instrument of corruption rather than of dictatorship. Army officers in Parliament are placemen, and they encourage the growth of a military establishment outside parliamentary control . . ." (Pocock 1973, p. 125).[14]

The critique widened after the new arrangements between King William and Parliament produced a complementary set of institutional changes in fiscal policy and government administration. They included the Bank of England, professionalization of tax collection and administration, and the development of new methods to fund the growing national debt.[15] Continuous warfare with France created a military-industrial complex in England. Between 1700 and 1800 government expenditures rose from 5 percent of income to 20 percent of income.[16] This unprecedented expansion of state power was equally the accomplishment of Parliament and the king, for Parliament controlled tax policy.

It was in the early eighteenth century that the concept of systematic corruption was articulated fully. Commonwealth theorists drew an explicit connection between royal manipulation of economic privileges and the securing of political power. The British had come through the civil wars of the seventeenth century with their belief in a balanced constitution intact and enhanced. They increasingly saw the House of Lords as a balance be-

13. I have drawn on Pocock's "Machiavelli, Harrington, and English Political Ideologies" in this section (1973, pp. 104–47). The argument is developed further in *The Machiavellian Moment* (1975, pp. 406–22).

14. Since the influential position of the aristocracy depended on their provision of military service, the country could have an independent nobility or a professional army, but not both. "For the power of *Peerage* and a *Standing Army* are like two buckets, the proportion that one goes down, the other exactly goes up . . ." From *A Letter from a Person of Quality to his Friend in the Country,* as quoted in Pocock (1973, p. 118).

15. On the Bank of England and the financial revolution generally see Dickson (1967); on the bureaucratization of tax collection see Brewer (1989); and for the national debt see North and Weingast (1989).

16. Mathias and O'Brian (1976) review the history of government revenues and expenditures in eighteenth-century Britain.

tween a competing monarchy and the House of Commons.[17] Independence of the three parts was required to maintain the balance. The commonwealthmen saw the economic innovations of the financial revolution
as mechanisms by which the crown exerted influence in the Commons and
subverted parliamentary independence. The king's tools were parliamentary patronage, the public credit, and political parties. If the king obtained
enough influence in Parliament to suborn its independence, liberty would
be lost and tyranny and slavery would follow.[18]

Rising defense expenditures increased the number of patronage positions
in the Army, Navy, Treasury, Customs, and Excise at the disposal of the executive. By the time of the American Revolution, close to half of the House
of Commons were placemen, pensioners, or represented electoral districts
under the control of the king and his ministers.[19] The steadily growing public
debt created a class of creditors with a direct interest in the financial stability of the government, many of them members of Parliament. The large
profits to be made in marketing and servicing the debt went to the favored
few financial houses, banks, and chartered trading companies, all of whom
had connections in both the executive and Parliament. There was ample reason to doubt the independence of individual members of Parliament. And
finally, the manipulations of politicians like Walpole created groups within
the government whose interest "is that of men attached to the government;
or to speak more properly, to the persons of those who govern; or, to speak
more properly still, to the power profit, or protection they acquire by the
favour of these persons, but enemies to the constitution" (Bolingbroke 1997,
p. 85). The creation of a political party within Parliament that was headed
by the king, organized by his ministers, financed by corporate privileges, and
coordinated by the national debt, threatened the end of balanced government and the establishment of a unitary executive tyranny.[20]

17. This is the theme of Weston (1965).
18. "It is certain then, that if ever such men as call themselves friends of the government,
but are real enemies of the constitution, prevail, they will make it a capital point of their
wicked policy to keep up a standing army. . . . To destroy British liberty with an army of
Britons, is not a measure so sure of success as some people may believe. To corrupt the Parliament is a slower, but might prove a more effectual method; and two or three hundred mer-
cenaries in the two Houses, if they could be listed there, would be more fatal to the constitution, than ten times as many thousands in red and in blue out of them. Parliaments are the
true guardians of liberty. For this principally they were instituted; and this is the principal article of that great and noble trust, the collective body of the people of Britain reposes
in the representative. But then no slavery can be so effectually brought and fixed upon us as
parliamentary slavery. By the corruption of Parliament, and the absolute influence of a King,
or his minister, on the two Houses, we return to that state, and are really governed by the ar-
bitrary rule of one man" (Bolingbroke 1997, pp. 92, 93–94).
19. See the essays on "Parliamentary Patronage," pp. 46–56, and on "Placemen and Pensioners," pp. 118–26 in Namier and Brooke (1964).
20. The commonwealthmen opposed all political parties as a manifestation of corruption.
To confuse matters, at the same time one of the parties that developed in Britain was the Whig
Party, which is distinct from the Whig/Commonwealth thinkers. Bolingbroke, as noted, was
a prominent Tory politician as well as a prominent Whig philosopher.

The British in the eighteenth century certainly enjoyed better government than they, and perhaps the world, had ever seen. Britons on both sides of the Atlantic extolled the virtues of the British constitution. John Toland called the British government "the most free and best constituted in the world." John Adams claimed, "no Government that ever existed was so essentially free." Even the Frenchman Montesquieu talked of "this beautiful system."[21] The Whigs believed in the perfect balance of the British constitution. In this light, it is easy to dismiss commonwealth claims of corruption as paranoia. To do so, however, overlooks that Whigs were not concerned about the current state of Britain. Commonwealthmen feared what would happen next. They had no historical yardstick to judge whether the changes that British society and government were undergoing in the eighteenth century were good or bad. Commonwealthmen believed, with the deepest conviction, that if executive influence in Parliament was allowed to go unchecked, then the next stage in British government would inevitably be tyranny and slavery.

The heart of the commonwealth attack on corruption criticized the government's relation to the economy. Adam Smith attacked the system of government-granted mercantilist privileges (Smith 1981). In *Cato's Letters,* Trenchard and Gordon (1995) challenged the use of chartered corporations to promote economic activity that potentially created economic rents (by limiting entry) that could be used by the Crown to cement economic interests to its cause (no. 3, 1720, 44–45).[22] "For as to that class of ravens, whose wealth has cost the nation its all, as they are manifest enemies to God and man, no man can call them his neighbours: They are rogues of prey, they are stock-jobbers, they are a conspiracy of stock-jobbers!"[23] The financial revolution brought with it numerous instances of special privileges granted by the government.[24] The combined charges of systematic corruption, suborning the independence of politicians and Parliament, and individual corruption, including the venality and greed of stock-jobbers and speculators, packed a powerful message.

21. Quotations from Wood (1969, p. 11).

22. "Companies and joint-stocks are always established for the encouragement and benefit of trade; though they always happen to mar and cramp trade" (Trenchard and Gordon [1720] 1995, *Cato's Letters,* no. 9, p. 69).

23. The title of *Letter* no. 6, December 10, 1720, conveys the sentiments of Trenchard and Gordon: *How easily the People are bubbled by Deceivers. Further Caution against deceitful Remedies for the publick sufferings from the wicked Execution of the South-Sea Scheme.*

24. As Dickson summarized: "Finally, it is worth noting that while few aspects of the Financial Revolution were of greater political and economic utility than the development of a market in securities in London, none united contemporary opinion more against it. It was denounced as inherently wicked and against the public interest. The phrase 'stock-jobbing', freely used to denote every kind of activity in the market, had clear overtones of self-interest and corruption. An anthology of comments by contemporaries would be remarkably uniform, indeed monotonous, in its tone, and uninformative about how the market actually worked" (1967, pp. 32–33).

By the mid-eighteenth century commonwealthmen decried the corrupting evils of executive patronage, the public credit, and political parties. Commonwealth ideals were important elements of the political conversation in the eighteenth century. They defined, with clear, bright lines, what was and was not constitutional. Britain, of course, was in the midst of a phenomenal rise to world power, and most Britons were happily apathetic about the supposed corruption of their government. In Briton, the commonwealthmen "were not in any sense of the word an organized opposition. . . . Without leaders and organization the reformers failed. When they achieved these they still failed to attract sufficient public support and interest. A part of their failure must be attributed to their detestation of party. . . . The Real Whigs were not a coherent party. They professed almost as many creeds in politics as in religion." Yet "In America the academic ideas of the Whigs of the British Isles were fruitful and found practical expression."[25]

1.2   Corruption, Revolution, and Constitutions

> Sir, we have done everything that could be done to avert the storm which is now coming on. We have petitioned; we have remonstrated; we have supplicated; we have prostrated ourselves before the throne, and have implored its interposition to attest the tyrannical hands of the ministry and Parliament.
>
> The battle, sir, is not to the strong alone; it is to the vigilant, the active, the brave. Besides, sir, we have no election. If we were base enough to desire it, it is now too late to retire from the contest. There is no retreat but in submission and slavery! Our chains are forged. Their clanking may be heard on the plains of Boston! The war is inevitable—and let it come!
> —Patrick Henry, *Address to the Virginia Provincial Convention,* March 23, 1775

> The notion of a legislative power exercised conjointly by kings, lords and commons is a notion of legislative sovereignty undeveloped in classical republican theory; its presence in the *Answer* is a reminder that the notion of "separation of powers," though invented largely in England, could not be effective there and could be realized in the United States only after rejection of parliamentary government.
> —J. G. A. Pocock (1987, p. 310)

We have reached the point where British and American paths divide. The "republican synthesis" in American history provides a convincing ex-

---

25. Robbins (1959) quotes from pages 381, 382, and 385.

planation for why Americans revolted and what "made their revolution so unusual, for they revolted not against the English constitution but on behalf of it" (Wood 1969, p. 10).[26] The desire to preserve the existing constitution made the American revolution one motivated by fear rather than hope. The widespread perception of English corruption, on both sides of the Atlantic, inexorably drove the Americans to independence once a wedge opened between Parliament and the colonies in 1763. The fear in the American colonies was that England, "once the land of liberty—the school of patriots—the nurse of heroes, has become the land of slavery—the school of parricides and the nurse of tyrants."[27] At its root, the fear driving the American Revolution was Polybian. The influence of the executive in Parliament had unbalanced the constitution. What inevitably followed monarchy, no matter how pure the intentions of those who produced the monarchy, was tyranny. As Patrick Henry declared: "Our chains are forged. Their clanking may be heard on the plains of Boston!"

Any government organized along commonwealth lines should immediately have put in place a constitution with balanced government. In May of 1776, the Continental Congress asked the states to write their own constitutions. By July 3, New Jersey had drafted a new constitution which, among its many features, distinctly articulated the separation of powers:

> XX. That the legislative department of this government may, as much as possible, be, preserved from all suspicion of corruption, none of the Judges of the Supreme or other Courts, Sheriffs, or any other person or persons possessed of any post of profit under the government, other than Justices of the Peace, shall be entitled to a seat in the Assembly: but that, on his being elected, and taking his seat, his office or post shall be considered as vacant.[28]

The Constitution of Maryland, ratified in November 1776, stipulated in Section 6 of the Declaration of Rights: "That the legislative, executive and judicial powers of government, ought to be forever separate and distinct from each other." Separation of powers was the most visible way that Americans addressed systematic political corruption, but the entire structure of early state constitutions, with their articulated branches, attempted to systematize balanced government.

The powers assumed by the states in their constitutions were not powers

---

26. Wood (1969, p. 10). The republican synthesis literature is neatly summarized and discussed in Shalhope (1972, 1982).

27. The quotation is from a letter from Charles Lee to Robert Morris, January 3, 1776, as quoted by Wood (1969, p. 32).

28. New Jersey, Constitution of 1776, Article 20. The New Jersey Constitution of 1844, Article 3, Section 1, read: "1. The powers of the government shall be divided into three distinct departments—the legislative, executive and judicial; and no person or persons belonging to, or constituting one of these departments, shall exercise any of the powers properly belonging to either of the others, except as herein expressly provided" (Wallis, *NBER/Maryland State Constitution Project*).

necessarily denied to the national government. But once states defined their powers they could not be taken by the national government without substantial political cost. The second national constitution, written in 1787, gave the national government broad and generous powers. But only in the areas of military and international affairs, public lands, international trade and commercial policy, and (to a lesser and immediately disputed extent) financial and monetary policy, did the national government possess well-defined *exclusive* powers. Even in these areas, with the exception of military defense and international relations, the national government subsequently found it extremely difficult for political reasons to exercise its constitutional powers.[29] National government action inevitably raised the specter of systematic corruption.

The ability of states to legislate, regulate, or promote almost any aspect of economic and social behavior meant that the states, and not the national government, became the focal point of economic policies. Americans were embarking on two new experiments in government: written constitutions and widespread government support of private organizations. The first experiment is a central part of American history. The second experiment, successful as it was, is so taken for granted that we rarely recognize how important government support of private organizations was for American social and economic development. As de Tocqueville famously noted: "Americans of all ages, all stations in life, and all types of dispositions are forever forming associations. There are not only commercial and industrial associations in which all take part, but others of a thousand different types—religious, moral, serious, futile, very general and very limited, immensely large and very minutes. . . . In every case, at the head of any new undertaking, where in France you would find the government or in England some territorial magnate, in the United States you are sure to find an association" (1966, p. 513).

The American colonists brought the ancient English constitution with them, but not a king or an aristocracy, two of the critical elements in the constitutional balance. This led to a more egalitarian society, a deep belief in the right of individuals to assemble, and more vigorous private sector organizations. In Europe, the right to form voluntary organizations was not universal; one found governments and territorial magnates at the head of organizations because they possessed the sometimes implicit, but often explicit, privilege to form organizations. The ability to form corporations was limited to the social and economic elite. Limited entry created the economic rents that made royal grants of privilege to the monied interests so valuable. In America, the freedom to assemble, the ability to form religious, political, economic, and social organizations did not go undisputed after the revolution. Deciding how much public support should be given to

---

29. This point is developed further in Wallis (2005b) and Wallis and Weingast (2005).

private organizations was important and, at least in the economic and political world, very contentious.

America's balanced state constitutions recognized the Harringtonian imperative of balancing power within the government in the same proportion as land ownership was balanced in the population. "Power results from the real property of society."[30] The equality of land ownership posed new and vexing problems for American politicians, problems without English antecedents. The distribution of land did not mirror the distribution of social prestige or the presumed distribution of leadership talents within the "natural elite." Freedom of assembly, freedom of speech, and freedom of petition were fundamental rights. How far did these rights extend into the politically competent, independent, landowning citizenry? Who had the right to vote, to incorporate a business, or form a political party? Britain's financial revolution did not represent a move toward an economy or society with more open entry; it restricted entry. Adam Smith and the classical economists built their criticism of government policy on mercantilist limitations on access to economic organization. Kings and ministers used limited access to create economic rents, then used the spoils from the rents to purchase political influence, and thus eroded the independence of Parliament and corrupted the entire political system. Corporations and stock-jobbers represented the very essence of both systematic and venal corruption. How was the United States to deal with the identical problem?

1.3   Corruption and the First Crisis of National Politics

> "It is hard to imagine how by deliberate intent, Alexander Hamilton's economic program for the new republic could have been better calculated to exacerbate these [commonwealth] fears. . . . They inevitably brought to mind the entire system of eighteenth-century English governmental finance, with all the consequences that entailed for minds shaped by British opposition thought."
> —Banning (1978, p. 128)

Straightening out the nation's finances instigated the first battle over corruption in the new republic. Hamilton's proposed financial policies— refunding national and state debts, a national bank, a moderate revenue tariff, and excise taxes—all stimulated opposition and debate when Congress considered them in the first Congress, which ended in March of 1791. Each of Hamilton's measures raised fears of corruption in classic commonwealth terms, but all of them passed. The debate over the meaning of

---

30. Joseph Galloway to the Continental Congress, as quoted by Jensen (1940, p. 66), quoting John Adam's Notes on Debates, *Works of John Adams,* 2:372.

the new financial system in the summer of 1791, however, produced a conflagration of fears about systematic corruption, and led to the creation of an opposition party in the United States. All of the policy measures at issue were economic, and the critical element in the debate was the effect of the economic policies on politics.

We have already seen how the financial revolution in England created a funded national debt, a bureaucracy of excise and tariff collectors, a national bank, and an interlocking set of financial intermediaries and chartered corporations that marketed and traded in government debt. As the bureaucracy expanded, so did opportunities for executive patronage. The ability to tie the interests of the financial community to the policies of the government through the medium of the national debt and corporate charters allowed the Crown to extend its influence and undermine the independence of Parliament. The danger of the English system of finance was to fundamental liberties; it was systematic corruption, and the identification of financial interests with the Crown was the mechanism of corruption.

Hamilton's arguments for America's new financial system had ominous overtones. In the *Report on the Public Credit* in January 1790, Hamilton proposed that "If all the public creditors receive their dues from one source . . . their interests will be the same. And having the same interests, they will unite in support of the fiscal arrangements of the government."[31] Hamilton proposed precisely the type of arrangement with the monied interest that commonwealthmen feared in Britain. A typical response to Hamilton's proposals came from the Virginia legislature's memorial to Congress on December 16, 1790:

> That it is with great concern they find themselves compelled, from a sense of duty, to call the attention of Congress to an act of their last session, entitled "An act making provision for the debt of the United States," which the General Assembly conceives neither policy, justice, nor the constitution, warrants. Republican policy, in the opinion of your memorialists, could scarcely have suggested those clauses in the aforesaid act, which limit the right of the United States, in their redemption of the public debt. On the contrary, they discern a striking resemblance between this system and that which was introduced into England at the Revolution—a system which has perpetuated upon that nation an enormous debt, and has, moreover, insinuated into the hands of the Executive an unbounded influence, which, pervading every branch of the Government, bears down all opposition, and daily threatens the destruction of every thing that appertains to English liberty. The same causes produce the same effects.

31. "Report on the Public Credit" *American State Papers, Finance*, vol. I, p. 15. See Ferguson (1961) for an analysis of how constitutional issues and the public debt interacted in Hamilton's thinking.

In an agricultural country like this, therefore, to erect and concentrate and perpetuate a large moneyed interest, is a measure which your memorialists apprehend must, in the course of human events, produce one or other of two evils: the prostration of agriculture at the feet of commerce, or a change in the present form of Federal Government, fatal to the existence of American liberty. (*American State Papers, Finance,* vol. I, p. 90)

The Virginians questioned whether "Republican policy," that is, commonwealth ideas, could have suggested such a financial program and drew a direct connection between Hamilton's plan and English executive corruption, which has "insinuated into the hands of the Executive an unbounded influence." In typical commonwealth style, the memorial raises the alarm that Hamilton's plans threaten the "existence of American liberty."

As Banning noted (1978), it would have been difficult to consciously design a financial program that provoked commonwealth fears of executive influence more directly than Hamilton's. The debate about the implications of the financial plan after it was passed in 1791 opened a division within the national government.[32] On the Federalist side the Adamses, joined by Hamilton, praised the British constitution and argued against extending democracy too far. On what would become the Republican side, Jefferson and Madison, abetted by Thomas Paine and Phillip Freneau, attacked the Adamses as monarchists and Hamilton as an aspiring Prime Minister. The Republicans castigated the financial plan as an attempt by Hamilton to use his position as Treasury Secretary to secure control of the government through systematic corruption. Public acrimony between the participants set in motion the formation of distinct Federalist and Republican parties in national politics. The way in which the conflict was resolved placed corruption in governmental promotion of economic development at the center of American politics for the next seventy years. It took a long time for Americans to figure out how to write their constitutions. The conflict of the 1790s brought to prominence several contradictions in the American experiment with republican government.

Popular sovereignty versus tyranny of the majority. In the ratification debates, both the Federalists and the Anti-Federalists argued for popular sovereignty as a critical element in the new American system. Sovereignty, lodged with the people, could be delegated to representatives through election. Yet ultimately sovereignty remained in the hands of the voters. But to those steeped in commonwealth theory, tyranny of the many was just as much of a threat as tyranny of the one or the few. The exercise of popular sovereignty necessarily involved the risk of tyranny of the majority, a risk that Madison and Hamilton both appreciated. Madison hoped the ex-

---

32. The events of 1791 and their subsequent impact on national politics are described in Banning, (1978) and McCoy (1980).

tended republic would mitigate the risk, as he argued famously in Federalist #10. The greatest danger from majority rule lay in the possibility that a demagogue would arise, unify a majority of the voters behind him, and lead the government into despotism. Such a leader might override the checks and balances built into system by sweeping a majority through all the branches of government. Madison's hopes didn't last a decade: by the early 1790s the Federalists controlled all three branches of the national government.[33]

Political parties versus corruption. The Constitution itself offered a way for Jefferson and Madison to oppose the Federalists: the formation of an opposition party. The logic of the winner-take-all electoral process for President, as well as other offices, seemed to guarantee that two competing parties would eventually emerge.[34] Despite the strict separation of executive and legislative functions in the Constitution, the President and Congress still had to find a way to come to an agreement about how government was to be carried out, a coordination eventually accomplished through political parties. But the formation of an overt opposition party carried with it an explicit danger. The incumbent Federalists, with Washington at their head, could plausibly claim that their administration was nonpartisan. Parties and factions were inherently and systematically corrupt. For the Republicans to contest for control of the government as an organized party exposed them to the charge of per se corruption in the 1790s.[35]

Rather than stressing the need for competing parties, Madison and the Republicans emphasized the need for one government with the right policies. They claimed that they stood on the side of the angels in a debate over republican versus monarchical government and pure versus corrupt methods of governing.[36] Tarring Adams and the Federalists with being closet

33. "The success of the Federalist Party in gaining control of all three branches of the national government called into question the fundamental premise of the Madisonian federalism of 1787–8: that durable factious majorities would be far less likely to coalesce at the national level of politics" (Ferejohn, Rakove, and Riley 2001, p. 3).

34. "Yet even amid the presumed 'paranoia' of the 1790s, with insidious motives being ascribed all around, both Federalists and Republicans opted to seek advantage not through a strategy of exit but rather by exploiting potential opportunities within the Constitution itself. Both parties quickly discovered a strong incentive to convert the untested mechanism of presidential election into an occasion for political innovation. In 1787 no one had expected the presidency to emerge as the crucial focus for national political competition, but by 1796, and even more so by 1800, it was evident that control of the executive was essential to control of the government" (Ferejohn, Rakove, and Riley 2001, p. 7).

35. In particular see Hofstadter (1969, pp. 80–86) and the third chapter, "The Jeffersonians in Opposition." Madison, in a series of articles published in the *National Gazette,* attempted to provide an intellectual justification for parties. He drew on the classic distinction between the few and the many, arguing that the Republicans represented the many.

36. "A final aspect of these essays is worth remark, since it represents a strain in Republican thought which we encounter again and again: it is the effort to reduce the issue between the two sides to a dispute over the merits of republican government. Today this seems a false question; the issues of funding, assumption, the bank, taxation, and foreign policy seem real

monarchists played well to some voters, but it was the fear of executive influence in the legislature, wielded by Prime Minister Hamilton through the
coordinating mechanism of the Bank of the United States and the national
debt that posed the greatest threat. It was a threat that resonated with a
century of British political writing and decades of American paranoia over
corruption in the Britain. The negative political implications of the Republicans' existence as an organized political party were minimized by
stressing the rightness of their cause. "The situation of the public good, in
the hands of two parties nearly poised as to numbers, must be extremely
perilous. Truth is a thing, not of divisibility into conflicting parts, but of
unity. Hence both sides cannot be right. Every patriot deprecates a dis-
union, which is only to be obviated by a national preference for one of these
parties."[37] If the Republicans were truly right, then their cause was not a
partisan one but a righteous one, and when the country came to see the wisdom of their position there would no longer be a need for competing parties.

Corruption versus promotion of economic development. By building their
case against Hamilton and the Federalists along traditional commonwealth lines, the Republicans gained the moral force of a century of British
and American thinking about corruption in government. At the same time,
they boxed themselves into a fundamental dilemma. The Republicans were
just as pro-growth and development as the Federalists. Their arguments
against the Federalists were political, not economic. They were not arguing that Hamilton's plan wouldn't work in economic terms, but that Hamilton was taking the first step down the slippery slope to executive tyranny.
How then did the Republicans propose to promote economic development?

The only model available at the end of the eighteenth century was one
that had been used by European governments to promote economic development for centuries: by creating public service corporations. Those corporations were given public privileges in order to induce them to provide
public services. Their public privileges generated private rents by limiting
entry. Drew McCoy's book, *Elusive Republic,* makes abundantly clear that

---

and substantial enough without superimposing on them an artificial quarrel over a question
of monarchy and hereditary power which all but the tiniest handful of Americans agreed. But
the exaggerated passions of both sides can be understood if we remember that most politically
conscious Americans were acutely aware of being involved in a political experiment in republicanism that was attended by difficulties of the most acute kind and that might face many
hidden and unpredictable pitfalls. Both sides were nervous about the stability of republicanism in an extensive federal union pervaded by many differences of sensibility and interest"
(Hofstadter 1969, pp. 34–50). In this passage Hofstadter articulates the notion than any
movement away from the perfect balance is a move down a slippery slope "back towards
monarchy and the hereditary principle." My only qualification to Hofstadter is his overem-
phasis on the fear of monarchy relative to the fears of systematic corruption represented by
the funding system.

37. John Taylor, *A Definition of Parties* (1794, p. 2); cited in Hofstadter (1968, p. 100).

the central tenets of Jefferson's and Madison's economic vision required the construction of a financial and transportation infrastructure to bring the agrarian west into viable production. At the same time, foreign economic policy had to ensure growing external markets for American products abroad, so that yeomen farmers did not produce themselves into poverty.[38] There was no institutional vehicle to promote financial and transportation improvements but the corporation. If the Republicans condemned the corporation as an instrument of corruption at the national level, they left themselves without a way of promoting the very economic development that they sought and that voters demanded.

None of these contradictions were resolved in the first forty years of the country's history—all three were resolved in the 1830s and 1840s.

1.4 Corruption Everywhere: Jacksonian Democracy and the Whig Response

The Republicans' ability to govern by apparent consensus from 1800 to 1824 papered over the threat of a tyrannous majority by governing as a virtuous majority. Geographic, if not partisan, divisions soon appeared in Congress. The inability of the federal government to overcome the problem of internal geographic competition produced inaction at the federal level.[39] Responsibility for promoting development fell squarely on the states. The resurgence of national party politics in the 1820s and 1830s was a result of the fight between the Democrats and Whigs over economic issues and, fundamentally, over systematic corruption. Again, the national government failed to provide active leadership and, in the 1840s, it was state governments that finally solved the paradox of promoting economic development while avoiding systematic corruption.

State governments expanded their involvement in banking and transportation from 1790 onward.[40] It is tempting to attribute the rise of state promotion to an absence of federal promotion, but it seems clear that state activity was a continuation of the development of government capacity at the state level that began in 1776, with the call for new state constitutions. States began chartering banks, turnpike companies, bridge companies, fire companies, and all manner of religious, charitable, educational, and mu-

38. In particular see McCoy (1980) chapter 3, "Commerce and the Independent Republic," pp. 76–104. The opening chapters to McCoy lay out the Whig origins of Republican thought as clearly as Banning (1978). The essential role of corruption in McCoy's analysis is captured in the title to Chapter One: "Social Progress and Decay in Eighteenth Century Thought."

39. Wallis and Weingast (2005) investigate the causes of federal inaction.

40. The history of government promotion of transportation improvements, federal, state, and local, is Goodrich (1950, 1960). Larson (2001) supplements Goodrich's study of the politics of federal internal improvements. The history of banking is enormous. State banking is the subject of two recent books by Bodenhorn (2000, 2003).

nicipal corporations in the 1790s.[41] By 1836, when the national charter for the Second Bank of the United States expired, there were over 600 state-chartered banks. In the meantime, the federal government had chartered the First and Second Banks of the United States and a few small banks in the District of Columbia.[42] Between 1790 and 1860, state and local governments spent $450 million, financing the Erie Canal, the Baltimore and Ohio Railroad, and hundreds of other successful projects—as well as hundreds of failures. Over the same period, the federal government spent $60 million on transportation improvements, mostly small rivers and harbor projects. In 1841, aggregate state debts stood at $198 million, larger than the national debt had ever been.

Corporate charters were, of course, grants of special privileges to small groups of citizens. Initially, every charter required an act of the state legislature, and all corporations were, in the language of the time, special. Charters always raised the specter of corruption, and strong anticharter sentiments were usually expressed whenever a charter was contemplated (Larson 2001, p. 119). At the same time, there was widespread public sentiment for promoting economic development, and the corporation was seen as the vehicle for state promotion. As a result, corporate chartering policy often contained contradictory elements.

> Although anticharter arguments were frequently stated as if they applied to all corporations without exception, in practice opposition usually settled on some corporations only. Even the Pennsylvania legislators who campaigned against the BNA and the reincorporation of Philadelphia [the city] apparently raised no objections to the charters granted "every day," as one legislator put it in 1786, to "half a dozen or 20 people for some purpose or another." Similarly, in 1792 James Sullivan carefully distinguished the incorporation of a bank from that "to build a bridge, or to cut a canal," which he found unobjectionable. Banks were probably assailed more often than any other kind of corporation. But consider the position of a delegate to the Massachusetts constitutional convention of 1853 who launched a rhetorically powerful attack on corporations "of a business character." Among corporations "for other purposes," which were apparently exempted from his criticisms, he included railroads, insurance companies and banks!" (Maier 1992, pp. 73–74)

The right to assemble, the right to organize, was explicitly recognized by early American states. Their charter policies reflected public support of

---

41. In the decade of the 1800s, New York averaged eighteen incorporations per year, Ohio one, Maryland two, Pennsylvania six, and New Jersey, four. In the 1830s, New York averaged fifty-seven, Ohio forty-three, Maryland eighteen, Pennsylvania thirty-eight, and New Jersey eighteen (Evans 1948). There is a substantial historical and legal literature on American corporations: Davis (1961), Dodd (1954), Hurst (1970), Handlin and Handlin (1969), Seavoy (1982), Maier (1992, 1993), Lamoreaux (2004), and Dunlavy (2004).

42. For state involvement in banking in the early nineteenth century see Wallis, Sylla, and Legler (1994); Sylla, Legler, and Wallis (1987); and Bodenhorn (2000, 2003).

private organization. In itself, this made a significant, if unmeasured, contribution to the development of the American economy.[43]

But granting corporate charters was not without its costs, real and potential. In New York the Albany Regency, headed by Martin Van Buren, used bank charters to dominate state politics.[44] The Regency granted bank charters only to their political allies. In return, the bankers provided financial support to the Regency, enabling the Regency to maintain control of state government. It was a classic case of systematic corruption: a group of politicians using economic privileges to secure their control of the political system. New York was not unique. Unlike New York, however, most states that created rents by limiting entry chose to take their share of the rents in the form of tax revenues, not political influence.[45]

The presidential election of 1824 offered a chance to change the course of federal policy. The election was contested by William Crawford, John Quincy Adams, Henry Clay, and Andrew Jackson. Corruption was the theme of Jackson's campaign:

> Look to the city of Washington, and let the virtuous patriots of the country weep at the spectacle. There corruption is springing into existence, and fast flourishing, Gentlemen, candidates for first office in the gift of a free people, are found electioneering and intriguing, to worm themselves into the confidence of members of congress, who support their particular favorites, are bye and bye to go forth and dictate to the people what is right.[46]

Jackson won a plurality of the popular vote and the electoral vote. When the election went to the House, however, Clay threw his support behind Adams. Adams was elected, and subsequently appointed Clay Secretary of State. Jackson decried the "corrupt bargain": "so you see, the *Judas* of the West [Clay] has closed the contract and will receive thirty pieces of silver. His end will be the same. Was there ever witnessed such a bare faced corruption in any country before?"[47] Jackson's campaign for the 1828 election began in 1824, and its theme was corruption.

43. See Handlin and Handlin (1969) for a clear statement of how corporation policy in Massachusetts was used to support private organizations.

44. See Bodenhorn, this volume, Seavoy (1982), and Benson (1961) for the political uses of bank chartering in New York.

45. Wallis, Sylla, and Legler (1994) present a simple model of "fiscal interest" that explains why some states chose to limit entry into banking in return for higher dividends on the bank stock they owned. Pennsylvania consciously limited entry into banking. New Jersey created a monopoly railroad, the Camden and Amboy, from which the state received substantial dividends (Cadman 1949). In Arkansas, two politically powerful families used a state bank for the same purposes as the Albany Regency (Worley 1950).

46. Eaton (1824, pp. 3–4) as quoted in Larson (2001, p. 154). The quote is from *Letters of Wyoming,* campaign pamphlets that began appearing in 1823, written by John Eaton, later Jackson's Secretary of War. "Eaton was constructing for Jackson out of older republican cloth a coat of virtue and simplicity that made other candidates appear to be draped in ancient, British-style corruption" (Larson 2001, p. 155).

47. Jackson to Lewis, February 20, 1825; as quoted in Remini (1967, p. 98).

Jackson's election in 1828 brought the three contradictions of American democracy into clear focus—tyranny of the majority, political parties, and the connection between economic development and systematic corruption. General Jackson was the military hero who, to his enemies, offered the perfect image of a demagogue and the dark side of democracy. The Democratic party built to elect Jackson did not disappear after 1828; competitive party politics became a permanent part of American politics and raised the specter of corruption, faction, and party. Finally, the opposition party that emerged during Jackson's first term, what became the Whig party headed by Henry Clay, chose to contest Jackson in the arena of economic policy. The first defining question for Whigs and Democrats was whether the national government should renew the charter of the Second Bank of the United States. The question boiled down to whether a national bank was an instrument of systematic corruption.

The economic and political history of the Bank War is well known.[48] The debate between Jackson and his opponents was carried out in terms of systematic corruption. Jackson's veto message railed against the special privileges conveyed to the Bank, laid out Jackson's position on the battle between the aristocratic wealthy and the masses of the population, and articulated the abuse of privilege as an evil of government.[49] But he did not begin speaking of systematic corruption until the Bank War broke into open conflict with his plans to remove the federal deposits. On September 18, 1833, Jackson had Secretary Taney read a statement to the Cabinet that Jackson and Taney had prepared on why the deposits should be removed:

> The Bank of the United States is in itself a Government which has gradually increased its strength from the day of its establishment. The question between it and the people has become one of power—a question which its adherents do not scruple to avow must ultimately be decided in favor of the Bank. . . . The mass of people have more to fear from com-

48. See Remini (1967) and Temin (1969). The debate in economic history over the effects of the Bank War, Jackson's other economic policies, and the causes of the macroeconomic rages on. For a summary of the literature, and a strong argument that Jackson's domestic economic policies contributed to the Panic of 1837, see Rousseau (2002).

49. "It is to be regretted that the rich and powerful too often bend the acts of government to their selfish purposes. Distinctions in society will always exist under every just government . . . but when the laws undertake to add to these natural and just advantages artificial distinctions, to grant titles, gratuities, and exclusive privileges, to make the rich richer and the potent more powerful, the humble members of society—the farmers, mechanics, and laborers—who have neither the time nor the means of securing like favors to themselves, have a right to complain of the injustice of their government. There are no necessary evils in government. Its evils exist only in its abuses.

If we can not at once, in justice to interest vested under improvident legislation, make our government what it ought to be, we can at least take a stand against all new grants of monopolies exclusive privileges, against any prostitution of our Government to the advancement of the few at the expense of the many, and in favor of compromise and gradual reform in our code of laws and system of political economy." Jackson's Veto Message, July 10, 1832 (Richardson 1897, pp. 1153–54).

binations of the wealthy and professional classes—from an aristocracy which thro' the influence of riches and talents, insidiously employed, sometimes succeeds in preventing political institutions, however well adjusted, from securing the freedom of the citizen, and in establishing the most odious and oppressive government under the forms of a free institution.[50]

Jackson recalled the classic phrases of systematic corruption. The Bank itself was a government: a small group (in this case Biddle and Clay) were using the powers of government to create a powerful economic interest, and gains from monopoly rents thus created were being used to subvert the process of government and threaten the liberties of all citizens by establishing an odious and oppressive government.

His opponents replied in kind. In the election of 1832, they styled themselves National Republicans, and by late 1833 the Whig party was born. In a speech in December 1833 protesting Jackson's removal of federal deposits, Henry Clay concluded:

The eyes and the hopes of the American people are anxiously turned to Congress. They feel that they have been deceived and insulted; their confidence abused; their interests betrayed; and their liberties in danger. They see a rapid and alarming concentration of all power in one man's hands. They see that, by the exercise of the positive authority of the Executive, and his negative power exerted over Congress, the will of one man alone prevails, and governs the republic. The question is no longer what laws will Congress pass, but what will the Executive not veto? The President, and not Congress, is addressed for legislative action. . . . We behold the usual incidents of approaching tyranny. The land is filled with spies and informers, and detraction and denunciation are the orders of the day. People, especially official incumbents in this place, no longer dare speak in the fearless tones of manly freemen, but in the cautious whispers of trembling slaves. The premonitory symptoms of despotism are upon us; and if Congress do not apply an instantaneous and effective remedy, the fatal collapse will soon come on, and we shall die—ignobly die—base, mean, and abject slaves; the scorn and contempt of mankind; unpitied, unwept, unmourned![51]

Clay did not accuse Jackson of venal corruption. Clay and the Whigs charged Jackson with executive usurpation, of systematically corrupting the political process. Following commonwealth theory, tyranny and slavery would inevitably follow.

During the early 1830s, when permanent two-party political competition developed, both parties accused the other of systematic corruption. It

50. From "Paper read to the Cabinet" in the Jackson Papers, L. C.; as quoted in Remini (1967, p. 119).
51. Henry Clay's speech on the "Removal of Deposits," December 30, 1833. *Register of Debates,* 21st Cong., 1st sess., p. 94.

was the most salient issue for American voters. The contest between Clay and Jackson, and the longer struggle between Whigs and Democrats, was fought over classic commonwealth concerns: executive usurpation, the monied conspiracy, corporations, and the appropriate role of government in promoting economic development. The major issues between Democrats and Whigs were economic, but the foundation for the debate over economic policy was a larger debate over systematic corruption.

Jackson's administration resolved two of the paradoxes of American democracy. First, from Jackson onward, demagogues were accepted, as long as they were elected President.[52] Jackson permanently increased the power of the Executive branch. He claimed that the President most effectively represented the collective will of the entire people, as shown in the only nationwide election. Second, political parties became an accepted part of the political system. Suspicion of partisan motivation and the dangers of faction and party remain to the present day, of course.[53] But the national government could not resolve the third paradox—corruption and the promotion of economic development. Jackson's solution to corruption in banking was to not have a bank. He extended the existing federal policy of inaction. Except in the earliest days of the Washington administration, the national government, Congress and executive, were unable to design or execute a program of active government promotion of economic development.

Promotion of economic development was left to the states. By the end of Jackson's second term, states throughout the country were deeply involved in investing in and promoting banks and transportation systems. The investment boom of the 1830s was ended by the depression that began in 1839. By 1842, eight states and the territory of Florida were in default. The crisis in public finance naturally brought investigations into its causes. Venal corruption caused fiscal problems in a few states: Mississippi, Florida, and Arkansas. Most states, however, blamed faulty institutions: they blamed corruption on how democracy was working out in practice.[54]

American state governments were the first governments of their kind in

52. Sprague colorfully expanded on the dangers of Jackson. "The people love their constitution, their liberties, and themselves. They are always politically honest. . . . But they are not infallible . . . oftentimes a military chieftain, having wrought real or fancied deliverance by successful battles—fervent gratitude, unbounded admiration, the best feelings of our nature, rush towards him. . . . In the paroxysm of their devotion, they are ready at his shrine to sacrifice their rights, their liberties, their children, and themselves." Senate Debate, 23rd Cong., 1st sess., on the Removal of the Deposits, January 29, 1834, *Register of Debates,* pp. 386–87.

53. Hofstader (1968) is particularly illuminating on the rise of parties and the role played by Martin Van Buren in the process of rationalizing the need for parties in a democracy.

54. See Wallis, Sylla, and Grinath (2004) for a description of the default crisis and a discussion of its causes. We explicitly consider the role played by naivete and corruption and find that most states were neither. For examples of corruption, both systematic and venal, in American states between 1790 and 1860 and its effect on financial system development, see Wallis (forthcoming).

history. Governed by written constitutions, they operated within the framework of a national government that provided military defense and international relations, a basic legal system, and very little else. States believed that republican government was good. They wanted to promote economic growth, but they worried incessantly that the corporations and privileges they created for that purpose benefitted a favored few to the detriment of the many and undermined the integrity of their governments. States were forced to solve the paradox of corruption and the promotion of economic development. Their solution was elegantly simple: let everybody have a corporate charter who wants one.

Their history endowed American state governments and their citizens with the idea that some problems of government were not caused by bad men, but by bad governments. They were Aristotelian and Polybian in their understanding that the constitution of a government, the *stamina vitae,* created incentives for the actors, politicians, and citizens to pursue particular ends. They were the first modern people to possess extensive experience with written constitutions.[55] The early nineteenth century was an era of continual political debate about the structure of government.

States were the first governments with extensive experience in chartering corporations. The first and most important connections between governments and corporations were fiscal. This was true in Britain, with the mercantilist privileges that Adam Smith complained about. It was true in the American states from the beginning. If governments were going to sell monopoly privileges and corporate charters for revenue, then inevitably each charter required a price, a negotiation, a bargain.[56] This was a feature of any system of government where charters created limited entry into a line of business. Democratic governments could create and sell corporate privileges. Taxpayers liked receiving government services paid for by charter fees, taxes on capital, or dividends on stock. But by its very nature the cre-

---

55. By the 1830s most of the original states had experience with two or more state constitutional conventions and the state ratifying conventions for the national constitution. Only North Carolina and Massachusetts stayed with their first constitution through the Civil War. By 1860, states had written the following number of constitutions: Connecticut, two; Delaware, three; Georgia, three; Maryland, two; New Hampshire, three; New Jersey, two; New York, three; Pennsylvania, three; South Carolina, three; Vermont, two; Virginia, three. Of the new states: Kentucky, two; Tennessee, two; Maine was part of Massachusetts until 1820, when it wrote a new constitution. In addition to the new constitutions, there were several constitutional conventions that produced constitutions that were not ratified by the voters.

56. Andrew Jackson's first complaint in his veto of the proposed charter renewal for the Second Bank of the United States was that the government wasn't getting a good enough deal: "Every monopoly and all exclusive privileges are granted at the expense of the public, which ought to receive a fair equivalent. . . . If our Government must sell monopolies, it would seem to be its duty to take nothing less than their full value, and if gratuities must be made once in fifteen of twenty years let them not be bestowed on the subjects of a foreign government nor upon a designated and favored class of men in our own country." Veto Message, July 10, 1833 (Richardson 1897, pp. 1140–41).

ation of corporate privileges created the opportunity for political groups to create economic privileges that could be used to distort the political process. The commonwealthmen claimed that this happened in Britain with the national debt, it happened in New York with the sale of bank charters to the political friends of the Albany Regency, it was a systematic feature of any government that sold corporate privilege. State governments came to understand that if they remained in the market for selling corporate charters, if they remained willing to consider developers' proposals that promised tax-free provisions of railroads and banks, inevitably some politicians, even well-meaning politicians, would make some serious mistakes. Voters could easily be induced to vote for expenditures that promised large returns without levying taxes. States also came to understand that allowing entry reduced the rents associated with corporate privileges, without eliminating the wider social benefits of creating corporations.

The states' solution to the paradox of corruption and economic development was as simple as it was ingenious. First, states eliminated the pressure to create special corporate privileges by enacting constitutional provisions requiring legislatures to pass general incorporation laws. These laws allowed unlimited entry into corporate status via an administrative procedure. Second, states passed constitutional provisions requiring that all state borrowing required a bond referendum: mandating that the higher taxes necessary to service the bonds be approved by the voters before the bonds were issued. Third, most states forbade state and local investment in private corporations. Between 1841 and 1852, twelve states wrote new constitutions. Eleven of the twelve contained procedural debt restrictions and eight mandated general incorporation acts. In banking, general incorporation acts produced free banking (the first free banking acts were in Michigan and New York in 1837 and 1838). Nine states prohibited incorporation by special legislative acts altogether, prohibiting state legislatures from creating corporations with special privileges.[57]

The point of these reforms was not to eliminate state and local government investments in finance and transportation. Governments could borrow as long as they were willing to raise taxes. The reforms were not designed to limit the creation of corporations. General incorporation acts made it much easier to get a charter. The reforms were designed to reduce or eliminate the private economic rents that were created when the political system limited entry. The reforms intended to reduce the political manipulation of the economic system, not by making such manipulations illegal or unconstitutional, but by reducing the payoff to political machinations. Institutions supporting unlimited entry, free competition,

---

57. The history of these constitutional changes is presented in Wallis (2005). The general relationship between public finance and corporations is discussed in Wallis (2003). For a history of incorporation laws see Evans (1948), and for a larger discussion of the nineteenth-century corporation see Hurst (1970).

and competitive markets were put in place by American states in the 1830s and 1840s. They were the solution to a political problem, not an economic problem. The effect of the reforms, however, was to put in place a critical institutional underpinning of modern economies. It was the uniquely American solution to the paradox of systematic corruption and the promotion of economic development.

1.5   Venal Corruption and Progressive Era Reforms

> Almost any history textbook that covers the Progressive era and was written at least twenty years ago tells how early-twentieth-century Americans discovered how big business interests were corrupting politics in quest of special privileges and how an outraged people acted to reform the perceived evils.
> —McCormick (1981, p. 247)

By the Progressive Era, the fear of systematic corruption, the corruption of economics by politics, had faded. Venal corruption remained, of course, and, as the title of McCormick's essay suggests, there was a growing concern with the "discovery that business corrupts politics." The Civil War, the rise of an integrated national economy, and the development of a thriving manufacturing sector all could have unbalanced and corrupted America's governments. But they did not produce tyranny or dictatorship, and by the 1890s Americans had become more confident in the inherent balance and resilience of their system of government. Corruption no longer seemed to be an inframarginal threat; the system was no longer at risk. When progressive reformers complained about the evils of big business's influence on politics, they no longer warned that slavery and tyranny were just around the corner. Their confidence in the American system was reflected in the constitutional changes made during the era: at the national level the direct election of senators by popular vote and women's suffrage, and at the state and local level the spread of initiatives, referendums, and recalls, and the rise of home rule. Progressive Era constitutional reforms all emphasized an increased role for popular participation in the political process, reforms that were unthinkable a century before.

Benjamin Parke DeWitt, progressive reformer and historian, wrote in his history of the Progressive movement in 1915:

> In this widespread political agitation that at first sight seems so incoherent and chaotic, there may be distinguished upon examination and analysis three tendencies. The first of these tendencies is found in the insistence by the best men in all political parties that special, minority, and corrupt influence in government—national, state, and city—be removed; the second tendency is found in the demand that the structure or machinery of government, which as hitherto been admirably adapted to

control by the few, be so changed and modified that it will be more difficult for the few, and easier for the many, to control; and, finally, the third
tendency is found in the rapidly growing conviction that the functions of
government at present are too restricted and that they must be increased
and extended to relieve social and economic distress. These three tendencies with varying emphasis are seen to-day in the platform and program of every political party; they are manifested in the political
changes and reforms that are advocated and made in the nation, state,
and the cities; and because of the universality and definiteness, they may
be said to constitute the real progressive movement. (DeWitt 1915,
pp. 4–5)

The first Progressive tendency—that special, minority, and corrupt influence in government be removed—could have been written in Rome in 200
BC, Florence in 1500, London in 1720, Philadelphia in 1787, Albany or Indianapolis in the 1840s, or today for that matter. The venal will always be
with us, and venal corruption can only be prevented by eternal vigilance.
The third tendency, a call for government policies to relieve social and economic distress, translated into new social programs like workmen's compensation and mother's pensions in the 1900s and 1910s, but reached its
full measure in the New Deal.[58]

The second tendency, to make changes in the structure and machinery
of government, constituted the heart of the Progressive reform agenda.
DeWitt's language indicates the distance that Progressives had come from
Commonwealthmen. The structure of machinery of government "be so
changed and modified that it will be more difficult for the few, and easier
for the many, to control." A century earlier such a suggestion would have
been a call for unbalanced government—in short, a call for corruption.
The Progressive movement was an anticorruption reform movement,
nonetheless it promoted policies the founding fathers would have regarded
as systematically corrupt.

The Progressive movement produced reforms in three distinct constitutional areas. First, the Progressives altered the relationship between corporations and governments through active regulation and changes in chartering. Second, they expanded direct participation in government; at the
national level through women's suffrage and the direct election of senators,
and at the state and local level through the initiative, referendum, and recall to bring direct democracy into the policy process. Third, they altered
the relationship between state and local governments through home rule
amendments and the local charter movement. These reforms shared several elements. They allowed both public and private sector organizations
more flexibility to choose the form of their internal organization. They in-

---

58. See Wallis, Fishback, and Kantor, this volume, for a discussion of social welfare in the
New Deal and the end of corruption in relief administration.

creased the acceptable range of interaction between government and the economy, allowing governments to interfere and regulate business, or to withdraw their regulation. Finally, the entire process was to be monitored by more democracy, by putting more power in the hands of the many. The Progressives believed in balanced government. But it was the checks and balances of the national and state constitutions, not the balance of social orders and classes reflecting the interests of the one, the few, and the many.

State chartering policy links the Progressive and Jacksonian eras. The widespread adoption of general incorporation acts in the 1840s liberalized access to corporate charters and the number of corporations in America exploded, relative to both early American history and contemporary European economies.[59] But general incorporation acts liberalized entry while putting more severe restrictions on the structure of corporations. All corporations created under a general act shared common features. In states that banned special incorporation altogether, a corporation that wanted to change its internal voting rules, shareholder rights, or its management structure was severely constrained.[60] For example, corporations were typically prohibited from owning stock in corporations domiciled in other states. All this began to change in New Jersey in the late 1880s.[61]

In a series of acts between 1888 and 1896, New Jersey created liberal general incorporation. These acts allowed corporations to merge and hold stock in other corporations, to operate outside of the state, and to define their internal governance structure within much wider bounds. Corporations flocked to New Jersey, swelling the state's revenues and opening up new opportunities for corporate structure throughout the country. What followed was the great merger movement. Between 1895 and 1904 there was a rapid consolidation of the nation's largest manufacturing firms. Over half of the consolidations involving more than $1 million in capital took place in New Jersey (Grandy 1989, pp. 678 and 681–83).[62] New York and Delaware soon followed New Jersey's lead, liberalizing their incorporation laws and trying to lure businesses into their states.

Attributing the Progressive Era to the merger movement would be silly, although there is a remarkable coincidence of timing. "Yet, given the long-term forces involved, it is notable how suddenly the main elements of the

59. For a comparison on corporate chartering in France and the United States, see Lamoreaux and Rosenthal (2004). Their point that the options open to structure firms in France was much more flexible than the options open to firms in the United States is a key argument in this section.

60. For a discussion of general incorporation acts see Dunlavy (2004), Million (1990), and Mark (2000). The actual structure of corporations under general acts is an area of which legal and economic historians are almost completely ignorant. Dunlavy's paper and her current project examining a large sample of corporate charters is beginning to shed light on this critical area.

61. For the history of New Jersey corporations, see Cadman (1949). For the specifics of New Jersey's changing corporation policy, see Grandy (1989).

62. For a general history of the merger wave see Lamoreaux (1985) and Nelson (1959).

new political order went into place. The first fifteen years of the twentieth century witnessed most of the changes; more precisely, the brief period from 1904 to 1908 saw a remarkably compressed political transformation. During these years the regulatory revolution peaked; new and powerful agencies of government came into being everywhere" (McCormick 1981, p. 252). When a small number of unprecedentedly large corporations sprang into being during the merger wave, the national and state governments responded to the public perception that corruption was again a problem in American politics. But they responded much differently in the first decades of the twentieth century than they did in the nineteenth century.

Giving more control to the many was the mechanism by which "special, minority, and corrupt influence in government—national, state, and city—[could] be removed" (DeWitt 1915). The constitutional machinery of the progressive constitutional reforms were electoral and democratic. At the national level, the direct election of senators by popular majorities and suffrage for women were the key progressive accomplishments. At the state level, the adoption of the initiative, referendum, and recall gave voters direct control over legislation and officials. Initiative, referendum, and recall were adopted at the local level as well, but the critical change was the widespread adoption of home rule provisions and new methods of chartering local governments. These transferred control of local governments from state to local governments, providing voters with the ability to directly shape local government policies to suit the ends of local majorities.

Battling venal corruption and regulating the excesses of the plutocrats charged the Progressive movement with a populist morality and a renewed faith in majoritarian democracy. It is striking how much of the Progressive rhetoric, perhaps in combination with the symbols of the temperance movement, focuses on bad men rather than on bad institutions. The medicine prescribed by progressives to cure corruption would have seemed insane to a founding father. Systematic corruption flowed from the ability of politicians to use the economic system to further their political ends. Electoral excess, tyranny of the majority, and mob rule were serious threats that had to be balanced by the creation of other centers of power in the political system. Progressive reforms celebrated popular sovereignty, the concept that the voters were the ultimate judges of government policy. Deciding whether politicians and policies were venally corrupt could be left to popular choice. The many would decide whether the few had violated their mandate to govern on behalf of the common good. Majorities really would rule.

How could this happen? One constant element in earlier discussions of systematic corruption in America and Britain was that it inevitably leads to tyranny and slavery. Such language is not to be found in the Progressive Era. Between 1840 and 1890 American crossed a divide. On the early side of the divide governments could never be trusted. Politicians would always, if the chance presented itself, use the powers of government to manipulate the economic system in order to consolidate their control of the political system. Consolidation of political control upset the delicate balance of government and, with Polybian certainty, led to tyranny and slavery. Balance in government could never be assumed. Small changes in the distribution of power could quickly lead to imbalance. The defense of liberty required eternal vigilance. On the later side of the divide, balance in government is no longer fragile. Tyranny and slavery are still possibilities, but highly improbable ones. By allowing, indeed mandating, more competition and entry into the economic and political system, Madison's extended republic, as modified by the states, had produced a stable balance within government.

In classic commonwealth political theory, increasing government regulation raised as many red flags as did special corporate charters. Regulation created the opportunity for creating rents, and rent creation created the possibility for political manipulation of the economy. One could see James I or Charles II supporting Progressive policies, not Whig commonwealthmen. If, on the other hand, political and economic competition limit rent creation and dissipation, they also make it safer for the government to regulate in positive and negative ways. Competition and entry create their own balanced equilibrium.

This could only have happened if Americans came to trust their government more than they ever had in the colonial, revolutionary, or early national periods.[63] Progressive Era reforms increased political entry by widening the scope of popular democratic political institutions: direct election of senators, women's suffrage, the initiative, the referendum, the recall, and home rule. At the same time, Progressive Era policy reforms created much wider opportunities for rent-seeking by politicians and economic actors, trusting, apparently, that voters could monitor the new powers given to their representatives. The threat of systematic corruption, so prevalent for three centuries in British and American political and economic thinking, had receded to the point of disappearance from the political debates of the Progressive Era.

1.6   The End of Systematic Corruption

One way to think about developing countries is that they are poor because their government officials are venally corrupt. If only the right people and policies could be put in place, economic growth would ensue. A more pessimistic and realistic view is that developing countries are systematically

---

63. This "trust" is historically relative; Americans retain a profound ability to mistrust government.

corrupt. They are plagued by governments that systematically manipulate the economy to produce economic rents to further the political interests of the people and parties in power. This is not a matter of bad people causing problems. This is a fundamental flaw in the constitutional structure, the *stamina vitae,* of these societies.

The United States came by its fear of systematic corruption legitimately. It was born in a constitutional crisis rooted in Whig paranoia about the threat to fundamental liberties of all Britons embodied in the executive usurpation of Parliamentary independence. The emerging institutions of modern financial capitalism—a national debt, a central bank, a stock market, and a host of financial intermediaries—were not the causes of corruption. The institutions of modern financial capitalism were the instruments of systematic corruption, tools in the hands of the Crown and its evil ministers. British corruption threatened fundamental liberties. The storm warnings of tyranny and slavery were flying in 1776. Today, of course, we see the eighteenth century as the dawning of a new era of personal and economic liberty that produced modern economies and societies. Early Americans could not afford to be complacent.

The founding fathers seized the first chance to write their own constitutions in 1776, crafting a series of state constitutions implementing precepts of balanced government. They didn't get it right the first time. Between 1776 and 1852 the original thirteen states wrote twenty-nine constitutions and the national government wrote two. Congress implemented Hamilton's financial plan in 1791, deliberately modeled on the British financial system: a national debt, a central bank, and assumption of state debts. Within a year, national politics fragmented over the charge that Hamilton and the Federalists were establishing a Prime Ministry with Hamilton at the center of a web of influence and interest. The national government remained gridlocked for decades over how, and whether, economic development should be promoted. When the national government's experiment in central banking came to an end with Jackson's veto of the charter of the Bank of the United States in 1832, the issue was still systematic corruption. Clay claimed that "we shall die—ignobly die—base, mean, and abject slaves; the scorn and contempt of mankind; unpitied, unwept, unmourned!" if Jackson went unchecked.

Meanwhile, in the 1790s states began chartering banks, churches, and all varieties of corporations. By the 1820s states were building canals, experimenting with railroads, borrowing money, and investing their own funds in corporations. By the 1830s there were over 600 state-chartered banks, and state debt for internal improvement investment was double the national debt accumulated during the Revolution and the War of 1812. State activism did not go unchallenged. Corporations were still regarded as potential vehicles for corruption. Bank chartering under New York's Albany Regency was a classic example of systematic corruption: a political faction using the creation of economic privilege to secure its control of the political system. The central theme in Jackson's rise to prominence was an attack on corruption, an attack on government-created privilege. Of course, most American governments were not thoroughly systematically corrupt, but there were warning signs everywhere, New York included. Americans did not fear that their governments were corrupt: they worried that their governments would become corrupt if they did not take measures to protect and strengthen the institutions that supported balanced government.

When the internal improvement boom collapsed after 1839, states carefully reexamined the policies that had led them to issue $200 million in state bonds. States again turned to their constitutions and implemented a series of reforms that mandated general incorporation acts guaranteeing free entry into corporate privileges, modified the procedures by which state and local governments borrowed money, and prohibited government investment in private corporations. With few exceptions, the constitutional reforms were not bans on state promotion of economic development. They did not prevent governments from chartering banks, building canals or railroads, or, in the Progressive Era, building municipal water systems, sewer systems, and school systems. Constitutional reforms were explicitly designed to cut away the roots of systematic corruption, by limiting the government's ability to create economic rents through limiting entry and granting special economic privileges.

Republican and Federalists in the 1790s, Whigs and Democrats in the 1840s, were just as concerned with venal corruption as the Progressives in the first decade of the twentieth century. But venal corruption was not the most dangerous problem facing America before the Civil War. Tyranny and slavery were all around the world of the early nineteenth century. France went from absolute monarchy, to revolution, to dictatorship, and back to monarchy. Spain's New World empire collapsed in a wave of revolutions, many inspired by the United State's example. New World revolutionary governments often adopted constitutions explicitly modeled on the United States, checks and balances and separation of powers included. But tyranny, not liberty, was typically the fruit of revolution in Latin and South America. Americans feared that any movement away from balanced government would bring, with Polybian certainty, an erosion of republican government and the rise of tyranny and slavery.

By 1890, however, not only was the American experiment in limited government a demonstrable success, but the country's institutions had persisted through a bloody civil war, with liberty intact and chattel slavery ended. Fear of tyranny and slavery was justifiably receding. A modern industrial economy and the world's largest integrated market posed a new set of problems for governments. After tentative first steps at economic regulation in the 1870s and 1880s, the national government effloresced in the first half of the twentieth century, as the papers in this volume show so clearly. Giving the national government control over food and drugs would have seemed insane to the founding fathers, Federalist and Republican. Such regulation opened up vistas of rent creation beyond the imagination of James I or Charles II.

Yet, for all the fear of corruption that filled the rhetoric of Progressive reformers, the corruption documented so ably in this volume is distinctly venal corruption. The Progressives were not afraid that a faction within government would use the creation of economic privileges to seize control of the government. They were concerned that economic interests were using their growing size to wrest concessions from governments. They worried about the efficiency of American government, about the quality of representation, of equity, access, and fairness. They worried that economics corrupted politics. They did not worry about politics corrupting economics.

The landmark accomplishment of the western democracies in the nineteenth and twentieth centuries has been the creation of stable, limited government. No society with a systematically corrupt political system has limited government. The economic system is always at risk, entry is limited, competition is fettered, and economic policies are shaped by politicians to maintain their political control of the government. Crony capitalism is not a manifestation of venal corruption—it is a symptom of systematic corruption. Developing countries do not have markets that work well, because the open access and competition necessary to make impersonal markets work cannot flourish when entry is limited to create the privileges that hold the political system together. What lessons does the United States have to teach about corruption? The fundamental lesson is how to construct a government that does not depend on manipulation of the economy for its continued existence.

References

Aristotle. 1996. *The politics and the constitution of Athens.* Ed. Stephen Everson. New York: Cambridge University Press.

Bailyn, Bernard. 1967. *The ideological origins of the American Revolution.* Cambridge, MA: Harvard University Press.

Banning, Lance. 1978. *The Jeffersonian persuasion.* Ithaca, NY: Cornell University Press.

Benson, Lee. 1961. *The concept of Jacksonian democracy: New York as a test case.* Princeton, NJ: Princeton University Press.

Bodenhorn, Howard. 2000. *A history of banking in antebellum America.* Cambridge: Cambridge University Press.

———. 2003. *State banking in early America: A new economic history.* Oxford: Oxford University Press.

Bolingbroke, Henry St. John. 1997. *Political writings.* Ed. David Armitage. New York: Cambridge University Press.

Brewer, John. 1989. *The sinews of power: War, money, and the English state, 1688–1783.* New York: Knopf.

Cadman, John W. 1949. *The corporation in New Jersey: Business and politics, 1791–1875.* Cambridge, MA: Harvard University Press.

Clague, Christopher. 2003. The international campaign against corruption: An institutionalist perspective. In *Collective choice: Essays in honor of Mancur Olson,* ed. Jac C. Heckelman and Dennis Coates, 187–218. New York: Springer.

Davis, John P. 1961. *Corporations: A study of the development of the origin and development of great business combinations and their relation to the authority of the state.* New York: Capricorn.

DeWitt, Benjamin Parke. [1915] 1968. *The Progressive movement: A non-partisan, comprehensive discussion of current tendencies in American politics.* Repr. Seattle: University of Washington Press.

Dickson, P. G. M. 1967. *The financial revolution in England: A study in the development of public credit, 1688–1756.* London: Macmillan.

Dodd, Edwin Merrick. 1954. *American business corporations until 1860; with special reference to Massachusetts.* Cambridge, MA: Harvard University Press.

Dunlavy, Colleen A. 2004. From citizens to plutocrats: Nineteenth century shareholder voting rights and theories of the corporation. In *Crossing corporate boundaries: History, politics, and culture,* ed. Kenneth Lipartito and David B. Sicilia, 66–93. New York: Oxford University Press.

Evans, George Heberton. 1948. *Business incorporations in the United States, 1800–1943.* NBER General Series no. 49. Baltimore: Waverly Press.

Ferejohn, John, Jack N. Rakove, and Jonathan Riley. 2001. *Constitutional culture and democratic rule.* New York: Cambridge University Press.

Ferguson, E. James. 1961. *The power of the purse: A history of American public finance, 1776–1790.* Chapel Hill: University of North Carolina Press.

Goodrich, Carter. 1950. The revulsion against internal improvements. *Journal of Economic History* 10 (November): 145–69.

———. 1960. *Government promotion of American canals and railroads.* New York: Columbia University Press.

Grandy, Christopher. 1989. New Jersey corporate chartermongering, 1875–1929. *Journal of Economic History* 49 (September): 677–92.

Handlin, Oscar, and Mary Flug Handlin. 1969. *Commonwealth: A study of the role of government in the American economy; Massachusetts, 1774–1861.* Cambridge, MA: Belknap Press.

Harrington, James. 1992. *The commonwealth of Oceana and a system of politics.* Ed. J. G. A. Pocock. New York: Cambridge University Press.

Hofstadter, Richard. 1969. *The idea of a party system.* Berkeley: University of California Press.

Hurst, James Willard. 1970. *The legitimacy of the business corporation in the law of the United States, 1780–1970.* Charlottesville: University of Virginia Press.

Jensen, Merrill. [1940] 1970. *The articles of confederation.* Madison: University of Wisconsin Press.

Klitgaard, R. 1988. *Controlling corruption.* Berkeley: University of California Press.

Lamoreaux, Naomi. 1985. *The great merger movement in American business, 1895–1904.* New York: Cambridge University Press.

———. 2004. Partnerships, corporations, and the limits on contractual freedom in U.S. history: An essay in economics, law, and culture. In *Crossing corporate boundaries: History, politics, and culture,* ed. Kenneth Lipartito and David B. Sicilia, 29–65. New York: Oxford University Press.

Lamoreaux, Naomi, and Jean-Laurent Rosenthal. 2004. Legal regime and business's organizational choice. NBER Working Paper no. 10288. Cambridge, MA: National Bureau of Economic Research, February.

Larson, John Lauritz. 2001. *Internal improvement: National public works and the promise of popular government in the early United States.* Chapel Hill: University of North Carolina Press.

Machiavelli, Niccolo. 1996. *Discourses on Livy.* Trans. H. Mansfield and N. Tarcov. Chicago: University of Chicago Press.

Maier, Pauline. 1992. The debate over incorporations: Massachusetts in the early republic. In *Massachusetts and the new nation,* ed. Conrad Wright, 76–77. Boston: Massachusetts Historical Society.

———. 1993. The revolutionary origins of the American corporation. *William and Mary Quarterly,* 3rd ser., 50 (January): 51–84.

Mark, Gregory. 2000. The role of the state in corporate law formation. *International Corporate Law Annal* 1:5–9.

Mathias, Peter, and Patrick O'Brien. 1976. Taxation in Britain and France, 1715–1810: A comparison of the social and economic incidence of taxes collected for the central government. *Journal of European Economic History* 5:601–50.

McCormick, Richard L. 1981. The discovery that business corrupts politics: A reappraisal of the origins of Progressivism. *The American Historical Review* 86 (April): 247–74.

McCoy, Drew R. 1980. *Elusive republic: Political economy in Jeffersonian America.* Chapel Hill: University of North Carolina Press.

Million, David. 1990. Theories of the corporation. *Duke Law Journal* 1990:201–62.

Murrin, John M. 1994. Escaping perfidious Albion: Federalism, fear of corruption, and democratization of corruption in postrevolutionary America. In *Virtue, corruption, and self-interest,* ed. Richard K. Matthews, 103–47. Bethlehem, PA: Lehigh University Press.

Namier, Sir Lewis, and John Brooke. 1964. *The House of Commons, 1754–1790.* London: Parliament Trust.

Nelson, Ralph L. 1959. *Merger movements in American industry, 1895–1956.* Princeton, NJ: Princeton University Press.

North, Douglass C., and Barry R. Weingast. 1989. Constitutions and commitment: The evolution of institutions governing public choice in seventeenth century England. *Journal of Economic History* 49 (December): 189–210.

Pocock, J. G. A. 1972. Virtue and commerce in the eighteenth century. *Journal of Interdisciplinary History* 3 (Summer): 119–34.

———. 1973. *Politics, language, and time.* New York: Atheneum.

———. 1975. *The Machiavellian moment: Florentine political thought and the Atlantic republican tradition.* Princeton, NJ: Princeton University Press.

———, ed. 1977. *The political works of James Harrington.* Cambridge: Cambridge University Press.

———. 1985. *Virtue, commerce, and history.* Cambridge: Cambridge University Press.

———. 1987. *Ancient constitution and the feudal law.* New York: Cambridge University Press.

Polybius. 1962. *The histories of Polybius.* Vol. 1. Trans. Evelyn S. Shuckburgh. Westport, CT: Greenwood Press.

Remini, Robert V. 1967. *Andrew Jackson and the bank war.* New York: W. W. Norton.

Richardson, James D. 1897. *The messages and papers of the presidents.* Washington: Bureau of National Literature.

Robbins, Caroline. 1959. *The eighteenth-century commonwealthman.* Cambridge, MA: Harvard University Press.

Rose-Ackerman, Susan. 1978. *Corruption: A study in political economy.* New York: Academic Press.

Rousseau, Peter. 2002. Jacksonian monetary policy, specie flows, and the panic of 1837. *Journal of Economic History* 62 (June): 457–88.

Seavoy, Ronald E. 1982. *The origins of the American business corporation, 1784–1855.* Westport, CT: Greenwood Press.

Shalhope, Robert E. 1972. Toward a republican synthesis: The emergence of an understanding on republicanism in American historiography. *The William and Mary Quarterly* 29 (January): 49–80.

———. 1982. Republicanism and Early American historiography. *The William and Mary Quarterly* 39 (April): 334–56.

Shleifer, Andrei, and Robert Vishny. 1993. Corruption. *Quarterly Journal of Economics* 108 (3): 599–617.

Skinner, Quentin. 1978a. *The foundations of modern political thought.* Vol. 1, *The Renaissance.* New York: Cambridge University Press.

———. 1978b. *The foundations of modern political thought.* Vol. 2, *The age of reformation.* New York: Cambridge University Press.

———. 1998. *Liberty before liberalism.* New York: Cambridge University Press.

Smith, Adam. [1776] 1981. *An inquiry into the nature and causes of the wealth of nations.* Indianapolis, IN: Liberty Fund.

Sylla, Richard, John B. Legler, and John Joseph Wallis. 1987. Banks and state public finance in the new republic. *Journal of Economic History* 47 (2): 391–403.

Temin, Peter. 1969. *The Jacksonian economy.* New York: W. W. Norton.

Tocqueville, Alexis de. 1966. *Democracy in America.* Trans. George Lawrence. New York: Harper and Row. (Orig. pub. 1835, 1840.)

Trenchard, John, and Thomas Gordon. 1995. *Cato's letters.* Ed. Ronald Hamowry. Indianapolis, IN: Liberty Fund.

Wallis, John Joseph. 2003a. Market augmenting government? The state and the corporation in 19th century America. In *Market-augmenting government: The institutional foundations for prosperity,* ed. Omar Azfar and Charles Cadwell, 223–65. Ann Arbor: University of Michigan Press.

———. 2003b. The public promotion of private interest (groups). In *Collective choice: Essays in honor of Mancur Olson,* ed. Jac Heckelman and Dennis Coates, 219–46. New York: Springer-Verlag.

———. 2005. Constitutions, corporations, and corruption: American states and constitutional change, 1842 to 1852. *Journal of Economic History* 65 (March): 211–56.

———. Forthcoming a. American government and the promotion of economic development in the national era, 1790 to 1860. In *Government and the American economy,* ed. Price Fishback.

———. Forthcoming b. Answering Mary Shirley's question: Or why the World Bank should pay attention to American history. In *Economics, political institutions, and financial markets,* ed. Stephen Haber and Barry Weingast.

———. *The NBER/Maryland State Constitution Project.* http://129.2.168.174/constitution/.

Wallis, John Joseph, Richard Sylla, and Arthur Grinath. 2004. Sovereign default and repudiation: The emerging market debt crisis in the U.S. states, 1839–1843.

NBER Working Paper no. 10753. Cambridge, MA: National Bureau of Economic Research, September.

Wallis, John Joseph, Richard Sylla, and John Legler. 1994. The interaction of taxation and regulation in nineteenth century U.S. banking. In *The regulated economy: A historical approach to political economy,* ed. C. Goldin and G. Libecap, 121–44. Chicago: University of Chicago Press.

Wallis, John Joseph, and Barry Weingast. 2005. Equilibrium federal impotence: Why the states and not the American national government financed infrastructure investment in the antebellum era. NBER Working Paper no. 11397. Cambridge, MA: National Bureau of Economic Research, June.

Weston, Corinne Comstock. 1965. *English constitutional theory and the House of Lords, 1556–1832.* London: Routledge and Kegan Paul.

Wood, Gordon S. 1969. *The creation of the American republic, 1776–1787.* Chapel Hill: University of North Carolina Press.

Worley, Ted R. 1950. The control of the real estate bank of the state of Arkansas, 1836–1855. *The Mississippi Valley Historical Review* 37 (3): 403–26.

2

Limiting the Reach of the Grabbing Hand
Graft and Growth in American Cities, 1880 to 1930

Rebecca Menes

> The people had been taught to expect but little from their
> rulers: good water, good light, clean streets, well paved, fair
> transportation, the decent repression of vice, public order and
> public safety, and no scandalous or open corruption, would
> more than satisfy them . . . the public was getting something
> for its money,—not full value, but a good percentage.
> —Lincoln Steffens ([1904] 1957, p. 144)

American cities present us with a puzzle. Between 1880 and 1930 the cities
were notorious for corruption. Corruption generally undermines government performance and cripples economic growth, but American cities
prospered. The cities grew rapidly, attracting new residents from the rural
United States and from abroad. American firms built new factories in the
cities, developing new products and new processes and making the United
States the leading industrial power in the world. The city governments accommodated the new growth, leading the world in the provision of clean
water, sewers, paving, education, gas, electricity, public safety, public
health, and mass transportation (Teaford 1984).

Corruption deters economic activity and investment, just as a tax does,
because it lowers returns to economic activity. However, corruption can do
more damage than a tax of the same size. Corruption is unpredictable and
can increase as the economic returns to an activity increase. Corruption
can lower the quality of government. Corrupt governments may provide

Rebecca Menes is an assistant professor of economics at George Mason University, and a
faculty research fellow of the National Bureau of Economic Research.

The term "Grabbing Hand" is borrowed from Shleifer and Vishny (2002).

lower quantity and quality of the public goods and social services, such as infrastructure and education, that support economic growth. Corruption can suppress economic growth by encouraging officials to interfere with private business. Corrupt officials discourage entry and investment in the private sector by demanding bribes for licenses and inspections and by accepting bribes from businesses that wish to have local markets manipulated in their own interest. And corruption can undermine the police and courts, protecting criminals, subverting the enforcement of private contracts, and decreasing the security of property (Kaufmann 1997; Krueger 1993; Murphy, Shleifer, and Vishny 1993; Shleifer and Vishny 1993).

At the end of the nineteenth and beginning of the twentieth century, American urban politicians took advantage of their opportunities. Municipal contracts and franchises were notoriously corrupt, regulations were applied unevenly, and access to rail and water was available only for a price. In most cities, politicians and officials accepted bribes from organized crime, and in some cities, politicians and officials organized the crime themselves—especially gambling, prostitution, and illegal sales of alcohol. How did corruption *not* cripple growth? There is no single answer, but corrupt officials faced strong incentives to limit their corruption and to provide good government in spite of corruption. The open borders of the cities, the ballot box, and the bond market punished greedy politicians who ignored the limits. Rapid city growth rewarded the circumspect grafter with opportunities for what one famous Tammany Hall politician termed "honest graft" (Riordan [1905] 1994, p. 53).

In this essay, I first discuss the evidence for corruption in American cities over time and across the nation, showing that corruption did indeed peak between 1880 and 1930. Second, I compare the conditions in American cities with what we now believe to be the causes and consequences of corruption. Third, I introduce a guide to corruption as it was practiced in the United States between 1880 and 1930. Fourth, I discuss two important democratic responses to corruption, political machines and political reform.

2.1   History of American Urban Corruption

Were American cities unusually corrupt during what we now call the Reform or Progressive Era—broadly speaking, from the 1880s until the New Deal? Contemporary observers believed they were. Authors such as Lincoln Steffens and James Bryce reported that city governments had grown more corrupt than previously, that they were generally more corrupt than state or national governments, and that they were more corrupt than foreign city governments—at least, more corrupt than the governments of northern European cities (Bryce 1895, 2:163; Steffens [1904] 1957; Teaford 1984, p. 1). Ever since the New Deal, interest in many aspects of city government, including corruption, has declined. The decline may reflect a fall in corruption, or a fall in concern as the relative importance of local government declined. The histories of individual cities suggest that corruption did subside in most of the larger cities. However, it would be more convincing to find a single historical source that allows a comparison of corruption in cities across time.

The most comprehensive political history of large American cities over time is the *Biographical Dictionary of American Mayors, 1820–1980,* edited by Melvin Holli and Peter d'A. Jones. I use this history to determine whether American cities were unusually corrupt between 1880 and 1930. The *Biographical Dictionary* includes the histories of the 678 mayors of fifteen large American cities.[1] The book is not an antiquarian exercise but an academic work by two leading urban political scientists. The authors are forced by the discipline of the format to evaluate each mayor, the obscure and dull as well as the famous and colorful. Each entry includes a personal history, election or elections, and the leading issues, accomplishments, and failures of the mayor's administration, including corruption.

Government corruption is the misuse of public power for private purposes. Based on this definition, I code each mayoral administration according to two measures: (a) whether any member of the administration was reported to be corrupt, including the mayor, and (b) whether the mayor was personally corrupt.[2] I do not separate the administrations into honest and dishonest periods. If corruption ever occurred, the administration and/or the mayor is considered corrupt for the entire term of office. This classification seems more realistic than calling the government corrupt only in the year someone was caught. I now turn to consider the relationship between the measures of corruption and the city characteristics. The major limitation to this analysis is the size of the population, only fifteen cities, but it cannot be expanded since this is the historical population of large American cities.

According to the *Biographical Dictionary,* corruption in the fifteen large

1. The cities are listed in table 2.1. There is no single year in which these fifteen cities were simultaneously the largest fifteen, but viewed from the vantage of 1980 they are the fifteen most important. For ease of discussion I shall refer to this group as simply the fifteen large American cities.

2. The coding includes venal corruption and vote fraud, but not patronage or political violence. The Biographical Dictionary captures corruption that involved the mayor or senior members of the administration. The source is not perfect. Especially good grafters may have escaped detection, honest politicians were occasionally unfairly smeared, and in periods of extreme political or economic upheaval only the most serious corruption may have been noticed. The 1930s and 1960s may suffer from this last bias. However, the evaluation is far more consistent, across cities and years, than any other source I have found for the United States. When the mayor is coded as honest, I mean he was personally honest. He may or may not have condoned corruption in his administration. By this measure, Mayor Daley, Sr., of Chicago was honest. I do not code for the combination of corrupt mayor and honest administration, since it was not observed. I will employ the male pronoun for the corrupt mayors, as none of the handful of women mayors were reported to be personally corrupt.

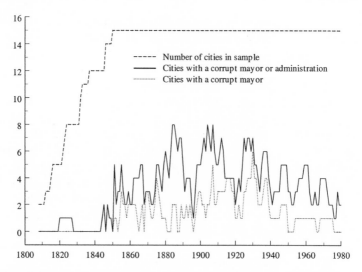

Fig. 2.1   Presence of administrative and mayoral corruption in fifteen large U.S. cities

Source: Corruption measures are derived from Holli and Jones (1980).

Note: See text for discussion and table 2.1 for the identity of the fifteen cities.

American cities peaked during the Reform Era, 1880 to 1930. In figure 2.1 I plot the change over time in the two measures of corruption, starting in 1820. According to these measures corruption was nearly nonexistent before 1850, rose between 1850 and 1880, remained at a relatively high level—fluctuating but with no overall trend—between 1880 and 1930, and then declined from the 1930s through the 1970s. In table 2.1 I summarize the presence of corruption (the first measure, mayoral and/or administrative corruption) for each of the fifteen cities.[3] Between 1851 and 1880, on average nearly one out of four of these cities was corrupt; between 1880 and 1930 the level rose by nearly 50 percent, to more than one out of three; after 1930 the reported level declined, falling back to about one out of four.

Corruption in the fifteen large cities is correlated with city size, but not with region or with city growth. In table 2.2 I report the population and rate of growth for each of the fifteen cities. In general, the larger cities were more corrupt. In the last row of table 2.2 I report the correlation between

---

3. Tables 2.1 and 2.2 omit 1820–1850. Before 1850, corruption is reported in only three cities, New Orleans, San Francisco, and Pittsburgh. However, this may underestimate the presence of corruption, because the population of cities is incomplete before 1850. However, even when we adjust for the number of years reported for each city, corruption was rare before 1850. For the 332 city-years covered before 1850, only fifteen city-years, or 4.5 percent, were corrupt according to the first measure. The cities for which corruption is reported are also somewhat unusual. Pittsburgh was still a small town more than a city. Politics in New Orleans and San Francisco was complicated by the transition from colonial legal systems (French and Spanish, respectively) to American.

Table 2.1   **Fraction of city-years under a corrupt mayor or administration, by city,
                    for fifteen large U.S. cities**

City	Corruption 1850–1880	Corruption 1881–1930	Corruption 1931–1980
Baltimore	0.43	0.18	0.08
Boston	0	0.46	0.14
Buffalo	0	0.04	0.30
Chicago	0.50	0.76	0.92
Cincinnati	0.27	0.12	0
Cleveland	0	0.24	0.20
Detroit	0.03	0.26	0.12
Los Angeles	0.27	0.22	0.12
Milwaukee	0.20	0.28	0
New Orleans	0.33	0.64	0.54
New York	0.67	0.58	0.18
Philadelphia	0.17	0.68	0.42
Pittsburgh	0.23	0.32	0.06
San Francisco	0.33	0.20	0.16
St. Louis	0	0.20	0.04
Average	0.23	0.35	0.23

Notes: Corruption is measured as the percentage of years during the period in which the city
had a corrupt administration or mayor. The fifteen large American cities are those whose political histories are included in the *Biographic Dictionary of American Mayors: 1820–1980*
(Holli and Jones 1980). See text for discussion of the corruption variable.

population at the beginning of each period and corruption during the period. The correlation is always positive, hovering around 0.6 until 1930,
then dropping to 0.28 between 1930 and 1980. Despite the small number of
cities, this result is not driven by outliers. Between 1850 and 1880 three of
the five largest cities were among the most corrupt; between 1880 and 1930
four of the five largest cities were among the most corrupt. Only after 1930,
when the governments of both Boston and New York improved (slightly),
were three of the five most corrupt cities also relatively small.[4] Corruption
was not consistently related to location. Northeastern, midwestern, western, and southern cities all experienced periods of corrupt government.[5]

The American growth paradox remains. There is no evidence that corruption was good for growth, but likewise no evidence that corruption was
bad for growth. Across the fifteen cities there is no statistical relationship
at all between corruption and growth. As I show in the last row of table
2.2, the correlation between growth and corruption bounces around,

4. The positive correlation is not because random chance produces more corruption in the
larger administrations of large cities. Each city has only one mayor, but mayoral corruption
is also positively correlated with city size.

5. The two California cities may exhibit a slightly different pattern over time. Corruption
appears to peak earlier, between 1850 and 1880, in Los Angeles and San Francisco.

Table 2.2   Population and growth rates of fifteen large U.S. cities, by period, and correlated with corruption

City	1850–1880		1881–1930		1931–1980		1981–2000	
	Pop. in 1850 (1000s)	Annual growth (%)	Pop. in 1880 (1000s)	Annual growth (%)	Pop. in 1930 (1000s)	Annual growth (%)	Pop. in 1980 (1000s)	Annual growth (%)
Baltimore	169	2.25	332	1.77	805	−0.05	787	−0.95
Boston	137	3.25	363	1.53	781	−0.66	563	0.23
Buffalo	42	4.33	155	2.61	573	−0.94	358	−1.01
Chicago	30	9.40	503	3.81	3,376	−0.23	3,005	−0.18
Cincinnati	115	2.64	255	1.14	451	−0.31	385	−0.76
Cleveland	17	7.47	160	3.45	900	−0.90	574	−0.91
Detroit	21	5.70	116	5.20	1,569	−0.53	1,203	−1.18
Los Angeles	2	6.46	11	9.41	1,238	1.75	2,967	1.10
Milwaukee	20	5.84	116	3.22	578	0.19	636	−0.32
New Orleans	116	2.06	216	1.51	459	0.39	558	−0.70
New York	516	2.83	1,206	3.50	6,930	0.04	7,072	0.62
Philadelphia	121	6.48	847	1.67	1,951	−0.29	1,688	−0.53
Pittsburgh	47	4.04	156	2.91	670	−0.91	424	−1.18
San Francisco	35	6.36	234	2.00	634	0.14	679	0.67
St. Louis	78	5.01	351	1.70	822	−1.19	453	−1.32
Average	98	4.90	335	3.0	1,449	−0.2	1,423	−0.4
Correlation with corruption	0.59	−0.13	0.61	−0.09	0.28	0.00	0.02	

Notes: The population figures are from Gibson (1998). Growth in first three periods is correlated with corruption during the period. Growth in the last period (1981–2000) is correlated with corruption 1931–1980. Population at the beginning of each of the first three periods correlated with corruption during the period.

sometimes negative, sometimes positive, but never far from zero. Yet all fifteen cities were growing between 1850 and 1930, while corruption was rising. Corruption began to fall after 1930, just as growth rates stagnated. The puzzle remains.

Are these rates of corruption high or low? On the one hand, even during the worst years of urban corruption, at most eight of the fifteen cities are reported as corrupt. On the other hand, the *Biographical Dictionary* only reports corruption that occurs at a relatively high level of the administration, so these numbers represent a minimum estimate of the presence of corruption. None of the cities were immune to corruption during the Reform Era. Even Buffalo, the least corrupt of the cities, spent two years under a corrupt administration. However, none of these cities were always corrupt. Even Chicago, the most corrupt, spent twelve years under reportedly honest administrations. In short, the evidence suggests that corruption was common, but so was resistance to corruption. The political histories also show that political competition and regime change were common in American cities. Even during the most corrupt periods, the corrupt mayors and council members operated in a world where they could be voted out of office.

2.2   Growth and Corruption: American Cities Since 1820

In this section I explore the forces that encouraged corruption and those that suppressed it. Economists and political scientists have explored the relationship between corruption, poor government, and growth. Corruption can undermine growth as a tax does, by lowering the returns to economic activity. Corruption also undermines growth because it leads to poor government (Kaufmann 1997; Wei and Shleifer 2000). One explanation for the relative success of American cities is that, despite corruption, they had relatively good government, but this only replaces one puzzle with another. Why, in American cities, did corruption not lead to poor government?

From 1880 to 1930 the dominant economic feature of American cities was growth.[6] Corruption may be bad for growth, but growth attracts corruption, especially the kind of growth enjoyed by American cities. It was the period of the merger movement and the robber baron, a period of growing concentration in industry and of growing monopoly profits. Technological advances also made cities more attractive locations, including improvements in transportation, water, sewers, public health and safety, education, roads and bridges, and professional police and fire departments. The improving city amenities meant cities were creating their own

---

6. I am equating population growth with economic growth. Although this is not accurate for a country, it is accurate for a city embedded in a large economy with free movement of capital and labor. Cities with high wages and high returns to capital grew in size. Cities with low wages and low returns lagged.

rents. Finally, the growth in city populations and the increasing diversity of city populations strained the old structures of city government and provided opportunities for entrepreneurial politicians to accommodate the diverse interests, for a price.

The strongest force suppressing corruption and encouraging good government was competition between cities. From 1880 to 1930, American cities competed with each other to attract growth. The competition between cities limited urban corruption. The cities were (and are) small open economies. They competed with each other to attract new firms and new business. They depended on local taxes, and when they borrowed money, they did so on their own credit. The local firms depended on markets outside the city. Cities could not control imports and could not manipulate markets outside their borders, nor could they control the passage of capital and labor across their borders.

As Shleifer and Vishny (1993) have explained, competition between governments reduces corruption. If a business faces one corrupt politician, the politician can charge the "monopoly" bribe and extort any economic profits enjoyed by the firm. If the business can deal with any one of a number of politicians to get what it requires, then the competing politicians will bid down the bribe. However, if each business must make deals with many politicians, then the bribes can get quite high. Like up- and downstream monopolists, the politicians will overcharge, driving firms out of business and lowering the overall observed level of bribes but increasing the burden of corruption. This simple model has many applications to American cities. The cities were exquisitely aware that they competed with each other for new businesses and new residents. Voters cared whether their cities prospered, and politicians cared about reelection. Corruption also grew more lucrative as the city grew, so corrupt politicians had even more incentive than honest politicians to encourage city growth (McGuire and Olson 1995; Olson 1991).

The open economy of the city also encouraged local elites to favor good government and pro-growth policies. Open borders limit the favors that a corrupt government can grant to a local industry that depends on markets outside the city. As Krueger (1993) points out in her essay on "vicious and virtuous circles," government officials and businessmen can be allies. She compares growth in developing nations that chose to pursue import substitution policies to growth in nations that chose export-oriented policies. In the import-substituting countries (common in Latin America), local business owners became dependent on the government trade restrictions and lobbied to have them maintained. Over time the economy fell further and further behind, forcing ever more restrictive policies to keep the import-substituting industries alive, a "vicious circle." On the other hand, countries (such as the "Asian tigers") that started with export-oriented policies developed a political elite whose preferred policies were good for growth, a "virtuous circle." Firm owners in Korea and Japan are as involved in politics as those in Argentina or Mexico, but the firms in the "virtuous," export-oriented countries find it in their interest to encourage an efficient economy with good provision of public goods, low tariffs and taxes, and other pro-growth policies. In American cities, the local elites did not stay out of politics, but they were export oriented and they wanted good government and growth (Hays 1964).[7]

Another limit to corruption before the New Deal was the fiscal independence of cities and the resulting municipal dependence on the local tax base and the national bond market. Although legally creatures of the state, cities depended on their own taxes, not on state or federal funds, both for regular expenses and to back loans to build infrastructure. From 1880 to 1930 cities did a lot of building, which was largely funded through the municipal bond market. The municipal bond market was one of the first parts of the financial industry to come under government regulation. During the financial difficulties of the 1870s a number of cities were forced into default. As a result, many state governments passed reforms that limited municipal borrowing (Monkkonen 1996). In a large number of states, the debt was limited to a set proportion of the taxable real estate of the city, generally 5 percent. In other states, the city could not issue bonds without a voter referendum or without establishing a mechanism of guaranteed tax receipts for the repayment of the bond (Nelson 1907). Everywhere the cities were forced to open their books. These rules reassured investors, who were quite willing to buy municipal bonds. Their confidence in the cities was well placed. No city of any significant size defaulted between the 1870s and the Great Depression (Monkkonen 1996).

The border imposed one more limit on urban corruption. The city was a creature of the state, and subject to state law. Both the state and later the federal government could investigate and prosecute city officials. The court system was relatively protected, and the rule of law was generally enforced in American cities.

Considering the limits to corruption, we might wonder that politicians were able to profit from political control. However, some conditions between 1880 and 1930 favored corruption. The ability of firms and residents to leave the city constrained corruption, but the cost of escaping the legal boundaries of the city was higher during the Progressive Era than it was before or after. In many cities, the border followed development out through annexation. Suburban willingness to accept annexation shows that residents and firms located outside city boundaries valued city services more than they feared city corruption. Technology also determined the value firms placed on urban locations. After the 1880s, two developments accel-

7. Reform-Era American businesses did want export-oriented policies from the federal government. Pressure from business kept the U.S. import tariffs high.

erated the concentration of economic activity in cities: the national rail system created a true national market, and the electric streetcar allowed large numbers of workers to live in the suburbs and work in the central cities. City wealth and urban and suburban real estate values grew (Mills and Hamilton 1994; Warner 1978). These developments made it more difficult for large firms to leave the political boundaries of the city and therefore increased the sustainable level of corruption. The growing dependence on large, steam-driven plants also kept firms near the railroads that delivered coal.

By the 1920s the car and the truck began to allow residents and firms to leave central cities for suburban or (later) ex-urban locations. After the 1950s, trucks and the interstate highway system largely replaced rail for lightweight long-distance freight. The auto released workers from the streetcar (Bottles 1987; Garreau 1991; Mills and Hamilton 1994). The new transportation options did not destroy the central cities. The population of most larger, older cities peaked only in 1950 or later, and the population of many large central cities has now stabilized as rising service-sector jobs replace the lost manufacturing jobs. But the internal combustion engine has decreased the level of corruption a central city can support before the firms and wealthier residents leave. The development of the electrical grid and the electric motor released manufacturing plants from coal, and from the railroads that delivered coal.

Before 1930 the higher quantity and quality of government goods and services found in the larger cities also encouraged residents and businesses to stay inside the city borders. After 1930 the central cities began to lost this advantage to the suburbs. During the period from 1880 to 1930 government responsibilities were growing rapidly. In the early part of the period, central cities appear to have had an advantage in producing many of the new public goods and government-provided services. Water and sewer systems were especially costly and difficult for the growing suburbs to build, but even education required significant capital outlays, to build new schools, especially expensive new high schools. Over time the central cities' advantage declined, as suburbs improved the quantity and quality of public goods. In many states, changes at the state level forced cities to share large systems, like water. Suburban municipalities learned how to borrow money and build their own infrastructure. And the populations of the suburbs rose until many were small cities of their own, able to support quality government goods and services.[8] As residents and firms moved to the suburbs, the central cities found themselves with aging infrastructure and relatively larger populations of poor residents, which shifted the advantage in government quality away from the central cities. The level of sustainable corruption dropped.

---

8. Today it is estimated that the economies of scale in most urban government services are exhausted around 100,000 in population (Mills and Hamilton 1994, p. 335).

Competition constrained corruption but did not eliminate it. Cities were not perfect substitutes for one another. It could cost a firm quite a bit to relocate. The large cities, such as New York, Chicago, and Boston, were the most valuable business locations. They were home to the largest banks, the main wholesale markets, the largest populations, and the most varied and sophisticated labor markets. Many firms needed to be in the biggest cities, giving the politicians in those cities monopoly power. This may explain the observation that the largest cities were the most corrupt.

2.3 Types of Corruption

I now consider how these forces shaped corruption and the quality of government in American cities during the Progressive Era. Contemporary reports and popular histories of American cities have always featured tales of bribery, embezzlement, graft, kickbacks, political influence peddling, insider trading, and criminal cover-ups, collected by enterprising investigative journalists, crusading district attorneys, and ambitious rival politicians. Secondary histories have placed these examples into the historical narrative. One original source is important enough to merit separate discussion: Lincoln Steffens's series of essays for *McClure's* magazine, *The Shame of the Cities* ([1904] 1957). Steffens's essays, written between 1901 and 1903, were intended to show readers where to look for corruption. Steffens was not an unbiased observer. He believed that American businessmen, not poor or ethnic voters, were the source of corruption, and he spent no time looking for political machines. He was suspicious of every government responsibility and every private-sector partner, and his essays paint a detailed and remarkably comprehensive picture of venal corruption in American cities at turn of the twentieth century.

The corruption common in Reform Era cities can be divided into four basic categories: (a) embezzlement, (b) graft on public contracts and franchises, (c) regulatory corruption, including graft on crime, and (d) insider trading.

The most striking aspect of embezzlement is how little occurred during the Progressive Era. Between 1880 and 1930 reports of outright theft are puzzlingly rare. Steffens reports only three examples, and only one is substantiated. In Pittsburgh, $300,000 disappeared from the city attorney's office. Cancelled checks suggested that at least $100,000 of this money went directly to Boss Flinn. Although $100,000 is the equivalent of $2 million in 2004, it is dwarfed by Flinn's building contracts with the city.[9] The

9. All the conversions from period to modern dollar values are computed using the consumer price index (CPI). The conversion rates used are available on the economic history services website, www.eh.net. For discussion of the historical estimation of the CPI, see McCusker (2003).

paving contracts alone were worth \$3.5 million, or \$70 million in 2004 dollars (Steffens [1904] 1957, pp. 119–21).

Contemporaries noticed the politicians' self-control. It is one of the main points of William Riordan's charming book of interviews with Tammany politician George Washington Plunkitt. "The books are always all right," Plunkitt explains; "the money in the city treasury is all right. Everything is all right. All they [the reformers] can show is that Tammany heads of departments looked after their friends, within the law, and gave them what opportunities they could to make honest graft" (Riordan [1905] 1994, p. 56). Contemporary investors also found that city governments could generally be trusted. City bonds were considered safe and were issued at low interest from the 1880s on.

Open books kept the city administration honest. Opening the books was one of the earliest, least controversial, and most successful reforms of the Reform Era. At first individually, and then by mandate of the federal government, cities opened and published their accounts. In 1902 the Bureau of the Census began publishing an annual series of city expenditures, assembled from the city books by accountants hired and trained by the bureau. Only thirty-one years earlier, the Tweed Ring had been able to keep New York City's accounts secret. It would be another thirty-one years before publicly traded companies would be forced to open their books.

The second form of corruption, graft on contracts and franchises, was more rewarding. Enterprising government officials (elected and appointed) found it easier to skim from the legitimate provision of government goods and services. After 1880, local governments were responsible for providing, or arranging for the provision of, a rising array of goods and services. Sometimes the city government contracted with private firms to provide goods and services, such as street cleaning and medicines for government hospitals. In other cases the government arranged for private firms to provide the services directly to the public, through government departments or municipally owned firms. Embezzlement was rare, but corrupt contracts were not. Even before the Civil War the mayor was expected to deliver the city printing contract to the publisher of the most loyal newspaper.[10] By the early twentieth century, according to Steffens, city money was deposited in favored banks in St. Louis, Philadelphia, and New York. In St. Louis, city hospitals bought drugs and city poorhouses bought groceries from favored suppliers. The St. Louis boss, Colonel Butler, after a career of questionable activity, was finally convicted of paying a \$2,500 bribe to members of the Board of Health for a garbage contract (Steffens [1904] 1957, pp. 23–24, 40, 147, 207).

The most lucrative contracts were in construction. Many political bosses

10. This little piece of patronage was so standard that the Biographical Dictionary entry only mentions it if the mayor messed it up.

invested in construction firms. In Pittsburgh, Boss Flinn "went in for public contracts." He built buildings, streets, and bridges for the city (Steffens [1904] 1957, pp. 115–24). In Philadelphia, Boss Martin's business partner, Porter, handled the construction contracts (Steffens [1904] 1956, p. 145). In New York "Tammany has a good system of grafting on public works" (Steffens, p. 210). The early twentieth-century Tammany boss, Charles Francis Murphy, was a silent partner in his brother's construction firm, New York Contracting and Trucking. In 1905, the firm and its subsidiaries received $15 million worth of city contracts (Allen 1993, p. 211).

Reformers attempted to prevent these thefts, but they were less successful than they were against embezzlement. Although laws were passed requiring competitive bidding, Steffens reports for Pittsburgh and Philadelphia that bids were rigged and jobs designed to favor a particular bidder. Bidding was also manipulated by collusion. G. W. Plunkitt reports colluding with fellow bidders on a government surplus auction (Riordan [1905] 1994, p. 55). Rules that required competitive bidding could keep costs down, but they encouraged poor quality. Concerns about quality led reformers to adopt the unusual reform of replacing private producers with city departments or city-owned firms. As an economy measure, substituting private provision with municipal ownership is a questionable tactic, as municipal employees have little incentive to cut costs, but they also have little incentive to cut quality (Glaeser 2001).

Although according to Steffens corrupt contracts both raised costs and lowered quality, Reform Era American cities apparently avoided the most costly problem associated with corrupt contracts—that the opportunity for graft encourages governments to choose the wrong projects. Modern corrupt nations divert resources from projects with high social return but low opportunities for graft to projects with lower returns but better opportunities (Kaufmann 1997, p. 119; Mauro 1995; Shleifer and Vishny 1993). The earliest reformers did complain of excessive building. In New York City, the reform Mayor Havemayer, elected after the Tweed scandals of the early 1870s, thought the Brooklyn Bridge an immense waste of taxpayer money. The voters rewarded his position by returning Tammany Hall to power in the next election. By the turn of the twentieth century the reformers were no longer complaining about excessive construction of infrastructure or provision of services. Neither Steffens nor his contemporaries mentions the problem of too much infrastructure; a number of reformers complained of too little (Hays 1964). Apparently, corrupt politicians found it easiest and safest to steal from projects that the voters and bond buyers thought were worth building.

Cities have been far less careful in the late twentieth century. We can compare the construction of New York City's first subway to the construction of the Los Angeles subway. The New York Interborough Rapid Transit (IRT) line was begun in 1900 and finished four years later, opening

October 27, 1904. The IRT line was 23.5 miles long, with two underwater tunnels, one to the Bronx and one to Brooklyn. The $40 million for the construction was paid by the city, which raised the money through bond issues. The $20 million for equipment was the responsibility of the line operator, the McDonald Company (*New York Subway Souvenir* 1904). Together, the cost was equivalent to about $1.1 billion in 2004 dollars, of which a decent percentage appears to have been corruption (Glaeser 2001). But it was worth building. By December, the system was averaging 300,000 passenger trips per day. Originally planned for a maximum ridership of 600,000 trips per day, ten years later, the system was providing 1.2 million trips per day (Hood 1968). By any measure, the subway was a success.

The Los Angeles subway, on the other hand, has been described as "a fiasco of epic proportions" (Claiborne 1998). In the 1970s the federal government, eager to decrease consumption of gasoline, offered to subsidize subway construction. Los Angeles broke ground in 1986, the first segment of the Red Line opened in 1993, and three more segments followed, in 1996, 1999, and 2000, for a total system length of 17.4 miles (Trinidad 2004). The total cost of the Red Line has been about $5 billion dollars, about half of which has been covered by the federal government (Claiborne 1998; Trinidad 2004). Most of the $5 billion dollars was not corruption, but that did not make it a good investment. The system was planned to handle 300,000 riders per day, but in 2004 the average weekday total was only 102,000 (APTA 2004). The subway does have value, but the $5 billion would probably have been better spent on upgrading and expanding the heavily used Los Angeles metro area bus system.[11]

Construction contracts were lucrative sources of graft, but city franchises could be worth even more. Several important new industries emerged at the end of the nineteenth century, including gas, electricity, and the streetcar. In many European countries these new services were the responsibility of the government, but in the United States they were usually provided by private firms working under franchise to the city government. The gas, electric, and traction firms required franchises to run lines on, under, or over the city streets. Owning a construction firm could make a man rich. Owning a city-franchised utility or streetcar line could elevate a man to the exalted wealth of the Gilded Age elite. Streetcar magnates married Vanderbilts (Whitney) and left their names attached to libraries (Huntington, Widener), museums (Whitney again), and scientific institutions (Yerkes Observatory). As entry into these industries was controlled by the city government, corruption was inevitable.

11. In a final twist, the Los Angeles Bus Riders Union successfully sued the Los Angeles Metropolitan Transportation Authority (MTA) for bias, under the Civil Rights Act of 1964. The Los Angeles MTA has signed a consent decree, agreeing to transfer funds from the rail system, with its relatively white and middle-class ridership, to the bus system with its overwhelmingly minority and poor ridership.

Steffens caught the street railway industry in the midst of a period of competition and consolidation. He found city officials taking advantage of their power over the streetcar franchises in five of his six cities: St. Louis, Pittsburgh, Philadelphia, New York, and Chicago. The consolidations had reopened the franchises, and the cities took advantage. Blackmailing a streetcar company by monkeying with the franchise even had a name: it was called a mace (Steffens [1904] 1957, pp. 156–58).

Municipal corruption was only one aspect of traction corruption. The streetcar companies engaged in the same sorts of corporate shenanigans as their bigger cousins, the long distance railroads. The managers, owners, and financiers manipulated the price of the common stock, set up construction firms to build the streetcar rails and overpaid themselves, and speculated in real estate along the streetcar lines (Hendrick 1919; Jackson 1985). In many cities, owners of the streetcar lines could make more money out of real estate speculation than from the line itself. "Borax" Smith in Oakland, Henry Huntington in Los Angeles, and Senator Francis Newland in Maryland built streetcar lines whose purpose was to sell suburban real estate (Jackson 1985, p. 124).

The danger posed by government monopoly is usually that the government will suppress entry and raise prices in order to protect the value of the monopoly. In the developing world this tendency is one of the reasons that corruption appears to suppress economic innovation (Murphy, Shleifer, and Vishny 1993, p. 413). But that does not appear to have been a serious problem for American cities before World War I. Although the system was corrupt, streetcar lines were built quickly and covered many miles. The street railways, powered by horses and cables, began to spread after the Civil War, but the real growth came after Frank Sprague perfected the overhead electric line in 1887. Within fifteen years, all major cities and many relatively minor ones had electric streetcars. In 1901–2 the traction systems in large cities (population above 350,000) provided on average 243 trips per year for every man, woman, and child in the city (Teaford 1984, p. 236). In much of Europe, where owners of streetcar lines were forbidden to speculate in abutting real estate, lines were built more slowly and were not as long (Jackson 1985, p. 124; Teaford 1984, p. 236).

The model of competing corrupt officials proposed by Shleifer and Vishny (1993) may explain why city governments were not able to limit entry. In most cities franchises were distributed by the city council. The owner who sought a franchise did not have to bribe every council member, only a majority, so the politicians were forced to compete with each other for the bribes. In St. Louis, according to Steffens, the president of the Suburban Railway Company, Charles Turner, approached the city boss, Colonel Butler, about expanding the grants to his streetcar line. Turner found Butler's price of $145,000 too steep, and he sought a different political broker. A Mr. Stock agreed to handle the deal for only $135,000, which

Stock would distribute among a sufficient number of councilmen to pass the bill. For Turner this would prove a foolish economy. According to later testimony, the value of the franchise extension was something between $3 and $6 million. Butler was the boss of the St. Louis machine; Stock was a lobbyist for the brewery industry. Stock was not able to prevent a legal setback, a court mandate that held up the new franchise, nor was he able to keep his "ring" of councilmen in line. Somebody leaked the story to the press, although without naming names, in hopes of forcing the final payment. The anonymous leak alerted a politically ambitious state prosecutor, Joseph W. Folk. Folk put pressure on Turner, the president of the streetcar line, and the whole conspiracy quickly unraveled (Steffens [1904] 1957, pp. 28–30).

There is also evidence that voter pressure prevented the governments from limiting entry, even when the bosses controlled the legislature. By 1900 New York City had nearly 1,300 miles of surface and elevated lines, much of it owned by Tammany supporters. In deference to their supporters, the government had blocked the building of a subway for most of the 1890s, but not even Tammany Hall could hold out against the demand for improved mass transit. Public opinion forced the city government to authorize the start of construction on the IRT in 1900 (Katz 1968, p. 10).

Corruption and profits on city franchises rose and fell together; the fall was almost as swift as the rise. By World War I nearly every state regulated franchises, including the streetcars (Hendrick 1919, p. 44; McCormick 1981). The regulators made it more difficult for city governments to play games with franchises, but they also prevented the utilities and traction companies from raising prices. The inflation of World War I, followed by the automobile, hit the streetcar industry hard in the 1920s. The deflation of the Great Depression took some pressure off prices, but ridership fell when one-quarter of the workforce was out of work. Ridership recovered during World War II but fell again in the 1950s. In the decades after World War II most streetcar systems were bought out by city governments and converted to buses. The electric and gas utilities did not go out of business, but they were increasingly regulated; state-appointed commissions policed the firms and their debt and investments, and regulated prices.

The third basic category of corruption regularly practiced by urban politicians was graft from the manipulation of laws and regulations. Regulatory corruption occurs when a private individual bribes a representative of the government to ignore legitimate regulations or when a government official extorts payment by threatening to impose regulation with unusual severity or to withhold approval for an activity.

Among the most lucrative laws were those banning or regulating what the Progressive Era called "vice" and what we call "victimless crime": prostitution, gambling, and the sale of alcohol and drugs. Graft on crime was not invented during the Reform Era, and it has not disappeared. However, between 1880 and 1930 the responsibility for crime graft reached unusually high up the hierarchy of government. Mayors and bosses, not just corrupt police, benefitted. Steffens reports that in "New York and most other cities" police blackmail was the dominant form of graft, and at least a few Tammany leaders were surprised to learn from the Lexow Committee investigations that the police collected $4 to $5 million per year ($80 to $100 million in modern dollars).[12] In Pittsburgh, however, "[vice] is a legitimate business, conducted, not by the police, but in an orderly fashion by syndicates"—that is, by organized crime. Steffens's informant claimed that the annual bribe of $250,000 went directly to the Pittsburgh bosses, Flinn and Magee (Steffens [1904] 1957, pp. 115–16).[13] In Minneapolis, according to Steffens, the government was the syndicate. The boss, "Doc" Ames, did not run a machine, was not planning on reelection, and was simply stealing everything he could lay his hands on through his control of the police department. Ames was caught and convicted fairly swiftly. More successfully, Tom Dennison, a professional gambler and the boss of Omaha, organized the vice trade and ran it like a department of the city government. He remained in power for almost three decades, doing especially well under Prohibition, until he was indicted for murder (Menard 1989).

By the 1920s the political bosses were largely replaced by mob bosses, who specialized in crime. The mob paid off the government, but the government no longer controlled the industry. The establishment of formal police departments during the nineteenth century may have initially increased graft on crime, since the police were a natural organization for shaking down gamblers, prostitutes, and saloon keepers, but police corruption was not popular with voters. The police were generally the first department to come under civil service rules, although this did not always end political interference. Police corruption has not disappeared, but it is now rarely organized by the city mayor, boss, or police superintendent. Likewise, Prohibition may also have originally encouraged a closer relationship between the city government and criminals. Unofficial tolerance of vice served to bridge otherwise apparently irreconcilable political conflicts that arose out of the cultural and ethnic diversity of late nineteenth- and early twentieth-century American cities. But in the 1920s national Prohibition increased the returns to scale in crime. National Prohibition was also accompanied by a rise in the level of violence associated with organized crime, perhaps driven by increased profits or by cheaper automatic weapons. The level of violence required to establish and maintain a position in the liquor business during Prohibition was not, apparently, some-

---

12. The Lexow Committee was one of a series of committees that have investigated corruption in New York City. It was organized in 1894 at the instigation of the Society for the Prevention of Crime, which was established in New York in 1877.

13. Since the population of Pittsburgh was about one-tenth the population of New York, the syndicates were paying about half the per capita rate paid in New York.

thing most city administrations could stomach, with a few notorious exceptions (such as Boss Dennison in Omaha).

The cost of graft on crime is not the graft, and it is generally not limited to the cost of the crime. Rather, graft on crime undermines the police and the rule of law, and fosters violence. Today alcohol is legal, but the trade in illicit drugs is lucrative and violent and is a serious problem in many central cities and in a number of developing countries.

City governments regulated more than crime. The city government, usually the council, controlled an array of grants to use city streets and to access railroad yards and docks (Teaford 1984). According to Steffens, corrupt politicians and appointees were willing to put their regulatory power to lucrative purpose. In St. Louis the legislators in the upper and lower chambers of the city council had a regular schedule of prices for "all possible sorts of grants. . . . There was a price for a grain elevator, a price for a short switch; side tracks were charged for by the linear foot, . . . a street improvement cost so much; wharf space was classified and precisely rated . . . nothing was passed free of charge" (Steffens [1904] 1957, pp. 22–23). In Pittsburgh, with a stronger boss, a businessman went straight to Chris Magee if he wanted one of the "little municipal grants and privileges, such as switches, wharf rights, and street and alley vacations" (Steffens, p. 109).

This graft—the granting of rail and wharf access and the right to build over city streets—gave the city government access to the profits generated by large manufacturing firms and railroads. Steffens was convinced that "Big Business everywhere is the chief source of political corruption" (Steffens [1904] 1957, p. 204). Since Steffens viewed corruption as a moral failing, he held both parties equally responsible. Manufacturing firms, however, did not want to have to pay the city in order to access the railroad or waterfront. Similarly, regulatory corruption is a serious impediment to business in many countries, where a successful firm can expect to pay an endless stream of bribes to secure the necessary permits and licenses and forestall sudden inspections and threats of closure. The graft that Steffens documented, however, was generally a one-time extraction. The business paid to gain access to a city-controlled asset. The legal right to access the asset was granted by a vote of the city council, so a businessman knew that, once the council voted, the right was his.

But the kind of regulations that allow for repeat graft, such as regulations regarding health, employment, construction, and liquor, were among the many reforms passed during the period. The police and the growing army of inspectors hired to enforce the new rules took advantage of their responsibilities. Steffens reports deals with "shopkeepers who don't want to be bothered with strict inspections" in Philadelphia and architects and builders in New York who could buy off the inspectors, "generally . . . on the basis of the [Building] department's estimate of a fair half of the value of the savings in time or bad material" (Steffens [1904] 1957, pp. 148 and

208). The mechanisms limiting this sort of graft are not entirely clear, but it may be that city governments limited this corruption in order to protect growth. However the constraints were imposed, regulatory corruption in the United States does not appear to have been so bad as to either cripple business or undermine the new building and health codes introduced by the reformers. Hurricanes and earthquakes revealed individual failures, but not the systemic failures that such disasters can reveal in the third world today. During the Reform Era, American cities grew steadily larger and more densely populated, and yet healthier and safer (Teaford 1984; Troesken 2004).

The flight of industry to the suburbs has probably decreased the burden of regulatory corruption in cities. Offices are the sector of the economy least susceptible to regulatory shakedown. Steffens noticed that regulatory corruption was limited in New York City because "most of the big businesses represented in New York have no plants there. . . . [T]he biggest and the majority of our financial leaders, bribers though they may be in other cities and even in New York State, are independent of Tammany Hall, and can be honest citizens at home" (Steffens [1904] 1957, p. 204). This suggests that regulatory corruption has been lessened by the movement of manufacturing out of the cities. It is also possible that regulatory corruption has distorted the distribution of economic activity between city and suburb.[14]

The final form of corruption regularly pursued by city politicians was insider trading, which occurs when a party to private information uses the information to make an advantageous purchase or sale. In Philadelphia, according to Steffens, there are "real estate dealers who like to know in advance about public improvements." George Washington Plunkitt enthusiastically engaged in insider trading: "Supposin' it's a new bridge they're goin' to build. I get tipped off and I buy as much property as I can that has to be taken for approaches. I sell at my own price later on. . . . Wouldn't you? It's just like lookin' ahead in Wall Street or in the coffee or cotton market. It's honest graft" (Riordan [1905] 1994, p. 54). In 1900, insider trading was common on Wall Street, and not clearly illegal. Politically, inside tips were a useful and largely untraceable currency: they allowed a politician to make money, to provide a favor or bribe to someone else, or to receive a payoff himself. Insider trading is now illegal, which has decreased the practice but not eliminated it.

Insider trading weakens property rights and may have discouraged investment in urban real estate. On the other hand, it was a mechanism that aligned the interests of politicians with the growth of the city. Politicians who had invested in local real estate or owned stock in local firms had a

14. On the other hand, if other costs are low enough, manufacturing can live with corruption; otherwise, manufacturing would not be moving from the United States to China.

powerful incentive to pursue policies that encouraged growth. There is evidence that this relationship did not disturb voters. Los Angeles was unusually dependent on investment in infrastructure for its growth. The Los Angeles voters regularly elected businessmen and real estate developers they could trust to vote for pro-growth policies. For example, in 1898 the voters elected landowner and developer Frederick Eaton as mayor. He was an early booster of an aqueduct to bring water from the Owens River to the city. No one was disturbed that the water would also increase the value of his large land holdings (Holli and Jones 1980, p. 108).

These were the dominant forms of graft practiced in American cities during the fifty years from 1880 to 1930. I am not arguing from this evidence that graft was good for the American economy, but rather that it was relatively benign, as corruption goes. City politicians would have been perfectly content to steal more, even at the cost of growth, but they were limited by the forces already identified—the open border, the voters, and the bond market. To make this point, let us consider two unusual examples of graft, when politicians escaped some of the usual constraints. Both cases involve attempts to monopolize local markets.

Border corruption is the manipulation for private benefit of trade in goods, capital, or labor across the border. It is the one important category of graft that was largely unavailable to city government. In general city governments, unlike national governments, could not pursue import substitution as a policy; they could not favor inefficient local firms over efficient foreign firms or manipulate the currency. This limitation prevented some of the most harmful forms of corruption observed today in the developing world (Krueger 1993). However, because four of the five boroughs of the city are on islands, New York City wielded an unusual amount of control over its own border—at least over waterborne trade. In 1899 the boss of Tammany Hall, Richard Croker, and a number of his lieutenants decided to use this control to monopolize the ice trade. At the time, ice was harvested in the winter in New England and upstate New York. It was stored in sawdust or straw and brought to New York City by boat as needed, with demand peaking in the summer. Croker and his conspirators arranged for the American Ice Company to purchase every ice company of any consequence in New York City. In early 1900 the *New York World* revealed that a large number of Tammany politicians owned stock in the American Ice Company. Mayor Van Wyck held about $678,000 worth; Croker's deputy, John F. Carroll, owned about $500,000 worth; and Croker and his wife about $250,000, along with a number of other politicians, including (future Tammany boss) Charles F. Murphy and Murphy's real estate partner, Peter F. Meyer. These last two controlled the key asset in the scheme—the New York docks. Murphy and Meyer closed the docks to the few firms that had not signed up with the American. On April 4, 1900, the

World broke the news that the Ice Trust would double the price of ice, from thirty cents to sixty cents per hundredweight.

But the Ice Trust quickly unraveled, revealing the limits on even the most powerful political machines. In 1900 ice was an urban necessity, not a luxury. The high price was especially hard on the poor—Tammany Hall's most ardent supporters. The *World* forced Mayor Van Wyck and the dock commissioners to appear in court (a power that the *World* had thanks to a reform law written into the city charter after the scandals of the Tweed ring). The individuals admitted they owned stock, although they denied they had been given the stock in exchange for political favors, but shortly afterward the American Ice Company announced it was reducing the price of ice to forty cents per hundredweight. However, the political damage could not be entirely undone. Tammany's most loyal supporters felt betrayed, and Tammany lost the 1901 mayoral election to the Republican reform candidate, Seth Low (Allen 1993, pp. 199–205).

The second example goes better for the monopolists, although it is not clear that any actual corruption was involved. In general, American politicians were in favor of new business and innovation. However, innovation was understood to involve a technological improvement made by a large firm, or by a small inventor who then created a large firm. Few in the cities recognized the "jitney" as a potentially valuable innovation.[15]

In 1914 the streetcar companies faced their first serious competition for urban commuters. By the beginning of World War I the franchise wars that Steffens had observed were largely over. In most cities the streetcars were a regulated monopoly or duopoly. The five-cent flat fare was nearly universal, generally written into the franchise contract. The five-cent fare entailed cross-subsidization; the streetcar companies made money on the short trips in downtown but lost money on the commuters they carried out to the distant suburbs, but the five-cent fare was extremely popular with voters. Then, in Los Angeles, a few out-of-work laborers who owned secondhand cars began to shadow the streetcars in downtown, offering to carry commuters for the same price the streetcar charged, five cents. The jitney craze was born. Within a year the innovation had spread to most of the larger cities in America. The jitneys, usually secondhand Ford touring cars, could carry half a dozen to a dozen riders. Driving a jitney was a marginal employment. Drivers were willing to work for low returns. Some drivers, often construction workers, switched to operating a jitney when they were unemployed. Other drivers picked up riders only on their morning and evening commutes. The streetcar companies could buy omnibuses and

---

15. The history of the jitneys is derived from three sources: a contemporary analysis of the economics of jitneys by F. W. Doolittle (1915) and two more recent analyses (Eckert and Hilton 1972; Schwantes 1985).

compete with hired drivers, but not at five cents a ride. On the other hand, the jitneys could only compete on the short, heavily traveled inner city routes. The outer suburbs still depended entirely on the streetcars.

The results were disastrous for the streetcar companies. For example, by 1915 the two Seattle traction firms reported heavy losses. The Seattle Electric Company estimated it was losing $2,450 per day to the jitneys, while the Puget Sound Traction Light & Power Company estimated it would lose nearly 21 million fares in 1915 to the jitneys. The losses cut severely into profits, since the streetcar companies could not cut back on service without putting themselves at an even greater disadvantage vis-à-vis the jitneys. The simplest solution to the jitney challenge would have been to change the flat fare. But voters liked the flat fare. Instead, in city after city, regulations were enacted that eliminated the jitneys. On the face of it, regulation was not unreasonable. The jitney industry was plagued by high accident rates and, very occasionally, criminal behavior on the part of jitney drivers. Even the jitney drivers themselves, through their new industry associations such as the International Jitney Association (there were chapters in Canada) supported reasonable requirements for inspection and insurance and driver licenses. However, it was easy to impose regulations that put the jitneys out of business. By the end of 1915, only eighteen months after the first jitneys had appeared in Los Angeles, anti-jitney legislation had been passed in 125 out of 175 cities with important jitney industries. By October of 1918, the jitney cars had declined to 10 percent of their peak numbers, and by the 1920s they had disappeared entirely in nearly every city.[16]

What can we learn about corruption, rent seeking, and innovation from the jitney experience? First, the beneficiaries of an innovation may not recognize the innovation, especially if it is invented by unemployed laborers. The voters did not recognize that the regulatory response was protecting the streetcar companies at the expense of city residents. Second, the rules represented only a brief reprieve for the streetcar companies. Although most systems resisted municipal ownership until after World War II, the industry would never again enjoy the profits of the pre-automobile era. Third, the regulation created one of Krueger's "vicious circles." The jitney episode stopped the development of a small-scale commercial transport industry. The swift suppression of the jitneys was assisted by the regulatory framework that had so recently been established to protect the city residents from franchise corruption. The new rules created constituents—taxi drivers and employees of the municipal transit systems—who benefit from the restrictions imposed by anti-jitney legislation. Long after the streetcar rails have been ripped up or paved over, entry into the taxi industry is still

16. Saginaw, Michigan continued to tolerate the jitneys. By 1921 the jitneys, consolidated into something like a modern bus company, had driven the streetcar out of business. Of course, the dominant employer in Saginaw was General Motors.

strictly regulated. It is illegal, in most cities, for an independent owner to operate a small bus that picks up passengers on the street. Likewise, it is illegal to charge your neighbors to join your car pool. Today the highways are clogged with commuters, each driving to work alone. Few commuters have any idea that there was, briefly, a small-scale commercial alternative to either owning a car or taking a city bus.

2.4   Democracy, Machine Politics, and Reform

In this section I trace the evolution of two related democratic institutions: the rise and fall of the political machine and the slow but fundamental changes in the structure of city government achieved by the reform movement. A political machine relaxed, but did not eliminate, the power of voters to punish corrupt politicians. A political machine did not relax the constraints imposed by the border and the bond market. Before World War I the Reform movement did not do much to suppress machine politics or (apparently) corruption. Before 1900 the reformers did not have a viable alternative to offer the voters. After 1900 reform began to reshape urban government but appears to have had little immediate impact on corruption. Over the decades, however, reform evolved from the simple attempt to prevent corruption into a complete theory of how a city government should work. In the end, the reformers created modern metropolitan government—both of the modern central city and of the modern suburb.

A political machine is an institution designed to win democratic elections by distributing patronage (city jobs and government favors) to supporters in exchange for votes. Political machines are the equilibrium outcome in many democracies. They have developed all over the world, from Mexico's Institutional Revolutionary Party (PRI) to Japan's Liberal Democratic Party (LDP). Political machines were common in the United States between the 1880s and the 1930s. Of the fifteen cities in the *Biographical Dictionary,* eleven had one or more periods of machine domination between 1880 and 1930.[17] In my own research, I have found that between 1900 and 1920 machines dominated, at a minimum, one-quarter of the cities with populations greater than 50,000 (Menes 1997). Political machines were most common in the largest cities. They were found in every region of the country, although they were least common in the West. However, elections remained competitive, even in cities like Chicago, Boston, and New York with large and influential machines. Political bosses were regularly defeated, sometimes by reformers, more commonly by rival machines. The truly dominant machines, political organizations that ruled for decades without facing significant opposition, such as the Daley machine

---

17. The four nonmachine cities were Buffalo, Detroit, Los Angeles, and Milwaukee. All four of these cities did have periods of significant political corruption.

in Chicago, largely developed after World War I or later. During the Progressive Era, competitive elections forced even machine politicians to pay attention to the quality of government.

William M. Tweed created the first urban machine. He turned a popular and politically influential social club, Tammany Hall, into a patronage organization that distributed favors to voters. The institution spread in the 1880s, remained common for about fifty years, and then began to decline after 1930. Some machines lived on for decades, but few new machines were organized after the Great Depression (Reid and Kurth 1992).[18]

What constrained the machine-dominated city governments, if it was not the reformers? In previous work I have modeled the behavior of political machines (Menes 1997). Buying votes allows a politician to steal and still win at the polls, but it does not remove all limits on corruption. The higher the theft, the more it costs to buy the election, so there is an equilibrium level of theft under a machine. The economic and geographic limits to corruption also constrained the machine-dominated city governments; the border and the bond market did not respond to patronage payoffs. My work suggests that these constraints forced even a machine-dominated government to produce the desired quantity and quality of goods and services (Menes 1999). The structure of the machine also provided a mechanism for limiting the freelance corruption of lesser politicians and bureaucrats. The machine provided a structure that allowed complaints to flow up the organization from the precinct and ward captains to the boss and control to flow down the city government from boss to politicians and city employees.[19]

Political machines did not have a monopoly on corruption. There were many dishonest politicians who operated without machines. "Doc" Ames of Minneapolis, Michael Curley of Boston, and Boss Ruef of San Francisco all ran corrupt administrations but failed to assemble Chicago-style precinct-level organizations (Bean 1968; Steffens [1904] 1957; Holli and Jones 1980). There were also many personally honest machine politicians. Mayor Daley, boss of Chicago, the Tammany-ite New York State governor Al Smith, and President Truman, loyal member of the hopelessly corrupt Pendergast machine in Kansas City, were all personally honest. However, political competition between machines forced even honest machine bosses to tolerate corruption within their organizations. A machine boss who limited his organization put himself at a disadvantage against other bosses who allowed more corruption. Charles F. Murphy, boss of Tam-

---

18. The Democratic machine in Pittsburgh is probably the most effective machine organized after 1930. The Pittsburgh Democrats used New Deal work relief to build a patronage organization strong enough to defeat the previously dominant Republicans (Stave 1970).

19. This is one of the "latent functions" identified by Robert Merton ([1957] 1972). Jane Addams (1898) describes voters who tolerate corruption because they know they have a "friend" in city hall.

many Hall after the defeat of Croker in 1901, disliked vice and strongly discouraged Tammany's connections to crime, but Murphy could not afford to alienate every ward boss who benefitted from crime graft. He eliminated Croker's corrupt police chief, Bill Devery, and Martin Engel, whose district contained an unusually large number of brothels. However, he left gambling alone. It was a specialty of his friend, close ally, and potential rival, "Big Tim" Sullivan (Allen 1993, pp. 186 and 212–13).

The trade-off between maximizing wealth and maximizing power was the central trade-off for most political machines. The rapid rise and fall of the Tweed Ring in New York City shows that it was technically possible to steal more than was politically sustainable.[20] Between 1867 and 1871, Boss Tweed and his associates stole an astonishing amount from the city budget, something between $40 million and $100 million (Mandelbaum 1965, p. 86). In modern terms, this is something between $800 million and $2 billion. This estimate does not include what the conspirators earned from trading in city real estate or what they received in bribes from franchise, railroad, and construction firms grateful for regulatory favors. But Tweed's theft depended on secrecy; he was stealing more than the voters or the bond market would sustain. In 1871 a rival politician was able to steal the city books and pass them on to the *New York Times*, which gleefully published evidence of Tweed's thievery. The city's access to credit evaporated, and Tweed's ring fell in a matter of months. Tweed died in jail seven years later.

The recovery of Tammany Hall under the leadership of "Honest" John Kelly illustrates the possibilities open to a machine politician who understood the limits that politics, economics, and finance placed upon corruption. In 1873, only two years after the fall of Tweed, Kelly defeated the reform administration of Mayor Havemayer and returned control of the city to Tammany Hall. Kelly realized there was plenty to be earned in patronage, moderately inflated contracts, and insider deals without threatening to bankrupt the city. He reorganized Tammany Hall, centralizing control of the machine and imposing fiscal discipline on both the machine and the city. In recognition of his ability, and his honesty, in 1876 Kelly was the bipartisan choice for city comptroller; for five years he carried out his duties with strictest honesty.

Political corruption created a demand for political reform. I am not going to attempt even a brief intellectual history of American progressivism. There are a few points, however, that are relevant to our discussion of corruption and growth. First, reform was a slow business. Nearly half a century was required after urban corruption began to rise in the 1850s before reform matured from the simple idea of "cut the budget and throw the ras-

---

20. The three main sources used for the history of Tweed and Tammany Hall are Mandelbaum (1965), Allen (1993), and a nearly contemporary history by Maurice Werner (1928).

cals out" to a set of policies designed to rebuild city government into a structure that would be both resistant to corruption and able to meet the rising demands on urban government. The early reforms adopted in New York City are typical: the reformers generally tried to take power away from whatever body of politicians had proven corrupt. In 1857, reformers stripped the corrupt Assembly of much of its power, handing the Assembly's fiscal responsibilities to a smaller, bipartisan board of supervisors. But the supervisors could also be bought, as Tweed proved. In 1872, after Tweed, the reformers tried again to create a corruption-proof administration; they weakened the mayor and divided decision making among three overlapping interdepartmental boards and the comptroller. The result was a government that was resistant to corruption because it could not, on its own, get much done. This charter almost required an outside centralizing and decision-making body, like Tammany Hall.

There were a few successful early reforms passed between the fall of Tweed and the rise of the muckrakers thirty years later, largely changes that constrained the behavior of individuals. After the financial problems of the 1870s, many states had imposed limits on municipal borrowing. The secret ballot and open government accounts were standard by 1900. These reforms reinforced the mechanisms by which economic, geographic, and democratic constraints acted on individual politicians and voters.

The development of structural reform, the rearrangement of the internal structures of government, and the expansion of government responsibilities required the development of a theory of government. They also required the development of a number of other institutions, including civic associations and lobbying groups and, most important, an independent and nonpartisan press, in which new ideas could be invented, refined, and spread. The new professional organizations and nonpartisan press began to emerge in the 1890s. The "muckrakers," crusading journalists who exposed corruption, dominated popular journalism during the first five years of the twentieth century. This set off the first wave of important structural reforms, which peaked between 1904 and 1908 and continued through the 1910s (McCormick 1981).

Very broadly, the new reforms can be divided into four categories: structural reforms intended to remake the internal arrangements of government, regulatory reforms intended to remake the relationship between government and business, electoral reforms intended to eliminate patronage and fraud from elections, and social reforms intended to improve the lives of Americans. Reformers had great faith in experts and in the model of large bureaucratic business applied to government. They modeled a good deal of structural reform on large corporations. They favored the executive branch over the legislative and favored organizing the city government into functional divisions—departments, semi-independent boards and authorities, regulatory commissions, and municipally owned industries. They tried to insulate city employees from political pressure through civil service rules, trusting that if the right people were hired they would naturally want to do the best possible work.

It is difficult to ascertain the impact of reform before 1930. First, the reforms were endogenous. Each city selected which reforms it chose to adopt. Second, it is difficult to know what effects to look for, since many Progressive reforms were changes that we would expect to increase corruption, such as municipal ownership of utility and transit firms and increases in the regulation of business. Today most economists and political scientists recommend limiting temptation by privatizing government-owned firms and limiting government regulation of firms (Kaufmann 1997). It is possible that American reformers did not have as sophisticated an understanding of corruption as we have today; however, decades of political thought had gone into the American reforms. More likely is the interpretation offered by Glaeser (2001). The reformers were as interested in creating a government that could get things done as they were in preventing corruption. Previous attempts to police city contracts and franchises had proven it was easier to cut costs then to maintain quality. City employees, on the other hand, had less incentive to cut costs and more incentive to increase production as well as employment. Suppressing corruption was only one of the many goals of the Progressive Era reforms that were passed during the first two decades of the twentieth century.

A slightly different picture of reform emerges if we lift our eyes from the older central cities to the suburbs and the younger cities of the South and West. These municipalities adopted a very different set of reforms than were adopted in large northern and midwestern cities like Chicago and New York. Many suburbs and southern and western cities abolished their mayor-council governments and adopted the "business-like" commission or city manager forms. They did not expand regulation to the same extent, and they largely eschewed municipal ownership. Entirely private provision of local public goods, rather than either city contracts or municipal provision, spread in the suburbs. Today in many communities, homeowners' associations hire and supervise such services as garbage collection and maintenance of common space. These reforms might be expected to lower corruption, and today corruption is generally considered to be lower in suburbs and in Sun Belt cities than it is in the older central cities of the North and Midwest, despite the higher wealth and economic growth of the suburbs and sun belt (Bridges 1997).

2.5   Conclusion

The experience of American cities shows that the quality of government matters as much as the simple presence or absence of corruption. The challenge for modern policymakers is determining how to build good government. Some of the economic, geographic, and political conditions that protected American city governments—the open borders, free elections, and fiscal independence of the cities—can be adopted as policy choices in modern nations. But the American experience also shows that strong democratic and civil institutions, and especially a strong and independent press, suppress corruption and improve government performance. Building these institutions is a more complex, and longer-term, project. Finally, the American experience shows the importance of aligning the interests of local elites and politicians with the interests of the majority of the population. In America real estate investments tied together the fortunes of the politicians, the wealthy, and the relatively ordinary city residents. In modern nations, the rule of law—especially reformed land ownership laws, providing secure title to land not only for the elite but also for the middle class and the poor—might encourage better government.

The policy lessons for structural reform of government are less clear. In the United States reform of city government may have contributed to the better provision of public goods and even to the suppression of corruption, but it did not guarantee future economic growth. Detroit, Cleveland, and Buffalo were national leaders in urban reform, electing long-lasting reform administrations and adopting important structural reforms.[21] During the Progressive Era the three cities also enjoyed relatively honest government. But honest government did not guarantee future success. Between 1930 and 2000 the population of fifteen cities in the *Biographical Dictionary* shrank an average of 7 percent. Over the same period, Detroit, Cleveland, and Buffalo shrank by 39 percent, 47 percent, and 49 percent, respectively.[22] I am not suggesting that reform caused the population collapse in these cities, but honest government was not enough to guarantee growth.

Corruption is an opportunistic infection. It is a problem where civil and political institutions are weak. The experience of American cities, corrupt and growing, reveals the importance of local institutions—of democracy; free trade; unfettered financial, labor, and product markets; secure property rights; the rule of law; free press; and a politically active citizenry organized into a plethora of groups and associations—in constraining corruption and encouraging corrupt governments to govern well. Whether this is a reason for optimism or pessimism is not clear. On the one hand, these results suggest that we do not need to eliminate corruption, and we can focus instead on building strong institutions to constrain it. On the

---

21. All three of these cities elected mayors who became national leaders of reform: Grover Cleveland was elected mayor of Buffalo in 1882, Hazen Pingree was elected mayor of Detroit in 1890, and Tom Johnson was elected mayor of Cleveland in 1901.

22. Only two other cities lost as high a proportion of their population: By 2000 Pittsburgh had lost 50 percent of the 1930 population and St. Louis had lost 59 percent of the 1930 population. Population figures are from Gibson (1998).

other hand, strengthening weak institutions in a poor and poorly governed city or nation is not a simple task.

References

Addams, Jane. 1898. Why the ward boss rules. *Outlook* 58 (April): 879–82.
Allen, Oliver E. 1993. *The tiger: The rise and fall of Tammany Hall.* Reading, MA: Addison-Wesley.
American Public Transportation Association (APTA). 2004. American Public Transportation Association heavy rail ridership report, second quarter. http://www.apta.com.
Bean, Walton. 1968. *Boss Ruef's San Francisco: The story of the Union Labor Party, big business, and the graft prosecution.* Berkeley: University of California Press.
Bottles, Scott L. 1987. *Los Angeles and the automobile: The making of the modern city.* Berkeley: University of California Press.
Bridges, Amy. 1997. *Morning glories.* Princeton, NJ: Princeton University Press.
Bryce, James. 1895. *The American commonwealth.* New York: MacMillan.
Claiborne, W. 1998. L.A. subway tests mass transit's limits. *Washington Post,* June 10, A1.
Doolittle, F. W. 1915. The economics of jitney bus operation. *Journal of Political Economy* 23 (7): 663–95.
Eckert, Ross D., and George W. Hilton. 1972. The jitneys. *Journal of Law and Economics* 15 (2): 293–325.
Garreau, Joel. 1991. *Edge City: Life on the new frontier.* Garden City, NY: Doubleday.
Gibson, Campbell. 1998. Population of the 100 largest cities and other urban places in the United States: 1790 to 1990. Population Division Working Paper no. 27. Washington, DC: U.S. Bureau of the Census.
Glaeser, Edward. 2001. Public ownership in the American city. NBER Working Paper no. W8613. Cambridge, MA: National Bureau of Economic Research.
Hays, Samuel. 1964. The politics of reform in municipal government in the Progressive Era. *Pacific Northwest Quarterly* 55 (October): 157–69.
Hendrick, Burton J. 1919. *The age of big business.* New Haven, CT: Yale University Press.
Holli, Melvin G., and Peter d'A. Jones. 1980. *Biographical dictionary of American mayors, 1820–1980.* Westport, CT: Greenwood Press.
Hood, C. 1968. The impact of the IRT on New York. In *The Interborough Rapid Transit System (original line),* Survey Number HAER-122, Historic American Engineering Record, National Park Service, 2–144. Electronic facsimile at the Library of Congress, American Memory Project, http://memory.loc.gov/ammem/index.html. Searchable version residing in electronic form at http://www.nycsubway.org.
Jackson, Kenneth. 1985. *Crabgrass frontier.* New York: Oxford University Press.
Katz, W. 1968. The New York rapid transit decision of 1900: Economy, society and politics. In Survey Number HAER-122, Historic American Engineering Record, National Park Service, 2–144. Electronic facsimile at the Library of Congress, American Memory Project, http://memory.loc.gov/ammem/index.html. Searchable version residing in electronic form at http://www.nycsubway.org.

Kaufmann, Daniel. 1997. Corruption: The facts. *Foreign Policy* 107 (Summer): 114–31.

Krueger, Anne O. 1993. Virtuous and vicious circles in economic development. *American Economic Review* 32 (2): 351–55.

Mandelbaum, Seymour J. 1965. *Boss Tweed's New York.* New York: Wiley.

Mauro, Paolo. 1995. Corruption and growth. *Quarterly Journal of Economics* 110 (August): 681–712.

McCormick, Richard L. 1981. The discovery that business corrupts politics: A reappraisal of the origins of progressivism. *American Historical Review* 86 (2): 247–74.

McCusker, John J. 2003. Source note for CPI. *Economic History Services,* March. http://www.eh.net/hmit/compare/sourcecpi.php.

McGuire, Martin C., and Mancur Olson, Jr. 1995. The economics of autocracy and majority rule: The invisible hand and the use of force. *Journal of Economic Literature* 34 (1): 72–96.

Menard, Oliver D. 1989. *Political bossism in mid-America: Tom Dennison's Omaha, 1900–1933.* Lanham, MD: University Press of America.

Menes, Rebecca. 1997. Public goods and private favors: Patronage politics in American cities during the Progressive Era, 1900–1920. PhD diss., Harvard University.

———. 1999. The effect of patronage politics on city government in American cities, 1900–1910. NBER Working Paper no. 6975. Cambridge, MA: National Bureau of Economic Research.

Merton, Robert S. [1957] 1972. The latent functions of the machine. Repr. in *Urban bosses, machines, and progressive reformers,* ed. Bruce Stave, 27–37. Lexington, MA: D. C. Heath.

Mills, Edwin S., and Bruce W. Hamilton. 1994. *Urban economics.* 5th ed. New York: Harper Collins.

Monkkonen, Eric H. 1996. *The local state: Public money and American cities.* Stanford Studies in the New Political History. Palo Alto, CA: Stanford University Press.

Murphy, Kevin M., Andrei Shleifer, and Robert W. Vishny. 1993. Why is rent seeking so costly to growth? *American Economic Review* 83 (May): 409–14.

Nelson, Samuel Armstrong. 1907. *The bond buyers' dictionary.* New York: S. A. Nelson. *The New York Subway Souvenir.* 1904. New York: Burroughs. Available in electronic form at http://www.nycsubway.org.

Olson, Mancur, Jr. 1991. Autocracy, democracy, and prosperity. In *Strategy and choice,* ed. R. J. Zeckhauser, 131–57. Cambridge: MIT Press.

Reid, Joseph D., Jr., and M. M. Kurth. 1992. The rise and fall of urban political patronage machines. In *Strategic factors in nineteenth century American economic history,* ed. C. Goldin and H. Rockoff, 422–45. Chicago: University of Chicago Press.

Riordan, William L. [1905] 1994. *Plunkitt of Tammany Hall.* Repr. St. James, NY: Brandywine.

Schwantes, Carlos A. 1985. The West adapts the automobile: Technology, unemployment, and the jitney phenomenon of 1914–1917. *The Western Historical Quarterly* 16 (3): 307–26.

Shleifer, Andrei, and Robert W. Vishny. 1993. Corruption. *Quarterly Journal of Economics* 108 (August): 599–617.

———. 2002. *The grabbing hand: Government pathologies and their cures.* Cambridge, MA: Harvard University Press.

Stave, Bruce M. 1970. *The New Deal and the last hurrah.* Pittsburgh: University of Pittsburgh Press.

—, ed. 1972. *Urban bosses, machines, and progressive reformers.* Lexington, MA: D. C. Heath.

Steffens, Lincoln. [1904] 1957. *The Shame of the Cities.* Repr. New York: Hill and Wang.

Teaford, Jon. 1984. *The unheralded triumph: City government in America, 1870–1900.* Baltimore: Johns Hopkins.

Trinidad, Elson. 2004. Metro red line. http://www.westworld.com/~elson/larail/red .html.

Troesken, Werner. 2004. *Water, race and disease.* Cambridge: MIT Press.

U.S. Bureau of the Census. 1929. *Financial statistics of cities having a population of over 30,000:1927.* Washington, DC: Government Printing Office.

Warner, Sam Bass, Jr. 1978. *Streetcar suburbs.* 2nd ed. Cambridge, MA: Harvard University Press.

Wei, Shang-Jin, and Andrei Shleifer. 2000. Local corruption and global capital flows. *Brookings Papers on Economic Activity,* Issue no. 2:303–54.

Werner, Maurice R. 1928. *Tammany Hall.* Garden City, NY: Doubleday.

3

Digging the Dirt at Public Expense
Governance in the Building of the
Erie Canal and Other Public Works

Stanley L. Engerman and Kenneth L. Sokoloff

3.1 Introduction

It is generally accepted that no human society, at least since the early
days of the Garden of Eden, has been free of *corruption*. Although con-
ceptions of what range of behaviors is encompassed by the term vary
widely, there is a grand tradition of laying responsibility for many social ills
on it. One such social ill is the lack of economic growth, and economists
have in recent years sought to elucidate mechanisms through which various forms of corruption might bring about inefficient actions, preventing a
society from fully realizing its productive potential, at a point in time or
over time. Such studies normally treat corruption as a phenomenon of
public officials' taking private advantage of their public offices but recognize that both public and private figures are typically involved.[1] Public officials tailor or administer laws, regulations, contracts, and other policies in
ways calculated to benefit particular private interests in return for bribes
(or other sorts of personal material gain). Such arrangements may be good
for the public officials and the particular favored private interests, but bad

Stanley L. Engerman is the John H. Munro Professor of Economics and a professor of history at the University of Rochester and a research associate of the National Bureau of Economic Research. Kenneth L. Sokoloff is a professor of economics at the University of California, Los Angeles, and a research associate of the National Bureau of Economic Research.

The authors gratefully acknowledge valuable comments from David Dollar, Ed Glaeser,
Claudia Goldin, Stephen Haber, Karla Hoff, Daniel Kaufmann, Zorina Khan, Naomi Lamoreaux, and participants in the NBER Conference on Corruption and Reform. Sokoloff was
a visiting fellow at All Souls College as well as a visiting scholar at the Russell Sage Foundation during his work on the project, and he benefited much from their support.

1. In some contexts, fraud, or deceit or cheating between private parties, might also be considered a form of corruption. However, in the modern literature this class of activities is generally viewed as a consequence of poor enforcement of the "rule of law."

for overall economic performance (and social welfare) if they contribute to misallocation of resources (public or private), irregular protection of property rights that deters individuals from exerting effort or investing in physical or human capital, or barriers to entry or other impediments to competition, innovation, and use of best practice.[2]

There seems little disagreement that, in theory, higher levels of corruption should impede economic performance, but empirical investigation of this relationship has been largely confined to establishing strong correlations in contemporary data. This work has been very informative, but skeptics argue that the results might be due to high levels of productive performance reducing corruption, either through institutional change or though affecting perceptions, rather than by reductions in levels of corruption bringing about better economic outcomes. For this reason, it is not surprising that many scholars are turning to economic history to improve our understanding of the social processes involving corruption. Extending the study of corruption along a time dimension offers the possibility of obtaining a more precise fix on the importance of corruption for understanding long-run patterns of economic growth or performance more generally. It should also allow for a closer examination of what sorts of conditions are more conducive to corruption, whether the forms of corruption change over time as circumstances change, whether some forms are more destructive of prospects for economic progress, and whether (and how) specific types of institutions or conditions reduce the prevalence of corruption.

Although the study of corruption may be much enhanced by turning to history, several key problems remain. The first is definition. Where does one draw the line between corrupt and noncorrupt behavior? Can an action that is legal be corrupt? Should private actions that deviate from meritocracy or economic efficiency, and systematically advantage or disadvantage a particular agent or group, be considered corrupt, or should the classification be reserved for behaviors involving public officials? If the latter, should the standard for corruption be the familiar "taking private advantage of public office"? What does private advantage encompass? Should any action by a public official that affects the interests of a party with whom the official has a personal or pecuniary relationship be so classified? The second problem is one of measurement. Even if one is able to formulate a definition that is conceptually sound, how does one empirically implement it such that a study of how corruption varies over time, place, and other circumstances is feasible?

2. Daniel Kaufmann and his colleagues at the World Bank have been pioneers in trying to devise systematic measures of corruption, and relating it to performance, at both the micro and macro levels. See, for example, Hellman, Jones, and Kauffmann (2000). Also see La Porta, Lopez-de-Silanes, Shleifer, and Vishny (1999); Murphy, Shleifer, and Vishny (1993); Shleifer and Vishny (1993); and Glaeser and Shleifer (2003).

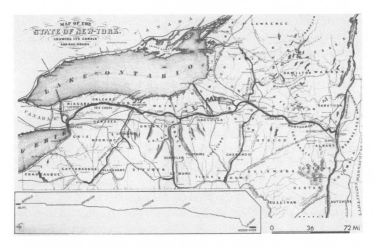

Fig. 3.1   **Map of New York canals and railroads, c. 1858**

Recognizing the difficulty of framing a broadly acceptable general definition of corruption, we choose to focus our study of corruption on a specific context—the building of the Erie Canal, and other canals, by New
York State during the antebellum period (see figure 3.1 for a map of the
New York State canals and the railroad system c. 1858). The logic of this
approach is that it will be easier to develop a reasonable working definition
of corruption in a particular setting, and our goal is to explore the issue of
whether corruption in this major public works program of the era led to a
marked misallocation of resources, generated excess rents for the well connected and politically influential, or otherwise constituted a significant ob-
stacle to economic growth. Large-scale public works projects such as the
Erie Canal (which was sometimes referred to as the "big ditch") are widely
regarded as nurseries for, if not hotbeds of, corruption. Well-directed
bribes (varying in form), or clever orchestration of logrolls, can generate
appropriations for public investments whose social returns would not seem
to warrant the costs that the respective population has to bear. Moreover,
even for projects having a solid economic basis, problems in governance,
or principal-agent issues more generally, provide opportunities for public
officials to extract personal returns at public expense through the precise
design of the plan (such as the route of the canal) and the manner in which
contracts for construction or operations are extended, written, and enforced. Thus, overall economic performance can be impacted adversely
from excessive investment in public works, poor project selection, and
public authorities' acquiescence to higher-than-necessary costs in carrying
out the work, as well as by the dissipation of resources in rent seeking and
other secondary effects.

The movement by a number of northeastern states during the first half of the nineteenth century to undertake the construction of a massive network of roads, canals, and railroads, in an attempt to attract and gain control of trade with the Midwest, is perhaps the most dramatic example of the intense competition among states that the federal nature of U.S. government encouraged.[3] Boston, New York, Philadelphia, Baltimore, Washington, and New Orleans (as well as Montreal) all sought to tap the trade with the Midwest, and did so with various combinations of canals and railroads. The great triumph of New York City is what makes the Erie Canal (but some might say it is the reverse) a critical part of the American historical experience. Much attention, deservedly, is given to its successful construction and operation as one of the success stories among state economic policies. Less attention has been devoted to the importance of political factors in its origins, and to the blemishes in the story of its construction. While it was clearly a great success and one of the leading reasons why New York City became the principal port of the United States and upstate New York a major agricultural and industrial center for a century, questions about the prevalence of corrupt practices in the development of the Erie Canal and other canals were raised during the era.

There has been a considerable historical literature devoted to corruption in the economy in the postbellum United States. Colorful terms such as "the robber barons," "the Great Barbecue," and "the Gilded Age" have been applied to the late nineteenth-century links between government and the economy, and texts are filled with the story of the Union Pacific, the Chapters of Erie, and the great battles among the railroad tycoons seeking advantageous routes and rates. Curiously, however, despite some attention to the operation of the so-called "spoils system" and legislative bribery in chartering banks and other businesses, many scholars have treated the antebellum era as relatively corruption free. There are, of course, discussions of the background to Hamilton's economic policies, especially the assumption of the state and central government revolutionary war debts by the federal government, and the Yazoo land scandal is depicted by some as symptomatic of other land speculations, but the general impression is that corruption was, if not less prevalent, less costly than in later years.[4] In part, this may reflect the fact that governments were smaller during this era and that most of the relevant activity took place at the state and local levels, rather than federal. The perception that corruption was not such a problem during the early nineteenth century also traces back to Tocqueville,

---

3. In addition to the works cited elsewhere in this article, for recent discussions of the general movement for internal improvements in transportation, see Shaw (1990), Majewski (2000), and Larson (2001).

4. On the Yazoo scandal, see Magrath (1966), and for a discussion of the debates on the assumption of the debts, and other aspects of the Hamiltonian policy after the Revolution, see Nettels (1962), pp. 89–129.

with his emphasis on high rates of citizen participation in (and monitoring of) local affairs, competition between different communities and states (as well as political figures and parties), and an ideology celebrating democracy and open access. In such a setting, one might expect opportunities for rent seeking to be rather limited.[5] Whether this judgment reflects the reality, or whether corruption by large railroads and manufacturing firms merely provides a more exciting story than those forms of corruption that occur in smaller decentralized polities, is an issue deserving of more investigation.

Recently Edward Glaeser and Andrei Shleifer (2003) have asked whether this view that corruption was not so severe during the early years of the republic is well founded. In suggesting that the traditional image is idealized, if not mistaken or naive, they are raising fundamental questions about the nature of the relationship between corruption and economic development. Are high levels of corruption so detrimental to prospects for economic growth that developing societies must focus on reducing them if they are to have much hope of realizing sustained material progress? Or is pervasive corruption a feature or symptom of a pre- or early-industrial society that will decrease with economic growth as higher incomes support changes in institutions that lead to improvements in the "rule of law"? The case of the United States has often been cited in arguments that low levels of corruption, or secure property rights, are a virtual precondition for sustained growth.[6] The provocative notions of Glaeser and Shleifer challenge economic historians to determine just how prevalent corruption was during the antebellum period. Our work is but one part of a general effort to respond to that challenge by extending our knowledge of the record of corruption in the American past.

The paper is organized in a straightforward fashion. The next section reviews the history of the building of the Erie Canal, and of how the enormous success of this unprecedented public investment in transportation in-

---

5. See Tocqueville (1961), particularly chapters 5 and 8. Another related and relevant feature of antebellum political structures in the United States is the extremely high turnover rates of elected representatives. L. Ray Gunn (1988) argues that the extremely brief tenures of legislators during the early and mid-nineteenth century led to legislatures that were focused primarily on local and sectional concerns, as committees were weak and legislators closely tied to their communities: "the legislature mirrored an increasingly fragmented, mobile, individualistic society, which seemed to derive its very energy from the competitiveness of local communities. As a consequence, policy demands were themselves highly fragmentary, representing local or sectional interests and only rarely expressing the possibility of a 'general' interest. Thus, the legislature more nearly approximated a public market in which the agents (legislators) of local and special interests bargained and traded for considerations favourable to their clients (constituents) than a deliberative assembly making public policy for the common good . . . But it should be noted that this was a wholly acceptable, indeed desirable, condition in the context of American ideas about representation." See Gunn, p. 80.
6. For examples, see North (1981) and Rosenberg and Birdzell (1986).

frastructure inspired more public investment in canals, in New York and elsewhere. We note how the administrative procedures adopted for the letting and monitoring of contracts in constructing the Erie Canal do appear to have led to rather effective use of public funds, but that the oversight of public resources may have eroded during the canal mania that followed. In the third section of the paper we make use of the ratio of actual expenditures on public works relative to the original projected costs as a gauge of the quality of governance of public resources. We contend that the ratio is a useful measure of an important phenomenon closely related to corruption, and that it has the additional advantage of permitting comparisons over time and other circumstances.[7] Estimates of the ratio for a range of public works extending from the Erie Canal to the present day are presented, and it is shown that cost overruns seem to be much larger (in absolute and relative terms) in the modern era than during the early nineteenth century. In the concluding section, we note how a comprehensive study of the governance of resources in public works would examine the social rates of return on investment, but that our evidence points to the possibility that the governance of public works projects may be worse today than it was before. The significance of this finding is, moreover, enhanced by the observation that the government has come to play a markedly more substantial role in the economy than it did previously.

3.2 The Building of the Erie Canal

Canals were only one of a large range of economic activities, most notably in the provision of social overhead capital, provided or permitted by state governments during the antebellum era. Unlike the railroads that would come later, canals were generally both built and operated by governments. Railroads were granted state charters (allowing them to raise funds in the private capital markets that only gradually evolved over time) as well as awarded subsidies in the forms of land, bonds, or cash, but most were privately owned, built, and operated. Given the central role of government in canal construction and operation, as well as the pronounced geographic patterns of the benefits they yielded, it is easy to understand how the political factors involved in making decisions and in obtaining the necessary votes to implement them could have led to overbuilding of canals, which raised overall costs even in the absence of outright fraud and corruption. With so many parts of New York State desirous of procuring access to low-cost water transportation, how was the route of the Erie

---

7. This interpretation is not unique to us. Susan Rose-Ackerman (1999, p. xi) has commented: "people [at the World Bank] told me that when a review of a program mentioned 'governance problems,' 'unexplained cost overruns,' or 'excessive purchase of vehicles,' this meant that corruption and simple theft were a problem."

Canal (and other canals) selected? How was legislative approval of the plan for the rules and regulations controlling the actual construction and operation of the canal accomplished?[8]

The great commercial success of the Erie Canal and its contribution to the growth of New York City often leads us to overlook the uncertainty and political controversy that surrounded the project. Not only was the Erie Canal a public project of an unprecedented scale (363 miles) and cost to society, but the route was also not the obvious first choice for a canal to link the Midwest and Lake Erie with the Hudson River.[9] Apparently, the shorter, cheaper, and more certain route would have linked a canal around Niagara Falls with another leaving Lake Ontario for the Oswego River. Indeed, this was the approach recommended for New York State by Albert Gallatin (1968) in his 1808 *Report on Canals,* where he otherwise did an excellent job in detailing a plan for the antebellum canal network that would ultimately be constructed.[10] There was a strong logic for the Erie route, however, especially from the point of view of the state government (see figure 3.1). Not only was there a possibility that the canal Gallatin proposed might lead to a diversion of the trade in midwestern produce to Canada (Montreal), not New York City, but the Erie route also had the advantage of having a higher expected payoff because of the considerable new land in western New York that it would bring into profitable production. Indeed, the funding of the Erie Canal was aided by substantial land grants from the Holland Land Company, and others, as an inducement to build the canal through their lands.

The Erie Canal was well short of being voted in unanimously, as the issue came to be entangled in sectional and political disputes. Indeed, the margin of victory in the 1817 roll call was very thin. The mid-Hudson val-

8. Our descriptions of the debates over the building of the Erie Canal, and of the discussions of various forms of alleged corruption, are drawn from our reading and examination of a variety of primary and secondary sources, including *Report* (1818, 1847, 1851, 1868, 1875, 1876); *Laws of the State of New York* (1825); Whitford (1906); Renwick (1842); "Internal Improvements in the State of New York" (1850); Hammond (1846); Shaw (1966); Bernstein (2005); Walker and Walker (1963); Sheriff (1996); Miller (1962); Hanyan and Hanyan (1996); Goodrich, Rubin, Cranmer, and Segal (1961); and MacGill and staff (1917).

9. George Washington is often credited with suggesting, during the 1780s, a canal to link the Great Lakes to Atlantic ports. The route ultimately selected was extraordinarily ambitious, however, in that no canal of near that length had previously been constructed in either Europe or the Americas. Although there were many short canals in England, by far the longest was in France, a 148-mile-long waterway in Languedoc—spanning less than half the distance the Erie did. The longest canal in the Americas extended for less than one-tenth the length. See Goodrich (1960) for more discussion.

10. The building of a link between the Hudson and Lake Erie similarly presented a choice of methods. Clinton advocated a waterway, while Morris—another powerful member of the State Commission—preferred an inclined plane-canal from Lake Erie to Utica, and then a connection with the Hudson via the Mohawk River. This approach was dropped in 1816, however.

ley farmers were opposed to the canal because of the threat of extensive Midwestern and upstate produce entering into New York City. The quite strong opposition of New York City is a bit more difficult to comprehend. In part, given the great uncertainty of whether the stimulus to economic development would be sufficient to justify such a massive public work— more than twice as long as the then longest canal in the western world and more than ten times that in the United States at the time—economic success (or even its completion within a reasonable time) was not obvious beforehand. Even Thomas Jefferson, whose boldness and vision were reflected in the Louisiana Purchase, in 1808 considered the project a century ahead of its time.[11] With those in New York City fearful that they would bear a heavy tax burden for a social investment with little return, it should perhaps not be so surprising that their representatives stood fast against the construction of such a large-scale public work. A second reason for the lack of support from New York City reflected the intense political disagreements within the state. With DeWitt Clinton (who became governor in 1817) and his Federalist followers pushing vigorously for the canal to generate economic growth, as well as to further his political interests, the Democrats, then in control of the city, were instinctively opposed so as to prevent any political credit accruing to their rival party. Political struggles of this sort, between representatives from different regions and parties, continued in subsequent debates over expenditures on canal construction, repair, and enlargement, as well as over political patronage of canal employment.

A key issue was, of course, how to finance the canal. While the federal government had earlier indicated a willingness to provide support for interstate public works, a formal request for assistance from New York State was rejected by the national government on the grounds that funding the project would be inappropriate because the benefits would go to residents of only a limited area. New York then organized a petition asking for a general program to help states finance public improvements, but this too was turned down. New York State also attempted to raise funds from those states, such as Vermont, Kentucky, and Ohio, that could expect to benefit from building the canal, but the effort yielded only moral support. Finally, in April 1817, six weeks after President Madison had vetoed legislation that would have provided New York with some funds, the state legislature adopted a measure calling for the building of the canal and accepting that New York State would bear full responsibility; the first dirt was dug on July 4. The five canal commissioners (previously appointed under an act of 1810) who had prepared an extraordinarily detailed plan, including the route, technical specifications, and estimates of cost, were vested with the

11. See Shaw (1966), pp. 35–37. Granted, Jefferson expressed this opinion when reneging on an earlier promise to help finance canals.

authority to direct the construction and to borrow the money on the credit of the state. The law provided that this debt would be paid off from a Canal Fund, overseen by all of the officers of the state except the governor. The revenues for this fund were to come from tolls from the canal, a tax on salt manufactured in the state, duties on goods sold at auctions, a tax on steamboat passengers, grants, donations, and a tax on real estate located within twenty-five miles of the canal (this latter tax appears never to have been implemented). The need to levy taxes within New York State led to inevitable conflicts between those who expected to receive direct benefits and those who expected not to benefit, as well as over how to tailor revenue enhancements. For example, an initial proposal to raise funds through a more general tax on property was voted down.

One method of attracting votes from the representatives of districts not in a position to directly benefit from the canal was the use of traditional logrolling to provide assurances that their support would be remembered in decisions about future, if not concurrent, transportation projects. Extensive legislative maneuvering was required to obtain approval of the act to construct the Erie Canal, contributing to the inclusion of authorization to build the Champlain Canal (linking the Hudson to Lake Champlain) in the 1817 act. However, logrolling seems to have played a much more important role after the completion of the Erie and Champlain, as a mania for canals developed and the legislature authorized surveys for seventeen proposed canals in 1825, and the actual construction of five additional shorter canals over the next decade.[12] It has been widely noted that the geographic patterns of voting on the various bills were salient, and that the question of whether a proposed canal would traverse near the home county explained more about how legislators voted than did their party affiliation or the advice of state officers about financial feasibility.[13] Representatives of counties along the Erie Canal were understandably reserved or hostile to new projects that were thought likely to offer competition for traffic.[14] Three of these five extra waterways proved to be (as anticipated) financial

12. By 1836, even after two reductions in tolls, the Canal Fund was able to pay off the entire debt incurred in building the Erie and Champlain canals. The five lateral canals included the Oswego Canal (begun in 1825 and completed in 1829), the Cayuga and Seneca Canal (1827 to 1828), the Crooked Lake Canal (1829 to 1833), the Chemung Canal (1829 to 1833), and the Chenago Canal (1833 to 1836). See figure 3.1.

13. See the discussions in Hammond (1846) and Sowers (1914) about voting patterns. A telling example of the weight of economic feasibility in the deliberations of this period comes from the case of the Chenango Canal. Despite a report from the canal commissioners stating that its tolls would be unlikely to cover either the interest on the debt necessary to construct the canal or the variable costs of operating it, and warnings from the state comptroller and the governor about its inadvisability, the legislature ultimately voted to order the canal commissioners to proceed with construction.

14. In a similar fashion, once the Erie Canal was built, Clinton and Martin Van Buren, who had both vigorously pursued federal support, reversed their stances and systematically opposed federal aid for internal improvements. See Seavoy (1982), pp. 3 and 83.

failures and added to the state's debt. Indeed, in 1876, the New York Canal Investigation report notes that "the lateral canals . . . [have] been the sole cause of the fact of the present indebtedness of the State by reason of the canals."[15]

As inefficient (or corrupt) as logrolling might seem, this approach to getting measures through the legislature was, and remains, far from novel. Logrolling along geographic lines was a common feature of crafted political alignments throughout the antebellum period, wherever (most notably Pennsylvania, Ohio, and Kentucky, as well as New York) there was legislative consideration of internal improvements.[16] When successful (from the perspective of those seeking to obtain authorization for an economically desirable public investment), logrolling meant that there were higher costs than necessary to construct the core project.[17] A failure to achieve success by logrolling saved on costs to the state government (by avoiding the commitment of public resources), but often—because of the difficulty of raising private funds to carry on with the investment—meant the loss of the benefits that would have flowed from the internal improvement. In a context of legislators voting the interests of their constituents, logrolling may not merit classification as an intrinsically corrupt practice. Rather, the key issue about logrolling is the social return to the package of public investments for which the political tactic obtains authorization.

Payment of bribes to secure approval of the Erie Canal was not mentioned in the extensive legislative hearings on the construction and operations of the canal, nor in the many scholarly treatments of this major public works project that have been published since. In contrast with descriptions of bank charters being issued during this era in return for bribes, in cash or by sale and repurchase of securities, exchanging votes for remuneration seems to have been insignificant in this case, perhaps because of the opportunities for land ownership in appropriate locations. Where corruption and fraud were more visible concerns of the state, or of those entrusted with responsibility for public funds, was in the construction and operation of the canal. Rather than having the work done by state employees, the policy was to contract out the construction to private firms or individuals who furnished their own tools and hired their own workers. A rather small group of engineers (most of whom were canal commissioners) was responsible for most of the technical or design issues, and they and their assistant engineers oversaw the work of the various contractors. Partly because the

15. See *Report* (1876), p. 11. The report continues: "but for that fact, the State would be to-day entirely free from any canal debt."
16. For discussion of the experiences in Pennsylvania and Ohio, see Hartz (1948) and Scheiber (1969).
17. Of course, there may be cases where no economically desirable public investment is at stake, and success at logrolling leads to allocating resources to a set of socially undesirable projects.

enterprises of the era were of modest size (and often strapped for funds to procure necessary supplies and materials), each contractor was to handle only a short stretch of the canal (no more than a few miles, and sometimes as short as a quarter-mile).[18] This policy also meant that expenditures were widely spread to benefit many contractors in local areas, a nontrivial consideration during the protracted economic contraction that plagued the country through the early years of the project (up until 1821 or 1822). The engineers who were charged with inspecting and approving the quality of the work before the contractor was paid (generally on a monthly basis, and in advance conditional on performance up to that point) typically boarded at homes near the construction site and made their disbursements in small bills drawn from local banks.[19]

Although a theory for why this organization of the construction would keep costs low was offered by some observers at the time, the basic reason for its adoption was likely the reality that the work was performed over a vast geographic expanse and that construction firms of this era were small and highly localized.[20] It was, accordingly, left up to the engineers responsible in each area to provide for construction by placing for bid contracts pertaining to rather short spans. On one hand, the lack of central control and monitoring of contracting procedures, the small size of the firms hired, and the not uncommon personal familiarity between the engineers and the contractors could well have fostered corrupt practices. From another perspective, however, it could be argued that the conditions were unfavorable to malfeasance. Not only did the technology of constructing canals make it relatively easy to make comparisons of cost per mile across supervising engineers or contractors, and to detect those stretches of canal that were below standard (further facilitated by strict procedures and guidelines for the testing of the quality of the work), but the absolute amounts to be gained from individual episodes of corruption must have been small.

A ceremony to officially mark the completion of the entire canal took

18. Each contract was to be put up for bid and assigned to the lowest bidder, and each contained detailed specifications appropriate to the individual situation (with the tasks including clearing land, excavating, and the construction of locks, embankments, culverts, towpaths, fences, etc.). For more treatment of the procedures, see Shaw (1966) and Walker and Walker (1963), pp. 40–44, for the relevant discussion from the 1818 *Report of the Commissioners.*

19. The most prominent scandal associated with the construction of the canal concerned the activities of Myron Holley, the treasurer of the Canal Committee, and the commissioner who was perhaps most active at negotiating contracts and disbursing payments to contractors. Although he was attacked by some observers for partisanship in the award of contracts as early as 1820, in 1824 it was discovered that he was unable to account for $30,000 of public monies and had used public funds to purchase property near the canal. For more discussion, see Shaw (1966), pp. 169–72.

20. Another explanation for the use of relatively small contracts rather than a sole, general contractor emerged during the Progressive Era, with the intent to curb the powers of contractors and avoid corruption on public jobs, albeit at the cost of imposing difficulties of coordination. While many states soon repealed this legislation, New York still operates under the Wicks Law, which requires separate contracts for each function to be performed.

place to universal acclaim in 1825, but the financial and economic success of the Erie was evident to observers well before. Indeed, it was not long after the middle section of the canal had been opened, and substantial toll collections began to roll in, that the securities issued to mobilize funds for the remainder of the project were attracting the interest of investors as distant as London. The primary basis for the enormous social returns to this public investment was of course the demand for the transportation services that the canal provided at radically lower cost than the alternatives.[21] But the cost effectiveness of the construction effort also deserves attention. Despite the massive and unprecedented scale of this public works project, the provincial attitudes of most of those involved, and the direction by canal commissioners who were at best self-taught engineers, the Erie Canal (and its companion, the Champlain Canal) were constructed at only about 46 percent above the estimated costs at the time of authorization. Although this overrun seems quite formidable in the abstract, it is (as suggested by the comparison with other public works projects presented in table 3.1) quite modest by the standards of modern experience and sensibilities.

The problems of excess expenditure, if not corruption, in New York State grew much more severe after the completion of the Erie. As mentioned above, the Erie Canal was so successful in stimulating economic development along its route, and in generating surpluses from tolls, that state legislators were swept up with a general enthusiasm for constructing many more canals throughout New York with borrowed funds.[22] Within five years, they authorized going forward with a series of additional canals despite reports from canal commissioners that predicted that at least some of the planned canals would not produce sufficient tolls to cover expenses, and despite a series of increasingly tough warnings from the comptroller and governor about committing to projects unlikely to be able to cover costs. To make matters worse, as the annual expenses of the state government grew over time, the legislature, reluctant to raise taxes, increasingly relied on tapping the revenue or accumulated surplus from canal tolls and exotic financial measures such as borrowing from the Common School Fund at lower than market rates. Despite the ominous fiscal balance, however, in 1835 and 1836 the legislature again defied the advice of the governor by authorizing not only a major enlargement and improvement of the Erie Canal (which was widely acknowledged to be of insufficient size given

21. See Fogel (1979) for discussion and estimates of the extraordinary cost advantages of canals and railroads over transport by horse and wagon. More specifically, the costs for transporting grain or flour from Buffalo to New York City are generally said to have fallen by 85 to 90 percent. So great was the impact of the Erie Canal that Carter Goodrich (1960, p. 55) judged its opening as "the most decisive single event in the history of American transportation."

22. It is interesting that this movement to build more canals got started about the same time that the franchise was extended in New York by eliminating wealth requirements. See Engerman and Sokoloff (2005).

Table 3.1 Actual expenditures to projected costs on major public works: 1817 to 2004

Time period	Public works	Projected cost (current U.S. $ millions)	Actual expenditures (current U.S. $ millions)	Ratio of actual to projected cost
1817–1825	Erie Canal (New York State)	5.75	8.40	1.46
1824–1829	Chesapeake and Delaware Canal (U.S. government)	1.35	2.20	1.63
1825–1835	Ohio and Miami canals (Ohio)	5.13	5.93	1.16
1835–1862	Enlargement and improvement of Erie Canal (NY State)	12.42	30.00	2.42
1838–1843	Croton Aqueduct (City and County of New York)	8.46	11.45	1.35
1883–1926	Mississippi River Levee Line (U.S. government)	11.45	>229.00	>20.00
1902–1913	Panama Canal (U.S. government)	145.00	298.00	2.06
1931–1936	Hoover Dam (U.S. government)	48.89	54.70	1.12
1952–1953	Interstate highways (U.S. & state governments)	25.00	477.50	19.10
1966–1975	Louisiana Superdome (Louisiana)	35.00	163.00	4.66
1971–1975	Renovation of Yankee Stadium (New York City)	24.00	100.00	4.17
1991–2004	Boston Central Artery/Tunnel or "Big Dig" (U.S. government)	2800.00	>14600.00	>5.21

Notes: Our projected cost figures generally pertain to the estimated construction costs at the time the projects were approved. The periods specified for the projects begin with the year of approval (or cost estimate) and end with the completion of the project. For each project we have specified the government that was the initiator of the project, or the major funding source. The cost figures for the Erie Canal include the cost of the Champlain Canal. The projected costs were prepared in March 1817 and were those in place when the legislature approved the plan in that year. For those estimates and the actual cost of constructing the two canals, see "Internal Improvements in the State of New York" (1850, p. 386). For the Chesapeake and Delaware Canal, see Gray (1967, p. 51); the cost estimate we use here is the one prepared by the consulting engineers, which leads to a slightly lower ratio of expenditures to estimated costs. For the Ohio and Miami canals, see Bogart (1924, pp. 28–29 and 76). For the estimates for the Croton Aqueduct, see King (1843, pp. 176 and 221). For the estimates of projected (prepared by the Mississippi River Commission in 1883) and actual expenditures on building the levee line to control flooding on the Mississippi River, see Frank (1930) and the U.S. House Committee on Flood Control (1927–28). This project was not completed by 1927. For the projected costs of constructing the Panama Canal (presented in 1901 by a commission appointed by President McKinley, and voted on by Congress in 1902), see J. Bishop (1913, pp. 428–29). For a more optimistic estimate, see McCulloch (1977, pp. 610–11). For a more pessimistic estimate, see Moulton (1915). Our cost figures do not include the $40 million that was paid to obtain the land, property, and rights of an unsuccessful French effort to build the canal. For discussion of the estimated cost of the Hoover Dam (taken as the winning bid by the contractor), and the ultimate cost of the construction to the government, see Stevens (1988, p. 252). For the figures on the Louisiana Superdome, see Quirk and Fort (1992, p. 279). Also see Danielson (1997, p. 158). The figures for interstate highways pertain to the Federal-Aid Highway Act of 1952 and come from Weingroff (1996, p. 4). For an extended discussion of the background and development of the New York City project to renovate Yankee Stadium, as well as of how the costs of the project were underestimated, see Sullivan (2001, chap. 7). For the estimated costs of the "Big Dig" (a highway/bridge/tunnel project in Boston and the "single largest civil-engineering project in American history"), see Franklin (2003, p. 28).

the heavier-than-expected volume of traffic) but also several other water-way projects and a $3 million loan to aid the New York and Erie Railroad.[23] Even with a change in the party in power (from Democrats to Whigs), a courageous and insightful state comptroller, and the encouragement to concentration of the mind provided by the financial crisis of 1837 and the protracted downturn that followed (along with the associated fall in canal revenue), the legislature continued to pursue policies of extravagance. The ability of the state to service its debt and obtain new credit, not coincidentally, eroded dramatically.

It was not until 1842 that New York, on the brink of insolvency, began to take strong action.[24] The "stop and tax law of 1842" both assessed a general tax on wealth and suspended state expenditures for the construction of public works (paying only for maintenance and repairs). As the state made progress in paying down its debt and restoring fiscal balance, it also took steps to prevent the recurrence of such profligacy by the government. In 1846 a new constitution was adopted, and among the many important new provisions were restrictions on borrowing, establishments of guidelines for the use of sinking funds to pay off canal and other government debts, and other reforms directed at improving governance.[25] The same concern with trying to identify the sources of the fiscal crisis, as well perhaps as a spirit of reform more generally, also gave rise in 1846 to the first serious investigation of the construction and operations of the canals. Another motivation may have been an interest on the part of legislators to shift responsibility for the debacle in state finance.

The Select Committee of the Assembly that convened in 1846 was zealous about "investigating frauds in the expenditures of the public moneys upon the canals of this state" and desirous of identifying problems that would attract public attention and provoke enactment of, if not resolution by, new laws and procedures (*Report* 1847, p. 3). The investigators focused on the possibilities of corruption associated with the construction of the canals as well as on the use of canal-related jobs as a form of political patronage (with the allocation of supervisory, inspector, and other positions associated with operating the canals changing with shifts in parties in power). The chronological scope of the inquiry was broad, extending back

23. For discussion, see Shaw (1966), pp. 239–42. For more on the New York and Erie Railroad, see Pierce (1953), pp. 13–16.

24. During the early 1840s, one-third of the states defaulted on their bonded debt, and while several resumed payments of interest and principal within a few years, four repudiated their debt. See McGrane (1935). New York did not default.

25. For example, the new constitution increased transparency (and perhaps limited logrolling) by specifying that private or local bills could not deal with more than one subject and that the subject had to be expressed in the title. Also, money could only be paid out of the treasury "in pursuance of an appropriation," and any such appropriation had to be explicit about the sum appropriated and the object to which the fund would be applied. See Sowers (1914), pp. 72–74, for more discussion.

to the construction of the Erie Canal several decades before. The major sources of corruption highlighted in these hearings were fraud in allocating contracts to "friends, acquaintances, and neighbors," forging of vouchers for reimbursements of materials, padded payrolls, stolen materials, and use of claims concerning the need for extraordinary repairs to circumvent state limits (*Report* 1847, p. 6). The committee established that problems emerged very early in these public works projects. As noted above, the most notorious example involved Myron Holley, one of the first canal commissioners, who in 1824 had been charged with (and admitted to) being unable to account for some public funds and using some of them to purchase land in the canal region. Also worthy of note was the discovery that the books of the canal commission for the period 1822–28 were missing (or that no records had been kept during those years) and that several of the individuals asked to testify about the construction of the Erie declined to do so.

What stood out in these hearings, and in the other major hearings that were to be held in the years to come on the subject of the construction and operations of the canal policies, is that the quality of controls had become more lax over time, allowing the influence of politicians (as regards who served as engineers and who received contracts) and corrupt practices by engineers to become more pronounced.[26] Although other factors, such as the originally unscheduled cessation of construction between 1842 and 1847, certainly played an important role in accounting for cost overruns, the findings of the investigators suggest that poor governance (encompassing acceptance of incompetence or inefficiency), if not an increased prevalence of outright fraud, help to explain why the costs of enlarging and improving the Erie Canal ballooned from the initial projection of $12.42 million to over $30 million (and the time required for the work from twelve years to twenty-seven years). The testimony to, and analysis provided by, the series of investigating committees convened by the New York Assembly

---

26. For example, the report of the Select Committee expressed concern about what happened under the charge of Frederick C. Mills, chief engineer on the construction of the Genesee Valley Canal. Near the close of his work, his brother Hiram P. Mills was employed as resident engineer on the stretch of the canal extending from Mount Morris to Olean. The contracts for the construction on this part of the canal were let in the fall of 1838: "it will therefore, be seen that the work on that section was immense, and that a majority of it was rock excavation from the mountain side, whence the rocks excavated could be cast directly off into the river channel. The contract for that work being a very desirable one, there was much competition for it; and the manner of conducting the business of letting that contract to the successful competitor, deserves particular attention. The contract was awarded to Nicholas Van Derwerken, who it is said, was not possessed of the means necessary to the prosecution of such an undertaking, and who was without experience as a contractor. How it happened that he became the lowest bidder does not directly appear, except by the proposition itself; but the course then pursued in regard to it by H. P. Mills, the resident engineer, leaves the impression very strong that there was connivance between him and Van Derwerken. After the work was awarded to Van Derwerken on his proposition, the contract for it was taken jointly by Van Derwerken and Robert Powers, his brother-in-law, who had previously been a partner with H. P. Mills." See *Report of the Select Committee* (1847), pp. 4–49.

and/or Senate were published in 1847 (1,242 pages), 1851 (332 pages), 1868 (1,018 pages), 1875 (677 pages), and 1876 (770 pages), and in less complete reports on contracts and frauds in other years (starting in 1840).[27]

The 1876 report reported on the following "various forms of mismanagement, neglect, fraud, and malfeasance":

> (a) the approval or toleration of "unbalanced bids"; (b) improper action of commissioners in making new contracts, and in extending or canceling old ones; (c) agreement to contracts that were adverse to the interests of the State, and for the benefit of contractors; (d) blind, hasty or corrupt legislation in making appropriations for repairs, claims, and awards; (e) failure of engineers to make true cost estimates, and connivance with bidders or contractors in making false ones; (f) carelessness or neglect on the part of the Canal Board in ascertaining whether proposed work had proper legal sanction; (g) appropriation of property of the State by contractors, or by superintendents; (h) approval, by superintendents, of bad or worthless work; (i) wrongful or careless awards by canal appraisers; (j) the legal fiction of "extraordinary repairs" which misstates a matter of fact, misleads successive Legislatures, and prevents the completion of the enlargement; and (k) the lack of responsibility on the part of canal officers, owing to a defective system of subdividing duties, which rendered it difficult to hold a wrong-doer to strict account. (*Report* 1876, pp. 12–16)

The various hearings uncovered a number of instances of these kinds of mismanagement and malfeasance, as well as the likelihood that there had been some confiscation of fees and tolls collected by canal workers.[28] Their conclusions, framed in general terms, were that the controls intended to prevent behaviors inappropriate or otherwise wasteful in the use of public funds were imperfectly designed, not strictly adhered to, and irregularly enforced. Because we have all come to expect such problems, at least to some extent, in the administration of large public (and private) enterprises, it is in no way surprising that thorough investigations uncovered their existence. What would be more informative and useful, however, is a gauge that would allow us to evaluate the magnitude of these problems and to examine whether their seriousness varies over type of project or time.

27. See *Report* (1876), p. 11, and Hasse (1907).
28. These same sorts of problems with internal improvement projects were noted in other states. For example, in 1840 the Pennsylvania Canal Commissioners listed twenty ways in which "positive proof was obtained to substantiate . . . charges of attempts to defraud the Commonwealth." In his study of corruption in *The State Works of Pennsylvania,* Bishop observes (1907b, pp. 229–44) that "we have no assurance that there would have been greater purity under corporate management," and that "public works were used by the political party in power as an invaluable instrument of political corruption, destroying the morale of citizens and squandering the resources of the state." He concludes that "those who are abashed by the present-day disclosures of corruption in the management of cities and powerful corporations, and who therefore sigh for the 'good old days' of political purity, have to face the fact that these did not exist in Pennsylvania . . . at least during the period of state ownership and control of public works." See also Bishop (1907a) and Bowers (1983).

3.3   Gauging the Quality of Governance of Public Resources

Several features of this record of canal building by New York State stand out. First, although legislators were perhaps wanton in their authorization of public transportation projects, it is significant that a potentially more corrosive form of rent seeking appears not to have imposed major costs on the state. The legislature does not seem to have been capable of limiting access to low-cost transportation, and in so doing to greatly advantage one specific region or segment of the population at the expense of others—and at the expense of the overall growth of the state economy.[29] On the contrary, even when precarious state finances should have strengthened the case for skepticism about marginal projects, legislators all too often failed to summon up a majority against. Their failure in enforcing such restrictions, or monopolies, on access to low-cost transportation, was not because of an absence of advocates. The representatives of the areas that already had access to canals were generally among those legislators who opposed the authorization of new ones along routes that would have competed for traffic. Similarly, they, as well as others who had interests in canal operations, also sought restrictions on the speed of the expansion of a new competing innovation, the railroad. Various limitations were in fact imposed on the railroads when they threatened toll collections on canals, though they were withdrawn in the early 1850s.[30] Partially offsetting such restrictions were, of course, subsidies to encourage the construction and expansion of specific railroads. Excess transportation capacity and collapsing rates were the consequence.

The observation that legislators were not effective at restricting access to transportation by water or rail reflects the fact that the open political system made it very difficult for those geographic areas or companies who sought to obtain and maintain strong competitive advantages, or monopolies, on such a basis. It further suggests that if there were social costs to corrupt practices in the building and operation of New York canals they likely consisted primarily of excessive costs of construction and/or opera-

---

29. The liberal policy about authorizing canals is not unlike the policies concerning the establishment of banks and corporations. The passage of free incorporation and free banking acts reduced the ability of the legislatures to create highly profitable monopolies by restricting entry. Because the monopoly rents would have gone in large measure to legislators with the power to charter firms, the free incorporation and banking laws meant that the legislators were accepting a lower stream of rents. The social and political pressures that led to such policies may have narrowed the scope for, and economic consequences of, corruption in the antebellum economy.

30. See MacGill and staff (1917), pp. 353–56. First were requirements that they carry only passengers, and passenger baggage, not freight. They were followed by restrictions against railroads operating during the summers when the canals were open, and finally by a requirement that railroads pay canal tolls for traffic carried. Similar types of restrictions, lasting until 1861, were introduced for railroads in Pennsylvania. See Dunlavy (1994), pp. 79–80 and 138–39.

tions, or from investments in marginal canals that yielded low social re-turns. It is beyond the scope of our study to estimate the social returns to each of the New York canals, but we would note that the work of Albert Fishlow suggests that the rate of return on investments in New York canals was well above the cost of capital.[31] His estimates would seem to imply that the overall cost of the misallocation of public funds on these canal projects was likely not all that monstrous.

Our focus is instead on the issue of whether, and by how much, corrupt practices or incompetence tolerated by public officials increased the costs of constructing the canals. Precise measures of this theoretical concept are of course difficult to tease out of the data. The approach we employ here is to use the ratio of the expenditures on public works projects relative to the estimated cost at the time of authorization as a rough gauge of the quality of public governance in such activities. This ratio is, of course, very differ-ent from the amount by which the costs of construction exceeded the minimum feasible cost, but it has the advantages of being both relatively straightforward to retrieve and meaningful about the quality of public gov-ernance.[32] The implicit supposition for our approach is that conscientious public officials practicing good governance would make their decisions about whether to go forward on a public investment with the best available estimates of costs (and benefits). Errors in these estimates are obviously to be expected, as it is impossible to perfectly anticipate all of the circum-stances that develop in the course of major construction projects, and public officials, like other humans, are often prone to wishful thinking. Nevertheless, the estimated cost of a project at the time public authorities commit to carrying out an investment would seem to provide a reasonable baseline, on average, if there was good governance over public resources. Thus, we argue, a major source of systematic bias in the cost estimates is tolerance of incompetence, weak oversight or administration, actual cor-ruption, and other cost-inflating practices by public officials, or the qual-ity of governance more generally. Deliberate misrepresentation of the costs of a big public investment project reflects poor governance, in that public officials can get away with it (whether they are elected officials or not). Moreover, to the extent that costs rise (on average) after the authorization

31. Fishlow (2000), pp. 552–64 and 604–6. See also Goodrich et al. (1961), pp. 216–47, and MacGill and staff (1917). The social and private returns on building the Erie Canal were much larger than on the others, but in his assessment of six of the New York canals, Ransom (1964) concluded that three of the six were "successful" in financial terms. Fishlow also judged the early canals in Ohio successful. The problem was that too many feeder canals (as in New York) were built. Competition between the large number of waterways and railroads put sub-stantial downward pressure on tolls.

32. How much the ultimate costs of a project exceed the estimated costs at time of author-ization, and how that ratio has varied over time and across projects, has been the subject of earlier studies. See, for example, Merrow (1988) and Flyvbjerg, Bruzelius, and Rothengatter (2003).

of a public investment project, it would seem reasonable to attribute it primarily to poor management or oversight of the uses to which public funds are being put—whether due to corruption or tolerance of incompetence and other cost-inflating practices. The measure we rely on, therefore, should be regarded as one that relates more to the quality of public governance than to the level of corruption narrowly understood.

Although we emphasize how the cost overrun ratio is informative about the quality of public governance, it must be admitted that there are other reasons—some quite innocuous—why the ratio might differ from unity or even vary systematically. First, there might be unanticipated inflation, such that nominal expenditures could total more than original forecast, even if expenditures expressed in constant dollars had not risen.[33] Second, the costs of a public works investment might exceed the projected amount, because of a redesign that added new elements that added to costs. A third consideration, one that could in principle lead to increases or decreases in costs, is that technology (or regulations) might advance in unexpected ways. Yet another possible contributor to cost overruns is the deliberate preparation of downward-biased estimates of the costs of projects so as to increase the likelihood of their being approved by public authorities. There might also be problems having to do with management, which may stem from the complexity or scale of projects being undertaken—rather than to the quality of public governance. All of these factors need to be taken into account in the interpretation of any costs overruns or systematic patterns therein.

As we have already stated, and as is highlighted in table 3.1, the seriousness of the cost overruns in the construction of New York canals seems to have increased after the completion of the Erie Canal. Whereas expenditures on the Erie totaled roughly 46 percent more than projected at the time the legislature authorized going ahead, the ultimate cost of the enlargement and improvement of the Erie was more than 140 percent greater than the plan approved in 1835 (a decade after the Erie was originally opened). That the cost overrun was much larger in the later work is consistent with the evidence of erosion of oversight, and of greater prevalence of corrupt practices, over time uncovered by the various investigations conducted by the New York State Assembly and Senate. At least part of the higher-than-expected costs of completing this project must have been due to the interruption in work, between 1842 and 1847, brought on by the state fiscal crisis.[34] It is notable,

33. One might initially presume that this issue would lead to substantial cost overruns during periods of inflation. However, often, such as in the United States over recent decades, the projected expenditures generally took account of expected inflation in forecasting nominal expenditures. See the discussion in Merrow (1988).

34. Although the difficulty of obtaining information prevents us from giving the issue more extensive treatment, it does appear that extreme cost overruns were typically associated with delays in completing the respective projects. The Mississippi River Levee Line and the Boston Central Artery/Tunnel projects are examples of projects whose construction fell well behind schedule, and the Hoover Dam is an example of one completed well ahead of schedule.

moreover, that the cost overrun on the Erie Canal improvement project was far greater, relative to the estimated figures at time of authorization, than those incurred on several other antebellum canals—the Chesapeake and Delaware Canal (63 percent) and the Ohio and Miami canals (16 percent) as well as on the major project that vastly expanded the supply of fresh water to rapidly growing New York City—the Croton Aqueduct.

Given that these canal projects were extremely large, relative to the scale of enterprise, the depth of capital markets, and the size of the economy, the increase in the costs of carrying out these works could not have been insignificant in absolute terms. But it is difficult to gauge the import of the cost overruns without some basis for comparison. For this reason, to aid in the evaluation of the significance of the cost overrun ratios for the Erie and other antebellum canal projects, table 3.1 also includes the ratios calculated for other large public works projects over the course of the history of the United States.[35] Our selection of the public works to include in the table was not random, but we sought to retrieve the information on a range of well-known projects extending from the canal era to the present day.[36]

The record of cost overruns on public works revealed in table 3.1 suggests that the construction of the Erie Canal, and of other public works built during the antebellum period, was not plagued by extraordinary problems in managing costs. On the contrary, the cost overrun ratios drawn from the period before the Civil War are generally among the lowest we have observed; only the Hoover Dam, a Great Depression–era public works project, does as well by this gauge (the Panama Canal also does bet-

35. Some may find it interesting that the cost overrun ratios we computed for the unsuccessful French effort to build a canal across the Isthmus of Panama and for the infrastructure Montreal needed to host the Olympics were among the highest we have seen. See Toohey and Veal (2000), p. 77. We confine our attention here, however, to public works in the United States.

36. We have not included in table 3.1 all of the public works for which we obtained cost overrun ratios, but the basic qualitative pattern (and rough quantitative pattern) would be robust to their inclusion. For other examples from the late nineteenth and early twentieth centuries, and discussion of related issues, see Moulton (1915). Another example, developing as this paper is being written, is the increase in the cost of the eastern span of the San Francisco Bay Bridge (which was damaged in an earthquake) being carried out under the auspices of the California Department of Transportation. Although the project is not scheduled for completion until 2010, the cost overrun ratio is already at 3.0. We have also not included the Union Pacific Railroad, which was built during the 1860s by private enterprise with substantial subsidies specified in 1862, and then increased in 1864, from the federal government. The primary reason for its omission is that the organization of the project was very different from that of the Erie Canal and of the other more conventional public works treated here. However, a close examination of the history of this effort by the government to obtain a transcontinental railroad before private investors thought it sufficiently attractive to undertake on their own suggests that most of the corruption involved one set of railroad promoters extracting rents at the expense of other private investors. It is not obvious how to estimate the cost overrun to the government with any precision, but we judge the overrun to certainly have been no more than 100 percent, and probably much less. The case does not appear inconsistent with our qualitative conclusions about the general trend over time. For a very insightful examination of the Union Pacific, see Fogel (1960). Also see White (1895), Moody (1920), and Klein (1987).

ter than the project enlarging and improving the Erie Canal). If there is any trend, it is that cost overruns have become somewhat worse over time, especially after World War II. The cost overrun ratios vary between 1.16 and 2.42 across the five antebellum projects (averaging 1.60) but vary between 4.17 and 19.10 across the four projects constructed since 1950.[37] The difference in the distributions is indeed very stark. If the ratios do provide a meaningful indicator of the quality of public governance, then the implication would seem to be that conditions were better during the early nineteenth century than in the late twentieth century.

As many would find such a judgment surprising, it is necessary to critically assess whether we should believe the trend in our estimates. Although more observations would obviously be desirable, the strength of the pattern we have noted and the general consistency of our results with those of other studies give us confidence that the qualitative result will hold up under further research scrutiny.[38] For example, Bent Flyvbjerg, Nils Bruzelius, and Werner Rothengatter have conducted studies of both 258 railway and road projects and large nontransportation projects between 1927 and 1998, and found cost overruns to be generally higher, and often much higher, than what we found for the United States during the antebellum era. The cost overruns, moreover, seem to have grown slightly over the period under investigation.[39] In his study of fifty-two major investment projects (most of which were in mining, manufacturing, and energy) carried out across a range of countries during the 1970s and 1980s, Edward Merrow (using a concept or procedure that produces lower estimates than our approach) found overruns of 88 percent in real terms on average, and markedly higher for public or mixed public-private projects than for private.[40] Although such estimates of cost overruns on late twentieth-century public works projects generally fall below those suggested in table

37. The high ratio for the interstate highway system is especially striking. It appears to have resulted primarily from the initial law's having been written in an open-ended way, such that it obligated the federal government to pay for many more highway projects than had been anticipated. According to Weingroff (1996), the 1952 act authorized $25 million for the next two years to pay for an interstate system on a fifty-fifty matching basis between the federal government and the state governments. Within one year, however, the states had built considerable mileage, and the federal share of total costs was $477.5 million. We regret that our estimated cost overrun on the interstate highway system public works pertains only to the very early stages of the program. We have not yet been able to obtain the information that would permit us to calculate a cost overrun ratio for the entire system.

38. From our readings of the histories, the cost overruns, even those of the modern era, seem to be primarily due to higher-than-estimated costs of carrying out or implementing the designs or work laid out in the original plans, as opposed to the addition of new features to the original plan. The one exception (we cannot be sure) may be the cost overrun on the interstate highway program. See the sources cited in the note to table 3.1 for more details.

39. See Flyvbjerg, Bruzelius, and Rothengatter (2003), p. 18.

40. See Merrow (1988). He and his team calculated cost overruns from the detailed engineering plans typically made after authorization. They also found that projects that were larger ex ante had proportionally higher cost overruns.

3.1, they do provide rather strong support to our key observation—that such cost overruns were typically lower in the antebellum era than they are today.[41] Another issue in interpreting the high cost overrun ratios in the modern public works projects is whether the higher rates of inflation during the 1970s and 1980s may lead them to overstate the increase in the real costs of a project over what was originally forecast. This problem may be relevant for assessing the estimated cost overruns for the Louisiana Superdome, the renovation of Yankee Stadium, and the Boston Central Artery/ Tunnel project, but in all of these cases no reasonable adjustment for changes in the price level could alter the qualitative finding.[42]

In our view, the finding that cost overruns on public works were relatively modest during the antebellum era, as compared to those today or in other eras in American history, has a solid empirical basis.[43] The next and more fundamental question, however, is what this intriguing pattern means.

The straightforward interpretation, one for which we have already expressed support, is that the governance, or control over the use, of public funds was stricter during the early nineteenth century than it is today. It is difficult to explain the more substantial cost overruns during the modern

41. Current municipal policies regarding sports stadiums, if not airports and convention halls as well, resemble the mercantilist policies of local and state governments during the era of internal improvements. This entails competitive bidding for teams and large subsidies to influence location decisions, and has generated intense controversy about the social returns to such public investments. The cost overrun figures we present for several of the earliest public investments in stadiums are somewhat higher than the ones that pertain to more recently constructed stadiums. However, the costs of constructing sports stadiums have ballooned as the mania for publicly built stadiums has spread. It may be that the commitment of public resources to build ever-more-extravagant stadiums for use by private teams on easy terms is the most telling feature in this record about the quality of governance of public resources. See Quirk and Fort (1992, 1999).

42. For example, even after adjusting for inflation, the cost of the Boston Central Artery/ Tunnel project more than tripled. See the discussion in Altshuler and Luberoff (2003), chapter 4, and especially p. 119. As the task of retrieving all of the information necessary to deflate the expenditures on the public works are quite formidable to us, and as the qualitative results seem likely to be robust, we have not gone any further as of yet. Both the Hoover Dam and Erie Canal projects are cases where the bias from changes in the price level may have served to bias the cost overrun ratio downward, but again the basic qualitative results are unlikely to be sensitive to adjustments for changes in the price level.

43. Boss Tweed and his New York City machine are not infrequently invoked to illustrate the extent of corruption in the late nineteenth-century United States. It is not clear how representative they were of the country overall, but the histories are rather convincing about how poor public governance in New York City was under the Tammany Democrats. How does Tammany fare under our gauge? Although the complex accounts make it difficult to compute a precise cost overrun ratio, it seems that the amounts paid out for the construction of the famed New York County Courthouse ("the House that Tweed built") were more than forty times the amount forecast at the time of the original authorization (which took place before the Tweed Ring was formed). In contrast, the generally comparable courthouse (as regards size and accoutrements) built at about the same time in neighboring Brooklyn (Kings County) had a cost overrun of only about 40 percent and was built at less than 10 percent of the cost of the one in New York. See New York Times (1871) and Callow (1966).

era, in particular, without acknowledging either that the processes of vetting these public works projects were badly flawed (if not dishonest) or that oversight by the public authorities was so poor as to permit grossly inefficient use or private extraction of public resources.[44] The source of this contemporary institutional failure is not easily identified, but cost overrun ratios during the late twentieth century that seem routinely very high by early nineteenth-century standards imply that public officials (or the taxpaying electorate) have lost control. What the basis is for the relatively good performance of the public sector during the antebellum period is likewise unclear.

There are a myriad of possible explanations, ranging from the virtues of democracy and high rates of participation in civic affairs to the natural constraints on corruption and gross incompetence that come along with relatively low per capita incomes and small enterprises (as well as a small government sector). We are as yet unable to distinguish between them, and the absence of information on the social returns to different public works is another reason why our assessment must be considered tentative, but the evidence on cost overruns does seem consistent with de Tocqueville's (1961) conception that democracy in America meant good governance.

3.4   Conclusion

The Erie Canal was, for its time, a mammoth public works project undertaken largely because the scope of the investment was beyond what a private firm could manage. As with most public works, there were ample opportunities for public officials to realize private gains from the effort,

---

44. Among the scholars who have examined cost overruns on recent public works and other large investment projects, there are two schools of thought about the principal causes and the source of the evident trend toward proportionally higher cost overruns. One school emphasizes how forecasts of costs are deliberately underestimated so as to increase the probability of project approval. The notion seems to be that public authorities are less transparent or less able to monitor themselves than they were previously, perhaps because there are a greater number of organized interests that stand to benefit from a project approval and aid public officials in preparing deceptive cost estimates. For examples of those who hold this view, see Flyvbjerg, Bruzelius, and Rothengatter (2003) and Altshuler and Luberoff (2003). The latter (p. 246) quote Martin Wachs, "one of the nation's most thoughtful and balanced observers of urban transportation policymaking": "I have interviewed public officials, consultants, and planners who have been involved [in transit project cost and ridership forecasting] and I am absolutely convinced that the cost overruns and patronage overestimates were not the result of technical errors, honest mistakes, or inadequate methods. In case after case, planners, engineers, and economists have told me that they had to 'revise' their forecasts many times because they failed to satisfy their superiors. The forecasts had to be 'cooked' in order to produce numbers that were dramatic enough to gain federal support for projects whether or not they could be fully justified on technical grounds." Also see Wachs (1989). Although acknowledging that the much worse performance of public projects was telling, Merrow (1988) argues that changes in the regulatory environment and in feasible technology have also played an important role in causing cost overruns. For discussion of U.S. highway policy, see Burch (1962).

and many did. On the whole, however, the construction of the Erie (and the companion Champlain Canal) appears to have been well conceived and executed; it not only paid off more than its construction costs through tolls, but it also generated substantial welfare improvements for the residents of New York in the form of producer and consumer surplus and a wide range of positive externalities. Although there was obviously some fraud and mismanagement, the public authorities carried out the work at costs relatively close (by the standards of public projects) to those projected at the point of authorization. The experience of the Erie provides something of a model of what a public works project could feasibly be.

The problems arose after the completion of the Erie, and out of a common reaction to emulate success. Noting how the areas along the route of the Erie had grown quite prosperous, many other parts of New York wanted their own transportation improvements. The legislature approved some of the proposals, and committed to building some canals that may have been beneficial to those counties that were served but whose costs were at least partially borne by taxpayers elsewhere (as toll revenue was insufficient). The consequences of inadequate attention to the amount of traffic that would be procured were compounded by the oversupply of transportation lines as both new waterways and railroads proliferated, and by the impact of a severe and prolonged economic contraction that began in 1837. How much of the misallocation of public funds to such projects should be attributed to corruption or poor governance can be debated, as private agents too often make similar miscalculations in their estimation of the probability of duplicating the success of innovative investments (and did so during this era in buying some of the canal bonds), but matters were made worse by the evident deterioration in cost controls. The resources devoted to the post-Erie projects (both new canals and the enlargement and improvement of the Erie) mushroomed, with the ultimate costs far exceeding those originally budgeted for.

In an effort to try to place this episode in a broader perspective, we have computed the ratio of actual expenditures on construction relative to the estimated costs at the time of authorization for the Erie Canal, for the project to enlarge and improve it, and for a range of other public works in the United States to the present day. It is our contention that this measure, albeit quite narrow in focus, is informative about the quality of governance of public resources. In general, we expect the ratio to vary positively with the lack of transparency exhibited by public authorities as well as with their level of tolerance of incompetence or other cost-inflating practices manifested in the use of public resources. We highlight how, by this standard, the governance of public resources during the canal era of the early nineteenth century stands up well in comparison with what we have seen since. Indeed, the cost overrun ratios have risen sharply over the last half-century, coinciding with both a marked increase in the relative size of the government sector and sustained economic growth. These patterns reveal, in our view, how little scholars and policymakers understand about how the type, prevalence, and effects of corruption vary across different contexts, and how important it is that better measures and other means of systematically studying the phenomenon be developed.

References

Altshuler, Alan, and David Luberoff. 2003. *Mega-projects: The changing politics of urban public investment.* Washington, DC: Brookings Institution Press.

Bernstein, Peter L. 2005. *Wedding of the waters: The Erie Canal and the making of a great nation.* New York: Norton.

Bishop, Avard Longley. 1907a. Corrupt practices connected with the building and operation of the State Works of Pennsylvania. *Yale Review* 15 (February): 391–411.

———. 1907b. *The state works of Pennsylvania.* New Haven, CT: Yale University Press.

Bishop, Joseph Bucklin. 1913. *The Panama gateway.* New York: Charles Scribner's Sons.

Bogart, Ernest Ludlow. 1924. *Internal improvements and state debt in Ohio: An essay in economic history.* New York: Longmans, Green.

Bowers, Douglas E. 1983. From logrolling to corruption: The development of lobbying in Pennsylvania, 1815–1861. *Journal of the Early Republic* 3 (Winter): 439–74.

Burch, Philip H., Jr. 1962. *Highway revenue and expenditure policy in the United States.* New Brunswick: Rutgers University Press.

Callow, Alexander B., Jr. 1966. *The Tweed Ring.* New York: Oxford University Press.

Danielson, Michael N. 1997. *Home team: Professional sports and the American metropolis.* Princeton, NJ: Princeton University Press.

Dunlavy, Colleen A. 1994. *Politics and industrialization: Early railroads in the United States and Prussia.* Princeton, NJ: Princeton University Press.

Engerman, Stanley L., and Kenneth L. Sokoloff. 2005. The evolution of suffrage institutions in the Americas. *Journal of Economic History* 65 (December), 891–921.

Fishlow, Albert. 2000. Internal transportation in the nineteenth and early twentieth centuries. In *The Cambridge economic history of the United States.* Vol. 2, *The long nineteenth century,* ed. Stanley L. Engerman and Robert E. Gallman, 543–642. Cambridge: Cambridge University Press.

Flyvbjerg, Bent, Nils Bruzelius, and Werner Rothengatter. 2003. *Megaprojects and risk: An anatomy of ambition.* Cambridge: Cambridge University Press.

Fogel, Robert William. 1960. *The Union Pacific Railroad: A case in premature enterprise.* Baltimore: Johns Hopkins Press.

———. 1979. Notes on the social savings controversy. *Journal of Economic History* 39 (March): 1–54.

Frank, Arthur DeWitt. 1930. *The development of the federal program of flood control on the Mississippi river.* New York: Columbia University Press.

Franklin, Daniel, ed. 2003. *The world in 2004.* London: The Economist.

Gallatin, Albert. 1968. *Report of the Secretary of the Treasury on the subject of public roads and canals.* New York: Augustus M. Kelley. (Orig. pub. 1808.)

Glaeser, Edward L., and Andrei Shleifer. 2003. The rise of the regulatory state. *Journal of Economic Literature* 41 (June): 401–25.

Goodrich, Carter. 1960. *Government promotion of American canals and railroads, 1800–1890.* New York: Columbia University Press.

Goodrich, Carter, Julius Rubin, H. Jerome Cranmer, and Harvey H. Segal. 1961. *Canals and American economic development.* New York: Columbia University Press.

Gray, Ralph D. 1967. *The national waterway: A history of the Chesapeake and Delaware Canal, 1769–1965.* Urbana: University of Illinois Press.

Gunn, L. Ray. 1988. *The decline of authority: Public economic policy and political development in New York State, 1800–1860.* Ithaca, NY: Cornell University Press.

Hammond, Jabez D. 1846. *The history of political parties in the state of New York.* 4th ed. 2 vols. Cooperstown, NY: H&E Phinney.

Hanyan, Craig, and Mary Hanyan. 1996. *DeWitt Clinton and the rise of the People's men.* Montreal: McGill-Queens.

Hartz, Louis. 1948. *Economic policy and democratic thought: Pennsylvania 1776–1860.* Cambridge, MA: Harvard University Press.

Hasse, Adelaide. 1907. *Index of economic material in documents of the states of the United States: New York, 1789–1904.* Washington, DC: Carnegie Institution.

Hellman, Joel S., Geraint Jones, and Daniel Kaufmann. 2000. Seize the state, seize the day: State capture, corruption, and influence in transition. World Bank Policy Working Paper 2444. Washington, DC: The World Bank.

Internal improvements in the state of New York. 1850. *Hunt's Merchants' Magazine and Commercial Review* 28:259–69, 383–95, 497–508.

King, Charles. 1843. *A memoir of the construction, cost, and capacity of the Croton Aqueduct.* New York: Charles King.

Klein, Maury. 1987. *Union Pacific: Birth of a railroad, 1862–1893.* New York: Doubleday.

La Porta, Rafael, Florencio Lopez-de-Silanes, Andrei Shleifer, and Robert Vishny. 1999. The quality of government. *Journal of Law Economics and Organization* 15 (March): 222–79.

Larson, John Lauritz. 2001. *Internal improvements: National public works and the promise of popular government in the early United States.* Chapel Hill: University of North Carolina Press.

Laws of the state of New York in relation to the Erie and Champlain canals, together with the annual reports of the canal commissioners and other documents requisite for a complete official history of these works. 1825. 2 vols. Albany, NY: E. and E. Horsford.

MacGill, Carol S., and staff. 1917. *History of transportation in the United States before 1860.* Prepared under the direction of Balthasar Henry Meyer. Washington, DC: Carnegie Institution.

Magrath, C. Peter. 1966. *Yazoo: Law and politics in the new republic; The case of Fletcher vs. Peck.* Providence, RI: Brown University Press.

Majewski, John. 2000. *A house dividing: Economic development in Pennsylvania and Virginia before the Civil War.* Cambridge: Cambridge University Press.

McCullough, David. 1977. *The path between the seas: The creation of the Panama Canal, 1870–1914.* New York: Simon and Schuster.

McGrane, Reginald C. 1935. *Foreign bondholders and American state debts.* New York: Macmillan.

Merrow, Edward W. 1988. *Understanding the outcomes of megaprojects: A quanti-*

tative analysis of very large civilian projects. Santa Monica, CA: The RAND Corporation.

Miller, Nathan. 1962. *The enterprise of a free people: Aspects of economic development in New York State during the canal period, 1792–1838.* Ithaca, NY: Cornell University Press.

Moody, John. 1920. *The railroad builders: A chronicle of the welding of the states.* New Haven, CT: Yale University Press.

Moulton, H. G. 1915. The cost of the Erie Barge Canal. *Journal of Political Economy* 23 (May): 490–500.

Murphy, Kevin M., Andrei Shleifer, and Robert W. Vishny. 1993. Why is rent-seeking so costly to growth? *American Economic Review* 83 (May): 409–14.

Nettels, Curtis. 1962. *The emergence of a national economy, 1775–1815.* New York: Holt, Rinehart and Winston.

New York Times. 1871. How New York is governed: Frauds of the Tammany Democrats [pamphlet]. New York: *New York Daily Times.*

North, Douglass C. 1981. *Structure and change in economic history.* New York: Norton.

Pierce, Harry H. 1953. *Railroads of New York: A study of government aid, 1826–1875.* Cambridge, MA: Harvard University Press.

Quirk, James, and Rodney D. Fort. 1992. *Pay dirt: The business of professional team sports.* Princeton, NJ: Princeton University Press.

———. 1999. *Hard ball: The abuse of power in pro team sports.* Princeton, NJ: Princeton University Press.

Ransom, Roger. 1964. Canals and development: A discussion of the issues. *American Economic Review* 54 (May): 365–76.

Renwick, James. 1842. *Life of DeWitt Clinton.* New York: Harper and Brothers.

Report of the commissioners of the state of New York on the canals from Lake Erie to the Hudson River and from Lake Champlain to the same, presented to the legislature. 1818, January 31. Albany, NY: J. Buel.

Report of the Select Committee of the Assembly of 1846, upon the investigation of frauds in the expenditure of the public monies upon the canals of the state of New York. 1847, February 17. No. 100. *Documents of the assembly of the state of New York, seventieth session.* Vol. 3. Albany, NY: Charles van Benthuysen.

Report of Select Committee on reports etc., relative to canal frauds. 1851, April 17 and July 10. Testimony and exhibits taken by committee approved by the Assembly of 1850 to investigate certain alleged canal frauds. No. 158 and 156. *Documents of the Assembly of the state of New York, seventy-fourth session.* Vol. 6. Albany, NY: Charles van Benthuysen.

Report of the committee appointed by the Senate to investigate and inquire into the management of the canals of this state, the official conduct of any person now, or heretofore, officially connected therewith, and also the official conduct of persons comprising the canal contracting board. 1868, January 22. No. 32. *Documents of the Assembly of the state of New York, ninety-first session.* Vol. 4. Albany, NY: Charles van Benthuysen.

Report of Joint Committee of Senate and Assembly in relation to canal fraud investigation. 1875, May 5. No. 152. *Documents of the Assembly of the state of New York, ninety-eighth session.* Vol. 10. Albany, NY: Weed, Parsons and Company.

Report of the Joint Committee of the Senate and Assembly, relative to canal investigation. 1876, March 3. No. 78. *Documents of the Senate of the state of New York, ninety-fifth session.* Vol. 6. Albany, NY: Jerome B. Parmenter.

Rose-Ackerman, Susan. 1999. *Corruption and government: Causes, consequences, and reform.* Cambridge: Cambridge University Press.

Rosenberg, Nathan, and L. E. Birdzell, Jr. 1986. *How the West grew rich: The economic transformation of the industrial world.* New York: Basic Books.

Scheiber, Harry N. 1969. *Ohio canal era: A case study of government and the economy, 1820–1861.* Athens: Ohio University Press.

Seavoy, Ronald E. 1982. *The origins of the American business corporation, 1784–1855: Broadening the concept of public service during industrialization.* Westport, CT: Greenwood Press.

Shaw, Ronald E. 1966. *Erie water West: A history of the Erie Canal, 1792–1854.* Lexington: University of Kentucky Press.

———. 1990. *Canals for a nation: The canal era in the United States, 1790–1860.* Lexington: University of Kentucky Press.

Sheriff, Carol. 1996. *The artificial river: The Erie Canal and the paradox of progress, 1817–1862.* New York: Hill and Wang.

Shleifer, Andrei, and Robert W. Vishny. 1993. Corruption. *Quarterly Journal of Economics* 108 (August): 599–617.

Sowers, Don C. 1914. *The financial history of New York State from 1789 to 1912.* New York: Columbia University.

Stevens, Joseph E. 1988. *Hoover Dam: An American adventure.* Norman: University of Oklahoma Press.

Sullivan, Neil J. 2001. *The diamond in the Bronx: Yankee Stadium and the politics of New York.* New York: Oxford University Press.

Tocqueville, Alexis de. 1961. *Democracy in America* 2 vols. New York: Schocken Books. (Orig. publ. 1835.)

Toohey, Kristine, and A. J. Veal. 2000. *The Olympic games: A social science perspective.* Walingford, UK: CABI Publishing.

U.S. House. Committee on Flood Control. 1927–28. On control of destructive flood waters of the United States. *Flood Control Hearings.* 70th Cong., 1st sess., November 7–22, 1927 to February 1, 1928.

Wachs, Martin. 1989. When planners lie with numbers. *Journal of the American Planning Association* 55 (4): 476–79.

Walker, Barbara K., and Warren S. Walker. 1963. *The Erie Canal: Gateway to empire; Selected source materials for college research papers.* Boston: D. C. Heath.

Weingroff, Richard F. 1996. Federal-Aid Highway Act of 1956: Creating the interstate system. *Public Roads* 60 (Summer): 10–17.

White, Henry Kirke. 1895. *History of the Union Pacific Railway.* Chicago: University of Chicago Press.

Whitford, Noble E. 1906. *History of the canal system of the state of New York together with brief histories of the canals of the United States and Canada.* 2 vols. Albany, NY: Brandon Printing Company.

II

Consequences of Corruption

4

Corporate Governance and the Plight of Minority Shareholders in the United States before the Great Depression

Naomi R. Lamoreaux and Jean-Laurent Rosenthal

> The promoters . . . had their reasons for celebration. . . .
> [T]hey had set up the Crédit Mobilier, into whose chest the
> gains from contracts for the whole Union Pacific building had
> flowed. . . . The proceeds from government bonds, security
> sales, and sales of lands and town sites had all been swallowed
> up in the mounting costs of building or in other ways. For this
> work the directors of the Union Pacific had ingeniously con-
> tracted with themselves at prices which rose from $80,000 to
> $90,000 and $96,000 a mile, twice the maximum estimates of
> engineers. . . . Hence the jubilation of the Union Pacific ring.
> For what profits could they have awaited, if they had confined
> themselves purely to trafficking in freight or passengers
> through the empty prairies?
> —Matthew Josephson (1934, p. 92)

Naomi R. Lamoreaux is a professor of economics and history at the University of California, Los Angeles (UCLA), and a research associate of the National Bureau of Economic Research. Jean-Laurent Rosenthal is a professor of economics at UCLA.

The authors have benefited from the advice of Robert Allen, Steven A. Bank, Ruth Bloch,
Hongbin Cai, Judith Chevalier, Paul David, Lance Davis, Harold Demsetz, Stanley Enger-
man, Edward Glaeser, Claudia Goldin, Peter Gourevitch, Timothy Guinnane, Henry Hans-
mann, Ron Harris, Susan Helper, Philip Hoffman, Hugo Hopenhayn, Gonzalo Islas-Rojas,
Gregory Mark, Christopher McKenna, Joel Mokyr, William Novak, Gilles Postel-Vinay,
James Rebitzer, Larry E. Ribstein, Arthur Rolston, Roberta Romano, Kenneth Sokoloff,
John Wallis, and Matt Wiswall, as well as from the comments of participants in seminars at
the Yale Law School, Oxford University, Case Western Reserve University, UCLA, at a meeting of the Greater Chicago Economic History Group, at the conference on the Political Economy of Financial Markets held at Princeton University, and the NBER conference on Corruption and Reform. We are also grateful for the assistance of Eric Torres in searching
newspapers and other periodical sources.

4.1   Introduction

The Crédit Mobilier manipulation was a spectacular scandal. Directors of the Union Pacific Railroad had organized their own construction company and had awarded themselves contracts to build the transcontinental line. Although historians have long debated whether this arrangement yielded participants an exorbitant rate of return,[1] there is no doubt contemporaries thought it did. Even so, what made headlines was less this siphoning off of profits than the involvement of the federal government, which had granted the Union Pacific extensive tracts of public lands and also loans to finance construction. According to charges in the newspapers, the "railroad ring" had handed out shares in Crédit Mobilier to influential congressmen, buying political influence in order to forestall inconvenient scrutiny as well as to secure additional federal largesse (Josephson 1934; Bain 1999).[2]

The hoopla that surrounded these revelations of bribery has obscured for modern observers the extent to which conflicts of interest, like those at the heart of the Crédit Mobilier scandal, were endemic to corporations at the time. Although cases rarely made headlines unless they involved companies, such as major railroad or telegraph lines, that were important to the public welfare,[3] the legal record from the late nineteenth and early twentieth centuries suggests that directors of corporations large and small frequently negotiated contracts with other companies in which they had a financial interest,[4] elected themselves to corporate offices at lucrative salaries that they themselves set,[5] arranged mergers that earned themselves

1. Compare, for example, the accounts in Josephson (1934) and Bain (1999) with those of Kirkland (1961) and Summers (1993).

2. Intriguingly, details of the Crédit Mobilier manipulation had been reported in the press since at least 1869, but attracted little attention until the *New York Sun,* which opposed the reelection of President Ulysses S. Grant, broke the bribery story in September, 1872 (Bain 1999, pp. 599–600, 602, 627–28, 676).

3. Examples include "The Telegraph Combination," *New York Times,* August 22, 1877, p. 8; "More Trouble for Gould: Metropolitan Stockholders to Have an Inning," *New York Times,* November 5, 1882, p. 7; "He Shot Me Like a Dog," *New York Times,* December 29, 1883, p. 4; "Accused of Conspiracy: A Blow at Jay Gould and his Friends," *New York Times,* March 3, 1885, p. 2; "The Pennsylvania Interested: The Fight for the Cincinnati, Hamilton and Dayton," *New York Times,* May 3, 1885, p. 2.

4. For examples of cases involving such contracts, see *Smith v. Poor,* 40 Me. 415 (1855); *March v. Eastern Railroad,* 40 N.H. 548 (1860); *Flint and Pere Marquette Railway v. Dewey,* 14 Mich. 477 (1866); *Ashhurst's Appeal,* 60 Pa. 290 (1869); *Brewer v. Boston Theatre,* 104 Mass. 378 (1870); *Faulds v. Yates,* 57 Ill. 416 (1870); *European and North American Railway Co. v. Poor,* 59 Me. 277 (1871); *Kelly v. Newburyport and Amesbury Horse Railroad,* 141 Mass. 496 (1886); *Warren v. Para Rubber Shoe Co.,* 166 Mass. 97 (1896); and *Burden v. Burden,* 159 N.Y. 287 (1899). See also the much more extensive list of cases in Marsh (1966) and Mark (2003).

5. For examples of cases involving charges of excessive compensation, see *Dunphy v. Traveller Newspaper Association,* 146 Mass. 495 (1888); *Brown v. De Young,* 167 Ill. 549 (1897); *Von Arnim v. American Tube Works,* 188 Mass. 515 (1905); *Abbott v. Harbeson Textile Co.,* 147 N.Y.S. 1031 (1914); *Cole v. Wells,* 224 Mass. 504 (1916); *Almy v. Almy, Bigelow & Washburn,* 235 Mass. 227 (1920).

impressive capital gains while leaving other shareholders in the lurch,[6] and engaged in a wide variety of other actions from which they benefited at the expense of their associates. Examples included lending themselves corporate funds, issuing themselves additional shares of stock, and settling lawsuits against their companies that they had helped to bring in the first place.[7]

Following the conventions of this volume, we label this behavior fraud rather than corruption because it did not involve the use of government resources for private gain. Nonetheless, we would like to emphasize that, in the case of corporations, such a distinction would not have made much sense prior to the 1850s. Indeed, at the beginning of the nineteenth century, corporations were still regarded as quasi-governmental institutions. Businesspeople who wanted to form them had to seek special permission from the state, which tended only to be granted for projects deemed to be in the public interest, and many corporations obtained part of their capital stock from state treasuries. As the utility of the corporate form for ordinary business purposes became increasingly apparent, however, pressure mounted on legislatures to make the form more widely available—to prevent a favored few from engrossing its benefits. State governments responded to these political pressures first by making it easier to secure a special charter, and then (around the middle of the nineteenth century) by passing general incorporation laws that routinized the whole process, enabling anyone who so desired to form a corporation by fulfilling some standard requirements, filing a form, and paying a fee. In the process, the corporation lost its public character and came to be thought of as a wholly private institution (Hurst 1970; Maier 1993; Bloch and Lamoreaux 2004; Wallis 2005).

Despite this privatization, fraudulent extractive behavior by controlling shareholders in corporations potentially undermined the security of investors' property rights in much the same way as did corrupt extractive behavior by government officials. Like citizens, moreover, minority shareholders had only limited ability to protect themselves against abuse. Stan-

6. For examples of cases involving such charges, see *Peabody v. Flint,* 88 Mass. 52 (1863); *Converse v. United Shoe Machinery,* 185 Mass. 422 (1914); and *Bonner v. Chapin National Bank,* 251 Mass. 401 (1925). For a more extensive list of cases, see Carney (1980). These kinds of manipulations were more likely to make the newspapers, as, for example, when the directors and controlling shareholders of the Brush Electric Company of Cleveland, Ohio, arranged to sell their stockholdings to businessmen who controlled the Thomson-Houston Electric Company for $75 a share. The par value of the stock was $50, and its market price was estimated at that time to be $35. Minority shareholders were outraged that they were not included in the deal. *New York Times,* January 21, 1890, p. 1.

7. For examples of cases involving such charges, see *Hersey v. Veazie,* 24 Me. 9 (1844); *Smith v. Hurd,* 53 Mass. 371 (1847); *Abbott v. Merriam,* 62 Mass. 588 (1851); *Leslie v. Lorillard,* 110 N.Y. 519 (1888); *Continental Securities v. Belmont,* 133 N.Y.S. 560 (1912); *Dunlay v. Avenue M Garage & Repair Co.,* 253 N.Y. 274 (1930). A less venal example involved Col. Elliott F. Shepard, who bought control of the Fifth-Avenue Transportation Company for religious reasons in order to stop the running of stages on Sundays, evoking protests from minority shareholders who objected to the loss of revenues. *New York Times,* May 10, 1888, p. 5.

dard corporate governance rules based on the principle of one vote per share meant that shareholders who possessed enough stock to decide elections were effectively dictators.[8] If the majority pursued policies that members of the minority thought were wrongheaded or detrimental to their interests, there was little that the latter could do. Minority shareholders could not make the majority change their policies. Nor could they force a dissolution of the enterprise. Nor could they easily exit by selling their equity. In the case of publicly traded firms, they would only be able to sell off their holdings at a price discounted to reflect the majority's behavior; in the case of closely held corporations, often the only buyers for their shares were the same majority shareholders with whom they were in conflict.[9]

The intriguing puzzle is that, despite these problems, businesspeople kept forming corporations and minority shareholders kept investing in them. George Heberton Evans, Jr., has counted the number of corporate charters granted in a sample of key states and found a steady rise between the Civil War and the Great Depression. Indeed, the increase was so steep that Evans's index of incorporations (1925 = 100) had a value of only about 5 in 1870. In Ohio, for example, the number of charters increased from an average of 305 per year during the 1870s to 1,166 per year from 1895 to 1904, to 4,047 per year during the 1920s.[10] Although the growth was most rapid in the smallest size categories of firms, investors were increasingly willing to risk their savings in large corporations as well. As early as the 1870s, the authorized capital of new Ohio corporations valued at over $1 million averaged $37.6 million per year. The Ohio figures for later decades are not as informative because large corporations were increasingly choosing to organize first in New Jersey and then in Delaware. In New Jersey, the authorized capital of firms valued at over $1 million averaged $928.4 million per year from 1895 to 1904, and in Delaware, the comparable annual average was $18,814.2 million by the 1920s (Evans 1948, appendix 3). Moreover, as Mary O'Sullivan has shown, relative to gross domestic product (GDP) the value of new corporate equity issues on the New York Stock Exchange rose between the late nineteenth and early twentieth centuries to levels that, even without the boom years of the late 1920s, were higher than those in the second half of the twentieth century,

---

8. For a more extensive discussion of the importance of these rules, see Lamoreaux and Rosenthal (2005) and Lamoreaux (2004), which show that the courts made it difficult for firms in the United States to adopt nonstandard governance rules. For a comparison of voting rules in U.S. corporations with those in corporations in other countries, see Dunlavy (2004).

9. By the mid-twentieth century, it was becoming increasingly common for shareholders to protect themselves with buyout agreements. Even this remedy could be ineffective, however, if the majority prevented the corporation from accumulating the necessary surplus or manipulated the book value of the enterprise. It could also impose a costly burden on the firm (Hornstein 1950; Hillman 1982).

10. The trend seems to have been unaffected by the imposition of the income tax in 1916, which subjected investors in corporations to double taxation.

when the Securities and Exchange Commission protected investors in publicly traded corporations (O'Sullivan 2004).

The sheer magnitude of these numbers would seem to indicate that fear of expropriation did not significantly deter investment in corporations during this period. These numbers are not the whole story, however, for large numbers of partnerships were also formed during these years. Reliable data are not available until 1900, when the Census of Manufacturers reported information on organizational form, but at that time, 67 percent of all U.S. manufacturing establishments owned by more than one person were organized as partnerships and only 29 percent as corporations, with the remaining 4 percent consisting mainly of cooperatives (U.S. Census Office 1902, p. 503).[11] Although partnerships on average were significantly smaller than corporations (the census valued the total product of partnerships at $2.57 billion, as opposed to $7.73 billion for corporations), their numerical dominance is highly suggestive. The literature has generally treated partnerships as an inferior organizational form, one that mainly had utility for law firms and other similar businesses that depended on specialized human capital for their success (Alchian and Demsetz 1972; Gilson and Mnookin 1985; Grossman and Hart 1986; Hart 1995; Cai 2003; Blair 2003; Rebitzer and Taylor 2004).[12] The high proportion of partnerships in the manufacturing sector raises the question of whether businesspeople were deliberately choosing a suboptimal form in order to avoid the governance problems associated with corporations.

We address this question by exploring the decision to organize a new firm as a corporation or a partnership. In sections 4.2 and 4.3, we show that the legal rules governing these two forms meant that each alternative was subject to a different organizational problem. In the case of partnerships, the ability of any member of the firm to force a dissolution meant that partners were potentially subject to disruption. In the case of corporations, the power that controlling shareholders possessed to make decisions unilaterally meant that they could capture more than their fair share of the enterprise's returns. We develop a simple model of these alternative problems and show that the willingness of investors to participate in corporations, as opposed to partnerships, was affected by the extent to which their returns could be expropriated by controlling shareholders. We also show that investors' willingness to join a partnership, rather than not participating in

---

11. Economy-wide counts are not available until after 1916, when the Internal Revenue Service began to collect the income tax. In 1920, there were approximately 314,000 corporations in the United States, compared to about 241,000 partnerships, but it is likely that these figures greatly understate the total number of partnerships because all corporations, however small or unprofitable, were required to file tax returns, whereas partnerships only had to file if their income exceeded the threshold for the tax (U.S. Internal Revenue Service 1922, pp. 8–10).

12. For a rare contrary example of an article arguing for the superiority of partnerships over corporations, see Ribstein (2005).

the enterprise at all, was a function of the probability that a dispute among the partners would lead to a premature dissolution of the firm.

In section 4.4 we explore the limits that the legal system placed on the share of profits that controlling shareholders could engross. We find that, if anything, these restraints became laxer over the course of our period. Nonetheless, we argue, this change probably had little adverse effect on the pace of economic growth. The implication of our model is that organizational problems would only dissuade investors from putting their funds in firms whose expected returns were low. Because there was an abundance of good, highly profitable projects in the United States during the late nineteenth and early twentieth centuries, investors willingly participated in the formation of large numbers of new enterprises, including an increasing number of corporations.

4.2   Partnerships and the Problem of Untimely Dissolution

Under Anglo-American common law, partnerships were not legal persons and thus had no existence or identity that was independent of the specific individuals who formed them. Each partner possessed full ownership rights and, without consulting the other partners, could enter into contracts that were binding on the firm so long as those contracts were within the scope of the firm's normal business activities. Not only was this right to act unilaterally in and of itself a potential source of conflict within the firm, but it also meant that partners (all of whom were unlimitedly liable for the firm's debts) faced obligations that were beyond their control or perhaps even beyond their knowledge. Because businesspeople hesitated to enter into such relationships unless they could extricate themselves when their partners proved untrustworthy, partnerships typically existed "at will." That is, any member of the firm could force a dissolution simply by deciding that he or she no longer wanted to be part of the enterprise.[13]

As a result, partnerships potentially suffered from what we call the problem of untimely dissolution. Because each partner had full ownership rights and could act without consulting the others, there was a high probability that disagreements would arise that might induce one member of the firm to dissolve the enterprise. Such disagreements were potentially costly. At the very least, they might disrupt the functioning of what otherwise had been a profitable enterprise. More ominously, they might require the liquidation of firm-specific assets at prices below their value had the enterprise been able to continue. Because dissolution was so potentially costly, the at-will character of partnerships also created opportunities for

---

13. There are a number of treatises detailing the law of partnership during this period, but see especially Story (1859) and Gillmore (1911).

holdup. That is, a partner could attempt to extract a greater share of the firm's revenue just by threatening dissolution.[14]

Although partners could in theory contract around this problem by stipulating that the firm continue for a fixed period time, there was considerable uncertainty in the late nineteenth century about whether the courts would enforce such agreements (Gilmore 1911, pp. 571–73). For example, some courts refused to allow dissolution if the complaining party was the source of the dissension. In the words of an Illinois justice, "it would be inequitable to allow [such a person] advantage from his own wrongful acts," especially because "the results flowing from the premature dissolution of a partnership might be most disastrous to a partner who had embarked his capital in the enterprise" and who had been innocent of any "wrongful act or omission of duty" (*Gerard v. Gateau,* 84 Ill. 121 [1876]). Similarly, in *Hannaman v. Karrick,* a Utah justice insisted that a partner should not be "allowed to ruin the business of the firm from mere caprice, or of his own volition, without cause, and in violation of his agreement, and sacrifice the entire object of the partnership" (9 Utah 236 [1893]).

Other courts, however, refused to enforce the continuation of a partnership on the grounds that "it is a rule in equity that the court will not decree a specific performance where it has no power to enforce the decree" (Mechem 1920, pp. 196–98). As the Connecticut Supreme Court of Errors declared in *Morris v. Peckham* (51 Conn. 128 at 133 [1883]), "partnership articles will not be enforced . . . even where a time is fixed" because it was beyond the bench's power to ensure that all members of a firm performed their duties on an ongoing basis.[15] Moreover, many judges thought that it made little sense to force a partner to continue the association against his or her will because "no partnership can efficiently or beneficially carry on its business without the mutual confidence and co-operation of all the partners" (*Karrick v. Hannaman,* 168 U.S. 328 at 336 [1897]). Indeed, some

14. To give an early example, E. I. Dupont's partner, Peter Bauduy, attempted to boost his share of the firm's income by demanding to count as part of his contribution to capital a note he had endorsed for the benefit of the enterprise. Bauduy threatened dissolution and "could not be pacified" except by a new contract in which he "exacted from the concern some extra compensation and advantages." See "Answer of Eleuthere Irénée Dupont made in his own name as well as in behalf of Mess. E. I. Dupont de Nemours & Co. to the bill filed in chancery by Peter Bauduy against him and the said concern," 1817, Special Papers, Bauduy Lawsuit (Part I) (1805–1828), Longwood Mss., Box 45, Accession Group 5, E. I. du Pont de Nemours & Co., Series C, Hagley Library Manuscript Collections, Wilmington, Del.

For a more general discussion of holdup in partnerships, see Bodenhorn (2002). Bodenhorn argues that individuals mitigated this problem by selecting as partners individuals of similar age, productivity, and capital. We do not deny that businesspeople adopted a variety of strategies to reduce the likelihood of holdup, but the large number of dissolution suits in the legal record and the short life span of most partnerships suggests that the problem of untimely dissolution was very real.

15. In this particular case the duration of the contract at stake was not clear, but the judge declared the principle in the broadest possible terms. See also *Buck v. Smith,* 29 Mich. 166 (1874).

courts worried that restrictions on dissolution might themselves be pernicious and went so far as to declare that the right to dissolve a partnership at will could not be contracted away. Quoting an early New York decision, for example, the Michigan Supreme Court asserted that "there can be no such thing as an indissoluble partnership." To rule otherwise would be to expose a member of the firm to the opportunism of his or her associates. "The power given by one partner to another to make joint contracts for them both is not only a revocable power, but a man can do no act to divest himself of the capacity to revoke it" (*Solomon v. Kirkwood,* 55 Mich. 256 [1884], citing *Skinner v. Dayton,* 19 Johns. 513 [N.Y. 1822]).

The remedy that courts promoting this view offered to partners who had been victimized by threats of untimely dissolution was to sue for breach of contract rather than force a continuation of the firm. A partnership agreement was thus to be treated like any other contract: it could "be broken at pleasure, subject however to responsibility in damages" (*Solomon v. Kirkwood,* 55 Mich. 256 at 260 [1884]). Objecting to this position, the Utah court complained that such a remedy could never provide "complete justice" to the aggrieved party, for not only was "this mode of redress . . . usually slow and unsatisfactory," but the resulting "damages, in many cases, must necessarily prove to be utterly inadequate to compensate for the destruction of a profitable and growing business" (*Hannaman v. Karrick,* 9 Utah 236 at 241–42 [1893]).[16] Although this criticism had considerable merit, it did not carry the day. Indeed, it was the contrary view—that the only difference "so far as concerns the right of dissolution by one partner" between partnerships at will and those for specified terms was that "in the former case, the dissolution is no breach of the partnership agreement, and affords the other partner no ground of complaint," whereas in the latter "such a dissolution before the expiration of the time stipulated is a breach of the agreement, and as such to be compensated in damages" (*Karrick v. Hannaman,* 168 U.S. 328 [1897])[17]—that came to dominate and was enshrined in the Uniform Partnership Act (UPA) in the second decade of the twentieth century (Richards 1921).

The net effect of the enactment of UPA was to establish with greater certainty the principle that all partnerships, even those established for a fixed

---

16. Although in principle the injured party would be compensated forgone profits (see cases ranging from *Bagley v. Smith,* 10 N.Y. 489 [1853], to *Zimmerman v. Harding,* 227 U.S. 489 [1913]), the courts were necessarily conservative in estimating uncertain future profits (*Ramsay v. Meade,* 37 Colo. 465 [1906]).

17. Although partnerships were normally matters of state rather than federal law, this case had been appealed to the U.S. Supreme Court when Utah was still a territory under federal authority. In such matters, unlike constitutional issues, the Supreme Court did not make law for the nation, but the decision of such a prestigious court carried enormous weight. Justice Horace Gray's opinion in the case is particularly interesting because he went out of his way to criticize the Utah judge's view of partnerships, even though he admitted that it was not necessary for the adjudication of the appeal for him "to express an opinion upon this point."

term, were dissolvable at will. By defining some attempts to end partnerships prematurely as illegitimate breaches of contract punishable by an award of damages, the new legal rules did put limits on partners' ability to increase their wealth by holding each other up. Short of a systematic study of damage awards at the lower-court level, there is no way of knowing exactly what these limits were in actual practice or whether they had a significant effect on partners' behavior. We do know, however, that to the extent that a partner was able to make the case that another member of the firm was at fault or that general dissension among the partners made continued operation impossible, she or he would be able to escape damages entirely. Even courts that had been reluctant to dissolve partnerships before the expiration of their terms consistently asserted this rule. Hence the Utah judge in *Hannaman v. Karrick* admitted that "where there is such a breach between the partners as to render continuance impossible, or when dissension has dispelled the hopes, prospects, and advantages which induced its formation, or if for any just cause the partnership ought to be dissolved before the expiration of the term, then a court of equity is competent to grant relief" (9 Utah 236 [1893]). Similarly, the Illinois judge acknowledged in *Gerard v. Gateau* "that such embittered relations may exist as would render it impracticable to conduct the business, and justify a decree dissolving the partnership, admits of no discussion, on principle as well as upon authority" (84 Ill. 121 [1876]). Serious dissension among partners was, and always had been, grounds for dissolving a firm.

4.2.1 A Simple Model of Partnerships

In order to obtain a better understanding of the consequences of the at-will character of partnerships for businesspeople's willingness to participate in otherwise profitable enterprises, we model the partnership form of organization as suffering from the probability that a disagreement or holdup attempt among the partners would lead to an untimely dissolution of the firm. Imagine a firm whose total return per unit of capital is R, where $R > 1 + r$, the market rate of interest. We assume there is no asymmetric information. We also assume that a firm consists only of an entrepreneur and an investor, each of whom contributes capital ($K = K_E + K_I$). We relax this last assumption later on in order to consider explicitly the case where large-scale enterprises must raise capital from a greater number of investors.

If the firm is organized as a partnership, the two participants face costs associated with the probability that an otherwise successful enterprise will be forced to dissolve. We take this probability (d) to be given exogenously for each firm by the prevailing legal rules and by the existence of social institutions, such as the family or the community, that help govern relations among partners. If the firm is forced to dissolve, we assume that it must sell its assets on the cheap and that the return to the firm will be αR. We assume further that α is less than 1 and that it is the same for all firms. That is, in order to keep the analysis simple, we assume that firms differ only in the magnitude of the profits they can earn and in their dissolution probabilities. If the firm is organized as a partnership, then, its return on capital, R_p, is

$$R_p = (1 - d)R + d\alpha R.$$

Both the entrepreneur and the investor earn the same return as the firm. ($R_{PE} = R_{PI} = R_p$, where R_{PE} and R_{PI} are the returns to the entrepreneur and to the investor respectively.) Both, therefore, face the same participation constraint. That is, they will participate in the enterprise only if they expect to be able to earn at least as much as they could in the market—that is, $1 + r$:

$$R_{PE} = R_{PI} = (1 - d)R + d\alpha R > 1 + r$$

The implications of these participation constraints are apparent if we take α and r as given. As figure 4.1 illustrates, for each R there is a unique d^* (represented by the top upward-sloping curve) above which no partnerships will be formed.

As this analysis suggests, the partnership form is socially inefficient because the expected return that a firm can earn if it organizes as a partnership is below the return that could be earned if there were no problem of untimely dissolution. Because of this organizational cost, if the partner-

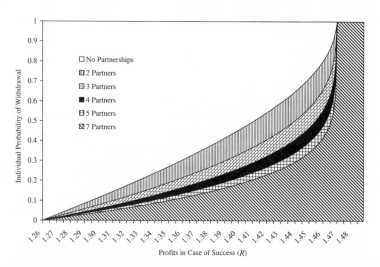

Fig. 4.1   How profit rates and the probability of withdrawal affect whether partnerships will form

Note: The probability of dissolution is $1 - (1 - d)^n$, where d is the individual probability of withdrawal and n is the number of partners. The values of R are illustrative only. Once $R = (1 + r)/\alpha$, partnerships are feasible irrespective of the number of partners. In our example $(1 + r)/\alpha = 1.47$.

ship were the only available form that businesspeople could choose, many firms that would be socially valuable would not form. The situation, moreover, is even worse if we relax our assumption that the firm consists of only two partners. If we assume that each member of the firm has an independent probability (d) of forcing a dissolution, then the probability that no dispute will occur is $(1 - d)^n$, and the probability of untimely dissolution, D, equals $1 - (1 - d)^n$, where n is the number of partners. As figure 4.1 shows, the more partners there are, the more likely it is that profitable business opportunities will go unrealized. By extension, projects that require large amounts of capital, and thus many investors, are unlikely to be undertaken as partnerships.

4.3   Corporations and the Problem of Minority Oppression

This unsatisfactory situation captures the essential details of the U.S. business environment in the early nineteenth century. By mid-century, however, most states had responded to the problem of untimely dissolution in partnerships by providing businesspeople with an alternative organizational form: the corporation. Unlike partnerships, corporations were by definition legal persons whose existence was in no way dependent on the ongoing participation of the people who founded them. Indeed, the identity of each and every one of a corporation's members could change without affecting the continuance of the enterprise (Freund 1896).[18]

Corporations solved the problem of disagreements among members of the firm by making the controlling shareholders effectively dictators. But this solution itself was potentially a source of problems. Because the only members of a corporation who could make decisions were officers who had been duly elected by the shareholders, any coalition that determined the election of officers also controlled the firm. This coalition could then use its power to benefit its members at the expense of other shareholders. Although the latter were only limitedly liable for the enterprise's debts and thus, in most cases, stood to lose no more than their investments, they had no means of preventing the controlling shareholders from expropriating some of their share of the returns.[19]

---

18. Of course, if an associate who had critical human capital withdrew, the business might be more likely to fail. Hence, corporations too were potentially subject to holdup. But we assume that this problem was small for corporations compared to partnerships and ignore it in our subsequent analysis.

19. We should point out that we are less concerned here with the specific legal forms that firms took than with the trade-off between these two transaction costs—untimely dissolution and minority oppression. We do not wish to deny that special types of partnerships did emerge (and were recognized by the courts) that had many features of corporations. Joint-stock companies are the most important example. But because the joint-stock company had disadvantages—for example, it was difficult to secure full limited liability—it was relatively rarely used once the corporate form became readily available. Similarly, businesspeople in the

We conceive of this problem of minority oppression as the main cost associated with the corporate form. Whereas we modeled the return to an investor in a partnership as a function of the profitability of the enterprise and the probability of untimely dissolution, we model the return to an investor in a corporation as a function of the profitability of the enterprise and the extent of these private benefits of control. Before we describe the two alternatives more formally, we offer a historical example as evidence that our stylized version of these two organizational forms captures the way both businesspeople and the courts thought about the choice between partnerships and corporations: the case of *Burden v. Burden,* decided by the New York Court of Appeals in 1899 (159 N.Y. 287).

The disputants in the case were brothers who had inherited an iron factory from their father in 1871. The brothers operated the business as a partnership for the next ten years but increasingly disagreed about its management until, by 1881, their relationship had deteriorated to the point where, in the words of the court, they "ceased to hold any personal conversation with each other and discussed their grievances in written communications only" (159 N.Y. 287 at 295). Finally, James A. Burden, the brother who had been trained as an ironmaster, decided that he could no longer bear the conflict and determined to force either a dissolution of the firm and a division of the property or the reorganization of the firm as a corporation that he would control. His brother, I. Townsend Burden, reluctantly agreed to the latter option, and the business was incorporated as the Burden Iron Company. James held 1,000 shares in the new concern and Townsend, 998. The remaining two shares went to James's associate, John L. Arts, who held a managerial position in the enterprise. In other words, in order to avoid the costs of dissolving a profitable enterprise, Townsend consented to become a minority shareholder in a corporation controlled by his brother. Although he continued to receive half of the profits that the firm paid out in dividends, he was completely frozen out of the management.

Townsend brooded over this outcome for three and a half years and then sued in equity, complaining that his lack of influence in the company had enabled his brother and Arts to run it in a way that was detrimental to his interests. In particular, he charged that "James and Arts [had] combined and conspired together, in violation of their duties as trustees, to the great damage of the Burden Iron Company, and to build up and sustain their own private interests" (159 N.Y. 287 at 306). Both the trial court and the

---

United States had the option of organizing their firms as limited partnerships, but the legislation regulating this option was so restrictive, and the courts so strict in their interpretation, that few were formed. Because the overwhelming majority of businesses in the United States organized either as ordinary partnerships or as corporations, it is this choice that we model. See Lamoreaux and Rosenthal (2005). For an extended discussion of the inadequacies of joint-stock companies and other variants of partnerships relative to corporations in Britain in the late eighteenth and early nineteenth centuries, see Harris (2000). For a similar analysis of the U.S. case up to the 1920s, see Warren (1929). See also Blair (2003).

appeals court were unsympathetic. Writing for the latter, Justice Bartlett acknowledged that "the plaintiff is doubtless quite right when he insists that he has been ignored in the management of the Burden Iron Company, and has no control, save to vote his stock, over properties of great value in which his interest is nearly one-half." But, he pointed out, Townsend "apparently fails to appreciate that his troubles are inherent in the situation." He had voluntarily agreed to give his brother control in order to prevent the untimely dissolution of an enterprise that was profiting them both. Generalizing from Townsend's situation, Bartlett explained that "the plaintiff is in the position of all minority stockholders, who cannot interfere with the management of the corporation so long as the trustees are acting honestly and within their discretionary powers." The plaintiff, he declared, "must submit" (159 N.Y. 287 at 308).

4.3.1   Modeling the Choice between Partnerships and Corporations

Given these starkly posed differences between partnerships and corporations, we return to our basic two-person model and make several additional assumptions. First, because it now matters who owns the largest share of the firm's equity, we assume that the entrepreneur owns more and has control of the firm—that is,

$$K = K_E + K_I \text{ and } K_E > K_I.$$

Second, we assume that the entrepreneur's control allows her to steal some fraction (ω) of the firm's profits, where the magnitude of ω is exogenously determined, in large measure by the legal system (which defines the boundary at which "private benefits of control" become fraud), but also by social institutions, such as the family or the community, that help govern relations among members of the firm. Finally, we assume that stealing affects only the distribution and not the level of the firm's profits, so that the return to a corporation is same as the return to the firm, which is greater than the return to a partnership.

$$R_C = R > R_P$$

Under these assumptions, so long as she can earn at least $1 + r$, the entrepreneur will always want to organize the firm and always as a corporation, because the return to a corporation is higher than that to a partnership and because her ability to steal earns the entrepreneur even more. The investor, however, will only be willing to invest in a corporation under the following conditions:

$$R_{CI} = R(1 - \omega) > 1 + r$$

Taking α, ω, and r as fixed, then this participation constraint implies there is a unique R^* such that investors will only participate in corporations if $R \geq (1 + r)/(1 - \omega) = R^*$.

If $R < R^*$, then firms will only form if they can be organized as partnerships. But entrepreneurs and investors will only be willing to organize partnerships to exploit otherwise attractive opportunities if the probability of untimely dissolution is not too high. That is,

$$R_P = (1 - d)R + d\alpha R > 1 + r.$$

If $R \geq R^*$, then corporations will be organized if the entrepreneur has the power to choose the form of organization, but for some range of R there will be a conflict between the preferences of the investor and those of the entrepreneur. Investors will prefer to organize the firm as a corporation if $R_{CI} > R_{PI}$. That is,

$$(1 - \omega)R > [1 - d(1 - \alpha)]R.$$

In other words, the investor prefers a corporation if

$$d > \frac{\omega}{1 - \alpha}.$$

The resulting distribution of organizational forms is displayed in figures 4.2 and 4.3. In figure 4.2 we hold ω fixed and allow d to vary. The vertical line indicates R^*, the threshold value of R below which corporations cannot form, and the upward-sloping line, $d^*(R)$, demarcates the boundary above which partnerships cannot form. Similarly, in figure 4.3 we fix d and allow ω to vary. In this case, R^* refers to the threshold value below which partnerships do not form (variation on the vertical axis does not affect

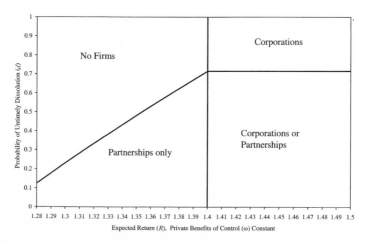

Fig. 4.2   The choice of organizational form as a function of the probability of dissolution, holding private benefits of control constant

Note: $d^*(R)$ is the line that separates the "no firms" area from the "partnership" area. The values of R and d are illustrative only. In this example, R^* (the expected return needed to form a corporation) is 1.4.

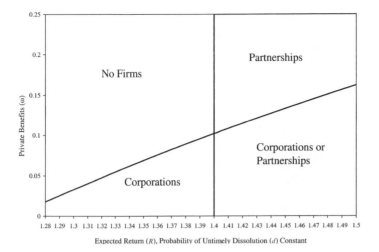

Expected Return (*R*), Probability of Untimely Dissolution (*d*) Constant

Fig. 4.3   The choice of organizational form as a function of the extent of private benefits of control, holding the probability of dissolution constant

Note: $\omega^*(R)$ is the line that separates the "no firms" area from the "corporations" area. The values of *R* and *d* are illustrative only. In this example, R^* (the expected return needed to form a corporation) is 1.4.

them), and the upward-sloping line, $\omega^*(R)$, defines the feasible area for corporations.

The figures underscore two important implications of our model. First, in equilibrium there is likely to be a demand for both organizational forms. Second, some firms do not form simply because of organizational difficulties. If ω is big, there will be a large range of firms for which profits are too low to induce investors to participate in a corporation. Whether or not these firms form depends on the magnitude of *d*. Clearly, therefore, it would be efficient to reduce *d* and even more salutary to reduce ω; in societies with high transaction costs of these types, improvements in institutions hence can have an important impact on growth. Nonetheless, it should be noted that the firms that do not form are those with relatively low returns. For firms with high enough returns, organizational difficulties are a nuisance but do not affect entry.

4.3.2   Extensions of the Model

In this section, we consider two extensions of the model: the case where the entrepreneur is poor and so owns less of the firm than the investor; and the case where there are more than two members of the firm. In an appendix, we consider a third possibility—that equity shares are endogenous and distinguishable from investment shares. There we consider the possibility that the entrepreneur could increase her profit by reducing the investor's equity stake until his return approached that of the market. We also consider the possibility that the entrepreneur could increase the range of profits over which the investor was willing to participate in a corporation by offering him a higher equity stake in order to raise his return. As we show, the entrepreneur would be constrained in pursuing this second strategy by her need to maintain control. Therefore, the closer her initial share to 50 percent, and the higher ω, the more likely the enterprise would organize as a partnership.

Suppose that the entrepreneur is the owner of a scarce asset (for example, an invention), but that she is poor, so $K_E < K_I$. This reversal does not change the model so far as partnerships are concerned, because for partnerships the participation constraint is the same for both the entrepreneur and the investor and does not depend on their respective ownership shares. For corporations, however, the change in relative equity stakes means that the investor will now have control. As a result, the investor's return will always be greater than that of the entrepreneur, and it is now the entrepreneur's participation constraint that binds. Because the entrepreneur's participation constraint is identical to that of the investor in the original model, reversing the relative equity stakes of the entrepreneur and investor does not alter the boundary of the region where corporations are feasible. It can, however, alter the entrepreneur's choice of organizational form when both partnerships and corporations are feasible and dissolution costs are low. In particular, if the entrepreneur gets to choose the form of organization and $R \geq R^*$ and $d \leq \omega/(1 - \alpha)$, she will now opt for a partnership instead of a corporation. The partnership is less socially efficient than the corporation, but it is the only way, in the environment that we have constructed, for the entrepreneur to protect herself from the expropriation that loss of control entails. The consequence is that she, the investor, and society will have to bear the costs associated with untimely dissolution in partnerships.

Suppose now that there are multiple investors in the corporation. If the entrepreneur retains control (that is, if the entrepreneur owns a majority of the stock in her own right or is part of a binding coalition that collectively owns a majority share), then the analysis is the same as in the basic model. If there is a controlling coalition but the entrepreneur is not a member of it, then the case is like that of the poor entrepreneur just described (though as the number of members of the firm grows large, and therefore partnerships become comparatively more costly, one would expect the entrepreneur instead to insist on membership in the governing coalition). In other words, the only significant deviation from our model occurs in situations where there is no predetermined group or individual that has control. We can conceive of this case theoretically by imagining that every member of the firm, including the entrepreneur, has an equal chance *ex ante* of being part of the governing coalition. Because everyone is equally likely to end up in a situation where she or he can extract private benefits of control, everyone has the same expected return, which is equal to the firm's return. This type of corporation would always be chosen over a partnership.

The entrepreneur, however, would always prefer to be sure that she would be part of a controlling coalition, because in that way she could obtain the private benefits that derive from control. If the relationship between the entrepreneur and the other members of the coalition was such that contractual guarantees of the group's stability were needed, there was a readily available mechanism in the form of a voting trust. Moreover, there was little uncertainty about the enforceability of such contracts, because voting trusts repeatedly were upheld by the courts.[20] One might expect, therefore, to find coalitions formed to control firms wherever profits were high enough to induce outside investors to participate. Where profits were too low to attract participation, one would expect the entrepreneur to forgo her certainty of control rather than form a less efficient partnership. Such forbearance, however, would only be feasible if there were at least three principals. If there were just two, one would inevitably have control, and the only solution to minority oppression would be a partnership.

4.4 Trends in the Limits on Private Benefits of Control

As we have already seen, despite the costs potentially imposed on investors by majority shareholders' private benefits of control, increasing numbers of corporations were formed during the late nineteenth and early twentieth centuries, and increasing numbers of investors willingly purchased their shares. One possible explanation for these trends is that the legal system placed additional constraints on the ability of controlling shareholders to deflect returns in their direction—that is, reduced the magnitude of ω. As we shall see, however, the changes that occurred during this period in the legal rules governing corporations appear to have worked in the opposite direction.

Just as the courts recognized that there was a problem of holdup in partnerships, they understood that minority shareholders in corporations were vulnerable to exploitation by the majority. But they faced two important problems that prevented them from offering the former much in the way of protection. The first was that minority shareholders did not have standing under the common law to redress their grievances by suing corporate officers and directors who abused their positions. Corporations were legal persons, and as a result, only they and not their shareholders could initiate

---

20. See, for example, *Brown v. Pacific Mail Steamship Co.*, 4 F. Cas. 420 (1867); *Faulds v. Yates*, 57 Ill. 416 (1870); *Brightman v. Bates*, 175 Mass. 105 (1900); and *Manson v. Curtis*, 223 N.Y. 313 (1918).

legal action.[21] Although abusers who were in positions of control were unlikely to allow themselves to be sued by their corporations, this problem was relatively easily surmounted by granting minority shareholders the right under certain circumstances to pursue a case in their own names in a court of equity, rather than at common law. The key precedent was *Robinson v. Smith* (3 Paige 222 [1832]), in which New York's chancellor explicitly extended to business corporations principles of trusteeship that had previously been used to protect beneficiaries of charitable entities. The chancellor posited that the directors of a corporation were equivalent to trustees and that the stockholders, having a joint interest in the corporation's property, were "cestui que trusts." Declaring that equity courts never permit wrongs "to go unredressed merely for the sake of form," he indicated that the stockholders might, after demonstrating that the corporation was controlled by those who were abusing their trust, file a bill in their own names, "making the corporation a party defendant."[22]

The second and more difficult problem that the courts faced was to protect minority shareholders without undermining the legal differences between corporations and partnerships—that is, without creating a situation in which disagreements among members of the firm could disrupt the functioning of corporations as easily as they did partnerships. For this reason, the courts were very conservative in defining what constituted an abuse of trust by those in control. For example, they quickly settled on the principle that shareholders could not sue officers and directors of corporations simply because they pursued policies that the former thought were wrongheaded or disadvantageous. Such disagreements were matters of business judgment and, as such, beyond the purview of the courts. Hence, when Thomas A. Edison sought to force the Edison United Phonograph Company to adhere to his own sense of how the business should be conducted by suing in equity to have the directors removed or, failing in that, to have the corporation dissolved, the court rebuffed his request: "No rule of law is better settled than that which declares that, so long as the directors of a corporation keep within the scope of their powers and act in good faith and

21. This principle underpinned the decision of Chief Justice John Marshall of the U.S. Supreme Court in *Dartmouth College v. Woodward* (17 U.S. 518 [1819]). Massachusetts Supreme Court Justice Lemuel Shaw explicitly articulated its implications for minority shareholders in *Smith v. Hurd* in 1847: "The individual members of the corporation, whether they should all join, or each severally, have no right or power to intermeddle with the property or concerns" of the firm. They also have no power to "call any officer, agent or servant to account." If there was an injured party, it was the corporation, the legal person whose rights were at stake, and only the corporation itself could take action to redress the damage (53 Mass. 371 at 384–87). For a similar English case, see Franks, Mayer, and Rossi, forthcoming.

22. For a more complete discussion of this case, as well as the *Dartmouth College v. Woodward* and *Smith v. Hurd* decisions, see Bloch and Lamoreaux (2004). That there was a similar trend in English law can be seen from the cases cited in *Robinson v. Smith* and also in the later U.S. Supreme Court decision *Dodge v. Woolsey*, 59 U.S. 331 (1856).

with honest motives, their acts are not subject to judicial control or revision" (*Edison v. Edison United Phonograph Co., 52* N.J. Eq. 620 [1894]). Unless the directors had clearly exceeded their statutory powers, the courts were unwilling to intervene in the affairs of a solvent corporation without compelling evidence that those in control had engaged in fraudulent or illegal acts that had inflicted serious damage on the corporation or its shareholders. Moreover, the burden of proof was on the shareholders bringing the suit. As the Massachusetts Supreme Court explained in the oft-cited case of *Dunphy v. Traveller Newspaper Association,* "it is always assumed until the contrary appears, that [directors] and their officers obey the law, and act in good faith towards all their members" (146 Mass. 495 at 497 [1888]).

That this interpretation of the *Robinson v. Smith* precedent operated to increase the magnitude of ω—that is, the private benefits that controlling shareholders could extract from their associates—is suggested by the changing way in which courts responded to situations in which directors had conflicting interests. There was a long-established principle of law that contracts tainted by conflicts of interest were voidable. This rule was an absolute one and applied to contracts that otherwise seemed completely reasonable, so that even though "the contract could not have been let on better terms, . . . the principle of law applicable to such a contract renders it immaterial . . . whether there has been any fraud in fact, or any injury to the company" (*Flint and Pere Marquette Railway Company v. Dewey,* 14 Mich. 477 [1866] at 487–88). Moreover, there is no question that the principle applied to corporations, as the U.S. Supreme Court emphatically affirmed in 1880 in *Wardell v. Railroad Company,* a case that arose as a result of a contract that officers of the Union Pacific Railroad had negotiated with a coal company that they themselves had organized. Writing for the court, Justice Field declared:

> Directors of corporations, and all persons who stand in a fiduciary relation to other parties, and are clothed with power to act for them, are subject to this rule; they are not permitted to occupy a position which will conflict with the interest of parties they represent and are bound to protect. They cannot, as agents or trustees, enter into or authorize contracts on behalf of those for whom they are appointed to act, and then personally participate in the benefits. (103 U.S. 651 [1880] at 658)

In this particular case, however, the action to void the contract was taken in the name of the corporation, whose directors had never formally approved it (the agreement had been drawn up and executed by the railroad's executive committee and had not been submitted to the board). Hence, the justices did not have to consider what the outcome of their decision would have been if the suit had been brought by a minority shareholder. The cases

Field cited in his decision suggest the outcome might well have been different,[23] and, indeed, there is evidence that state courts had for some years been applying what was in effect a reasonableness standard in such circumstances. For example, in the frequently cited case of *Hodges v. New England Screw Company,* the Rhode Island Supreme Court refused to invalidate the sale of assets by one corporation to another that was controlled by essentially the same people, determining that the plan was "judicious, and for the interest of the Screw Company" (1 R.I. 312 [1850] at 343). Moreover, the very next year after its *Wardell* decision, the U.S. Supreme Court established in the case of *Hawes v. Oakland* what was in effect a reasonableness standard. A stockholder victimized by such a conflict of interest could "sustain in a court of equity in his own name" only in the case of

> a *fraudulent* transaction completed or contemplated by the acting managers, in connection with some other party, or among themselves, or with other shareholders as will result in *serious injury* to the corporation, or to the interests of the other shareholders; Or where the board of directors, or a majority of them, are *acting for their own interest, in a manner destructive* of the corporation itself, or of the rights of the other shareholders; Or where the majority of shareholders themselves are *oppressively and illegally* pursuing a course in the name of the corporation, which is in violation of the rights of the other shareholders. (our emphasis, *Hawes v. Oakland,* 104 U.S. 450 [1881] at 460)[24]

As the phrases we italicized indicate, in order to secure the intervention of the courts, minority shareholders had to demonstrate that the actions taken by those in control were both fraudulent and seriously injurious.

Not only did the courts burden complaining shareholders with the task of proving that a contract tainted by conflict of interest was unreasonable, but there is evidence that they tended to give the controlling group the benefit of the doubt on the grounds that its members were unlikely deliberately to take actions that eroded the value of their own stock. Hence, the Rhode Island court asserted in the case of *Hodges v. New England Screw Company,* "we are the more confirmed in [our conclusion that the sale of assets was appropriate], when we recollect that the directors owned a large majority

---

23. For example, *Flint and Pere Marquette Railway v. Dewey* was brought by a corporation whose directors had ratified a contract proposed by the company's president without knowing that the president stood to profit from the arrangement. In its decision, the court raised the possibility that the contract might possibly be construed as binding if it had been ratified by the board "after a full explanation and knowledge of their interest and of all the circumstances" (14 Mich. 477 [1866] at 487).

24. In this decision the Supreme Court was deliberately qualifying a more liberal standard that it had articulated in the 1856 case of *Dodge v. Woolsey,* 59 U.S. 331. The qualification was a response to a flood of lawsuits that the earlier decision had stimulated and hence a good example of how the courts attempted to balance, on the one hand, their effort to limit the extent of the private benefits of control with, on the other, their desire not to encourage rent seeking by minority shareholders. For further discussion of these cases, see Bloch and Lamoreaux (2004).

of the capital stock of the Screw Company, and could not reduce the plaintiff's stock, without, at the same time, and in the same proportion, reducing the value of their own" (1 R.I. 312 [1850] at 343–44). Similarly, in *Faud v. Yates,* the Illinois Supreme Court found nothing wrong with a partnership agreement entered into by three stockholders of the Chicago Carbon and Coal Company. Collectively the three held a majority of the corporation's stock, and their agreement committed them to cast their votes in a block so that they could control the election of the board of directors. The partnership also leased the company's coal lands and operated its mines. In the view of the court, "The record wholly fails to disclose any injury to the other shareholders—any waste of the property," and therefore there was no reason to invalidate the agreement. But the court went even further and asserted that there was no conflict of interest involved because the incentives of the partners and of other shareholders were aligned. The partners, according to the court, "had a double interest to protect,—their interests as shareholders, and their interests as lessees. . . . As shrewd, skillful and prudent men, they were desirous of increasing the investment, and making the stock more valuable. Their interests were identical with the interests of the minority shareholders" (57 Ill. 416 [1870] at 420–21).

The courts were willing to intervene in cases where conflicts of interest led to contracts that were demonstrably fraudulent. This willingness placed limits on ω, but it is important to underscore that the shift was from a situation in which the courts would always permit such contracts to be voided to one in which complaining shareholders had to clear significant hurdles in order to obtain redress. It is difficult to get a precise idea of how high the hurdles were in actual practice without systematically studying the dispensation of cases at the lower-court level. We can, however, obtain some sense of the standards the courts applied from the case law. For example, one way in which plaintiffs could make the case that contracts tainted by conflicts of interest were fraudulent was to submit evidence that the resulting payments were substantially in excess of market levels. Hence Townsend Burden lost his case against his brother James in part because he was unable to show that James had paid too much for iron ore purchased from another company that he controlled. The trial court concluded that there was no evidence that these purchases were "made in bad faith or with any intent to defraud," but to the contrary that they had saved the Burden Iron Company money (*Burden v. Burden,* 159 N.Y. 287 [1899] at 306).

Even with such proof, complaining stockholders were in a much stronger position if they could also show that the controlling group had knowingly behaved improperly. Otherwise, their grievance was liable to be dismissed because the courts agreed that "mere errors of judgment are not sufficient as grounds for equity interference; for the powers of those entrusted with corporate management are largely discretionary" (*Leslie v.*

Lorillard, 110 N.Y. 519 at 532 [1888]). In *Brewer v. Boston Theatre,* the plaintiffs were able to make their case that several of the directors were fraudulently extracting profits from the corporation by showing that the latter had deliberately concealed their involvement in contracts from the other members of the board (104 Mass. 378 [1870]). Similarly, in *Almy v. Almy, Bigelow and Washburn,* the plaintiff was able to document that, after she had refused to sell them her stock, the controlling shareholders had tried to force her out of the company by, among other things, voting excessive salaries "to each and every member of the board, except the plaintiff Almy," as well as voting themselves other "gifts and gratuities" (235 Mass. 227 [1920] at 233).

As these last cases suggest, the courts did intervene in corporations and punish controlling shareholders who exploited their position to the detriment of other owners. Before they were willing to act, however, judges demanded compelling evidence of misdeeds. In *Flint and Pere Marquette Railway v. Dewey,* the Michigan Supreme Court had warned that if self-dealing contracts "were held valid until shown to be fraudulent and corrupt, the result, as a general rule, would be that they must be enforced in spite of fraud and corruption" (14 Mich. 477 at 488). That prophesy was borne out by the late nineteenth century. Although ω was bounded, it was positive and nontrivial. Moreover, its magnitude seems if anything to have increased during this period.

4.5   Conclusion

Partnerships and corporations each suffered from a different organizational problem. Because partnerships effectively existed only at the will of each of the members of the firm, they suffered from the potentially costly problem of untimely dissolution. That is, disagreements among members of a firm could lead one of the partners to withdraw from the enterprise, disrupting the operations of an otherwise profitable business and perhaps necessitating the liquidation of firm-specific assets. This problem may have grown worse over the course of the late nineteenth and early twentieth centuries because changes in the legal rules underscored the at-will character of partnerships, establishing with greater certainty the principle that all partnership contracts, even those for fixed terms, were revocable. The greater the number of partners, the greater the problem. Indeed, if partnerships had been the only available organizational form during this period, it is likely that it would have been extremely difficult to raise equity in the sums necessary for large-scale capital-intensive enterprises.

But partnerships were not the only available organizational form. By the mid-nineteenth century businesspeople in most states could readily organize their enterprises as corporations instead. Although disagreements among members of the firm could and did arise in corporations as well as in partnerships, the rules of corporate governance gave controlling shareholders what were in effect dictatorial powers. Majority shareholders could ignore the complaints of the minority if they so chose, and the latter had little choice but to grin and bear it. Members of the minority could not impose their will on the controlling shareholders, nor could they force a dissolution of the enterprise. This protection against untimely dissolution, however, came at a significant cost, for the same dictatorial authority that allowed the majority to disregard the views of the minority also gave controlling shareholders the power to expropriate more than their fair share of the company's earnings.

Although the media periodically published dramatic revelations of shenanigans by groups in control of corporations (aside from the Crédit Mobilier scandal, perhaps the most famous was Charles Francis Adams's *Chapters of Erie* [Adams and Adams 1871]), there appears to have been no major groundswell for reform until fallout from the 1929 stock market crash provoked Congress to create the Securities and Exchange Commission in 1934. Even then, however, the legislation applied only to large publicly traded corporations, and minority investors in privately held firms remained largely unprotected. There is some evidence that, by the 1930s, judges had become more receptive to shareholders' complaints than was the case earlier (Marsh 1966; Mark 2003), but major changes in the status of investors in private corporations would only come during the post–World War II period, when states began to revise their general incorporation statutes in ways that increased the ability of shareholders in close corporations to protect themselves contractually. During the third quarter of the century, many states also passed legislation granting shareholders new legal remedies against majority oppression and other similar ills (O'Neil 1978; Hillman 1982), and yet another wave of legislation at the end of the twentieth century provided small businesses with access to alternative organizational forms, most notably the limited liability partnership (LLP) and the limited liability company (LLC)—forms that potentially mitigated the contracting problems associated with both corporations and partnerships (Lamoreaux and Rosenthal 2005).

If protecting outside investors was unequivocally a good thing, one might expect the law to have evolved much more quickly in ways that increased minority shareholders' ability to defend themselves against expropriation by those in control of corporations. As we have seen, however, the changes that occurred in the law appear to have had precisely the opposite effect during the late nineteenth and early twentieth centuries. Because judges were intent on preventing disputes among members of the firm from disrupting the operation of corporations the way they did partnerships, they were not willing to allow disgruntled shareholders easy access to the courts. In fact, rather than give shareholders a legal weapon to use against corporate officers and directors, judges preferred to emasculate the long-standing common-law rule that contracts in which one party had a conflict of interest were voidable per se.

Although we have no way of estimating the magnitude of the private benefits that controlling shareholders could extract from their corporations without running afoul of the law, the legal record suggests that they were quite high. If they were low, moreover, we should have observed a steep decline in the number of partnerships during this period. Not only was there no such fall, but large numbers of partnerships continued to be formed. At the same time, the number of corporations also evinced a steady rise, as did investors' willingness to put their money in corporations.[25] Given that d and ω were both probably increasing rather than decreasing, the high rate at which firms were forming during the late nineteenth and early twentieth centuries is most likely attributable to the availability of large numbers of good (high-profit) projects. Everything that we know about this period of U.S. history—the rapid population growth, fall in transportation and communications costs, settlement of the continent, discovery of raw material resources, and dramatic pace of technological change—suggests that attractive entrepreneurial opportunities were indeed abundant. Many of these opportunities required capital in amounts sufficient to exploit economies of scale, making it especially important to have access to a form that would not suffer disruption as the number of investors increased. To the extent that these large projects also yielded returns that were high relative to government bonds or other similar assets, the private benefits of control that majority shareholders were able to extract were more an annoyance than a serious deterrent to investors. The Great Depression of the 1930s would dramatically alter this calculus, disrupting the legal equilibrium of the late nineteenth and early twentieth centuries and setting the economy off on a new path of institutional change, one whose outcome would be a set of statutes and precedents that were much more solicitous of the rights of minority investors. Perhaps not surprisingly, the number of corporations relative to partnerships would significantly increase.

---

25. Although newspaper announcements and other similar sources indicate that large numbers of partnerships as well as corporations were forming during this period, there are no data that enable us to measure trends in the relative numbers of partnerships and corporations before the income tax was imposed in 1916. The counts of the number of partnerships and corporations that the Internal Revenue Service published in its annual reports, *Statistics of Income,* indicate that the number of partnerships relative to corporations decreased in the 1920s, held stable in the 1930s, increased in the 1940s, and decreased in the 1950s. Only the last of these trends probably represented a significant shift in the businesspeople's preferred organizational forms. The others probably owed more to changes in tax levels that forced more (or less) partnerships to file returns. Corporations had to file regardless of whether they owed taxes, but partnerships did not.

Appendix

The Case of Endogenous Equity Stakes

The assumption that investment and equity stakes are identical seems reasonable in light of what we know about business practices in the nineteenth-century United States. It is also justifiable on theoretical grounds. If two members of a firm are similar in all respects except for the relative size of their investments, Nash bargaining would lead them to split the equity according to their contributions. The assumption of equal investment and equity stakes does, however, have two important implications. The first is that the investor earns above-market returns in nearly all of the firms that form. Hence, the entrepreneur could increase her profit if she could reduce the investor's equity stake until his return approached that of the market. Second, some firms that do not form could have done so if the entrepreneur had been able to offer the investor a higher equity stake in order to raise his return. In this appendix, we explore the consequences of relaxing the assumption of equal equity and investment stakes so that the entrepreneur can make a take-it-or-leave-it offer to the investor.[26] We assume throughout that $K_E > K_I$. Henceforth, E_E will be the equity stake of the entrepreneur, and E_I the equity stake of the investor.

In a partnership, the investor and the entrepreneur earn the same return on equity. Setting the investor's equity stake so that his participation constraint binds exactly implies that the investor's equity stake should be $E_{PI} = E_I(1 + r)/R_{PI}$, where $R_{PI} = [1 - d(1 - \alpha)]R$. Given K_I, allowing the entrepreneur to adjust equity stakes endogenously will mean that the investor's stake will decline as R increases, all other things being equal. Allowing such adjustments, however, has no effect on entry decisions for partnerships. Indeed, if $d < d^*(R)$, $R_{PI} < 1 + r$. But because $R_{PE} = R_{PI}$, $R_{PE} < 1 + r$, and the entrepreneur will not want to enter. Hence, investors in a partnership *never* have an equity stake that is larger than their investment stake.

In corporations, returns per unit of equity are not the same for the investor and for the entrepreneur because the latter enjoys the benefits of control. Setting the investor's equity stake so that his participation constraint binds exactly implies that $E_{CI} = E_I(1 + r)/R_{CI}$, where $R_{CI} = (1 - \omega)R$, or $E_{CI} = E_I(1 + r)/R(1 - \omega)$. As in the case of partnerships, when $R > R^*$, investors earn above-market returns, so allowing entrepreneurs to set equity stakes would lead to declining shares for investors as R increases. Un-

---

26. This change allows us to examine more complicated bargains than simple Nash bargaining. Nevertheless, we do not go so far as to allow side contracts to eliminate problems of minority oppression in corporations. The empirical record (particularly the persistence of large numbers of partnerships in all sectors of the economy and the extent of the litigation over minority oppression) simply will not support such a modification.

like the case of partnerships, however, entrepreneurs can affect entry decisions by varying equity stakes. Because the entrepreneur enjoys the benefits of control, some firms do not form because the investor's return would be less than the market's, even though the firm's return would have been greater than the market's. In these cases, the entrepreneur can transfer some of her return to the investor by increasing his equity stake just enough to encourage participation. There is, however, an important constraint on this strategy: the entrepreneur must not lose control. This constraint implies that, holding r, α, ω, K_I, and K_P fixed, there will be a unique R^{*m} below which corporations will not form. Because $R^{*m} < R^*$, allowing the entrepreneur to set equity stakes will increase the range of profits over which corporations form.

The entrepreneur wants to transfer just enough equity to the investor to make him indifferent between participating in the firm and investing in the market. If the investor's equity stake becomes larger than one half, he gains not just additional income rights but also the private benefits that come with control. This nonlinearity makes the entrepreneur's problem difficult when K_I is close to $K/2$. If the profitability of the firm (R) is too low, the entrepreneur may find it difficult to satisfy the investor's participation constraint if she forms a corporation. That is, as the firm's return rises, the equity stake that has to be given to the investor in exchange for a given contribution declines. Conversely, as ω increases, because the entrepreneur's private benefits of control increase, the investor must get a larger share of the equity for a given contribution in order to satisfy his participation constraint. This larger share in turn makes it more difficult for the entrepreneur to ensure that she retains control. Hence, the comparative advantage of the partnership form increases when the two members of the firm have relatively even investment stakes. When the cost of untimely dissolution is low, the entrepreneur will form a partnership instead.

References

Adams, Charles Francis, Jr., and Henry Adams. 1871. *Chapters of Erie and other essays*. Boston: J. R. Osgood.
Alchian, Armen A., and Harold Demsetz. 1972. Production, information costs, and economic organization. *American Economic Review* 62 (December): 777–95.
Bain, David Haward. 1999. *Empire express: Building the first transcontinental railroad*. New York: Viking.
Blair, Margaret M. 2003. Locking in capital: What corporate law achieved for business organizers in the nineteenth century. *UCLA Law Review* 51 (December): 387–455.
Bloch, Ruth, and Naomi R. Lamoreaux. 2004. The public-private distinction in American history: The privatization of the corporation and the problem of mi-

nority shareholders. Department of History, UCLA, and Department of Economics and History, UCLA. Unpublished manuscript.

Bodenhorn, Howard. 2002. Partnership and hold-up in early America. NBER Working Paper no. 8814. Cambridge, MA: National Bureau of Economic Research, February.

Cai, Hongbin. 2003. A theory of joint asset ownership. *RAND Journal of Economics* 34 (Spring): 63–77.

Carney, William J. 1980. Fundamental corporate changes, minority shareholders, and business purposes. *American Bar Foundation Research Journal* 1980 (Winter): 69–122.

Dunlavy, Colleen A. 2004. From citizens to plutocrats: Nineteenth-century shareholder voting rights and theories of the corporation. In *Constructing corporate America: History, politics, culture,* ed. Kenneth Lipartito and David B. Sicilia, 66–93. New York: Oxford University Press.

Evans, George Heberton Evans, Jr. 1948. *Business incorporations in the United States, 1800–1943.* New York: National Bureau of Economic Research.

Franks, Julian, Colin Mayer, and Stefano Rossi. Forthcoming. Spending less time with the family: The decline of family ownership in the UK. In *The History of Corporate Governance around the World,* ed. Randall Morck. Chicago: University of Chicago Press.

Freund, Ernst. 1896. The legal nature of corporations. PhD diss., Columbia University.

Gilmore, Eugene Allen. 1911. *Handbook on the law of partnerships including limited partnerships.* St. Paul, MN: West Publishing.

Gilson, Ronald J., and Robert H. Mnookin. 1985. Sharing among human capitalists: An economic inquiry into the corporate law firm and how partners split profits. *Stanford Law Review* 37 (January): 313–92.

Grossman, Sanford J., and Oliver D. Hart. 1986. The costs and benefits of ownership, a theory of vertical and lateral integration. *Journal of Political Economy* 94 (August): 691–719.

Harris, Ron. 2000. *Industrializing English law: Entrepreneurship and business organization, 1720–1844.* Cambridge: Cambridge University Press.

Hart, Oliver. 1995. *Firms, contracts, and financial structure.* New York: Oxford University Press.

Hillman, Robert W. 1982. The dissatisfied participant in the solvent business venture: A consideration of the relative permanence of partnerships and close corporations. *Minnesota Law Review* 67 (October): 1–88.

Hornstein, George D. 1950. Stockholders' agreements in the closely held corporation. *Yale Law Journal* 59 (May): 1040–56.

Hurst, James Willard. 1970. *The legitimacy of the business corporation in the law of the United States, 1780–1970.* Charlottesville: University of Virginia Press.

Josephson, Matthew. 1934. *The robber barons: The great American capitalists, 1861–1901.* New York: Harcourt, Brace and World.

Kirkland, Edward Chase. 1961. *Industry comes of age: Business, labor and public policy 1860–1897.* New York: Holt, Rinehart and Winston.

Lamoreaux, Naomi R. 2004. Partnerships, corporations, and the limits on contractual freedom in U.S. history: An essay in economics, law, and culture. In *Constructing corporate America: History, politics, and culture,* ed. Kenneth Lipartito and David B. Sicilia, 29–65. New York: Oxford University Press.

Lamoreaux, Naomi R., and Jean-Laurent Rosenthal. 2005. Legal regime and contractual flexibility: A comparison of business's organizational choices in France and the United States during the era of industrialization. *American Law and Economics Review* 7 (1): 28–61.

Maier, Pauline. 1993. The revolutionary origins of the American corporation. *The William and Mary Quarterly* 50 (January): 51–84.

Mark, Gregory A. 2003. A tentative history of the law governing managerial discretion: The concern with conflicts of interest. Rutgers-Newark University School of Law. Unpublished manuscript.

Marsh, Harold, Jr. 1966. Are directors trustees? Conflict of interest and corporate morality. *Business Lawyer* 22 (November): 35–76.

Mechem, Floyd R. 1920. *Elements of the law of partnership.* 2nd ed. Chicago: Callaghan.

O'Neal, F. Hodge. 1978. Close corporations: Existing legislation and recommended reform. *The Business Lawyer* 33 (January): 873–88.

O'Sullivan, Mary. 2004. What drove the U.S. stock market in the last century? INSEAD Department of Strategy and Management. Unpublished manuscript.

Rebitzer, James B., and Lowell J. Taylor. 2004. When knowledge is an asset: Explaining the organizational structure of large law firms. Case Western Reserve University, Weatherhood School of Management, and Carnegie Mellon University, John Heinz III School of Public Policy and Management. Unpublished manuscript.

Ribstein, Larry E. 2005. Why corporations? *Berkeley Business Law Journal,* forthcoming.

Richards, H. S. 1921. Uniform partnership act: Conclusion. *Wisconsin Law Review* 1 (April): 147–65.

Story, Joseph. 1859. *Commentaries on the law of partnership, as a branch of commercial and maritime jurisprudence with occasional illustrations from the civil and foreign law.* 5th ed. Boston: Little, Brown.

Summers, Mark Wahlgren. 1993. *The era of good stealings.* New York: Oxford University Press.

U.S. Census Office. 1902. *Twelfth census: Manufacturers, part I.* Vol. 7. Washington, DC: U.S. Census Office.

U.S. Internal Revenue Service. Various years. *Statistics of income.* Washington, DC: Government Printing Office.

Wallis, John. 2005. Constitutions, corporations, and corruption: American states and constitutional change, 1842 to 1852. *Journal of Economic History* 65 (1): 211–56.

Warren, Edward H. 1929. *Corporate advantages without incorporation.* New York: Baker, Voorhis.

Water, Water Everywhere
Municipal Finance and Water Supply in American Cities

David Cutler and Grant Miller

5.1 Introduction

Samuel Taylor Coleridge wrote about an ancient mariner stranded at sea, but he might as well have been writing about nineteenth-century American cities.[1] Although large-scale municipal water supplies first emerged in the United States at the beginning of the nineteenth century, water resource development and provision in many American cities remained abysmal many decades later. A large share of households continued to rely on private wells and privies, which generally resulted in "circular water systems" that recirculated household waste and perpetuated disease (Melosi 2000). Some larger cities and wealthier neighborhoods had initially enjoyed an escape from this vicious cycle. However, rapid urban growth, a weak understanding of disease transmission, and rudimentary sanitary engineering resulted in the deterioration of water provision and sewage removal to the point that they became large-scale circular water systems (Duffy 1990). Massive fires still wreaked havoc as early water systems failed to meet the needs of unprecedented urban growth (Anderson 1988).

David Cutler is dean of social sciences and a professor of economics at Harvard University and a research associate of the National Bureau of Economic Research. Grant Miller is assistant professor at the Stanford Medical School and a faculty research fellow at the National Bureau of Economic Research.

We thank conference participants for helpful comments and suggestions. Michael Edelstein, Claudia Goldin, and Sukkoo Kim graciously made historical data available to us. Research support from the National Institute on Aging grant number T32 AG00186 through the National Bureau of Economic Research is gratefully acknowledged. All errors are our own.

1. The title of our paper comes from the famous verse of Coleridge: "Water, water, every where / And all the boards did shrink; / Water, water, every where, / Nor any drop to drink" (*The Rime of the Ancient Mariner,* 1797).

Although Coleridge would have been out of place by the 1930s, many historical observers attribute the absence of piped water during the preceding decades to poor local governance and corruption in the public sector. As one put it, "It was the neglect and indifference of the city politicians and businessmen that permitted the unhealthy conditions to continue long after it was painfully evident that it affected all of the inhabitants of the city. . . . In fear of losing patronage, the politicians refused to cede some of their power to separate and independent public works and health agencies" (Alewitz 1989). Time variation in local government corruption and water system construction also suggests a negative correlation between the two. However, major investments in water systems coincided with a rapid rise in public ownership between 1890 and the 1920s. If bad local governance or corruption was responsible for the conspicuous absence of piped water for so long, why did public-sector involvement suddenly lead to so much apparent progress? An obvious answer might be that supplying water was just another means of corruption. Theft from the public (the way that corruption is defined in this volume) was commonly achieved by overpaying for inputs or contract work in exchange for kickbacks (Blake 1956; Steffens 1957).[2]

We contend that historical evidence fails to support corruption-based explanations for waterworks construction and public-sector involvement. First, we present case histories of municipal water systems that suggest that cities tapped new water supplies or greatly improved existing ones when private suppliers failed to perform well. We then discuss two major types of explanations for municipally led improvements in water systems.[3] One is changes in the value (or perceived value) of water systems. The late nineteenth and early twentieth centuries were times of major advances in the understanding of disease. It is possible that the public goods nature of clean water became clear during this era. But this explanation does not seem right; the link between dirty water and disease was apparent long before the acceptance of germ theory, even if the biological mechanism underlying the link was not well understood. Alternatively, increases in the population density of cities may have increased the need for clean water as public health conditions deteriorated. However, there do not appear to have been sharp changes in population density that coincided with waterworks expansion and public ownership.

The second type of explanation is that the costs of water systems were changing. Water systems are a natural monopoly, so private firms that win contracts for them have incentives to underprovide services (and charge a high price). As cities grew, welfare losses may have also grown. We suspect

2. Also see the Engerman and Sokoloff chapter in this volume.
3. This paper focuses on radical increases in the *quantity* of water supplied in the late nineteenth and early twentieth centuries. Cutler and Miller (2005) examine water quality and health.

this cannot be the whole explanation, however. Other utilities like the gas industry were predominantly private even though they were also natural monopolies. Contracting between the public and private sector in the era prior to municipal ownership may also have been difficult. Contracting costs between cities and private water companies were presumably rising, but the timing and pattern of public ownership across big and small cities suggests this is not the primary explanation. Private companies may have also feared expropriation by municipal authorities after making costly infrastructure investments (Troesken and Geddes 2003). However, private water companies were actually more likely to have expensive filtration plants than public ones (Troesken 1999), and no similar pattern of public ownership emerged in other utilities that required large investments. Other explanations such as reductions in corruption costs due to administrative reforms and the rise of a cadre of skilled municipal engineers also appear unsatisfactory.

We propose an alternative explanation for the rapid growth of water systems and public ownership that emphasizes the costs of capital and the development of local public finance. In the late nineteenth century, there was enormous latent demand for the expansion of waterworks—to serve neglected neighborhoods, to find clean water for drinking, and to ensure suffcient water supplies for fighting fires. The cost of building sufficiently large water systems was also enormous. Modern water systems frequently required transporting water from far away and investing in filtration plants. These costs were too large for private firms and sufficiently large that only the largest cities or cities with access to sophisticated municipal finance techniques could afford them.[4] While the largest cities invested in water systems prior to the late nineteenth century, we propose that the development of municipal bond markets was key to providing an adequate volume of water in many American cities. We present some evidence for this explanation using data on the cost of municipal water systems, the development of means of financing them, the time pattern of investment in water resources, and a time series of historical municipal bond yields.

In this essay, our approach is informal; we provide some selected trends, illustrations, and case studies to support our contention that the development of local public finance was primarily responsible for water system improvements. The second section presents a snapshot of how American cities typically addressed their water and sanitation needs before the adoption of modern water and sewage systems. The third section presents case histories of Boston and New York, suggesting that city governments intervened to provide water when existing private ones failed to perform well. The fourth section examines the development of local public finance and

---

4. Early in the nineteenth century before the development of municipal finance, private companies were perhaps better suited to building water systems.

its importance in the construction and expansion of water systems. The fifth and sixth sections review alternative explanations for local government ownership and control of water supplies and provide evidence refuting each; the seventh section concludes.

5.2   A Snapshot of Municipal Water and Sewer Systems in the Late Nineteenth and Early Twentieth Centuries

The following subsections discuss various aspects of municipal water and sewer systems around the turn of the twentieth century.

5.2.1   Household Wells and Privies

Households not connected to municipal water and sewer systems generally provided these services for themselves by digging wells and privies on their lots. Dry privies were generally used only for human waste and were generally placed a distance from homes. Cesspools received human and other types of wet waste and were generally placed in basements or immediately adjacent to homes, into which household drainage was emptied. (The terms *privy* and *cesspool* have come to be used interchangeably.) Privies and cesspools were generally constructed by digging a hole about three or four feet in diameter and at least five feet deep. Cesspool overflow was very common, saturating the surrounding earth with filth. Privy vaults were generally lined with brick, stone, or wood. Over a period of time, vaults would rot or begin to disintegrate; even in their prime, they were porous enough to allow contaminants to escape. The common result was the tainting of nearby groundwater into which household wells generally drew (Duffy 1990; Melosi 2000).

Not all waste material made its way directly into household water supplies or the surrounding soil. In many other cases, it journeyed to the streets in front of private lots. Liquid wastes were allowed to run into the open gutters of the alleys and into the streets. Here they mixed with cesspool contents removed from privies by hand and bucket and with dead animals and refuse (Duffy 1990). City governments would sporadically send horse-drawn carts through residential areas to remove the buildup of waste that collected in the streets and gutters. Removed waste known as "night soil" was used as a fertilizer through the turn of the twentieth century, when an overwhelming preponderance of scientific evidence had demonstrated such practices to be unhealthy. Cities gradually began to introduce a new suction method of emptying privies using airtight hoses and cart removal, although these services were not often provided on a sufficiently regular basis. The prevalence of cobblestone streets also exacerbated the problems of festering garbage and waste dumped onto streets. Cobblestone surfaces did not wash or drain well, and they made waste removal considerably more difficult and less effective (Duffy 1990).

5.2.2   The Requirements of Constructing Water Systems

The challenges of constructing large municipal water systems were quite formidable during the nineteenth century (indeed, they are not trivial today). A variety of complex decisions had to be made; each one involved extensive research and planning together with a precarious balancing act in volatile political environments. An appropriate water source had to be identified. For most cities, there were generally many candidates, including surface water (streams, rivers, and lakes) and groundwater sources of various sorts. Survey work by geologists and engineers was a difficult and time-consuming task, and their findings were often controversial and subject to political pressure. Each potential source required estimates of supply volume and purity (particularly difficult before science elucidated what "purity" meant). Engineers would then attempt to estimate how water from each source could be delivered to city populations. This involved acquiring water using pumps and dams, transporting it via large aqueducts, raising it to sufficient elevation to facilitate flow by means of gravity, and storing sufficient quantities of water in large city reservoirs to smooth water consumption across periods of high and low demand (Blake 1956).

With this information, each potential water source would then require rough cost estimates. Not surprisingly, these estimates were often quite inaccurate. Private interests also commonly exerted considerable influence over these estimates and surveys. In most cases, the expense of such waterworks projects were staggering regardless of the source chosen, totaling many times annual municipal revenue in some cases (Blake 1956). Given the amount of information required, the uncertainty surrounding it, the sheer size of the financial commitment, uncertainty about future city needs, and strong political pressures from various directions, it is not surprising that many decades of debate often preceded significant waterworks projects.

5.2.3   Sanitary Problems Linked to Municipal Water and Sewer Systems

During the 1870s and 1880s, major cities expanded or built new water and sewer systems, instituted systematic garbage collection, and began paving cobblestone roads with smoother materials like granite and occasionally asphalt. Clearly these services—municipal water and sewers in particular—held promise for addressing the woes caused by household wells and privies. But their promise was not to be immediately realized.

Sanitary engineering was developing as a field during the 1870s and 1880s, which meant that many of the eastern cities with sewers and drains constructed in earlier years were done so in a haphazard and inadequate manner (Melosi 2000). A considerable amount of waste continued to be dumped into city streets, and these wastes were generally swept or washed down drains and into sewers. Water systems generally provided inadequate water or inadequate water pressure to wash streets and flush sewers on a regular basis. Moreover, because most sewer systems were only designed to carry storm water, they often became clogged because they lacked sufficient capacity (many were not more than 2.5 or 3 feet in diameter; Duffy 1990). Rapid population growth during the nineteenth century greatly exacerbated the capacity problems of existing systems and often negated the benefits of investments made to improve existing systems. In addition to a large amount of waste introduced into sewers from city streets, the advent of water closets in the United States in the 1870s added considerable strain to already overburdened sewers. The end result was often backflow from sewers into streets and gutters; some observers began referring to sewers as "elongated cesspools" (Duffy 1990).

Perhaps the worst sort of backflow was the emptying of sewer systems directly into drinking water supplies. In the late nineteenth century, the primary sewer outfalls of many American cities emptied upstream of river water intakes or directly into large water bodies (like the Great Lakes) in close proximity to water intakes. The few cities that addressed this problem early on also suffered from the dumping of untreated sewage by upstream communities. This phenomenon essentially reproduced the household circular water systems on the municipal level (Duffy 1990).

5.2.4   Service Provision at the Household Level

Household water and sewer connections were often poorly constructed, resulting in waste and the continued spreading of filth. Annual flat fees were paid for piped water, giving households no incentive to fix leaky connections. Not until early in the twentieth century did many cities make efforts to meter household water, charging rates per volume of water used (or wasted) rather than flat fees. Water pressure, turbidity, and taste varied greatly from moment to moment, and isolated reports of other irregularities emerged from time to time (for example, fish being delivered through infrastructure pipes into bathtubs). As water closets began replacing simple privies and chamber pots after 1870, many of them resulted in more unsanitary conditions than the use of privies and cesspools. Many were not properly installed (permits to install water closets were trivial to obtain) and resulted in considerable sewage leakage (Melosi 2000).

5.2.5   Water Systems and Fires

The importance of water systems to combat major fires was an issue that emerged early in the nineteenth century. The growth of population and structures meant growth in the consequences of uncontrolled fires. Bucket brigades and water wagons were clearly inadequate to manage large conflagrations. In areas of cities served by water supplies, water for extinguishing fires was tapped in several ways. The most rudimentary method was to drill holes in wooden water pipes; these holes could be corked or opened as desired. A more sophisticated approach was the installation of fire hydrants. Arrangements for use of water ranged from cities paying hydrant rental fees to private water companies to water being made freely available for purposes of putting out fires. However, water pressure was inadequate to effectively combat fires with some regularity. Even in cities with well-developed water systems, they often did not extend to outlying areas, poor neighborhoods, and regions of high elevation. These areas were clearly particularly vulnerable to the destruction of fires, and fire insurance was more costly by several orders of magnitude (Anderson 1988).

5.2.6   Public Takeovers of Private Water Systems

Cities wishing to increase their involvement in the delivery of water essentially had two choices: build a water system if one did not exist or take control of existing private water systems. Municipal takeovers of existing private water systems generally involved either the outright purchase of private companies or the introduction of a municipal competitor to a private water company (essentially bankrupting the private company). The specifics of how this was done depended on the private company's charter. For example, if a private company had exclusive legal rights to provide water to residents of a city, these rights would generally have to be purchased. If a private company had exclusive legal rights to a given water source, a municipal water company could either buy this right or find another source. City governments could also petition state legislatures to revoke private water company charters under extreme circumstances.

Once a water company was municipally owned, it had to be operated. This usually required the establishment of a standing municipal water board that wasn't subject to changes with every electoral cycle (although appointment to boards was of course political), as opposed to being operated directly by a city council. Water boards would manage systems in conjunction with hired engineers and contractors. Rates would be set and collected from citizens and firms. Improvements or expansions would often begin with surveys and draft proposals prepared by engineers retained by the board. The board would decide which ones it preferred to pursue and would seek political permission and financing from the city council or other relevant municipal government authority. Once political permission was obtained and financing was approved, the water board would solicit bids for municipal contracts to actually conduct the work.

5.2.7   The Changing Landscape of Water Provision in Subsequent Years

The construction of water systems progressed rapidly at the end of the nineteenth century, and adequately engineered sewer systems gradually replaced the older ones designed for storm water early in the twentieth century. Near the end of the period that we examine, the 1932 federal Relief and Reconstruction Act authorized $1.5 billion to be lent to state and local governments for public works projects; a sizable proportion of these resources was spent on improving water and sewer systems (Melosi 2000). Not only did nearly all cities build and greatly improve water and sewer systems by this point in time, but access to them across diverse neighborhoods within cities was also greatly expanded.

The consequences of vastly improved water systems are very difficult to estimate empirically for a variety of reasons, but they undoubtedly include superior protection against fires, vast health gains, and other stimuli of economic development. The availability of water to combat fires was no longer perceived as a problem at all. Great strides in health improvement also coincided with (and appear to be driven by) water quality improvements (Cutler and Miller 2005). In the short span of five or six decades, the sanitary environment of many American cities was transformed from one of filth to one that resembles a modern city.

5.3   Case Histories of Boston and New York

The evolution of waterworks construction and ownership was different in every city. Keeping this in mind, we present case histories of Boston and New York below.[5] In both cases, waterworks were clearly used to further private interests in a variety of ways, both legitimate and otherwise. Boston and New York were reluctant to make the initial investments necessary to build water systems and preferred that private investors instead lead the way. The water supplies of both cities began with small-scale private ventures that proved to be inadequate to meet the needs of growing cities. In the end, the governments of both cities intervened to purse grander projects than private companies were willing to embrace in order to increase the available supply of water. Both examples illustrate the enormous scale of water projects.

5.3.1   Boston

In 1794 a group of entrepreneurs submitted a petition to the Massachusetts legislature to be incorporated to deliver water from Jamaica Pond to residents of Boston. The City of Roxbury, in which Jamaica Pond is located, opposed this proposal to no end. The following year the state legislature approved the application and incorporated the Aqueduct Corporation; the City of Boston passed a resolution approving the project as well. The company's charter gave it the right to obtain water from anywhere in Roxbury and deliver it to any part of Boston. It also contained two important restrictions: both Roxbury and Boston reserved the right to draw water free of charge to combat fires, and water rates were subject to court regulation.

---

5. Both case histories are drawn from Blake (1956).

The Aqueduct Corporation project proceeded quickly; it had obtained pine logs and awarded a contract for laying wooden pipes within months. Although historical accounts are unclear, customers appear to have been served with water by the middle of 1798. But the project failed to produce returns for its investors for twelve years. When its first dividends were paid, rates of return were only about 1.5 percent. Business gradually improved, however, and over the next thirty years, stock in the company yielded about a 4 percent annual return.

Although successful, this first water system only served about 800 families, and its pipes were small and were too shallow, causing them to freeze during the winter. Movement toward supplying most of the city with water had its origins in a fire in 1825 that destroyed fifty-three houses and stores and caused half a million dollars in damage. The city council responded by beginning serious debate on how an adequate water supply for the city might be obtained. The debate would continue for nearly twenty-five more years.

Boston's mayor at the time, Mayor Quincy, Sr., assembled a committee to investigate the matter. An engineer conducting surveys for the city reported that two sources would be most suitable: the Charles River above the falls at Watertown and Spot Pond in Stoneham. Spot Pond would not require the complications of pumping or reservoir storage because of its elevation. On the issue of ownership, the committee was split. Mayor Quincy also sought advice from the chairman of the Philadelphia Watering Committee (the success and scale of the Philadelphia waterworks was of course renowned); the chairman's answer both questioned the adequacy of the Spot Pond supply during dry months and strongly encouraged municipal ownership of any water system that Boston might pursue. On this advice, the mayor began denying petitions from entrepreneurs to establish private water companies. His own efforts were frustrated as well, however, and his tenure ended without further progress.

Several years later a new mayor named Theodore Lyman again brought the water issue to the forefront—and went on record favoring municipal ownership. Jamaica Pond was clearly too small a source to serve the entire city, so new surveys were begun. These new surveys were completed in 1834 and recommended larger, more distant sources over Spot Pond and the Charles River primarily because of concerns about volume. Farm and Shakum Ponds in Framingham as well as Long Pond were touted as the most suitable alternative water sources.

Mayor Armstrong, elected in 1835, frowned upon seeking water as far away as Framingham, so he assembled yet another committee to study the matter. He also charged the committee to make a recommendation for either public or private waterworks ownership. Their report favored building a more modest system than did earlier ones, making allowances for expansion as the city's population grew rather than investing in a larger system at the outset. It promoted Spot Pond with the proviso that if this supply became inadequate, the City of Boston could also draw water from Mystic Pond. Interestingly, attached to the report was the charter of the Boston Hydraulic Company, which had recently been incorporated by the Massachusetts legislature but was still subject to approval by the city council. Its charter gave it the authority to take water from any source north of the Charles River within twelve miles of Boston. It also gave the city the option of purchasing a considerable share of the new company's stock. The city council approved the charter but declined to buy any of its shares.

More mayors were elected, and more committees were appointed to study how to supply the city with water. In 1837, three city commissioners were appointed to develop a concrete water supply plan for the city. It considered four of the usual suspects: Spot Pond, Mystic Pond, Long Pond, and the Charles River. The Charles River was the most unattractive of the options because it would require more mechanical pumping—and was thought to be dirtier—than the others. The real choice was essentially between Long Pond and Spot Pond (which could be supplemented with water from Mystic Pond if necessary). The three commissioners could not agree among themselves; two of them recommended Spot Pond, and the mayor attempted to act on it.

In 1838, what was now the standing committee on water and the city board of aldermen approved a plan to draw water from Spot Pond under municipal ownership. Not surprisingly, the two private water companies strenuously objected and even pleaded that competition between them would best serve the city's interests. Small townships around Boston also vehemently protested, fearing that local interests would be hurt and that land for the project would be seized by condemnation. Investors in the Middlesex Canal (chartered in 1793 to build a waterway connecting the Merrimac River with Boston Harbor) also protested that water flow for their canal project would be diminished. The result of these objections was a series of protracted hearings.

In 1840 Mayor Jonathan Chapman was elected, and he frowned on the city's present water initiative because of the massive outlays required in light of the rapid growth of the city's debt in recent years. As the municipal effort was halted, private efforts were reinvigorated. In 1840, the rights of the Aqueduct Corporation were expanded to include Brookline and Brighton. The company also began modest expansions of its works and replaced its wooden pipes with more durable iron ones. But it also knew that it could never supply all sections of Boston from Jamaica Pond. Fearing a municipally owned water system, it began fostering other private interests in complementary systems that would supply other areas of the city.

In early 1843, a member of the city council whose family owned Spot Pond for many years resigned together with colleagues to form a company to serve Boston from the pond. Several months later the Spot Pond Aqueduct Company was incorporated. The company had exclusive rights to Spot Pond, and it would provide Boston with free water to fight fires. The City of Boston was entitled to purchase up to one-third of the company's stock or to seize the franchise and company property at any time at a price set by a predetermined formula. Because of an unusual feature of the charter that made stockholders individually liable for company debts, the city decided not to purchase any shares of the Spot Pond Aqueduct Company.

In 1844 a city initiative to tap water in Long Pond (the only source now considered by the city administration to possess adequate supply for the entire city) was revived. Additional costs of supplementing Spot Pond water with Mystic Pond water reportedly made Long Pond the most appealing source in light of Boston's continued rapid population growth. The two commissioners who originally constituted a majority in favoring Spot Pond had now changed their minds; Long Pond was now the unanimous choice recommended by a new commission report. After considerable wrangling in the legislature and a few compromise amendments, in 1845 Boston was given approval by the legislature to construct a municipal water supply that tapped Long Pond. However, supporters of the private companies campaigned vigorously against it, and it was defeated by popular vote in the referendum.

The Spot Pond Aqueduct Corporation attempted to fill the vacuum, and it submitted a proposal to the city council offering to sell the city its water rights and Spot Pond itself. In considering the company's offer, the city once again reconsidered all of its options for water and once again sought outside help in assessing both the city's future water needs and the quality of each potential source. John Jervis, the chief engineer of the Croton Aqueduct Project, was chosen to conduct the new surveys. While awaiting the Jervis report, parties favoring each source were attempting to position themselves as well as possible. Promoters of Spot Pond invited members of the city council to an extravagant reception and viewing of the pond, but the viewing had precisely the opposite effect of what was intended because the pond happened to be at its lowest level for the occasion. (The small quantity of water available from Spot Pond was of course its primary drawback.) The group later claimed that the Long Pond faction had placed large stones to obstruct the flow of water into the pond at the time of the event.

In the end, the report headed by John Jervis strongly supported the Long Pond proposal. Shortly afterwards Josiah Quincy, Jr., son of the mayor who had initially explored the construction of a municipal waterworks, was elected mayor and promised to pursue water from Long Pond. Under Mayor Quincy, the City of Boston had to obtain new authority from the state legislature again to pursue its project. It was virtually unopposed (save only by the township of Lowell), and in 1846 the legislature passed a new water act. A groundbreaking ceremony marked the beginning of the project shortly afterward. In 1848, Boston celebrated the arrival of its new water with a tremendous festival and a large fountain gushing in the center of Frog Pond in the Boston Common.

As a small side matter, there was discontent that the city's future water source had such a mundane name. A little research uncovered the pond's previous Indian name: Cochituate. Miraculously, the word's etymology was discovered to mean "an ample supply of pure and soft water, of a sufficient elevation to carry into the City of Boston, at a moderate expense" (Blake 1956). The mayor's proposal that Long Pond should subsequently be known as Lake Cochituate was enthusiastically embraced.

The completion of Boston's municipally owned water system created obvious problems for the private companies that still existed. In late 1848 the old Aqueduct Corporation asked that the city purchase its water rights and property, pleading that the city remember that private shareholders had made great sacrifice for the public good. The mayor originally planned to offer the corporation $100,000, but the city council knew that the old Aqueduct Corporation had no alternative but to sell its rights and property to the city. The council was therefore willing to go along with a purchase for $20,000, a price at which the company took great offense. The city and the Aqueduct Corporation failed to reach an agreement, and the company continued serving about 400 people who preferred water from Jamaica Pond to Cochituate water. In 1851, a new city body administering the waterworks negotiated to purchase the company for $45,000, and the company accepted the offer. This was effectively the end of private water in Boston, although some years later the city did sell the rights to supply the City of Roxbury with water from Jamaica Pond to a new private entity named the Jamaica Pond Aqueduct Corporation.

5.3.2   New York

Had it not been for the impediment of the Revolutionary War, a man named Christopher Colles might have succeeded in building a water system in New York late in the eighteenth century. After the war, numerous citizen movements pressed the city council to construct waterworks for the city. In 1798, a proposal by a physician, scientist, and engineer named Joseph Browne to dam and tap water from the Bronx River was seriously entertained. However, Joseph Browne also proposed that a private entity carry the proposed project forward. The city council considered it undesirable to place a private company in such a powerful position, so it instead decided to request authority from the state legislature to build a water system itself. Through clever maneuvering of state Assemblyman Aaron Burr, however, the bill that the state legislature produced authorized a charter for a private water company instead. Ironically, it was Alexander Hamilton whose advocacy then persuaded the city council to accept the bill as produced by the state legislature. One of the main points that furthered its case was the avoidance of enormous expense and taxpayer burden.

The Manhattan Company was then quickly incorporated; its new charter placed far fewer requirements on it than did other contemporary private water company charters of the day (again, courtesy of the efforts of Aaron Burr). The charter did stipulate, however, that if the company did not provide a continuous source of "pure and wholesome" water for all citizens desiring it within ten years, it would be dissolved. The other noteworthy feature of the charter was a carefully hidden section that gave the company the legal right to use all "surplus" capital for other purposes unrelated to water.

This obscure section of the charter opened the door for Aaron Burr to pursue banking through the Manhattan Company, which had been his intention from the beginning. Bank charters of the day were difficult to obtain through protracted political processes and were limited in duration; the Manhattan Company's charter had crept into existence below the political radar and was unlimited in duration. Although some other members of the state legislature apparently knew about the scheme, there was outrage when it was publicly discovered. Burr lost his position in a subsequent election, but the company lived on despite attempts of his political adversaries to undermine it.

To maintain its good standing, it was clear that the Manhattan Company had to provide water to some degree. The real question remained how adequate it would be. Despite serious concerns about its purity, the company decided to tap groundwater with the use of wells and pumps. Some water was flowing as early as 1800. Ironically, Joseph Browne was the lead engineer of the project. Problems and complaints about irregular and unpredictable service began almost immediately. The quantity of water provided was also inadequate for street washing and gutter flushing, forcing the city to rely on older wells for this purpose. The company provided free water to the city to fight fires, although its adequacy is unclear.

By 1804, the city council decided that the Manhattan Company's supply was inadequate to keep pace with city growth and began revisiting other proposals to draw water from more distant sources, such as the Bronx River. The company's banking business was booming, so its interest in water was waning even further. (Incidentally, by this time political and financial troubles had forced Aaron Burr to sell most of his stock in the company, and he had been removed from its board.) DeWitt Clinton, mayor of New York at the time, proclaimed in 1808 that the company had not fulfilled the requirement of its charter (that it provide "pure and wholesome" water for all citizens desiring it) and thought that, given the difficulties and low profitability of its water operations, it might be willing to sell its waterworks to the city. This would of course require the state legislature to amend the original charter for it to continue with its banking activities. Interestingly, DeWitt Clinton was also one of the Manhattan Company bank's directors. One of the points upon which negotiations hinged was the price to be paid to the Manhattan Company to acquire its waterworks. Many on the city council believed that it operated at a loss, although its books suggested that it earned an annual return of just under 7 percent on its original investment.

With this issue unsettled, the city council made an application to the state legislature to alter the Manhattan Company's charter and to receive authority to purchase the waterworks. Amazingly enough, in addition to serving as mayor and as a bank director, DeWitt Clinton was also a prominent state senator representing a southern district of New York. The legislature acquiesced to these requests. The Manhattan Company was given the right to lease or sell its waterworks and rights, the length of time it had to provide "pure and wholesome" water for all citizens desiring it was extended to twenty years, and its new charter gave it the right to continue with its banking and other activities even after divesting itself of its waterworks. Additionally, the charter would continue to be perpetual until the company sold the waterworks, at which point it would last for thirty years following the sale. The company therefore naturally tried to postpone the sale as long as possible.

Complaints about the company's water service were constant. Portions of the city (the ones with pipe infrastructure) received no water at all for prolonged periods of time. Repairs were made only to stave off crises of public outrage. Water availability to fight fires was so poor that public funding was used to build cisterns for collecting rainwater to be used to combat fires. Fires and disease epidemics (despite a poor understanding of the basis of disease) continued to push the inadequacy of water supply to the political forefront; public opinion was squarely opposed to the service provided by the company.

In subsequent years, the alliance between the Manhattan Company and the city government deteriorated. The city was highly indebted to the bank, and to meet its obligations it eventually resorted to selling off its stock in the company. DeWitt Clinton himself also slowly sold his company stock, and in 1813 he declined to be reelected as a bank director. By 1820, DeWitt Clinton was governor of New York, and both he and the state legislature supported drawing water for New York City from upland rivers. But the city council continued to be conflicted about how to proceed.

In 1823, after several years of surveys and considering its options, the city council supported another private initiative to charter the New York and Sharon Canal Company to build a waterway from Sharon, CT, to the Hudson River to join with a proposed canal to be built from Sharon to the Housatonic River. The state legislature approved the measure. Another private proposal to charter the New York Waterworks Company also gained momentum, alarming both the Manhattan Company and the Sharon Canal Companies. Although its charter was eventually approved, it was believed to be flawed because the Manhattan Company held exclusive rights to groundwater under Manhattan and the Sharon Canal Company held exclusive rights to surface water in Westchester County. The Manhattan Company clearly had the most to lose because of its profitable banking activities. Although it was unwilling to invest in drawing water from distant rivers, it did begin to seek new groundwater supplies by drilling a new well and began replacing its wooden pipes with iron ones.

To add to the confusion, a new report claimed that the water supplies of Rye Pond and the Bronx River, upon which both the New York Waterworks Company and Sharon Canal Company projects depended, was inadequate to meet the needs of New York City. After 1830, the water demand in New York had grown so much that serious attention began shifting from the Bronx River to the Croton River. Previous consideration of the Croton was limited by the daunting expense required to reach it.

With its eye on mounting a challenge to the Manhattan company, that year the city council appointed a committee to investigate whether or not the company had the right to discontinue providing water for fire plugs at will or any obligation to pay for its damage to streets and sidewalks—and, more generally, if it had met the conditions of its original charter. The committee found that water was available to only one-third of the paved and built city and that its failure to seek more copious sources was inexcusable—in short, that it had not met its obligations. An additional blow to the Manhattan Company was a communication to the city council by a body of well-known and respected doctors and chemists. It concluded that all of the groundwater in Manhattan was horribly contaminated with filth from graveyards and privies.

By 1833 it was clear that the city was going to build its own waterworks, and after a considerable amount of debate and conflicting geological surveys and engineering reports, the Croton was agreed upon as the most promising source. The Manhattan Company therefore offered to sell all of its water rights to the city, leaving the price open to negotiation. After a devastating fire in 1836, the city opened negotiations with the company to obtain a temporary supply for fighting fires while the Croton Aqueduct was under construction. No agreement was ever reached, however. At the same time, the state legislature found that the company had violated its charter.

In the end the Manhattan Company's rights were never purchased because, with the opening of the Croton Aqueduct in 1842, they were essentially not needed. The company had some legal claim to the groundwater in Manhattan, but the new source did not draw on Manhattan groundwater at all. When Croton water began flowing into the city, the company simply lost its customers. Ironically, it retained its wells for decades afterwards—not because it was actively providing water from them, but because it feared future challenges to its charter.

5.4   Municipal Finance and Public Ownership of Water Systems: History and Evidence

In the cases of Boston and New York, city government intervened to provide water when existing private companies failed to perform well—which generally meant failure to provide a sufficient supply to meet growing water demand. But Boston and New York were preeminent population centers in early America that were probably not representative of the typical American city. Growth in water quantity in the typical city occurred later and coincided with the sharpest rise in public waterworks ownership. One city in which this transformation occurred after the turn of the century—New Orleans—followed a course similar to that in Boston and New York (Troesken and Geddes 2003). A private company began providing New Orleans with water in 1878, but the company refused to extend its pipes to outlying areas of the city. Moreover, the water it did actually deliver was turgid and unfiltered. The city subsequently petitioned the Louisiana legislature to revoke the company's charter and eventually acquired the water system in 1908. Shortly afterward the system was expanded dramatically, and filtration plants were constructed.

Figure 5.1 and table 5.1 show that public ownership had been increasing throughout most of the nineteenth century, but that this trend accelerated from 1890 (when 43 percent of waterworks were publicly owned) through the 1920s (when 70 percent were publicly owned)—which coincides precisely with rapid growth in the number and adequacy of water systems. In particular, the period of fastest public ownership growth (ignoring the first few decades of the nineteenth century, when the absolute number of wa-

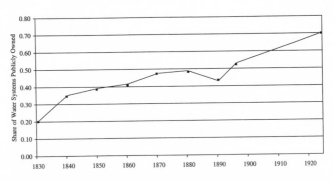

Fig. 5.1   The share of water systems publicly owned in American cities, 1830 to 1924

Sources: Overlapping series of number of waterworks taken from Galishoff (1980) and Melosi (2000); authors' calculations of the share publicly owned. Data are available on the decade from 1830 to 1890 and for 1896 and 1924; points in between are obtained by linear interpolation.

Table 5.1   **The number of publicly and privately owned waterworks in American cities, 1830 to 1924**

Year	Total		Public		Private		Percent public
			Number of waterworks				
1830	45	—	9	—	36	—	20
1840	65	(2)	23	(1)	42	(1)	35
1850	84	(2)	33	(1)	51	(1)	39
1860	137	(5)	57	(2)	80	(3)	42
1870	244	(11)	116	(6)	128	(5)	48
1880	599	(36)	293	(18)	306	(18)	49
1890	1,879	(128)	806	(51)	1,073	(77)	43
1896	3,180	(217)	1,690	(147)	1,490	(70)	53
1924	9,850	(238)	6,900	(186)	2,950	(52)	70

Sources: Overlapping series of number of waterworks taken from Galishoff (1980) and Melosi (2000); authors' calculations of the percent of waterworks publicly owned.

Note: Average annual increase in number of waterworks over the preceding period shown in parentheses.

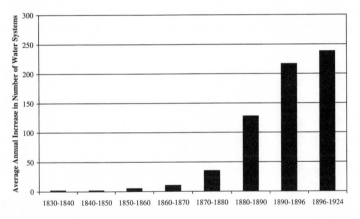

Fig. 5.2   Average annual increase in the number of water systems in the United States, 1830 to 1924

Sources: Overlapping series of number of waterworks taken from Galishoff (1980) and Melosi (2000); authors' calculations of average annual increases; data are available on the decade from 1830 to 1890 and for 1896 and 1924.

terworks was very small) was the 1890s. Figure 5.2 and table 5.1 show that the absolute annual increase in number of waterworks accelerated sharply around 1890. During the 1890–1900 decade, the number of miles of water mains in major cities with existing water systems also nearly doubled (figure 5.3).[6] This section first provides a brief overview of the development of

---

6. This is true in major cities for which data are readily available.

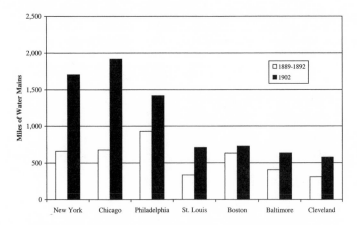

Fig. 5.3   Miles of water mains in selected cities, 1889–92 and 1902
Source: Teaford (1984).

local public finance during the nineteenth century and then presents suggestive evidence that it was the emergence of municipal bond markets that made water system improvements possible.

5.4.1   Local Public Finance during the Nineteenth Century

Although the precise date of the first municipal bond issuance in the United States is unknown, there were very few in the early nineteenth century. New York City issued its first securities around 1812, and bonds to support the construction of the Croton Aqueduct were issued in 1837 and 1838. Between 1830 and 1850, municipal indebtedness grew rapidly in both total and per capita terms (see table 5.2 and figure 5.4)—but almost exclusively in the largest cities. As table 5.3 shows, at least 93 percent of all city debt on record in 1843 (the first year for which these statistics are available for all cities) was issued by major population centers (Hillhouse 1936).

The explosive growth of municipal debt in the middle of the century was probably attributable to restrictions placed on state debt. Following financial difficulties during the depression of 1837 and a series of state defaults around 1840, the landscape of local public finance changed radically. Many state legislatures amended their constitutions to prohibit state borrowing for costly canals, turnpikes, railroads, and other improvements. As states were increasingly constrained by pay-as-you-go financing, municipal debt arose to fill the gap between what could be afforded and what was thought to be needed. (Not until after World War I were many state constitutional restrictions on debt officially relaxed.) A large share of municipal debt during this period was for railroad construction. This era of ex-

Table 5.2   **Real municipal debt in American cities, 1843 to 1932**

Year	Total municipal debt (millions of dollars)	Growth over preceding period	Per capita municipal debt (dollars)	Growth over preceding period
1843	625	—	265	—
1853	4,208	0.19	963	0.13
1860	4,055	0.00	652	−0.02
1870	6,629	0.05	669	0.00
1880	13,547	0.07	959	0.04
1890	17,126	0.02	775	−0.02
1902	31,899	0.05	979	0.02
1912	60,310	0.06	1,355	0.03
1922	77,678	0.03	1,357	0.00
1932	186,924	0.09	2,660	0.07

Sources: Nominal debt taken from Hillhouse (1936); historical consumer price index (CPI) taken from Carter et al. (2005) used to inflate debt to 2000 terms; authors' calculations of growth over the preceding period.

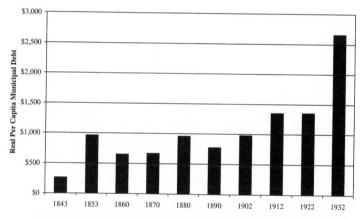

Fig. 5.4   Real per capita municipal debt in the United States, 1843 to 1932
Sources: Nominal debt taken from Hillhouse (1936); historical CPI taken from Carter et al. (2005) used to inflate debt to 2000 terms; historical populations 1840 to 1940 taken from http://www.census.gov/population/censusdata/table-4.pdf

pansion peaked in the late 1860s and early 1870s. Between 1868 and 1873, the net bonded debt of New York tripled; between 1867 and 1873 the bonded debt of Chicago also tripled. Debt tripled in Boston from 1868 to 1874; Cincinnati's debt grew by five times from 1868 to 1876, and Cleveland's debt grew by twelve times from 1867 to 1877 (Griffith 1974).

After these years of unchecked borrowing and spending, local economies turned sour during the panic of 1873. What ensued was the largest series of municipal bond defaults to that date. (Earlier economic slumps

Table 5.3   Debt in selected cities, January 1843

City	Total debt (dollars)
New York, NY	295,922,345
Philadelphia, PA	70,915,707
New Orleans, LA	39,982,622
Boston, MA	33,757,045
Baltimore, MD	29,989,809
Cincinnati, OH	25,927,297
Charleston, SC	24,097,285
Savannah, GA	12,445,467
Mobile, AL	11,667,284
Albany, NY	9,909,959
Troy, NY	8,210,311
Detroit, MI	5,424,264
Nashville, TN	2,642,424
Rochester, NY	2,228,838
Buffalo, NY	1,466,939
Vicksburg, MS	1,137,162
Providence, RI	507,652
All other cities	45,486,486

Sources: Nominal debt taken from Hillhouse (1936); historical CPI taken from Carter et al. (2005) used to inflate debt to 2000 terms.

had caused states to default on their obligations, but municipalities generally did not have much debt during these downturns; see Grinath, Wallis, and Sylla 1997.) The number of bond issues held void rose from 35 in 1870 to 101 in 1880 (Hillhouse 1936).[7] An estimated one-fifth of all municipal obligations could not be met following this depression; many of these municipal defaults during the 1870s were associated with railroads. The panic of 1873 and its ensuing debt problems were especially severe in southern cities struggling under Reconstruction. Some renegotiated their debt, while others gave up their charters or went into receivership (Griffith 1974).

Following the panic of 1873 and unprecedented revelations of widespread government corruption, many states and cities introduced new municipal debt limitations as a percentage of total property assessments. New York's bonded debt peaked in 1876 and fell by a quarter during the next decade (Teaford 1984). Other cities followed a similar pattern. Strikingly, Detroit's net debt fell from $961,000 in 1875 to $12,000 in 1885 (Teaford 1984). In subsequent years, however, these restrictions were circumvented in several ways. One was the passage of state constitutional amendments that one historian attributes to the municipal capture of state legislatures (Teaford 1984). These amendments allowed exceptions for a variety of spe-

7. Data on the total number of bond issues in these years are not readily available.

cial ventures including "self-supporting" municipal enterprises like waterworks (Griffith 1974). Another was the creation of special districts that were not technically a part of city government. Many local water authorities were incorporated in this way to be exempt from debt restrictions (Monkkonen 1995).

The panic of 1893 also contributed to the development of municipal bond markets and their ability to fund public waterworks. Businesses were hit the hardest, while municipal governments suffered less (Griffith 1974). Consequently, municipal bonds became relatively more attractive to investors. Interest rates fell, and cities were able to borrow large amounts to continue financing their growth. To quote one financial historian, "municipalities never enjoyed such a favorable market for their securities, for by the 1890s no investment was as sound as a municipal bond" (Teaford 1984). The granting of "home rule" to city governments by state legislatures also broadened their ability to borrow and spend. However, very little of this occurred before the turn of the century (Griffith 1974).

5.4.2   Evidence on Local Public Finance and the Supply of Water

One explanation for rapid water system expansion at the end of the nineteenth and beginning of the twentieth centuries is the development and growing sophistication of local public finance. Private water companies could not afford to build systems to serve entire municipal populations. Only the largest cities could afford adequate water supplies until the means for substantial borrowing were developed. Waterworks were exorbitantly expensive, even in comparison with other municipal utilities. In 1915, the mean value of municipal waterworks exceeded annual city government revenue, as shown in table 5.4. Mindful of the fact that many water systems were built long before 1915, the expenses of constructing a water system relative to annual municipal receipts were undoubtedly larger than shown here. Available statistics suggest that in 1905, waterworks were the largest debt line item of municipal government (U.S. Bureau of the Census 1907a).

Several different strands of evidence support this view. The timing of municipal investments in water provision by city size provides a first piece of evidence. Figure 5.5 shows municipal ownership over time by city size among all cities with publicly owned water systems in 1915. In general, large cities municipalized their waterworks earlier than smaller ones. For example, all of these cities with over 500,000 people in 1915 had a public water system by the end of the 1850s, while the share of smaller cities with public water systems at that time was below 20 percent.[8]

---

8. It is possible that city size responded to public investments in water, but readily available statistics do not allow for the bidirectionality of this relationship to be disentangled. See subsequent paragraphs for further discussion.

Table 5.4   **Reported book value of water systems and annual revenue in selected American cities, 1915**

	Value of water system (dollars)	Total municipal revenue (dollars)	Value-revenue ratio
All cities over 500,000 population	569,727,688	462,077,044	1.23
New York, NY	350,004,152	206,010,937	1.70
Chicago, IL	52,557,484	80,622,887	0.65
Philadelphia, PA	30,000,000	45,242,379	0.66
All cities 300,000 to 500,000 population	149,222,136	146,467,942	1.02
Buffalo, NY	15,702,219	15,184,834	1.03
Los Angeles, CA	36,058,144	24,405,199	1.48
Cincinnati, OH	17,366,561	13,785,166	1.26
All cities 100,000 to 300,000 population	186,574,699	171,787,677	1.09
Jersey City, NJ	12,448,453	6,792,713	1.83
Kansas City, MO	8,967,124	10,296,283	0.87
Rochester, NY	9,768,056	7,408,794	1.32
All cities 50,000 to 100,000 population	93,665,860	89,950,262	1.04
Ft. Worth, TX	3,937,893	1,694,390	2.32
Somerville, MA	1,017,365	1,916,006	0.53
Harrisburg, PA	2,487,150	1,481,848	1.68

Sources: Reported book value of water systems taken from U.S. Bureau of the Census (1907a); total municipal revenue taken from U.S. Bureau of the Census (1975); gross national product (GNP) deflator taken from Balke and Gordon (1989) used to inflate water system book values to 1915 terms; authors' calculations of value-revenue ratios.

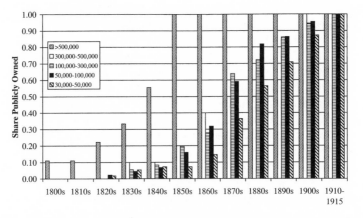

Fig. 5.5   Share of cities with publicly owned water systems by population and decade among cities with publicly owned systems in 1915
Source: U.S. Commissioner of Labor (1899).

If the municipal finance explanation was correct, one would also expect to see rapid growth in debt and revenue among small cities relative to large cities at the end of the nineteenth century (when figure 5.5 suggests that public ownership was rising faster among the smaller cities). Figure 5.6 shows that this is exactly what occurred. In the period from 1880 to 1902,

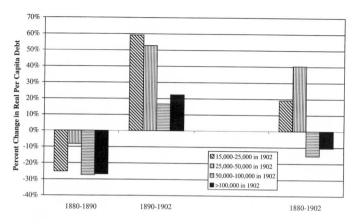

Fig. 5.6   Percent change in real per capita debt in American cities, 1880–1902, by municipal population in 1902

Sources: Nominal debt taken from U.S. Bureau of the Census (1907b); GNP deflator taken from Balke and Gordon (1989) used to inflate debt to 1902 terms; authors' calculations of percent changes.

debt in small cities grew by about one-third while debt in the largest cities fell by more than 10 percent.[9]

Of course this growth in municipal debt could have been due to either supply or demand factors. Our supply-side explanation is that financial innovation and investor interest made it possible for smaller cities to borrow much more at this time than earlier. Alternatively, it may have been that cities suddenly decided that they needed to borrow more and thus demanded additional debt. Although not readily available by city size, municipal bond yields during the late nineteenth century provide some means of distinguishing between supply and demand explanations for growth in municipal debt. The supply explanation implies that yields should have fallen with the increase in borrowing, while the demand explanation implies that yields should have increased.

Figure 5.7 shows mean nominal and real municipal bond yields in New England from 1857 to 1913.[10] In general, real bond yield fluctuations coincided with the business cycle. Real yields rose and then fell dramatically following the panic of 1873 and did not return to this level by the end of the century. Although there was a smaller increase in the middle of the 1890s,

9. The cities used to construct figure 5.6 were selected as follows. First, states with major population centers were chosen: California, Connecticut, Georgia, Illinois, Indiana, Kentucky, Louisiana, Maryland, Massachusetts, Michigan, Minnesota, Missouri, Nebraska, New Jersey, New York, Ohio, Pennsylvania, Rhode Island, Tennessee, Texas, and Wisconsin. All cities with a population of 15,000 or more in 1900 and with debt statistics in 1880, 1890, and 1902 were then chosen within these states.

10. Nominal municipal bond yields shown in figure 5.7 are taken from Macaulay (1938) and can also be found in NBER's Macro History Data Series #13020. Real bond yields were calculated using the implicit GNP deflator provided in Balke and Gordon (1989).

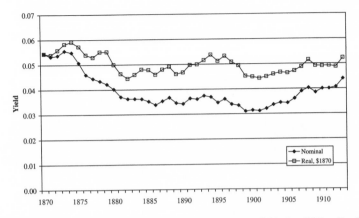

Fig. 5.7   Nominal and real mean annual municipal bond yields in all New England cities, 1870–1913

Sources: Nominal bond yields taken from NBER's Macro History Data Series #13020; GNP deflator taken from Balke and Gordon (1989).

this is presumably related to the panic of 1893. With the exception of business cycle fluctuations, real yields were low during the late 1890s and early twentieth century as municipal borrowing increased and municipal involvement in water accelerated. Lower yields during this period are generally consistent with a supply-side explanation that emphasizes the development of municipal bond markets. Evidence on alternative demand-oriented explanations is examined in the next section, but these factors should be reflected in the time series of municipal bond yields as well. The absence of high and rising real yields during this period of growing debt and increasing public involvement in water does not support them.

The decline in municipal ownership of water systems in the 1880s also lends some support to the municipal finance view. In the wake of the depression of 1873, the corruption scandals exposed at roughly the same time, and the subsequent rise in municipal bond issues held void, borrowing declined in all cities (shown in figure 5.6 for 1880 to 1890) as states imposed tight restrictions on municipal indebtedness. Although these indebtedness restrictions were only temporary obstacles, they were accompanied by the only decline in public waterworks ownership during the entire nineteenth century (see the decline from 1880 to 1890 shown in figure 5.1).

5.5   Alternative Explanations: Changes in Value (or Perceived Value)

One set of alternative explanations for the rapid expansion of water systems and increase in municipal ownership is that the value (or perceived value) of water systems increased. This would have increased demand for water services, and particularly in the presence of positive externalities, local governments may have been the appropriate providers of water.

5.5.1   Externalities and New Knowledge about Disease

There are clearly large external benefits of water supplies not captured by private water companies. The most obvious ones are disease reduction and improved capabilities of combating fires (a less clear one is that water systems were an economic stimulus through other pathways). On the surface, it is unclear why the existence of externalities would explain a sharp rise in municipal waterworks ownership beginning around 1890. Fires and epidemic infectious diseases had been serious problems in cities for as long as cities have existed. It is possible, however, that the bacteriological revolution of the 1870s and 1880s may have provided a new impetus for concerns about disease externalities. As knowledge of the basis of waterborne diseases became clearer, concerns about the socially inefficient incentives of private companies may have intensified.

But there are several reasons that call this line of reasoning into question. One is that dirty water was believed to be causally linked to disease long before the bacteriological revolution. The first demonstration of the link between unclean water and disease was John Snow's famous demonstration of how cholera spread from a single water pump in London in the 1850s. Snow had premonitions of the germ theory, but it took several more decades for the theory to be fully articulated.

The prevailing theory at the time, the miasma theory of disease, held that a variety of illnesses are the result of poisonous, malevolent vapors ("miasmas") that are offensive to the smell (Anderson 1984; Duffy 1990). The widespread acceptance of the miasma theory might have been based on Pavlovian learning. People exposed to foul odors were more likely to get sick, foul-smelling areas tended to have more sick people, and more people seemed to get sick during the summer seasons, during which offensive odors were more common. The leap of logic from correlation to causation led to misdirected sanitary interventions—and some successful ones as well.

The externality argument is also generally difficult to reconcile with the empirical observation that private water companies were more likely to possess expensive water filtration plants than were publicly owned companies early in the twentieth century (Troesken and Geddes 2003). And private water companies were ostensibly legally liable for damages attributable to large waterborne disease outbreaks (Troesken and Geddes), although it is not clear how enforceable this liability was in practice.

5.5.2   Population Density

As large numbers of Americans migrated to urban areas from the countryside, the population density of cities may have increased. Urban slums certainly emerged in the late nineteenth and early twentieth centuries. If the population density of cities grew rapidly, deteriorating public health conditions may have increased the demand for water. Similarly, the positive externalities of municipal water systems may have grown, giving local governments stronger reasons for getting involved.

Although reliable statistics on municipal population density before the 1890s are generally not available, there appears to have been no abrupt increase that coincided with water system growth. Data from a consistent panel of 119 cities from 1890 to 1950 suggest that the only large increase in municipal population density occurred between 1910 and 1920 (Kim 2002)—twenty to thirty years after major waterworks improvements began.

5.6 Alternative Explanations: Changes in Costs

In addition to changes in their value, another set of potential explanations for rapid water system growth and municipal ownership is that costs fell. The following section explores these possibilities.

5.6.1 Natural Monopoly

The cost structure of public utility provision is generally characterized by declining marginal costs. Hence, one firm could in principle serve an entire market most efficiently. Monopoly power held by a profit-maximizing firm of course commonly leads to inefficient service provision. As will all monopolists, a monopoly water supplier will raise prices to the profit-maximizing level and will restrict quantity to support those prices. Public ownership may be the natural response in the view of local governments.

However, a natural monopoly explanation fails to account for either the timing of the increase in municipal waterworks ownership or for why waterworks were increasingly city owned while gas and electrical utilities were not. On the timing, it is not clear why either welfare losses or local government losses should have suddenly accelerated around 1890, producing the observed increase in municipal waterworks ownership. Additionally, the cost structures of gas and electricity provision were similar, but these utilities were rarely privatized. Table 5.5 shows that gas companies were al-

Table 5.5	Public ownership of gas companies, 1890 to 1920		
Year	No. of companies	No. publicly owned	% publicly owned
1890	871	8	0.9
1900	896	15	1.7
1910	1282	122	9.5
1920	1008	45	4.5

Source: Troesken (1997).

most exclusively private from 1890 to 1920 when public waterworks ownership was rising most rapidly. Fewer statistics for electric companies are available, but around the turn of the century, nearly 70 percent of the 952 electric companies in the United States were privately owned (U.S. Commissioner of Labor 1899).

5.6.2   Contracting Failures

Although some dimensions of water provision can easily be observed and monitored, or stipulated ex ante in a contract (e.g., water pressure, rates, etc.), many others cannot. For example, it is difficult to specify in advance that certain new population centers not yet in existence should be served or what new water sources should be tapped to meet future demand growth. As the provision of water became increasingly complex and regulatory requirements became more onerous, contracting costs may have reduced the profitability of the water business, making it less attractive to private firms.

There are some suggestive findings that litigation against private water companies was positively related to municipal takeover during the period of rapid waterworks municipalization (Troesken and Geddes 2003). It is unclear why contract incompleteness would have become more problematic at the end of the nineteenth century, but there is some historical suggestion that contracts became more elaborate—and potentially more costly—shortly before 1900. For example, the National Municipal League's model Municipal Corporation Act was drafted in 1899 and subsequently adopted by many cities (Webber and Wildavsky 1986). However, a contracting cost explanation does not square with the continuation of predominantly private ownership in gas and electricity.

Holdup is another potential contracting difficulty. City governments may have had difficulty credibly committing not to expropriate the enormous infrastructure investments made by private water companies. Following the bacteriological revolution as technological innovations to combat waterborne disease were developed (such as filtration), the investments required to build and operate water systems increased substantially. Hence losses (or fears of losses) due to municipal expropriation could have potentially grown near at the end of the nineteenth and beginning of the twentieth centuries.

There is some evidence that municipal takeovers of private water systems were positively related to the extensiveness of a water system and negatively related to financial difficulties of private water companies (Troesken and Geddes 2003). One interpretation of this correlation is that cities were more likely to seize private waterworks that promised greater rents. Fear of expropriation could have also induced private companies to rationally underinvest in their water systems, resulting in inadequate service provision and an additional rationale for municipal ownership.

Countering this hypothesis is the fact that private water companies were more likely than public ones to own expensive filtration facilities. According to an 1899 federal government survey of water companies, 19 percent of the private companies had filters while only 6 percent of the public ones did (Troesken 1999). It is also unclear why municipal seizures or fear of expropriation would have risen in the 1890s and early twentieth century if it was truly a period in which corruption in municipal government was actually falling while contracts were growing more sophisticated. Moreover, the absence of municipal takeovers of other public utilities (gas and electricity) during this period also seems to contradict this view.

Finally, a recent analysis cites a positive cross-sectional correlation between population density and public ownership as evidence that contract evasion and appropriation problems were responsible for municipal control (Masten 2004). However, this would also be consistent with larger cities' (which were typically denser) having greater financial means to build or expand municipal water systems.

5.6.3   Corruption Costs and Administrative Reform

Administrative reform that began at the very end of the nineteenth century may have reduced the corruption costs associated with municipal ownership of waterworks. As a number of city government scandals were exposed in the 1870s, cities began experimenting with administrative reforms that aimed to reduce corruption. These reforms appear to have been at least partially responsible for the creation of standing boards to perform specialized functions like operating water systems. Board members were surely corruptible, but probably less so than city council members (who operated municipal water systems before professional boards emerged). It is not clear if delegation of authority to city boards was actually purposeful (to reduce corruption) or coincidental (driven by the increasingly technical and complex nature of city functions).

The problem with a corruption costs and administrative reform explanation is that the sharpest rise in public waterworks ownership occurred in the 1890s. Much of the effective administrative reforms came in the early decades of the twentieth century at the dawn of the Progressive Era. This was a primary objective of the National Municipal League's model Municipal Corporation Act that was first drafted in 1899 (Webber and Wildavsky 1986). Although corruption was surely present in historical water supply and management (McCarthy 1987), it seems to have relatively little direct bearing on public ownership or the expansion of water systems.

5.6.4   Growth in the Supply of Municipal Engineers

A final possibility is that exogenous growth in the supply of municipal engineers made it possible for cities to operate water systems on their own.

Table 5.6   Civil engineering degrees awarded in New York State by decade, 1830 to 1949

Decade	No. of civil engineering degrees awarded	Absolute change from previous decade
1830–39	61	—
1840–49	88	27
1850–59	124	36
1860–69	523	399
1870–79	605	82
1880–89	712	107
1890–99	973	261
1900–09	2,001	1,028
1910–19	3,330	1,329
1920–29	2,446	−884
1930–39	3,026	580
1940–49	2,760	−266

Sources: Number of awarded civil engineering degrees taken from Edelstein (2002); authors' calculations of change over previous decade.

Note: We believe the numbers provided represent both first and advanced degrees.

City governments may have desired to do so much earlier (out of either self-interest or public interest), but they simply lacked the human resources to do so.

The primary piece of evidence against this explanation is the fact that the public sector was in large part responsible for engineering and applied science training in the late nineteenth century. This means that increases in the number of engineers were probably not exogenous with respect to major public works projects.[11] The Morrill Land Grant Act provided large tracts of federal land to states to endow and support institutions of higher education specializing in agriculture and mechanical arts (Goldin and Katz 1999). During the 1870s and 1880s, the largest numbers of new engineering programs were established at land grant institutions (Edelstein 2002).

Historical data on the output of new engineers in the United States by area of specialization are not readily available. Data on the output of civil engineers in New York State (shown in table 5.6) suggest that the largest surge in the production of engineers occurred after the turn of the twentieth century. If the training of engineers in New York over time is representative of the national trend, growth in the supply of engineers does not hold much promise for explaining the rapid expansion and increasing public ownership of waterworks.[12]

11. An exogenous increase in the supply of engineers that accelerated the construction of waterworks would also be reflected in rising municipal bond yields as cities demanded additional debt. Figure 5.7 shows no clear evidence of this.

12. New York State most likely led many of the other states.

5.7   Conclusion

The quantity of piped water supplied in American cities grew dramatically near the turn of the twentieth century, and local government ownership seems to have been a driving force behind this surge in water system construction and expansion. Governments may have wanted to be involved earlier—and in fact were in the largest cities—but financial constraints appear to have prevented them from doing so. As innovation in local public finance made it easier for smaller cities to borrow, many American cities did in fact purchase or build waterworks. Even larger cities that already owned water systems were able to finance massive expansions to previously unserved neighborhoods. In an era of rampant corruption in local government (Steffens 1957), it is striking that government involvement in such a costly sector as water seems to have advanced the public interest considerably (if not the private interests of politicians as well). This observation is consistent with those of others that corruption—although undesirable and inefficient—can in fact go hand in hand with policies that improve public welfare if corrupt politicians seek both political support and a robust economy to exploit (Menes 2003).

References

Alewitz, Sam. 1989. *A social history of unsanitary Philadelphia in the late nineteenth century.* New York: Garland.

Anderson, Letty. 1984. Hard choices: Supplying water to New England towns. *Journal of Interdisciplinary History* 15 (2): 211–34.

———. 1988. Fire and disease: The development of water supply systems in New England, 1870–1900. In *Technology and the rise of the networked city in Europe and America,* ed. Joel Tarr and Gabriel Dupuy, 137–56. Philadelphia: Temple University Press.

Balke, Nathan S., and Robert J. Gordon. 1989. The estimation of prewar gross national product: Methodology and new evidence. *Journal of Political Economy* 97 (1): 38–92.

Blake, Nelson Manfred. 1956. *Water for the cities: A history of the urban water supply problem in the United States.* Syracuse, NY: Syracuse University Press.

Carter, Susan, Scott Gartner, Michael Haines, Alan Olmstead, Richard Sutch, and Gavin Wright, eds. 2005. *Historical statistics of the United States: Millennial edition.* New York: Cambridge University Press, forthcoming.

Cutler, David, and Grant Miller. 2005. The role of public health improvements in health advances: The 20th century United States. *Demography* 42 (1): 1–22.

Duffy, John. 1990. *The sanitarians.* Urbana, IL: University of Illinois Press.

Edelstein, Michael. 2002. The production of engineers in New York colleges and universities, 1800–1950: Some new data. City University of New York, Economics Department of Queens College. Unpublished manuscript.

Galishoff, Stuart. 1980. Triumph and failure: The American response to the urban water supply problem, 1860–1923. In *Pollution and reform in American cities, 1870–1930,* ed. Martin Melosi, 35–57. Austin: University of Texas Press.

Goldin, Claudia, and Lawrence F. Katz. 1999. The shaping of higher education: The formative years in the United States, 1890 to 1940. *Journal of Economic Perspectives* 13 (1): 37–62.

Griffith, Ernest S. 1974. *A history of American city government: The conspicuous failure, 1870–1900.* New York: Praeger Publishers.

Grinath, Arthur, John Wallis, and Richard Sylla. 1997. Debt, default, and revenue structure. NBER Historical Working Paper no. 97. Cambridge, MA: National Bureau of Economic Research.

Hillhouse, A. M. 1936. *Municipal bonds: A century of experience.* New York: Prentice-Hall.

Kim, Sukkoo. 2002. The reconstruction of the American urban landscape in the twentieth century. NBER Working Paper no. 8857. Cambridge, MA: National Bureau of Economic Research.

Macaulay, F. R. 1938. *The movements of interest rates, bond yields, and stock prices in the United States since 1856.* New York: National Bureau of Economic Research.

Masten, Scott E. 2004. Public utility ownership in 19th century America: The "aberrant" case of water. University of Michigan Business School. Mimeograph.

McCarthy, Michael P. 1987. *Typhoid and the politics of public health in nineteenth century Philadelphia.* Philadelphia: American Philosophical Society.

Melosi, Martin. 2000. *The sanitary city: Urban infrastructure in America from colonial times to the present.* Baltimore: Johns Hopkins University Press.

Menes, Rebecca. 2003. Corruption in cities: Graft and politics in American cities at the turn of the twentieth century. NBER Working Paper no. 9990. Cambridge, MA: National Bureau of Economic Research.

Monkkonen, Eric H. 1995. *The local state: Public money and American cities.* Stanford, CA: Stanford University Press.

Steffens, Lincoln. 1957. *The Shame of the Cities.* New York: Hill and Wang.

Teaford, J. 1984. *The unheralded triumph: City government in America, 1870–1900.* Baltimore: Johns Hopkins University Press.

Troesken, Werner. 1997. The sources of public ownership: Historical evidence from the gas industry. *Journal of Law, Economics, and Organization* 13 (1): 1–25.

———. 1999. Typhoid rates and the public acquisition of private waterworks, 1880–1920. *The Journal of Economic History* 59 (4): 927–48.

Troesken, Werner, and Rick Geddes. 2003. Municipalizing American waterworks, 1897–1915. *Journal of Law, Economics, and Organization* 19 (2): 373–400.

U.S. Bureau of the Census. 1907a. *Statistics of cities having a population over 30,000:1905 (Special Reports).* Washington, DC: Government Printing Office.

———. 1907b. *Wealth, debt, and taxation.* Washington, DC: Government Printing Office.

———. 1975. *Historical statistics of the United States: Colonial times to 1970, part 2.* Washington, DC: Government Printing Office.

U.S. Commissioner of Labor. 1899. *Water, gas, and electric-light plants under private and municipal ownership.* Washington, DC: Government Printing Office.

Webber, Carolyn, and Aaron Wildavsky. 1986. *A history of taxation and expenditure in the Western world.* New York: Simon and Schuster.

III

The Road to Reform

6

The Rise of the Fourth Estate
How Newspapers Became
Informative and Why It Mattered

Matthew Gentzkow, Edward L. Glaeser, and
Claudia Goldin

Burke said there were Three Estates in Parliament; but, in the Reporters' Gallery yonder, there sat a *Fourth Estate* more important far than they all. It is not a figure of speech, or a witty saying; it is a literal fact. . . . Printing . . . is equivalent to Democracy. . . . Whoever can speak, speaking now to the whole nation, becomes a power, a branch of government, with inalienable weight in law-making, in all acts of authority. It matters not what rank he has, what revenues or garnitures: the requisite thing is that he have a tongue which others will listen to; this and nothing more is requisite.
—Thomas Carlyle, *On Heroes, Hero Worship, and the Heroic in History* ([1841] 1993, p. 141, emphasis in original)

Matthew Gentzkow is an assistant professor of economics at the University of Chicago Graduate School of Business. Edward L. Glaeser is a professor of economics at Harvard University and a research associate of the National Bureau of Economic Research. Claudia Goldin is the Henry Lee Professor of Economics at Harvard University and director of the Development of the American Economy program and a research associate of the National Bureau of Economic Research.

We are indebted to many people. Magali Fassiotto compiled almost all of the data sets described in appendixes A and B and was ably helped by Neil Mehta and Tazeen Chaudhry. Li Han began the data work. Katharine Kaplan helped with various details. We thank Jesse Shapiro and Andrei Shleifer for suggestions and Paul Rhode for his comments at the conference. Jay Hamilton provided portions of the data described in appendix A. In our search for ways of demonstrating the relationship between newspapers and corruption James E. Rauch and Tomas Nonnenmacher offered us their data. Although these paths were not taken, we are grateful to them nonetheless.

6.1 Introduction

A free and informative press is widely agreed to be crucial to the democratic process. The impact of investigative reporting in the Watergate scandal and the role of the press in the exposure of Enron's accounting irregularities, among other legendary episodes, buttress the view that journalists can make a difference. Allegations of distortion and political bias in media (e.g., Goldberg 2001) are greeted today with hand wringing as a threat to government, even to society as a whole.

But from a historical perspective, the remarkable thing is not that the media remains somewhat biased but rather that there is now an expectation that the press will provide unbiased information. At the start of the republic, newspapers such as the *Aurora* were little more than public relations tools funded by politicians. In the nineteenth century, independence was a rarity. As late as 1870, 89 percent of urban dailies that covered political events proudly acknowledged their affiliation to one of the political parties.[1] Information hostile to a newspaper's political viewpoint was either ignored or dismissed as sophistry. Indeed, typical nineteenth-century news items seem more partisan than even the most rabid modern editorials. Today's media retain biases, but they are modest relative to the advocacy that was the norm of the nineteenth century.

Our concern here is with the causes and consequences of the rise of the informative press, a potent check on corruption. In section 6.2 we document the evolution of media bias using three types of evidence. First, we construct a basic measure of bias: stated party affiliation.[2] While stated political independence is no guarantee of independence, stated party affiliation is surely a guarantee of bias. The share of political newspapers that claimed to be independent rose from 11 percent in 1870 to 62 percent in 1920.[3] Another measure of bias is the use of charged language by the press. Negative words such as "slander," "liar," and "villainous" are used by papers to dismiss undesirable statements; words such as "honest," "honorable," and "irreproachable" are used to defend political heroes. Using textual analysis, we find a substantial drop in partisan and charged language across the late nineteenth and early twentieth centuries.

Because these aggregate measures are imprecise, we also examine the press coverage of two major scandals: the Crédit Mobilier scandal of the early 1870s and the Teapot Dome scandal of the 1920s. Our findings here

---

1. The earliest statistics on newspaper party affiliation come from the 1850 Population Census of Social Statistics. About 85 percent had an affiliation, a finding not much different from data on urban dailies in 1870.

2. The use of party affiliation as a measure of bias is similar to that in Hamilton (2004).

3. The 62 percent figure uses an inclusive measure of independence that includes papers that were listed as independent-Republican or independent-Democrat. The less inclusive measure is 40 percent.

support the results of the textual analysis: "spin," as measured by charged language and editorializing in news stories, was common in the coverage of Crédit Mobilier but was negligible during Teapot Dome. We also find subtler differences in media behavior between the two scandals. During the earlier scandal, many Republican papers omitted the critical early news that might have cast aspersions on their own party. When these papers eventually did print or acknowledge the stories, they were coupled with violent derogation of Democratic sources. By the 1920s Republican papers no longer coupled allegations of the corruption of their party members with condemnation of the character of the person making the charge. Although stories were still suppressed even during the 1920s, the growth of independent newspapers meant that most urban residents had access to the story.

After documenting the rise of the informative press, we turn to the causes of this change. In section 6.3 we follow Besley and Prat (2004) and present a supply-side model suggesting that newspapers weigh the rewards of bias—politicians' bribes or personal pleasure—against the costs of bias—lost circulation from providing faulty news. The key predictions of the model are that as the size of the market for newspapers rises and as the marginal cost of producing a paper falls, newspapers will become less biased and invest more in gathering information. The model also suggests that increased competition may further reduce bias.

In section 6.4, we present evidence suggesting that the rise of the informative press was the result of increased scale and competitiveness in the newspaper industry and that technological progress was the cause of these changes. We document the great increase in circulation, the rise in scale, and the overall rise in competition. We also provide evidence showing a link between these trends and the cost of newsprint and newspaper production. Finally, we provide some evidence linking the rise in the independents to growing news markets. We focus on the share of newspaper circulation that claimed to be independent and find that this share increased most rapidly in cities that had the largest increases in population.

6.2   The Rise of the Informative Press

The informative press emerged sometime between the 1870s and the early 1900s. We present information on the transition using three sources on bias and factual content of newspapers. The first is the number of newspapers that claimed to be independent, rather than being politically affiliated. The second is a time series of words in newspaper articles that suggest a decline in argumentative hyperbole, as opposed to reasoned presentation of facts. Finally we study newspaper reporting of two of the biggest national scandals in American history: Crédit Mobilier in the 1870s and Teapot Dome in the 1920s.

6.2.1   The Growth of the Independent Press

Newspapers today vehemently deny that they deliver anything but fair and balanced reporting. Such arguments were rarely heard during much of the nineteenth century, for newspapers never claimed to deliver the unvarnished truth. To the contrary, they proclaimed their close affiliation with one of the two major political parties. Although the assertion of "independence" by a press does not imply unbiased reporting, an outright declaration of party affiliation does seem to assure a political slant to the news. Throughout the mid-nineteenth century, the vast majority of newspapers were explicitly affiliated with one of the major political parties. Some were directly supported by a party, whereas others were supported by patronage positions, such as postmaster, and contracts with the government to print materials.[4]

Many of the pre–Civil War presses were bully pulpits for political bosses. Take Thurlow Weed, for example. He apprenticed as a printer, worked for the *Rochester Telegraph,* and then bought the newspaper, which he used to support his candidates. He soon set his sights higher and took charge of the *Albany Evening Journal,* a Whig party paper backed by the Anti-Masonic party. He used the paper to support Seward for New York State governor in 1838. Together with another well-known editor, Horace Greeley, he successfully worked to elect President Harrison in 1840 (Emery and Emery 1992, p. 104).

Sometime between 1870 and the early 1900s newspapers became demonstrably less connected to political parties. To explore changes in the party affiliation of the press, we have assembled data on newspapers in the largest U.S. cities between 1870 and 1920.[5] The data include any city that was among the largest 100 in any decennial census year during the period, for a total of 152 cities.

In 1870 only 11 percent of daily newspapers in large cities were identified as independent (see table 6.1, panel B).[6] Although the independents

---

4. Political parties before the 1830s, according to Cook (1998), financed the press through direct patronage (e.g., printing contracts). Although the government was initially a sponsor of the press, it later subsidized it through low postal rates. On political subsidies and when the independent press emerged, see also Kaplan (1993). Schudson (1978) contains a history of the informative content of the press, and Summers (1994) discusses the transition from a partisan to an independent press.

5. Our data set expands Hamilton's (2004), which he kindly gave us. The details of the construction of the data set are given in appendix A.

6. Throughout the paper, we exclude the foreign language press and dailies that were not general-interest newspapers (e.g., financial, fashion, theater, and gardening periodicals). We also exclude the minor political parties in table 6.1. In the newspaper directories from which our data are drawn, newspapers were listed by party affiliation, including independent, and after 1870 were also classified as independent-Republican or independent-Democrat. We have constructed two definitions of independent: a broad one that includes all three and a narrow one that includes only independent.

Table 6.1   **The growth of dailies, circulation, and independent newspapers: 1870 to 1920**

	All cities in sample					
	1870	1880	1890	1900	1910	1920

A. Newspapers by city

	1870	1880	1890	1900	1910	1920
Number of cities	140	149	150	150	150	150
Fraction cities with						
Dailies	0.743	0.866	0.947	0.967	0.973	0.967
Independent1 dailies	0.164	0.517	0.647	0.633	0.753	0.827
Independent2 dailies	0.164	0.436	0.527	0.527	0.627	0.653
Dailies by city						
None	0.257	0.134	0.053	0.033	0.027	0.033
One	0.129	0.148	0.060	0.047	0.073	0.100
Two	0.307	0.248	0.240	0.293	0.287	0.313
Three or more	0.307	0.470	0.647	0.627	0.613	0.553

B. Political affiliation of newspapers

	1870	1880	1890	1900	1910	1920
Fraction of dailies by party[a]						
Republican	0.527	0.386	0.336	0.360	0.332	0.219
Democratic	0.360	0.316	0.319	0.302	0.216	0.164
Independent1	0.114	0.298	0.345	0.337	0.452	0.618
Independent2	0.114	0.257	0.263	0.261	0.340	0.404
Circulation per capita						
All dailies	0.194	0.253	0.419	0.450	0.577	0.606
Independent1 dailies	0.051	0.135	0.215	0.217	0.300	0.441
Independent2 dailies	0.051	0.128	0.192	0.175	0.237	0.265
Independent fraction of circulation[b]						
Independent1	0.263	0.534	0.513	0.424	0.520	0.728
Independent2	0.263	0.506	0.458	0.389	0.411	0.437

C. Newspaper competition: Fraction of cities containing newspapers of the following types[c]

	1870	1880	1890	1900	1910	1920
Only D or R or I	0.289	0.279	0.162	0.145	0.205	0.386
(Only I)	(0.039)	(0.070)	(0.049)	(0.055)	(0.110)	(0.317)
(D or R) and I	0.058	0.171	0.232	0.269	0.411	0.407
D and R [not I]	0.529	0.194	0.204	0.255	0.130	0.076
D and R and I	0.125	0.357	0.401	0.331	0.253	0.131

D. Newspaper prices (real): Annual cost in 1982–84 dollars

	1870	1880	1890	1900	1910	1920
Unweighted	n.a.	57.41	64.34	62.23	53.02	35.74
Weighted by circulation	n.a.	71.76	60.90	55.90	44.76	33.33
Per square inch × 100, weighted	n.a.	n.a.	1.657	1.383	0.844	n.a.

Sources: N. W. Ayer and Son (various years), Rowell (various years). See appendix A. City population data from Gibson (1998). Deflator (see line 8) from Carter et al. (forthcoming).

Notes: The universe of cities is the union of the top 100 by population in every year. "All cities" includes every city that contained a population in the year given. Brooklyn and New York City are treated as separate cities after they merged. The cities of Charlestown, MA, and Allegheny, PA, exit the sample due to mergers. Results from a balanced panel of cities (those in the sample every year even if they do not include a daily in some year) are nearly identical. Daily newspapers include both aligned and independent papers but exclude specialized periodicals (e.g., financial, music, fashion, garden). We have also excluded minor political party newspapers (e.g., Socialist, Labor, Populist) and, most importantly, the foreign-language press. We use two definitions of "independent." "Independent1" includes independent-Republican (IR) and independent-Democratic (ID), as well as independent. "Independent2" includes only independent. The deflator is the CPI, 1982–84 = 100: 1880, 10.2; 1890, 9.1; 1900, 8.4; 1910, 9.5; 1920, 20.0. The "square inch" calculations divide by the size of the page times the number of pages in the newspaper. There are no data available for 1870 and 1880; that for 1920 is not in square inches. n.a. = not available.

[a]Republican, Democratic, and Independent sum to 1. The omitted categories using Independent2 are the IR and ID papers.

[b]Circulation per capita for the independents divided by the circulation for all dailies.

[c]Independent is defined here as Independent1.

were among the larger papers and accounted for 26 percent of circulation, the overwhelming majority of Americans in 1870 read papers that were openly partisan. The partisanship of the press changed substantially over the next half century. In 1920 62 percent of all big-city newspapers were independents, and 73 percent of all big-city circulation was (table 6.1, panel B using the broader definition of "independent"). Independent papers were anomalies in 1870, but fifty years later they had become the norm.

The largest increases in the independent press during 1870 to 1920 occurred at both the beginning and end of the period—the 1870s and the 1910s. The earlier decade contains responses to the excesses of the Grant administration, and the last decade includes part of the Progressive Era. Independent papers can increase as a fraction of the total because of an increase in new independents, the conversion of existing aligned papers, the exit of nonindependents, and mergers of aligned papers with independents. The breakdown in net additions to the independent press due to entry, exit, conversions, and mergers is given in table 6.2 for the five decades from 1870 to 1920. With the exception of the last decade (1910 to 1920), the vast majority of net additions came from start-up newspapers that began as independents.

There were many conversions of older papers, to be sure. Democrat and Republican newspapers became independent (or combined independence with a previous affiliation), and some nonaligned papers became aligned. But across the forty-year period 1870–1910 there were about three times as many newly established independent papers for every net conversion. Only in the last decade did conversions from other political parties play a major

Table 6.2   The increase in the independent press: 1870 to 1920

		Among independent newspapers				
Period	Total papers in end year	Net additions	Entry	Exit	Net conversions	Net change from mergers
1870–1880	373	81	68	13	29	−3
1880–1890	476	53	74	30	11	−2
1890–1900	486	0	38	39	5	−4
1900–1910	467	47	47	34	37	−3
1910–1920	421	49	26	31	62	−8

Sources: See appendix A.

Notes: The newspapers analyzed are all "political" papers in our sample of the top 100 cities by population in each year from 1870 to 1920. We limit "total newspapers" to include those with major political affiliations: Republican, Democrat, or Independent, defined as I, IR, and ID. Newspapers with other political affiliations (e.g., Socialist, Labor) are implicitly included in "Net conversions" if they switched to become independent or left the independent rank to become one of the "other" affiliations. The group from "other" and to "other" is a small number in all decades listed. "Net additions" is the number of independent papers in the later year minus that in the earlier year given. It is also equal to (Entry − Exit + Net conversions + Net change from mergers).

role in the rise of the independents. In the 1910–1920 decade the trend reversed and there were three times as many net conversions for every new independent paper. A majority (60 percent) of the conversions in the 1910s went from Republican to independent (evenly divided between independent [I] and independent-Republican [IR]).

The switch to independence did not necessarily imply a lack of bias, and many nominally independent papers revealed extreme political bias on occasion. Still, the fact remains that in 1870 papers trumpeted their bias and by 1920 they at least pretended to be unbiased. The image of independence had become a valued asset.

6.2.2   The Decline of Partisan Content

We now turn to the content and rhetoric of the news to determine whether the rise in declared independence was matched by comparable changes in reporting. Certain words are far more likely to appear in factually vacuous articles than in those that soberly report a fact. For papers on the defensive side of the issue these words include "lie" and its many synonyms.[7] The rhetoric on the offensive side uses the editorializing first person plural. Substantial intrusion of "we" into the text indicates that the newspaper is editorializing in the main body of the news.

Newspaper coverage of the famed Crédit Mobilier scandal of the 1870s, one of our case studies, provides illustrations of both types of bias. According to the Republican (thus on the defensive) *Albany Evening Journal:*

> The *Credit Mobilier* libel is the latest but not probably the last lie which the "truck and dicker" gentry will issue during the campaign. The libel was invented by knaves but it is retailed by fools. (September 16, 1872)
>
> The answer of Vice-President Colfax to the Credit Mobilier slander is manly and dignified. There was no need, however of any reply to this infamous calumny from him or from the others. . . . It is one of the infamies of this campaign that the supporters of Greeley stop at no outrage, however atrocious, at no falsehood, however monstrous, at no stab at character, however, dastardly. (September 26, 1872)

The first instance of the story as reported by the Republican *Philadelphia Evening Bulletin* contains six subheadlines including "Political Slanders," "How Leading Republicans are Vilified," and "The Whole Thing Proven to Be False," and the story began with "The attempt to fasten the charge of bribery . . . has already been shown to be utterly untrue" (September 14, 1872). This heavily rhetorical style of writing was the norm, not the exception, during most of the nineteenth century.

At the other end of the political spectrum were the anti-Grant papers, which spun their stories with the editorial "we." "At last *we* have one more utterance on the Crédit Mobilier scandal. . . . Mr. Wilson denies. . . . But

---

7. See appendix B for a list of the synonyms we have found in the 1870s.

. . . *we* know what his word is worth," wrote the *New York Tribune* (September 16, 1872, italics added), a Republican, anti-Grant newspaper. Some of the independents, such as the *Baltimore Sun,* wrote factual stories with little spin. But the *New York Sun,* also an independent, broke the story to the American public using six subheadlines including "The King of Frauds," "Colossal Bribery," "Congressmen Who Have Robbed the People, and Who Now Support the National Robber," and "How Some Men Get Fortunes."

By using a search engine capable of searching across several hundred electronically scanned newspapers, we are able to explore a wide range of newspapers for particular words to see if their use rose or fell over the period.[8] To deflate for the general amount of reporting we divide the number of instances that a word appears by the same for the neutral word "January."[9]

Among the various synonyms for "lie," we have chosen "slander" to use in the search, and at the opposite extreme in rhetoric we have used the word "honest."[10] Figure 6.1 shows the time path of "slander" and "honest" (using a three-year centered moving average) from 1850 to 1950 deflated by the word "January." The use of the word "slander" indicates editorial intervention and the aim of discrediting an opposing view, whereas "honest" is used to build respect.

Allegations of "slander" abounded in the 1850s, the start of the period depicted in figure 6.1, when the word appeared about 1/12 as often as the word "January." By the 1880s, however, the relative usage of "slander" had begun to decline, and by the 1920s "slander" appeared just 1/30 as often as our deflator word. Similarly, the word "honest" declined in usage by about one-half from the late nineteenth century to the 1920s. The highly opinionated style of reporting that was common in the 1870s had become uncommon by the early twentieth century.

General use of charged language also changed during the nineteenth century, as can be seen from a count of the word "honest" (and its variants) in books.[11] But the trend in literature substantially differs from that in the

8. We use Ancestry.com. Although several hundred newspapers are stored at this site, the number in the years we use ranges from about ten in the 1840s to fifty for most of the period after the 1880s. The newspapers, furthermore, are almost all from small towns and only occasionally include a big-city newspaper. The search engine counts a hit if a word is found at least once on a page. Other search engines, such as Proquest, count a hit if a word is found at least once in an article.

9. To deflate for reporting that is political, we have also used the number of all words beginning with "politic." We do not report those time series in figure 6.1 because they reveal similar time trends.

10. We traced all words beginning with "slander" (e.g., slanderous) and all words beginning with "honest."

11. We have used "The Making of America" collection, http://www.hti.umich.edu/m/moagrp/ at the University of Michigan and http://cdl.library.cornell.edu/moa/ at Cornell University, which is smaller, and restricted the search to "books" to exclude some literature, such as magazines and pamphlets, which would be similar in content to newspapers. We date the literature by the publication year and deflate by the neutral word "January."

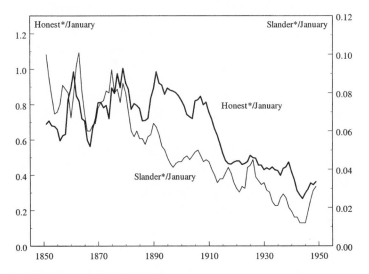

Fig. 6.1   Indicators of biased reporting

Source: Ancestry.com scanned newspapers using optical character recognition software. See introduction to this volume for more information on Ancestry.com and its newspapers.

Notes: "January" and all words beginning with "slander" and "honest" were searched. A hit occurs when at least one word is found on a newspaper page (this search routine is done by page, not by article). The newspapers covered vary by year, and each year contains anywhere from ten to fifty newspapers. Most of the newspapers are from small cities and towns.

political press. The use of "honest," relative to other neutral words such as "January," began high in the 1830s. It declined almost continuously to 1885 but then remained fairly constant until the end of the series around 1905. In the political press, on the other hand, the usage of the word "honest," relative to more neutral words, was uneven to 1890, after which it plummeted. Thus, general usage of charged and emotional words did change in the nineteenth century, but the change preceded that in the political press by about a half century. The change in the language used by political newspapers is consistent with the notion that the press became less biased and more independent late in the nineteenth century.

As interesting and suggestive as are these facts, they report broad trends with many possible interpretations. To assess the degree to which the bias and information content of the news media changed, we turn to case studies of the Crédit Mobilier and Teapot Dome affairs.

6.2.3   Case Studies of Political Scandal Reporting

In the pantheon of national political scandals in the United States a few stand out as momentous. Of these, we have chosen two that are separated by exactly fifty years and span the period of greatest expansion in national daily newspaper circulation per capita and in the number of daily newspa-

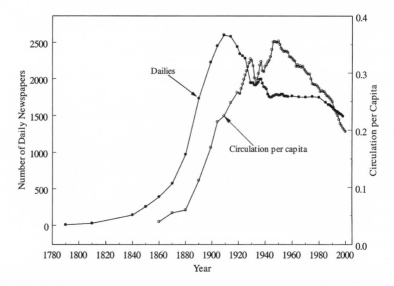

Fig. 6.2   Daily newspapers and circulation per capita: 1790 to 1998

Sources: Dailies, 1790–1925: Dill (1928), table V, p. 28; 1929–1998: Editor and Publisher (various years).

Notes: Daily circulation for 1850 to 1921 is imputed by converting newspaper subscriptions into circulation using the ratio of the two for 1921. That for 1921 to 1928 is interpolated. U.S. population is imputed from decennial censuses. These data are for the entire United States and are, therefore, diVerent from those in table 6.1, which are for large U.S. cities.

pers (see figure 6.2). The first of these scandals has become known as Crédit Mobilier and was exposed to the public in September 1872. The second has been called the Teapot Dome affair and was initially revealed in April 1922.

To understand how corruption scandals were reported by different types of newspapers and how their reporting changed over time, we have chosen nineteen daily newspapers. Of these, seventeen existed during the Crédit Mobilier scandal and seventeen existed during the Teapot Dome affair. The newspapers selected include most of the major presses in America, but we have also made an effort to obtain papers from cities that were small, that were distant from the center of national political activity, and that had only one daily paper (see appendix B, table 6B.3).

We have obtained every article covering the events during two critical periods in their history and have coded them to establish (a) whether particular "facts" were reported; (b) the size, in column inches, of the stories printed; (c) the degree of "spin"; and (d) the timeliness of reporting the facts. Spin is measured in two ways. The first counts the number of times the word "lie" and its various synonyms appeared in the first two paragraphs of each article (scaled by the number of articles). The second counts the number of times the first person plural (in any form; as in "we believe") was used in the first two paragraphs (also scaled by the number of articles). The first form of spin is anticipated to have been used more by the papers on the defensive, whereas the second form of spin would be expected to be used by those on the offensive. In both cases, spin is an editorial ploy and departs from factual reporting.

Because both of the scandals lasted for years—the Teapot Dome affair was not finalized until 1928—we have chosen two relatively brief periods for each scandal. The first period is several weeks around the breaking news of the story. The second is an equally brief period when an important detail or decision was announced. We call this the resolution period.

Both the Crédit Mobilier and Teapot Dome scandals were complex events and, to this day, have unresolved or undisclosed aspects. We have compiled various indisputable facts concerning the cases and study how these facts were reported by the various presses.

Crédit Mobilier

Crédit Mobilier was an independent corporate entity, set up as the construction arm of the Union Pacific Railroad, part of the great transcontinental railroad. Since stock in the Union Pacific Railroad was widely held, skimming off contracts by the Union Pacific would not greatly benefit particular individuals. But Crédit Mobilier was neither widely held nor traded. The Crédit Mobilier scandal concerned a congressman, Oakes Ames, whose financial stake in Crédit Mobilier led him to use stock of that company to bribe (or reward) other government officials.

The Crédit Mobilier scandal was broken by the *New York Sun* on September 4, 1872, with the publication of a letter, dated January 28, 1868, purportedly written by Congressman Oakes Ames of Massachusetts to one Colonel Henry McComb. The letter contained a list of names, including the current vice president, Schuyler Colfax, who had been a congressman in 1868, ten representatives, and four senators, to whom Ames had sold stock in Crédit Mobilier, placing the Crédit Mobilier stock "where it will produce the most good."[12] Among the list was James Blaine (Congress, R-ME), current speaker of the house; James Garfield (Congress, R-OH), later to become president; George Boutwell (Congress, R-MA), current secretary of the treasury; Henry Wilson (Senate, R-MA), the current vice-presidential candidate on the Grant ticket; and the chairs of most of the important House committees, including Ways and Means. Although the historical record established that Ames actually "sold" the stock, rather than gave it, to at least some of the individuals mentioned, the share price was approximately equal to the dividends paid out in just one year. Of great

---

12. The quotation is from the letter, as reported in the *New York Sun* and many other newspapers.

importance is that all but one was a Republican and a supporter of President Grant.

Oakes Ames and his brother had been major investors in the Union Pacific and were part of a group that held stock in Crédit Mobilier. Because the Union Pacific had received large grants and loans from the federal government and in 1868 appeared to need more, the letter from Ames to McComb in January 1868 suggested that Ames was shoring up further support or was rewarding his friends for past deeds.

McComb had revealed the letter to the *Sun* after a protracted legal and financial battle with Ames over the disposition of some Union Pacific stock. The timing of the revelation was of immense national importance since the 1872 presidential campaign between incumbent Grant and his challenger Horace Greeley had just begun to heat up. Greeley, moreover, was the founder of both the *New Yorker* and the *New York Tribune,* which he had once edited.

Sometime after the revelation of the letter, the House and Senate appointed committees to investigate the charges. That in the House was chaired by Representative Luke Poland (R-VT); that in the Senate was chaired by Senator Justin Morrill (R-VT). The Senate also appointed a committee, chaired by Senator Henry Wilson (also implicated in the Crédit Mobilier affair), to investigate the financial activities of the Union Pacific and Crédit Mobilier. In February 1873 the Poland and Morrill committees reported. The Poland Committee recommended that two representatives (Ames and Brooks, the only Democrat involved) be censured and expelled. The House censured but did not expel both, and the Senate voted to expel Paterson.

We have compiled a group of nine "facts" for the breaking news period of September 4–30, 1872 (see appendix B, table 6B.1). The first fact is the letter from Ames to McComb. The remaining eight facts are denials from the various officials named in the letter. The resolution period, from February 14 to 28, 1873, contains eleven "facts" concerning the congressional committee hearings and final reports.

Teapot Dome

The scandal that became known as "Teapot Dome" was innocuously broken by the *Wall Street News* (now the *Wall Street Journal*), which reported on April 7, 1922, that the U.S. government had leased lands near a place called Teapot Dome in Wyoming, one of the naval oil reserves, to Harry F. Sinclair of Mammoth Oil. Another naval reserve, in Elk Hills, CA, was also leased for oil exploration. The odd aspect of the leases was that naval oil reserves were under the jurisdiction of the navy secretary, Edwin Denby, yet the interior secretary, Albert Fall, approved the leases (both were Harding appointees). A week later the Senate called for hearings on the Sinclair lease.

Evidence suggesting an actual scandal erupted in late January 1924 when Edward Doheny, the head of the oil company that had received the Elk Hills lease, revealed that he had given Albert Fall an unsecured loan of $100,000 just prior to the oil deal. Harry Sinclair, the head of Mammoth Oil, also revealed, through his lawyer, that he had given Fall a loan just after the Teapot Dome lease. The resolution of the Teapot Dome affair took until 1928 when Albert Fall was found guilty of accepting a bribe. Fall had already resigned from office in March 1923, and Edwin Denby, the secretary of the navy, was forced to leave his position in March 1924.

We have compiled a list of eight facts for the breaking news period, April 7–30, 1922. These facts mainly concern the existence of the oil lease, its terms, the justification by the navy and interior secretaries for the lease, and Senate action on oil leases. The resolution period, January 21–28, 1924, contains nine facts concerning the revelation about the loans from Doheny and Sinclair to Albert Fall. See appendix B, table 6B.2 for a list of the facts for both periods.

Coverage of Crédit Mobilier by the Press

For the three-week "breaking news" period of Crédit Mobilier we have identified 224 articles in the seventeen newspapers, and in the two-week "resolution" phase we have found 543 articles among the same group of newspapers.[13] We have coded the articles with respect to the four characteristics: (a) size, (b) facts, (c) spin, and (d) timeliness (see appendix B on the coding). The results are summarized by affiliation of the newspaper in figure 6.3. Of the seventeen papers, eight were aligned with President Grant and the Republican Party, five either were aligned with the Democrats or were anti-Grant Republican papers, and four were listed as independent.[14]

In the breaking news period of the scandal the relative size of articles was considerably smaller in the pro-Grant (or Republican but not anti-Grant) papers than in the others and the number of facts was somewhat smaller (see figure 6.3, panel A, 1872).[15] The spin was extremely different between the two types of papers. The pro-Grant papers made use of the word "lie" and its synonyms with far greater frequency in the breaking news period,

13. These articles were found by our extraordinary research assistants, especially Magali Fassiotto, who scanned the microfilm. Only the *New York Times* and the *Wall Street News* could be used electronically with optical character recognition software.

14. Affiliations are from newspaper directories (see appendix A) and newspaper histories. The two Republican, anti-Grant newspapers are the *New York Tribune* and the *Chicago Tribune.*

15. The mean number of column inches devoted to the story (expressed as a fraction of the total size of the newspaper and multiplied by 10) was .110 for Republican papers, .425 for Democratic and anti-Grant papers, and .992 for independent papers. The mean percentage of key facts reported was .542 for Republican papers, .689 for Democratic and anti-Grant papers, and .667 for independent papers. The Democratic papers of the two lower South cities, Galveston and New Orleans, were exceptions to this pattern as they provided relatively less coverage of the scandal.

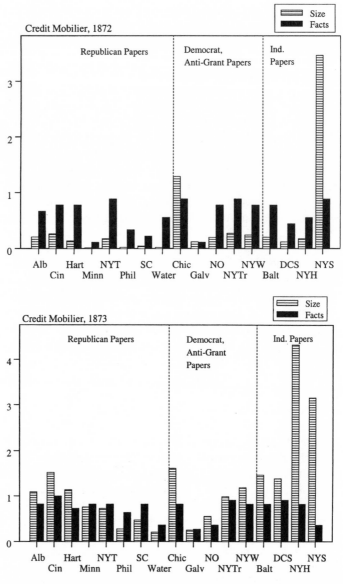

Fig. 6.3   Reporting of Crédit Mobilier: Size, facts, timeliness, and spin: *A,* Crédit Mobilier, 1872 and 1873: Size and facts; *B,* Crédit Mobilier, 1872 and 1873: Spin; *C,* Crédit Mobilier, 1872: Timeliness

B

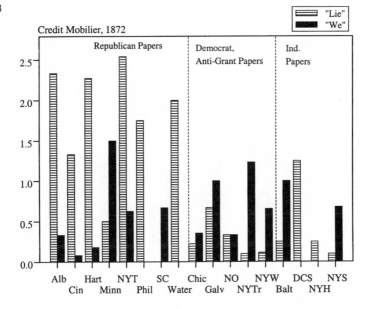

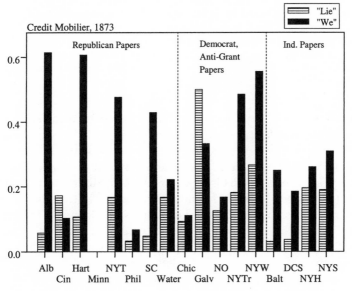

Fig. 6.3 (cont.)

C

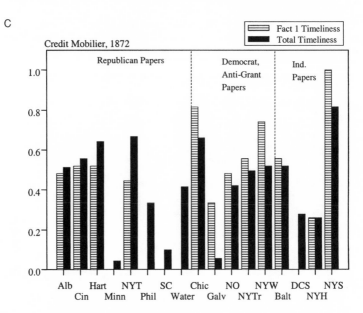

Fig. 6.3   (cont.) Reporting of Crédit Mobilier: Size, facts, timeliness, and spin: *A*, Crédit Mobilier, 1872 and 1873: Size and facts; *B*, Crédit Mobilier, 1872 and 1873: Spin; *C*, Crédit Mobilier, 1872: Timeliness

Sources and notes: See figure 6.4 and appendix B.

Note to panel C: There are almost no differences in "timeliness" among the newspapers in the sample in total and for the most important facts during the "resolution" period of February 1873.

whereas the Democratic and anti-Grant papers used the editorial "we" with greater regularity (see figure 6.3, panel B, 1872).[16]

When the letter from Ames to McComb was revealed by the *New York Sun* on September 4, 1872, it was viewed by many as mere political chicanery on the part of the Greeley campaign. For the entire period considered (September 4–30, 1872), fully four papers, all Republican, never reported the existence of the letter but simply alluded to it. The remaining four Republican papers were about two weeks late in reporting (see figure 6.3, panel C, 1872). In contrast, the Democratic and nonaligned papers reported the *Sun*'s publication of the letter more rapidly. The rest of the facts for the breaking news period were reported with about equal speed by all types of presses, but with different spin, since they were denials by various officials. Thus, the timeliness of the first fact differed greatly between the

16. The average frequency with which "lie" occurred (expressed as number of occurrences in the first two paragraphs per article) was 1.591 for Republican papers, 0.288 for Democratic and anti-Grant papers, and 0.463 for independent papers. The frequency of "we" was 0.424 for Republican papers, 0.715 for Democratic and anti-Grant papers, and 0.419 for independent papers.

two groups of papers even though the fraction of breaking news facts reported was about equal by political affiliation.

Differences in factual coverage among the various types of papers during the resolution phase of the story were not as great as in the breaking news period. The pro-Grant papers reported the facts with the same frequency as did the other papers. But other differences remained. The Republican papers gave considerably less room to the complete story and printed less of the Congressional testimony (figure 6.3, panel A, 1873).[17] The spin of the papers switched. In the resolution phase the pro-Grant papers used the editorial "we," whereas the others proclaimed more "lies" (figure 6.3, panel B, 1873).

In sum, newspapers in the 1870s had just begun their transition from being highly politicized organs, as they were in the antebellum era, to being more independent of political parties. When the Crédit Mobilier scandal broke, Americans in some parts of the country did not hear about it for weeks, and even when they were told the news, the facts were distorted for many. Distortions came about for several reasons; among them is that many papers were geographically removed from the nation's political and commercial centers and facts were still expensive to gather. The telegraph and wire services had cheapened the cost of gathering news, yet it was still an expensive proposition. Most of the distortion, however, came about because of the political alignment of the press.

Coverage of Teapot Dome by the Press

For the two-week breaking news period of Teapot Dome we have identified 104 articles in the seventeen newspapers, and in the week-long resolution phase we found 381 articles among the same list of newspapers (see appendix B, table 6B.2). We have coded these articles, as we did the others, with respect to (a) size, (b) facts, (c) spin, and (d) timeliness. The results are summarized by affiliation of the newspaper in figure 6.4. In the 1920s there were eight Republican newspapers, five Democratic papers, and four independent ones (including the one financial press—the *Wall Street News,* which broke the story).

By the 1920s American newspaper writing had come to look very much like the fact-based reporting of major newspapers we read today. As opposed to those in the 1870s, stories in the 1920s were factually reported when they were printed. Spin was not evident. In fact, we could not code spin by newspaper for the 1920s since we found practically no use of the word "lie" and of the editorializing "we." We did, however, find other ways in which reporting differed by type of newspaper.

---

17. The average space devoted to the scandal (expressed as a fraction of the total size of the newspaper multiplied by 10) was 0.688 for Republican papers, 0.919 for Democratic and anti-Grant papers, and 2.584 for independent papers.

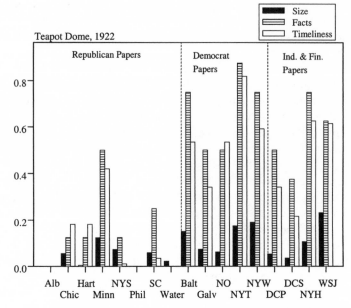

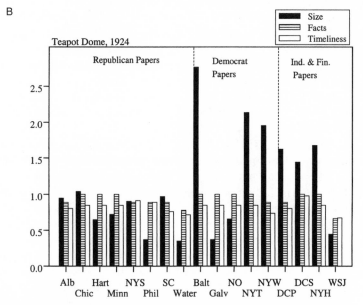

Fig. 6.4   Reporting of Teapot Dome: Size, facts, and timeliness: *A,* "Breaking news" period; *B,* Resolution period

Sources and methods: See appendix B.

Notes: Newspaper abbreviations are as follows:

   Alb   = *Albany Evening Journal*
   Balt   = *Baltimore Sun*

Fig. 6.4   (cont.)

Chic = *Chicago Daily Tribune*
Cin   = *Cincinnati Daily Gazette* (not in 1920s)
DCS = DC *Evening Star*
DCP = DC *Washington Post* (only in 1920s)
Galv = *Galveston Daily News*
Hart = *Hartford Courant*
Minn = *Minneapolis Tribune*
NO   = *New Orleans* (*Times-*) *Picayune*
NYH = *New York Herald*
NYS = *New York Sun*
NYT = *New York Times*
NYTr = *New York Tribune* (not in 1920s)
NYW = *New York World*
Phil   = *Philadelphia* (*Evening*) *Bulletin*
SC   = *Sioux City* (*Daily*) *Journal*
WSJ = *Wall Street News* (later the *Wall Street Journal;* only in 1920s)
Water = *Waterbury Daily American*

Newspapers are divided into groups by their stated political affiliations (in the Ayer directories). Supplementary information on the Republican Anti-Grant papers (Chic, NYTr) has also been used. The sole financial newspaper (the *Wall Street News*) is included with the latter papers in the 1920s because it broke the Teapot Dome story and would probably have been considered an apolitical newspaper at the time.

"Size" is the column length of the articles divided by the total size of the newspaper times 10. Thus, size is "relative size," adjusted for the fact that some newspapers were larger than others. Total size is length times width times the number of pages.

"Facts" is the fraction of the facts reported (see appendix B for the important facts) during the demarcated periods.

"Spin" is measured in two ways. In both cases a count of particular words is done for the first two paragraphs of all articles during the periods. In the first, the word "lie" and its various synonyms are counted. In the second, the words "we" and "us" are counted. The use of "lie" is generally used to spin the fact in the opposite direction. The use of "we" and "us" is generally used to put greater emphasis (that is, editorialize) on the fact. The total counts are scaled by the number of articles in the period for each newspaper.

"Timeliness" is measured by scoring the "facts," dividing by the maximum score, and then subtracting from 1. If a fact is reported on the first day that it could have been reported, the newspaper gets a 0 score and thus a 1 in "timeliness." If the fact is reported a day late, it gets a score of 1, if two days late, it gets a 2, and so on. The maximum days late is (1 + the full length of the period considered). The total score received by the newspaper is then divided by the maximum possible score and subtracted from 1. A zero means that the newspaper never reported the fact during the period considered.

During the breaking news period of the Teapot Dome scandal in 1922, all but one of the non-Republican newspapers printed more than one-half of the facts (the *DC Star* is the lone exception; see figure 6.4, panel A). Four of these papers printed three-quarters or more of the facts. Not only did these papers print the stories, but they also did so in a relatively timely fashion and devoted considerable space to the stories. By contrast, the Republican newspapers failed to print many of the stories. Albany, Philadelphia, and Waterbury, for example, printed no stories on the subject of oil leases during the more than two-week period after the *Wall Street News* published the story on the Teapot Dome lease. Three Republican papers published only one of the eight facts. By the 1920s these stories were available to all papers and could have been reported in a timely fashion. The absence of publication of the stories represents a degree of oversight that can fairly be called suppression of the news.

During the resolution phase in 1924 (see figure 6.4, panel B), the papers were less distinguishable from each other with one exception, which mirrors our findings in the Crédit Mobilier case. The non-Republican papers, especially some aligned with the Democratic party, gave considerably more (relative) space to the stories they printed.

The lesson from these case studies is that although reporting style greatly changed from the 1870s to the 1920s, the aligned papers in the 1920s still suppressed stories and gave far less room to the stories they had to print that damaged their candidates. Because both of our scandals involved Republican administrations, we do not know from this investigation whether the Democrat newspapers did the same, but we would hazard a guess that they did. The aligned press was often a biased and noninformative press. But the aligned press had become a far smaller fraction of all dailies and an even smaller fraction of circulation. Furthermore, even in cities that had aligned dailies, the existence of competition with the independent dailies would have fostered the informative press.

6.3   Understanding the Rise of the Independent Press

In documenting the rise of the informative press, we found both a reduction in overt bias and a substantial increase in the information content of newspapers. We now seek to explain the transformation, building on the growing literature that explores the economic forces that act to determine the degree of bias and the amount of information in news articles.

The information content of the news will reflect a trade-off between the demands of customers who seek knowledge and entertainment, and the incentives of suppliers who seek to earn profit and advance their ideological views. A growing theory literature, including Mullainathan and Shleifer (forthcoming), Gentzkow and Shapiro (2004), and Besley and Prat (2004), explores how these forces can lead firms to report biased news in equilibrium.

In this section, we follow Besley and Prat (2004) in modeling suppliers' incentives as a trade-off between (a) profits from consumers who are willing to pay for informative news and (b) direct payoffs from printing information favorable to one political side or the other. Although such direct payoffs to suppliers are not the only possible source of bias, they seem most consistent with historical evidence on the incentives faced by nineteenth- and early twentieth-century newspapers.[18]

18. A model that locates the source of bias on the supply side seems most consistent with the central empirical fact we document below: that the drop in bias in the late nineteenth and early twentieth centuries coincided with falling costs and increasing advertising revenue. Intuitively, if suppliers trade off direct gains from skewing news against market profits, any

The most obvious source of such direct payoffs from the political slant of information would be the individual political preferences of newspaper owners themselves. We previously cited Thurlow Weed's *Albany Evening Journal* and Horace Greely's *New York Tribune* as nineteenth-century examples of newspapers run by politically interested parties. Other examples include Colonel McCormick of the *Chicago Tribune* and Harrison Gray Otis and his descendants at the *Los Angeles Times* (prior to 1960), who had strong right-wing views and ensured that their papers supported those positions.[19]

An additional source of payoffs to firms would be outside influence from politicians or parties. This could take the form of direct bribes or kickbacks, as in the model of Besley and Prat (2004). Perhaps the most famous example of this kind of incentive is Secretary of State Thomas Jefferson's use of State Department funds to pay Philip Freneau to run the radically partisan pro-Jefferson, anti-Federalist *National Gazette*. Outside influence could also come from interest groups that provide biased information at low cost, or politicians who are able to use the threat of curtailing reporters' access to information to thwart unfavorable stories.

To develop the model formally, we assume that a newspaper first decides a level of investment that determines the probability, q, that the paper will acquire a story. The investment includes, for example, the number of reporters, reporter quality, and investment in infrastructure. The investment cost is denoted $K(q)$, where $K(0) = 0$, $K(1) = \infty$, $K' > 0$, $K'' > 0$. We assume that stories cannot be fabricated and that stories do not have spin. Instead, the primary ideological question that the newspaper faces is whether or not to *suppress* a story hostile to its viewpoint. The newspaper also determines how much to spend to uncover new stories.

A story has ideological content, ω, where $\omega \in \{-\infty, \infty\}$. The ideological content reflects the extent to which the story either helps or hurts politicians of different political hues. Conditional on having observed ω, the paper can either print the story $x = \omega$ or suppress it. Suppressing the story could be interpreted to mean not referring to the event at all or engaging in political editorializing that conveys no real information.

To capture the political bias of the newspaper, we assume that when the paper prints a story with ideological value ω the paper receives payoff $r\omega$. As just mentioned, this could reflect the political preferences of owners or

---

changes that increase the magnitude of market returns should reduce the degree of skewing. Models that locate the source of bias on the demand side do not necessarily imply such a link.

19. It is interesting to note that whereas through the early twentieth century the usual complaint was that newspapers were biased toward the right, allegations of bias today emphasize the liberal views of reporters who supposedly slant their stories to the left. One explanation for this switch, if indeed it occurred, could be an increase in reporters' incomes. If the chance to proselytize is a luxury good, then we should increasingly see reporters willing to accept lower wages for the chance to push their own bias, as reporters become generally wealthier.

outside influence from politically interested parties.[20] We assume, for simplicity, $r > 0$.

We assume that there are P consumers who always buy the paper, and an additional C consumers who buy the paper if it contains a new story. The newspaper receives advertising revenue a per reader. The marginal cost of printing a newspaper is c. Firm profits are thus $(C + P)(a - c) + r\omega - K(q)$ if they print an informative story with content ω and $P(a - c) - K(q)$ otherwise. We assume for simplicity that $a > c$. The model immediately yields the following proposition.

PROPOSITION 1: *There exists an ideological value* ω^* *at which the newspaper is indifferent between publishing or not publishing the story. For values of* ω *greater than* ω^*, *the newspaper strictly prefers publishing the story; for values of* ω *less than* ω^*, *the firm strictly prefers suppressing the story. The value of* ω^* *equals* $-C(a - c)/r$ *and therefore rises with c and r, and falls with a and C.*

PROOF: The gains from including the story in the newspaper equal $C(a - c) + r\omega$, and therefore when $\omega = -C(a - c)/r$ the firm is indifferent between publishing or not publishing a story. Since $C(a - c) + r\omega$ is monotonically increasing in ω, the firm strictly prefers publishing when $\omega > -C(a - c)/r$, and strictly prefers not publishing when $\omega < -C(a - c)/r$. The comparative statics follow from differentiating $-C(a - c)/r$.

The value of ω^* denotes the degree of bias that has been introduced into the newspaper because of its desire to publish stories that favor a particular political side. As ω^* rises, more stories are suppressed and the degree of bias increases. The comparative statics therefore suggest that the degree of bias is falling with net revenues per consumer $(a - c)$, falling with C (the marginal consumers that will be produced by a more informative paper), and rising with r (the degree of supply-side bias).

Although these comparative static results are not surprising, they illustrate a fundamental trade-off in newspaper bias. The possible benefits from selling more papers are weighed against the private gains from suppressing politically charged information. In this model, as the size of the market increases (causing C to rise) or as the gap between advertising revenues and costs rises, leading $(a - c)$ to rise, newspapers will become less biased. The variable C can also be interpreted to reflect competition among papers.

---

20. An important assumption built into this specification is that the direct political returns to suppressing or printing a story do not depend on the number of readers (i.e., C and P). This assumption seems an accurate description of some situations (i.e., payoffs from a politician who has a fixed value of winning an election), while for other situations (i.e., an editor who values the political views of each swayed reader) it is clearly a simplification. In the latter case, our results would require that political payoffs increase more slowly in C and P than market returns.

Suppose, for example, that most consumers prefer to read *some* newspaper regardless of its information content but would prefer an informative one over a noninformative one. Then a monopoly firm will sell to all readers regardless of information content, whereas a duopoly firm will strictly increase demand by providing information.[21]

We now turn to the equilibrium investment in information—the choice of q. Expected newspaper profits equal $(a - c)\{P + Cq[1 - F(\omega^*)]\} + qr\int_{\omega^*}^{\infty}\omega f(\omega)d\omega - K(q)$. Thus, the first-order condition is $K'(q) = [1 - F(\omega^*)]C(a - c) + r\int_{\omega^*}^{\infty}\omega f(\omega)d\omega$.

PROPOSITION 2: *Investment in information by the newspaper rises with C and a and falls with c and r.*

PROOF OF PROPOSITION 2: Since $K''(q) > 0$, the sign of the effect of any variable x on q will be the same as the sign of the effect of that variable on $\{1 - F[-C(a-c)/r]\}C(a-c) + r\int_{-C(a-c)/r}^{\infty}\omega f(\omega)d\omega$. Differentiation then reveals that q is rising with C and a, and falling with c and r.

Proposition 2 echoes proposition 1 and shows that as markets expand, we should observe more informative, as well as less biased, presses. Decreases in costs, c, will also increase the incentive to acquire information since the net returns from each reader are higher. If C rises with the level of competition, then information acquisition will also rise with competition. Lower levels of supply-side bias will also increase the tendency to acquire information. Because bias involves the suppression of information, a higher level of bias reduces the value of getting new information in the first place.

The framework has suggested that we look at (a) production costs, (b) market scale, (c) market competition, and (d) advertising revenues as forces that should determine the amount of information and bias in newspapers. We now turn to evidence on the news media in the nineteenth century to see which of these forces can help us to understand the rise of the informative press.

6.4   Evidence on the Causes of the Rise of the Informative Press

We turn now to the factors that the model predicts should impact the degree of bias and the amount of information in the press, such as production costs, market size, and advertising revenues. We will highlight the remark-

---

21. Besley and Prat (2004) show formally that in a model where firms receive payoffs from politicians to suppress harmful information, increased competition should reduce the degree of bias. In their model, if N firms are all suppressing information in equilibrium, a single deviator who prints the information gets the same payoff as a monopolist. The bribe that must be paid to each firm is thus independent of N, and the total bribe is increasing in N. In more competitive markets, politicians find it more difficult to suppress information.

able changes that occurred in each of these variables across the nineteenth and early twentieth centuries, although we acknowledge that these variables are interrelated and that we are treating each as a separate factor.

6.4.1   Production Costs

Perhaps the most important change in the production costs of newspapers in the nineteenth century was the reduction in the price of newsprint. The real price of newsprint fell by one-fifth from 1870, when the cost was $25 per pound, to 1910, when it was $5 (see figure 6.5). Up through the mid-nineteenth century virtually all newspapers were printed on relatively expensive newsprint made from cotton or linen rags. Although the price of rag paper began to decline in the 1830s with the invention of the Fourdrinier process, the price plummeted with the introduction, in 1867, of the process for making paper from wood pulp (Emery and Emery 1992,

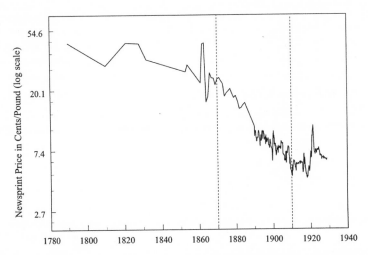

Fig. 6.5   Newsprint prices, 1790 to 1930 (cents/pound, deflated by the WPI 1967 = 100, log scale)

Sources: 1790 to 1890: Lee (1937), pp. 742–43; 1890 to 1929: NBER Historical Macro Database series m04093a,b, quarterly data on newsprint prices (http://www.nber.org/databases/macrohistory/contents/). Wholesale Price Deflator: 1790 to 1889, U.S. Bureau of the Census (1975), series E-52 (Warren and Person); 1890 to 1929, NBER Historical Macro Database, quarterly WPI. On an annualized basis, the NBER series from 1890 to 1915 is the same as U.S. Bureau of the Census (1975), series E-40. That for 1913 to 1929 is approximately series E-23 (BLS).

Notes: The NBER data are monthly, whereas the Lee data are at various intervals until 1860, when they are annual. The Lee and NBER series are linked at 1890. The overlap numbers are nearly identical. The Lee data for 1860 to 1890 are those paid by the *New York Tribune.* Before 1860, he pieced them together from several sources. The two series of newsprint data from the NBER Macro History Database are linked at 1914. The deflators are linked at 1890 by multiplying by 0.6854 (= 56.2/82) and again at 1913. The final deflator is constructed for 1967 = 100.

p. 188). With the exception of a sharp spike during the Civil War, prices declined rapidly and continuously from then to the 1910s.

Newsprint was the single largest component of costs. In the first year after the *New York Times* was founded in 1851, newsprint accounted for fully half of its operating costs (Mott 1962). Furthermore, the fraction of newsprint in *marginal* cost was considerably larger (the only other per-copy costs were ink and the pressmen's labor). A rough calculation suggests that the cost of the newsprint in a single four-page issue of the 1851 *New York Times* was approximately 1 cent, which was the same as the paper's cover price (the price was increased to 2 cents in 1852).

Changes in the price of newsprint, and the accompanying increase in circulation, made it profitable to invent and invest in high-speed printing technologies. These new technologies, similar to those in textiles a century before, widened bottlenecks. Once the price of newsprint declined (similarly for yarn), it was profitable to increase the speed of printing (weaving). And once printing speeds were faster, it paid to invest in producing even cheaper paper.

The most important innovations in nineteenth-century printing technology include steam-driven presses and presses using a cylindrical rather than a flat-bed printing surface. Both innovations were introduced in the mid-1800s and diffused rapidly after the Civil War. Hoe's famed "lightning press," the first of the cylindrical presses, was unveiled in the mid-1840s. The Linotype typesetting machine, which allowed type to be set automatically from a keyboard, was first used in 1886 and was still in use as late as the 1950s. Other innovations of the period include stereotyped plates that could be easily reproduced for simultaneous printing on multiple presses, automatic folders, and the half-toning process for printing photographs (see, e.g., Emery and Emery 1992, chap. 9, and Mott 1962, chap. 30). The typewriter, invented in the 1860s by C. L. Sholes, once an editor of the Milwaukee *Sentinel,* diffused rapidly in the editorial and reporting offices during the 1880s when its price fell (Current 1954).

As the throughput of printing machines increased, average fixed costs of operation plummeted. Although we have not located a time series on average fixed costs, we can approximate the change in costs by assuming that the lifetime of capital and its depreciation rate did not differ by type of machine.

In 1850 a six-cylinder type-revolving press could print 12,000 impressions an hour, and it cost (in current dollars) between $20,000 and $25,000. By the 1890s almost all printers owned "web" presses, which used a continuous roll of newsprint, printed on both sides of the page simultaneously, and automatically folded the paper. These presses were capable of doing from 24,000 to 48,000 twelve-page papers in an hour and cost from $40,000 to $80,000 (in current dollars). Expressing the capital cost in constant dollars and assuming no difference in the depreciation rate and lifetime by type of machine, average (per-page) fixed costs in 1890 were only 1/15 of what they were in 1870 (an average decline of about 7 percent annually).[22]

The maintenance cost of web presses was probably greater than that of earlier machines. But the newer presses automatically folded the paper, saving on labor costs, and were probably run for more days per year and more hours per day. We do not know the magnitude of these refinements, but it is unlikely that the enormous decrease in our estimate of average fixed costs would be substantially altered.[23] Printing technology, moreover, did not stand still. In 1895 Hoe introduced the "octuple press," which did 48,000 sixteen-page papers per hour, and in ten years the "double octuple" commenced operation, producing 144,000 sixteen-page papers per hour.

Of course, the best evidence that the expansion of newspapers was driven by cost-side changes is the actual sales price of newspapers. Although there is scant evidence on newspaper prices for the antebellum period, what does exist suggests a yearly subscription rate of from $87 to $110 (in 1982–84 dollars).[24] Price, circulation, and size-of-newspaper data are available in our data beginning with 1880 (see table 6.1, panel D). In 1880 the average annual (unweighted) subscription price was $57.41 (in 1982–84 dollars), and the price fell to $35.74 in 1920, although there was little change from 1880 to 1910. The price data weighted by circulation display a more extreme and continuous trend downward. Whereas the 1880 annual subscription price (in 1982–84 dollars) was $71.76, it was $55.90 in 1890, and $33.33 in 1920. Initially newspapers with the greatest circulations were the most costly, but they became the least expensive by the end of the period. From 1880 to 1920, therefore, newspaper prices for the average reader decreased an average of 1.92 percent annually.

The decrease in price is even steeper when scaled by the physical size of newspapers. Larger newspapers, not surprisingly, cost more. In the 1890–1910 period, during which we can obtain data on the number of pages and the size for each page, the price decline per unit area was an average of 3.37 percent annually (weighted and scaled) while the unscaled but weighted decline was 1.54 percent. Although scaling by size provides a reasonable quality adjustment, it is likely that the decrease we measure is on the high side relative to one that considered the marginal valuation by consumers of

22. The means of the ranges given were used and the CPI deflator was applied (Carter et al. forthcoming). The presses are assumed to run for the same number of days, and maintenance is assumed to be a fixed function of the initial cost. Most of the information on press output and prices is from Mott (1962).

23. Typesetting also decreased in cost with the implementation of Linotype machines. In 1890 Linotype was three times faster than by hand, and typesetters received $4 for a nine-hour day (Emery 1972, p. 338). Information on typesetting machines is too variable to estimate cost savings since the Paige machine cost $12,000 but the Thorne/Simplex machine cost just $2,000 (Mott 1962, p. 500).

24. Subscription rates are from Mott (1962, p. 203).

square inches of newspapers and that the decrease in cost per unit quality is somewhere between the weighted measure and the size-adjusted (and weighted) measure.

A third crucial set of innovations concerns communications. The constraints faced by early nineteenth-century newspapers in their quest to obtain timely information on events in the United States or across the Atlantic are hard to overstate. Virtually all news was transmitted by the exchange of local newspapers or letters from correspondents through the mails—carried either overland by horse or by sea. If these were delayed, as they often were by bad weather, newsmen could find themselves in the embarrassed position of the editor of the 1805 *Orleans Gazette* who wrote: "No mail yesterday—we hardly know what we shall fill our paper with that will have the appearance of news" (quoted in Mott 1962). A paper in Boston in these years could expect to wait almost a week for news from New York or Washington, a month for news from New Orleans, and several months for news from England (Mott 1962).

The situation was alleviated somewhat by transportation and communications advances such as the improved pony expresses, steamships, railroads, and even carrier pigeons. The key innovation, however, was the telegraph, first used in 1844. Telegraph wires soon connected all the major cities of the United States. With the completion of the transatlantic cable in 1866 instantaneous news was brought from Europe as well. The telegraph gave rise to the wire news services, among which the most important was the Associated Press, founded in 1848 as a joint venture by major New York City papers to share the cost of obtaining news by telegraph.

Also of great importance to the rise of the informative press was the employment of reporters and various types of editors. Up until the 1840s papers rarely employed reporters on a full-time basis. But by the 1850s, and more so after the Civil War when correspondents were employed to send in reports from the front, newspapers hired reporters in large numbers. By the 1870s, according to Emery and Emery (1992, p. 179), the average big-city daily employed a chief editor, a managing editor in charge of news, a city editor who supervised perhaps two dozen reporters, and a telegraph editor who sorted through wire stories, as well as a host of specialty editors and editorial writers. In the context of the model, the increase in staff should be seen as an increase in the amount of investment in information acquisition, or q.

6.4.2 Market Scale, Circulation, and Advertising Revenues

The substantial decrease in the cost of newspapers, together with an increase in average city populations and income, meant that the period from the end of the Civil War to the beginning of World War I saw enormous growth in the scale of newspaper markets. The number of subscriptions for the entire United States increased twelvefold between 1870 and 1920, from

2.6 to 33 million (see figure 6.2). This represents an increase from about one paper per day for every twenty inhabitants in 1870 to one per day for every four inhabitants in 1920. In America's larger cities the level of circulation per capita was higher, but the increase was about the same. There was about one daily per 5 urban residents in 1870 but one per 1.7 residents in 1920.[25] The average urban adult, therefore, was purchasing more than one newspaper per day, and likely reading even more.

While much of the increase in circulation was directly due to falling costs, lower prices, and higher incomes, some of the increase in scale was due to other demand-related factors. The population of America's cities grew rapidly during this period, and rising levels of education also may have increased demand for daily news.

The increase in total circulation can be separated into increasing circulation per capita and increasing population levels using a simple decomposition.[26] Focusing on our sample of large cities, total circulation rose from 1.37 million dailies in 1870 to 20.5 million in 1920. Circulation of dailies per capita increased from 0.194 in 1870 to 0.419 in 1890 to 0.606 by 1920 (see table 6.1, panel B).[27] Based on the decomposition, total circulation would have risen from 1.37 million to 4.27 million if only circulation per capita had changed and not population, meaning 15 percent of the rise in total circulation can be explained by increased per capita circulation holding population constant at 1870 levels. But if circulation per capita had stayed constant and population had grown, total circulation would have risen from 1.37 to 6.593 million. Thus, 27 percent of the share of the change in total circulation can be explained by the increase in population between 1870 and 1920. The remaining share of the increase—fully 58 percent—is due to the fact that both per capita circulation and population levels increased in tandem. Soaring circulation levels are largely explained by these concurrent effects.

The rise in readership was accompanied, not surprisingly, by a substantial increase in advertising revenue. Newspaper income became less dependent on sales to consumers and more dependent on advertising. Although a time series on advertising revenue does not exist, we have information on advertising rates for urban dailies in 1880. It is clear from the cross-section data that newspaper circulation was a primary determinant of advertising revenues. An increase in circulation by 10,000 papers

25. See table 6.1, panel B "circulation per capita," inverted to be expressed here as one paper per x residents.

26. Δ Total Circulation = Δ Per Capita Circulation $\cdot$ Initial Population + Δ Population $\cdot$ Initial Per Capita Circulation + Δ Per Capita Circulation $\cdot$ Δ Population

27. These figures, and all of table 6.1, apply to daily newspapers in the 100 largest U.S. cities in all years from 1870 to 1920 (see appendix A). By "political" newspapers we mean all daily papers except those that had special coverage, such as financial and theater.

was associated with a 28 percent increase in the advertising rate.[28] Thus, it is reasonable to think that advertising revenue continued to rise as total circulation soared. Advertising revenues, according to one source, accounted for 50 percent of newspaper income in 1880, rising to 64 percent in 1910 (Emery and Emery 1988). This increase does not correspond exactly to the parameter a in the model, which represents advertising revenues per reader, but it does confirm the view that attracting a large audience was the key to financial success for late nineteenth-century newspapers.

6.4.3   Market Competition

The rise in market size was accompanied by an enormous increase in the number of newspapers, as well as the number within each urban market. The magnitude of the national transformation is illustrated by figure 6.2, which shows the total number of daily papers printed in the United States. The number climbed steadily through the middle years of the nineteenth century and then exploded after 1870, from 500 to a peak of more than 2,500 around 1910.

Our data on urban dailies include the top 100 cities by population in each of the census years 1870 to 1920 for a total of 152 cities (see table 6.1, panel A for the number of cities in each year). In 1870 our sample contains 140 cities, and of these 25.7 percent (or 36) had no daily newspaper, 12.9 percent (or 18) had one daily paper, 30.7 percent (or 43) had two, and 30.7 percent (or 43) had three or more (table 6.1, panel A). In 1920, of the 150 cities included in the sample, just 3.3 percent (or 5) were left with no daily newspapers, and 10.0 percent (or 15) had just one paper, while 83 had three or more. Competition among newspapers of any political stripes had clearly increased. But perhaps more important, there were more competing newspapers among the parties and the independents.

The rise in competition is important for several reasons. Competition appears to have had the effect of inducing newspapers to provide more information relative to spin. Even when the behavior of newspapers did not change, more newspapers meant a greater supply of information for the

---

28. The regression is (with absolute values of t-statistics in parentheses; $R^2 = 0.813$) as follows:

$$\text{AdRate} = 4.039 + 4.55 \text{ Circulation} \cdot 10^{-3} + 0.205 \text{ City population} \cdot 10^{-3} - 0.839 \text{ Evening}$$
$$\quad\quad (2.82) \quad (17.6) \quad\quad\quad\quad\quad (14.1) \quad\quad\quad\quad\quad\quad\quad (0.56)$$
$$+ 2.066 \text{ Morning}$$
$$\quad (1.39)$$

where AdRate is dollars per ten lines of advertising, and evening and morning indicate the time of publication (the omitted category is another time of the day). The regression is run over 325 political (non–foreign language) dailies that were aligned with a major political party or were independent. See N. W. Ayer and Son (various years) and appendix A.

population. As long as one major newspaper in a city exposed corruption, the story would get out.

In 1870 25 percent of cities with a daily had just a Democrat (D) or Republican (R) newspaper (only 4 percent had just an independent paper), and an additional 53 percent had competing D and R papers but no independent paper (see table 6.1, panel C).[29] Thus, 78 percent of the 140 large cities in 1870 probably had largely biased, uninformative reporting of events such as Crédit Mobilier. By 1920, however, just 7 percent of cities with a daily had only a D or R (32 percent had just an independent), and 8 percent had competing D and R papers but no independent paper. In contrast, 54 percent (40.7 + 13.1) had an independent paper *and* at least one D or R paper.

Changes in local competition can also be seen through the use of the Herfindahl index. Using the appendix A data, we have calculated the average Herfindahl index in each city across the 1870–1920 period. The index is defined in its usual manner as the sum of the squared market shares times 10,000 and thus bounded by (0, 10,000], where a lower number indicates greater competition. The average Herfindahl index across cities is 6,916 in 1870, 6,531 in 1880, 6,410 in 1890, 6,215 in 1900, 6,295 in 1910, and 5,833 in 1920. As these numbers indicate, local news was never very competitive. These numbers are higher in each year than they would be if every market were split equally between two competitors. The cost of providing newspaper content (reporters' salaries) is a fixed cost and together with physical capital creates significant returns to scale (as in Berry and Waldfogel 2003). Nonetheless, the index declines in almost every decade. The decline is even more remarkable because the rapid decrease in the price of newsprint meant that the ratio of fixed to variable costs most likely rose over the period.

The rise in newspaper competition is, of course, not a puzzle. Declining costs and rising demand made it inevitable that there would be new entrants into the market. The presence of a robust market competing for consumers appears to have coincided with an increase in the amount of information contained in newspapers and a replacement of fact for vitriolic argument.

6.4.4   Cross-City Evidence

In the previous section, we documented a remarkable concurrence of different economic factors: declining costs and increasing scale, competition, and advertising revenues, all of which should (according to the model) have increased information and reduced bias. Given the interdependence of these variables, we cannot identify which of these variables is more important. We turn to cross-sectional evidence to examine the relationship among market size, information content, and political independence.

We provide two different forms of cross-city evidence. First, using the

---

29. We categorize the ID and IR papers as independents.

data from the Crédit Mobilier episode, we can examine the correlation between newspaper circulation and the various measures of information we extracted from newspaper coverage of the scandal. As mentioned above, we have four different potential measures of news quality: the percentage of facts recorded, the total number of stories, the relative size of the stories, and the timeliness of the reporting of the stories. We have these measures for both 1872 and 1873 and the circulation of the newspaper as of 1880. While we obviously cannot interpret the relationship among these variables as causal, our model would clearly suggest that circulation and informational content should be positively correlated.

In 1872, the relationships between all four of these variables and our measure of circulation are indeed positive.[30] If the *New York Herald* is excluded from the regression (it was a remarkably uninformative paper with an astonishingly high circulation) then all of these correlations are statistically significant (with the *Herald,* two are and two achieve borderline significance). Specifically, the correlation coefficient between circulation and the percentage of facts is 0.335 (0.415 without the *Herald*). The correlation coefficient between the number of stories and circulation is 0.529 (0.729 without the *Herald*). The correlation coefficient between the timeliness of the stories and circulation is 0.382 (0.557 without the *Herald*). The correlation between the relative size of the stories and circulation is 0.788 (0.946 without the *Herald*). Overall, newspapers with more circulation produced more facts and stories of importance, did so in a timelier manner, and devoted, relative to the size of the paper, more space to them.

As mentioned above, there is less heterogeneity across newspapers in 1873, when the reporting of the facts of the case became more complete. The relationship between circulation and the number of stories as well as their relative size remains positive. The relationship between circulation and facts and the relationship between circulation and timeliness are both negative and insignificant.

During the Teapot Dome episode, there is a generally positive connection between circulation and both coverage and timeliness (but not at conventional levels of significance). Newspapers with greater readership publish more facts. However, because coverage was generally more complete, the relationships are much weaker than in the 1873 era. Still, the Teapot Dome evidence continues to show that newspapers with more readers did a better job of providing more complete coverage of the events. Great coverage, however, was available to far more Americans.

A second form of evidence concerns newspaper independence across cities. If falling bias is the result of increasing newspaper scale and circula-

---

30. If instead of circulation we used a more plausibly exogenous measure—city population—we obtain correlations that are larger in size with the exception of the relative size of the stories.

Table 6.3   City population and the circulation share of independent
                   daily newspapers

Variable	Pooled		City fixed effects	
	Coefficient	Standard error	Coefficient	Standard error
Log city population	0.0710	0.0168	0.0937	0.0418
1880	0.166	0.0362	0.159	0.0422
1890	0.181	0.0396	0.161	0.0479
1900	0.164	0.0388	0.140	0.0557
1910	0.247	0.0440	0.211	0.0667
1920	0.395	0.0476	0.357	0.0760
Constant	−0.624	0.172	−0.852	0.428
R^2	0.206		0.600	
No. of observations	803		803	

Sources: See appendix A.

Notes: Dependent variable: fraction of city daily newspaper circulation that was independent (I + IR + ID). Independent newspapers are the Independent1 group (see notes to table 6.1). That is, independent newspapers include those that were strictly independent as well as those that were independent-Republican and independent-Democrat. Standard errors are robust standard errors, clustered at the city level (148 cities).

tion, then the number and circulation of independent newspapers should be increasing with city population levels and with the level of total readership by city. Hamilton (2004) has shown that in his sample (a subset of ours, including the fifty largest cities for each year from 1870 to 1900) the share of independent circulation was increasing in city population. We perform a similar analysis with our expanded data set, examining the relationship between city size, city circulation, and independent newspapers' share of circulation by city. In what follows, we report only the results using city population although those using city daily circulation are similar.

We report results in table 6.3 for a pooled cross-section time series regression on 148 cities across six decadal years (1870 to 1920). The results show the relationship between the logarithm of city population and the share of the city's circulation that is independent.[31] In the pooled analysis, we find that a 1 log point increase in population (roughly a 100 percent increase in population) is associated with a 7.1 percentage point increase in the share of circulation from the independent papers. The result holds in every decade and using either definition of independent (only I or the inclusive one that includes IR and ID): bigger cities had a greater fraction of their circulation that was independent.

---

31. In these regressions, we use the more inclusive measure of independence (I + IR + ID). The results are similar using the less inclusive measure (only I papers). The coefficient on log of city population is somewhat lower (although the mean of the dependent variable is as well), and the significance of the coefficient in the city fixed effects model is lower.

To check the robustness of these results, we also use city fixed effects. By doing so, we are identifying the effect using within-city variation. The results should be seen as testing whether cities that grew more rapidly had a greater increase in the share of circulation that was from independent newspapers. The estimated coefficient of 0.098, somewhat larger than from the pooled ordinary least squares regression, should be viewed as confirmation that increases in market size are associated with increases in the relative size of the independent press.

If these coefficients are accepted as reflecting the impact that population (or circulation) has on the relative circulation of independents, then we can determine how much of the rise in the Independents resulted from rising population (or circulation). In our sample of large cities, population increased from 7.1 to 34.4 million between 1870 and 1920. If the coefficient relating the share of independent newspapers to the logarithm of population is 0.098, then the increase in population would predict a 15.5 percentage point increase in the share of circulation that is independent. This predicted rise is about one-third of the total increase of 46.8 percentage points during the entire 1870–1920 period. Other factors we have identified above—falling costs, increasing advertising revenue, and so on—presumably accounted for much of the rest.

6.5   Summary: The Implications of the Informative Press for Corruption and Reform

We have documented significant changes in the news media during the late nineteenth and early twentieth centuries. A larger fraction of newspapers no longer had a party affiliation, and the press was far less likely to use partisan language in reporting. By comparing the coverage of the Crédit Mobilier scandal with the Teapot Dome affair, some fifty years later, we found that reporting became more complete, more timely, and generally less dominated by spin.

We also have argued and presented evidence suggesting that this transformation was the result of the rising scale and competitiveness in the newspaper industry. Declining costs and increased city populations caused a huge increase in scale. In 1870, a newspaperman might make more money pleasing a local politician than in selling papers and advertisements. By 1920 newspapers had become big business, and they increased readership and revenue by presenting factual and informative news. Following these financial incentives, newspapers changed from being political tools to at least trying to present a facade of impartial reporting.[32]

---

32. One might wonder why technological change and larger markets do not act in concert to spread unbiased and honest reporting everywhere today. Our answer is that some markets are small and also that the governments of many countries are able to use their power to influence the press.

We have not directly confronted whether these changes made a difference to political outcomes.[33] Gathering systematic evidence on this relationship remains a challenge for future work. Nevertheless, a range of anecdotal evidence suggests that growing press independence did have a significant impact on political outcomes, in particular on the incidence of corruption.

First, there are many notorious examples of the rooting out of corruption by the press. Both the Crédit Mobilier and Teapot Dome scandals were exposed by the press; the *New York Times* and *Harper's Weekly* successfully brought down Boss Tweed and Tammany Hall in 1871; and various papers, such as Pulitzer's *St. Louis Post-Dispatch,* were legendary for their campaigns against corrupt politicians.

Despite the spin and bias of individual papers in 1872, it is hard to doubt that the denizens of New York City were exposed to a steady stream of facts about the Crédit Mobilier scandal. By contrast, residents of smaller towns often had no opportunity to learn about major national events. While the rise of the informative press may not have mattered in large cities, it most likely did in most smaller cities and towns.

The prevalence of political investment in the press also provides indirect evidence that politicians thought the press was important. It seems unlikely that Alexander Hamilton would have been such a prolific polemicist if he did not see it as a tool for political success or that Thomas Jefferson would have put Freneau on the State Department payroll if Jefferson did not see Freneau's *Gazette* as an important tool in battling the Federalists. Whenever politicians used resources, such as government contracts or outright bribes, to influence papers they affirmed the fact that press coverage was thought to be significant.

For many nineteenth- and even twentieth-century politicians, newspaper publishing was an important stop on the path to political eminence. Consider the political careers of one-time newspapermen like Horace Greeley, Whitelaw Reid (*New York Tribune* publisher and unsuccessful vice presidential candidate in 1892), and Thurlow Weed. James Cox, who owned several papers and was governor of Ohio, ran unsuccessfully for president in 1920, losing to Warren Harding, a fellow newspaperman (the Harding family owned the *Marion Star*).[34]

Press exposure of major scandals often appears to coincide with electoral losses for incumbents connected to the scandal. Every significant Tammany Hall defeat coincided with a press campaign against municipal corruption. The meager Republican showing in the 1876 election (the only

---

33. On the role of the free press in controlling corruption in a cross-country analysis, see Brunetti and Weder (2003).

34. The *Marion Star* gave some coverage of the Teapot Dome affair for which Harding was implicitly involved. On April 21, 1922 (p. 2), it printed a small article on the questioning of the Teapot Dome oil leases by Senator Kendrick (fact #3, see appendix B).

election between 1860 and 1884 when the Democratic candidate won the national popular vote) may have been due to the exposure of the Grant-era scandals such as Crédit Mobilier. Progressive politicians succeeded in ousting incumbents when muckrakers, such as Lincoln Steffens, were regularly exposing corruption. While we cannot prove that a more informative press helped diminish corruption, it does appear that campaigns against corruption succeeded when they were supported by news coverage.

During the decades from 1870 to 1920 when corruption appears to have declined significantly within the United States, the press became more informative, became less partisan, and expanded its circulation considerably.[35] It seems a reasonable hypothesis that the rise of the informative press was one of the reasons why the corruption of the Gilded Age was reduced during the subsequent Progressive Era.

Appendix A

Newspaper Data, 1870 to 1920

We created balanced and unbalanced panels of cities and daily newspapers at decade intervals from 1870 to 1920. The cities were selected in the following manner. The top 100 cities by population in each year were compiled. We then increased the size of the balanced panel by adding information to the earlier years for cities that entered the sample later and also for cities that were in the top 100 earlier but not later. Some cities merged or were nonexistent in the earlier years. Thus, our total sample contains 152 cities, although the number of cities having a population is 140 in 1870, 149 in 1880, and then 150 for the remaining years. The balanced panel for all five years contains 138 cities.

We collected various types of information on all daily newspapers in these cities for the year closest to which we could obtain a copy of a national newspaper directory, such as N. W. Ayer and Son's *American Newspaper Annual* or George P. Rowell and Company's *American Newspaper Directory*. In most cases we were able to use the precise year. The information available for the newspapers is as follows: city, state, paper name, whether foreign-language press, type of paper, party affiliation, establishment date, subscription rate, advertising rate (for some years), size of paper in pages and square inches, circulation, and the accuracy of the circulation number (e.g., whether it was certified). By "type of paper" we mean whether the paper was nonpolitical, such as the financial and theater press, or whether it was political, either aligned with a party or independent or some mixture.

---

35. On the time-path of corruption, see Glaeser and Goldin (introduction to this volume).

Thus, by "political" we mean the regular, nonspecialty press. We generally grouped cities that later merged—for example, Brooklyn and New York City. We added data from the census on population and county name.

The full list of 152 cities (including those that later merged) is

AL	Birmingham	KS	Wichita
AL	Mobile	KY	Covington
AR	Little Rock	KY	Louisville
CA	Los Angeles	KY	Newport
CA	Oakland	LA	New Orleans
CA	Sacramento	MA	Boston
CA	San Diego	MA	Brockton
CA	San Francisco	MA	Cambridge
CO	Denver	MA	Charleston
CT	Bridgeport	MA	Chelsea
CT	Hartford	MA	Fall River
CT	New Haven	MA	Gloucester
CT	Norwich	MA	Holyoke
CT	Waterbury	MA	Lawrence
DC	Washington	MA	Lowell
DE	Wilmington	MA	Lynn
FL	Jacksonville	MA	New Bedford
GA	Atlanta	MA	Salem
GA	Augusta	MA	Somerville
GA	Savannah	MA	Springfield
IA	Burlington	MA	Taunton ·
IA	Davenport	MA	Worcester
IA	Des Moines	MD	Baltimore
IA	Dubuque	ME	Bangor
IA	Sioux City	ME	Portland
IL	Chicago	MI	Bay City
IL	East St. Louis	MI	Detroit
IL	Peoria	MI	Flint
IL	Quincy	MI	Grand Rapids
IL	Springfield	MI	Saginaw
IN	Evansville	MN	Duluth
IN	Fort Wayne	MN	Minneapolis
IN	Indianapolis	MN	St. Paul
IN	New Albany	MO	Kansas City
IN	South Bend	MO	St. Joseph
IN	Terre Haute	MO	St. Louis
KS	Kansas City	NE	Lincoln
KS	Leavenworth	NE	Omaha
KS	Topeka	NH	Manchester

NJ	Bayonne	OK	Tulsa
NJ	Camden	OR	Portland
NJ	Elizabeth	PA	Allegheny
NJ	Hoboken	PA	Allentown
NJ	Jersey City	PA	Altoona
NJ	New Brunswick	PA	Erie
NJ	Newark	PA	Harrisburg
NJ	Passaic	PA	Johnstown
NJ	Paterson	PA	Lancaster
NJ	Trenton	PA	Philadelphia
NY	Albany	PA	Pittsburgh
NY	Auburn	PA	Reading
NY	Binghamton	PA	Scranton
NY	Brooklyn	PA	Wilkes-Barre
NY	Buffalo	PA	Williamsport
NY	Cohoes	RI	North Providence
NY	Elmira	RI	Pawtucket
NY	New York	RI	Providence
NY	Newburgh	SC	Charleston
NY	Oswego	TN	Knoxville
NY	Poughkeepsie	TN	Memphis
NY	Rochester	TN	Nashville
NY	Schenectady	TX	Dallas
NY	Syracuse	TX	El Paso
NY	Troy	TX	Fort Worth
NY	Utica	TX	Galveston
NY	Yonkers	TX	Houston
OH	Akron	TX	San Antonio
OH	Canton	UT	Salt Lake City
OH	Cincinnati	VA	Norfolk
OH	Cleveland	VA	Petersburg
OH	Columbus	VA	Richmond
OH	Dayton	WA	Seattle
OH	Springfield	WA	Spokane
OH	Toledo	WA	Tacoma
OH	Youngstown	WI	Milwaukee
OK	Oklahoma	WV	Wheeling

Appendix B

Coding Newspaper Stories Concerning
Crédit Mobilier and Teapot Dome

The Historical Events and Facts

We have chosen two major historical events, known as Crédit Mobilier and Teapot Dome. Two relatively brief periods within each event were selected. The first period begins with the breaking story, whereas the second includes an incident that coalesced opinion, such as a congressional investigation or an admission of guilt. The periods span from one to almost four weeks. Their lengths by event were determined by to equalize the frequency of newspaper coverage between them. The dates used for each period per major event are as follows.

Crédit Mobilier Period 1: September 4 to September 30, 1872

The period begins with the release by the *New York Sun* of a letter from Rep. Oakes Ames to Henry McComb, once Ames's associate in Crédit Mobilier (written January 28, 1868), stating that Crédit Mobilier shares were placed "where [they] will produce most good to us." The names of congressmen, senators, and the vice president were written on the reverse side by McComb, supposedly from a list shown to him by Ames. The letter was given to the *Sun* by McComb. The remainder of the period is taken up with denials by those on the list.

Crédit Mobilier Period 2: February 14 to February 28, 1873

The events of this period include the conclusion of the House and Senate committees on the Crédit Mobilier scandal and the action of Congress regarding implicated sitting members (table 6B.1).

Teapot Dome Period 1: April 7 to April 30, 1922

The period begins with a seemingly innocuous release by the *Wall Street News* that the government, through Secretary of the Interior Albert Fall, had leased oil lands—including one in Wyoming known as Teapot Dome—to Harry Sinclair, owner of Mammoth Oil Company. The remainder of the period concerns Senate demands for more information on the leases.

Teapot Dome Period 2: January 21 to January 28, 1924

The main event of this period is the admission by Edward Doheny, whose company had received the Elk Hills oil leases, that he lent Albert Fall $100,000. Sinclair's lawyer also admitted to a loan to Fall by Sinclair (table 6B.2).

Table 6B.1   **Crédit Mobilier facts during two periods**

Period 1: September 4 to September 30, 1872

1 Sept. 4, 1872	New York (NY) *Sun* publishes letter (originally written 1/28/1868) from Rep. Oakes Ames (MA) to Henry McComb stating that shares were placed "where [they] will produce most good to us." Names of congressmen, senators, and the vice president were written on the reverse side by McComb, supposedly from a list shown to him by Ames.
2 Sept. 5, 1872	Sen. Blaine (ME), in the *Kennebec Journal,* denied ownership of CM stock.
3 Sept. 7, 1872	NY *Sun* revealed a second letter (written 1/25/1868) from Ames to McComb also with list of names of those receiving shares.
4 Sept. 11, 1872	Rep. Dawes, in a letter, thanks the editor of the *Syracuse Journal* for denouncing the *Sun* charges.
5 Sept. 13, 1872	Sen. Henry Wilson (MA), in a letter to the *Troy Whig,* denies speculating.
6 Sept. 15, 1872	General Garfield (R, OH) denied NY *Sun* charge and stated that he held no stock in CM or Union Pacific (UP).
7 Sept. 17, 1872	Ames, in a letter to his constituency, denied NY *Sun* charge.
8 Sept. 20, 1872	Rep. Scofield (PA) claimed he never received CM stock.
9 Sept. 25, 1872	Vice President Colfax, in South Bend, Indiana, speech, denied wrongdoing.

Period 2: February 14 to February 28, 1873

1 Feb. 14, 1873	Senate Committee chaired by Sen. Morrill heard testimony from McComb, Sen. Conkling (NY), and Sen. Patterson (NH).
2 Feb. 15, 1873	Senate Committee heard from Harlan regarding $10,000 from T. Durant (UP) to Harlan's campaign; testimony from Sen. Wilson (MA)
3 Feb. 17, 1873	Washington, DC Sunday *Herald* published the purported transcript of the Ames memorandum book.
4 Feb. 18, 1873	Poland Committee (House) recommended the expulsion of Oakes Ames and James Brooks (D, NY). Oakes found guilty of a misdemeanor.
5 Feb. 19, 1873	Senate Committee heard from Ames about Harlan.
6 Feb. 19, 1873	Poland Committee (House) heard from Vice President Colfax and Joseph Fowler (ex-senator, TN).
7 Feb. 20, 1873	Wilson Special Committee (Senate) on the Union Pacific reported on relations between the UP and CM.
8 Feb. 20, 1873	House referred to the Judiciary Committee the issue of impeaching the vice president.
9 Feb. 22, 1873	Morrill Committee (Senate) heard from Sen. Paterson; Sen. Harlan recalled.
10 Feb. 27, 1873	House voted to issue severe condemnations of Brooks and Ames but not to expel them.
11 Feb. 27, 1873	Morrill Committee (Senate) recommended expulsion of Sen. Paterson.

Notes: CM = Crédit Mobilier.

Table 6B.2	**Teapot Dome facts during two periods**

Period 1: April 7 to April 30, 1922

1 Apr. 7, 1922	The *Wall Street Journal* reported that the U.S. government leased Teapot Dome, one of the naval reserves, to Harry F. Sinclair of Mammoth Oil.
2 Apr. 14, 1922	Announcement of a Department of the Interior policy to store oil above ground.
3 Apr. 15, 1922	Senate passed Sen. Kendrick's (WY) resolution calling for detailed information on the Sinclair lease.
4 Apr. 17, 1922	Acting Interior Secretary Finney announced the terms of the lease: graduated royalties ranging from 12.5 to 50 percent.
5 Apr. 21, 1922	Sen. La Follette (WI) introduced a resolution calling for an inquiry into the leasing of oil areas to influential companies.
6 Apr. 22, 1922	A joint letter transmitted by Navy Secr. Denby and Finney that in leasing the oil reserves they were acting under the authority of Congress.
7 Apr. 28, 1922	Sen. La Follette charged that speculators on the New York Stock Exchange netted $30 million from advance information.
8 Apr. 29, 1922	Senate passes resolution directing the Committee on Public Lands and Surveys to investigate the leases.

Period 2: January 21 to January 28, 1924

1 Jan. 21, 1924	Archie Roosevelt (son of president) stated he severed ties to Sinclair.
2 Jan. 22, 1924	Subpoena issued for Fall and Zevely (lawyer to Sinclair) to testify before Senate. Sinclair requested to attend.
3 Jan. 23, 1924	Sen. Caraway (AR) called for immediate action on his resolution to cancel the Teapot Dome lease.
4 Jan. 24, 1924	Edward Doheny admitted that he had lent Fall $100,000 ["without security . . . eventuating in the contract awarded to Doheny on Apr. 25, following, through which he secured, without competition, a contract giving him a preference right to a lease of a large part of Naval Reserve No. 1"].
5 Jan. 25, 1924	Zevely testified about an additional $25,000 loan from Sinclair to Fall after the Teapot Dome lease.
6 Jan. 25, 1924	Senate ordered an investigation on Indian Land Lease entered into by Fall.
7 Jan. 27, 1924	President Coolidge stated he would appoint a special counsel.
8 Jan. 28, 1924	House recommended resolution granting $100,000 for Coolidge to investigate the leases.
9 Jan. 28, 1924	Sen. Robinson (AR) submits resolution calling on the president to request Navy Secr. Denby's resignation.

The Coding

Every article concerning the two events in the time periods listed was read and coded in the following manner to ascertain coverage, factual reporting, timeliness, and spin:

1. Size of article in column inches (excluding headlines).
2. Whether each fact given above was covered and on which day.
3. Spin is captured in two ways. We read the first two complete paragraphs of each article and coded the number of times the first person plural was used ("we," "us"). The use of the first person plural indicates editorializing. We also use the same paragraphs to count the number of times words such as "lie" and "false" were used (there were more than thirty different words in the 1870s articles that are synonyms for "lie").[36]

The Newspapers

We coded daily newspapers and included those that were instrumental in breaking the story (such as the *New York Sun* in the case of Crédit Mobilier). Where possible we included newspapers from smaller cities (such as Sioux City), those geographically distant from the East Coast (such as Galveston), and those in the nation's capital. We attempted to incorporate a mix of political parties, although Republican newspapers dominated in general.

The full list of papers follows together with the approximate number of separate articles published on the topic during the stated period (table 6B.3).

---

36. The full list of words is as follows: baseless, calumny, canard, charlatan, cheat, deception, deceitful, dishonest, dishonesty, fabrication, fake, false, falsehood, fib, fiction, fraud, groundless, hoax, humbug, hypocrisy, imposture, insincere, libel, meretricious, misrepresentation, myth, perjury, prevarication, quack, slander, specious, and untruth. All parts of speech were counted (e.g., noun, adjective, verb).

Table 6B.3   Newspapers used for coding Crédit Mobilier and Teapot Dome articles

| | Affiliation | | Number of articles for each period | | | |
| | | | Crédit Mobilier | | Teapot Dome | |
Newspaper	1880[a]	1920	9/9/1872–9/30/1872	2/14/1873–2/28/1873	4/14/1922–4/30/1922	1/22/1924–1/29/1924
Albany Evening Journal	R	IR	12	52	0	20
Baltimore Sun	I	ID	8	32	5	47
Chicago Daily Tribune	R	IR	31	54	9	15
Cincinnati Daily Gazette	R	—	12	29	ne	ne
DC Evening Star	I	I	4	27	4	25
DC Washington Post	D	I	ne	ne	4	19
Galveston Daily News	D	ID	3	6	4	13
Hartford Courant	R	R	11	28	1	21
Minneapolis Tribune	R	R	2	14	9	15
New Orleans (Times-) Picayune	D	ID	6	24	4	18
New York Herald	I	I	4	46	8	25
New York Sun[b]	I	IR	40	42	4	18
New York Times	R	ID	24	42	11	40
New York Tribune	R	—	30	33	ne	ne
New York World[b]	D	ID	26	45	6	38
Philadelphia (Evening) Bulletin	R	IR	4	30	0	15
Sioux City (Daily) Journal	R	R	3	21	2	20
Wall Street News (later Journal)	—	Financial	ne	ne	32	18
Waterbury Daily American	IR	IR	4	18	1	14
All listed newspapers, articles	—	—	224	543	104	381

Notes: ne = nonexistent for the period given. All newspapers were read from microfilm except the *New York Times* and the *Wall Street News,* which are on-line newspapers with optical character recognition (OCR) technology.

[a]1880 is used for political affiliation because many affiliations are missing for 1870. Note that the *DC Washington Post* began publication in 1877 and is not in the 1872, 1873 sample.

[b]There was both a morning and an evening paper in the 1920s. The microfilms used were for the morning paper.

References

Berry, Steven, and Joel Waldfogel. 2003. Product quality and market size. NBER Working Paper no. 9675. Cambridge, MA: National Bureau of Economic Research, May.

Besley, Timothy, and Andrea Prat. 2004. Handcuffs for the grabbing hand: Media capture and government accountability. London School of Economics. Mimeograph.

Brunetti, Aymo, and Beatrice Weder. 2003. A free press is bad news for corruption. *Journal of Public Economics* 87 (August): 1801–24.

Carter, Susan, Scott S. Gartner, Michael Haines, Alan Olmstead, Richard Sutch, and Gavin Wright, eds. Forthcoming. *Historical statistics of the United States: Millennial edition.* New York: Cambridge University Press.

Cook, Timothy E. 1998. *Governing with the news: The news media as a political institution.* Chicago: University of Chicago Press.

Current, Richard N. 1954. *The typewriter and the men who made it.* Urbana: University of Illinois Press.

Dill, William A. 1928. *Growth of newspapers in the United States.* Lawrence: University of Kansas Department of Journalism.

Editor and Publisher. Various years. *Editor and Publisher international yearbook.* New York: Editor and Publisher.

Emery, Edwin. 1972. *The press and America: An interpretative history of the mass media.* 3rd ed. New Jersey: Prentice-Hall. (Orig. pub. 1954.)

Emery, Edwin, and Michael Emery. 1988. *The press and America: An interpretative history of the mass media.* 6th ed. New Jersey: Prentice-Hall. (Orig. pub. 1954.)

———. 1992. *The press and America: An interpretative history of the mass media.* 7th ed. New Jersey: Prentice-Hall. (Orig. pub. 1954.)

Gentzkow, Matthew, and Jesse M. Shapiro. 2004. Media bias and reputation. Harvard University, Department of Economics. Mimeograph.

Gibson, Campbell. 1998. Population of the 100 largest cities and other urban places in the United States: 1790 to 1990. U.S. Bureau of the Census, Population Division Working Paper no. 27. http://www.census.gov/population/www/documentation/twps0027.html

Goldberg, Bernard. 2001. *Bias: A CBS insider exposes how the media distorts the news.* New York: Regnery.

Hamilton, James T. 2004. *All the news that's fit to sell: How the market transforms information into news.* Princeton, NJ: Princeton University Press.

Kaplan, Richard. 1993. The economics and politics of nineteenth century newspapers: Market segmentation and partisanship in the Detroit press, 1865–1900. *American Journalism* 11 (Winter-Spring): 84–101.

Lee, Alfred M. 1937. *The daily newspaper in America: The evolution of a social instrument.* New York: Macmillan.

Mott, Frank Luther. 1962. *American Journalism: A History, 1690 to 1960.* 3rd ed. New York: Macmillan.

Mullainathan, Sendhil, and Andrei Shleifer. Forthcoming. The market for news. *American Economic Review.*

N. W. Ayer and Son. Various years. *American newspaper annual.* Philadelphia: N. W. Ayer and Son.

National Bureau of Economic Research (NBER) Macro History Database. Wholesale price of newsprint paper. Series m04093a,b. http://www.nber.org/databases/macrohistory/contents/chapter04.html

Rowell, George P. Various years. *American newspaper directory.* New York: Geo. P. Rowell.

Schudson, Michael. 1978. *Discovering the news: A social history of American newspapers.* New York: Basic Books.

Summers, Mark Wahlgren. 1994. *The press gang: Newspapers and politics, 1865–1878.* Chapel Hill: University of North Carolina Press.

U.S. Bureau of the Census. 1975. Historical statistics of the United States from colonial times to the present. Washington, DC: Government Printing Office.

Bank Chartering and Political Corruption in Antebellum New York Free Banking as Reform

Howard Bodenhorn

He saw in the system what he thought a most dangerous political engine, which might in the hands of bad men be used for bad purposes.
—Luther Brandish, New York State assemblyman, quoted in the *Albany Evening Journal,* 19 January 1837

7.1 Introduction

Government policies toward business can be categorized into three types: minimal, maximal, and decentralized (Frye and Shleifer 1997). A minimal policy regime, often referred to as the "invisible hand," leaves most economic decisions to private agents, reserving the provision of only a few essential public goods to the state. In maximal, or "iron hand" regimes, the state is actively involved in economic activity, typically through the pursuit of industrial policies that direct resources toward sectors deemed important by politicians. Bureaucrats in maximal regimes may be corrupt, but corruption—defined here as the sale of public assets for private gain—is limited and does not impede economic growth (Murphy, Shleifer, and Vishny 1993; Mauro 1995). In the decentralized, or "grabbing hand," regime, the state is made up of many independent bureaucracies, each competing for rents, that together severely undermine economic activity.

In the half century between President Washington's inauguration and that of Van Buren, many states experienced abrupt transitions from fairly "iron handed" regimes to more "invisible" ones. Nowhere was this transition more apparent than in bank chartering policy, and nowhere was the

Howard Bodenhorn is a professor of economics at Lafayette College and a research associate of the National Bureau of Economic Research.

I thank Lee Alston, Michael Bordo, Andrew Economopoulos, Ed Glaeser, Stephen Quinn, Hugh Rockoff, Jay Shambaugh, Richard Sylla, John Wallis, Eugene White, and Robert E. Wright, as well as seminar participants at Rutgers, New York University, Yale, and the National Bureau of Economic Research for many useful comments and suggestions on earlier drafts. Special thanks go to Claudia Goldin, who provided extensive and valuable comments. I thank Pam Bodenhorn for valuable research assistance.

transition more pronounced than in New York State, which witnessed a shift from an iron-handed banking policy controlled by Van Buren's powerful Democratic Party machine in the early 1830s to a market-oriented policy instituted in 1838.

In the early nineteenth-century United States, bank chartering was high-stakes politics. Because states tended to limit the number of corporate franchises, the available rents were potentially large and prospective bankers spent freely in their efforts to obtain one. Reform proposals emerged throughout the antebellum era, but significant reform did not emerge until Michigan and New York took the lead in the late 1830s. These states' response became known as free banking. By 1860 some eighteen states had enacted a variant of free banking, modeled on the 1838 New York law. In this essay I describe the events leading up to the passage of New York State's 1838 free banking statute, showing how corrupt politics and an iron-handed chartering regime gave way to free market reform and a liberal general incorporation law. A restrictive franchise with a resulting partisan distribution of political privilege in post-Revolutionary New York led to electoral reform, culminating in a revised state constitution in 1821. Once the political issues were resolved, public attention turned to the political manipulation of economic opportunities. The debate about the role of government in the economy influenced the platforms of the three dominant contemporary political parties. Ultimately, free banking represented the confluence of Anti-Masonic populism, Democratic pragmatism, and pro-business American Whiggism.

Traditional explanations of why free banking appeared when it did fail to adequately account for why the 1838 bill passed when earlier bills had failed. The traditional interpretation, offered by Redlich (1968) and B. Hammond (1957), argues that free banking resulted from a combination of radical, laissez-faire, Jacksonian populism and an ill-informed, inflationist response to the panic of 1837.[1] Although New York's Democratic machine lost control of the party during the Jacksonian era, its strong egalitarian impulse predated the Jacksonians by a decade or more. Indeed, Jacksonian populism emerged as the party embraced much of the rhetoric and some of the policies of the Anti-Masons, a party built on an opposition to privilege and what New York governor William L. Marcy labeled political "spoils." Similarly, the inflationist explanation is lacking because calls for banking reforms that had much in common with the 1838 act predated the panic of 1837 by at least a decade. The panic mattered because it opened the door to the 1838 act, but not because it was an inflationist policy mistakenly believed to be a solution to panic-induced deflation. The panic mattered because it galvanized an electorate displeased with the corrupt practices of

---

1. Hammond notes a growing frustration with the political corruption discussed below, but he does not pursue the sources or depth of that frustration or its political and economic ramifications.

Van Buren's Democratic party machine. A Whig majority took control of the New York legislature in the autumn 1837 elections, and Whigs interpreted their newfound power and popularity as a mandate to effect reforms, including an overhaul of bank chartering policy. Thus, free banking did not spontaneously emerge in the late 1830s in response to Jacksonian populism and the panic of 1837. Rather, its passage was the consequence of a long chain of events and an evolving popular notion of equality of economic opportunity that emerged in the late 1810s and finally found full expression in the late 1830s. Using a narrative architecture, this article traces those events and shows how a growing popular discontent with corrupt politics led to the passage of New York's 1838 free banking act.

7.2 Bank Chartering: A Legacy of Corruption in New York, 1803–37

This section first discusses the general conditions under which New York state issued corporate charters and then turns to a discussion of bank chartering in the two decades prior to the enactment of free banking. In the early nineteenth century, corporate privileges were reserved for organizations, such as libraries, schools, churches, and bridge and turnpike companies, that served the common weal. By the second quarter of the century, however, corporations that served principally their owners received charters. Between about 1820 and 1838, Martin Van Buren's political machine manipulated the charter-granting process to serve its allies and advance its political agenda.

7.2.1 Early Chartering Practices

Between 1790 and 1810 corporate privileges were reserved for a select few organizations, mostly nonprofit associations. Religious congregations, schools, academies and colleges, medical societies, libraries, and benevolent societies received more corporate charters than any other type of association (Evans 1948). As the number of such organizations increased, the demand for acts of incorporation consumed a growing proportion of legislative time and energy, and between 1784 and 1811 New York enacted a number of general laws for the incorporation of nonprofit organizations. The law allowing free incorporation of religious institutions is of particular note because it promised denominational equality and the advantages of incorporation to all congregations free of government interference (Seavoy 1982, p. 3). Laws granting free incorporation to educational and benevolent institutions reflected the leveling and improving spirit of the post-Revolutionary era. The principal advantage of incorporation for a church, educational institution, or charity was that the institution could receive bequests and legacies as well as holding and legally defending property under joint title in the name of the (changeable) membership rather than holding it in trust.

Incorporation also promised several advantages for business, and corporate charters were eagerly sought by business promoters (Seavoy 1982, p. 4). As with nonprofit institutions, incorporation protected the collective ownership of real and personal property, encouraged the accumulation of large pools of capital, limited investor risk in speculative enterprises, and facilitated access to the courts. Post-Revolutionary New York reserved incorporation for new and large-scale businesses that did not compete with existing proprietorships and partnerships. Incorporation also established a supervisory role for the state. Turnpikes, canals, and bridges required special powers, including eminent domain, condemnation, and incorporation. Although the electorate looked favorably on such corporations, it also demanded public oversight to ensure that these firms neither abused their eminent-domain powers nor wandered from a previously approved route. Bank and insurance company charters granted these companies broad powers, but imposed numerous restrictions and often stripped shareholders of limited liability in the event of failure due to managerial incompetence or fraud. Incorporation implied a balancing act. On one hand, it was the state's responsibility to promote the commonweal, and the corporation was but one means to do so, mostly by promoting charitable and improvement associations (Handlin and Handlin 1947). On the other, promoting the commonweal sometimes required caution and restraint. Institutions capable of providing large social benefits were capable of imposing equally impressive costs. It was the state's responsibility to strike the balance.

Like most other states, New York only grudgingly relinquished its control over business incorporation. Although Gunn (1988, p. 49) contends that, between 1790 and 1820, the corporation evolved into "a modern, essentially private, instrument of economic organization," the evolution was slow and fitful. Before 1800 New York chartered just 28 for-profit corporations, including 13 turnpikes, 4 banks, and 3 canals. During the next decade, the state chartered 179 corporations, mostly turnpike, bridge, and water companies (Evans 1948, p. 17). It was only in the years surrounding the War of 1812 that the number of new manufacturing incorporations (153) exceeded the number of newly incorporated public utilities (134). Banking and insurance companies never represented more than a small fraction of the total number of incorporations. Twenty-five insurance companies were chartered between 1800 and 1820; just twenty-eight banks received charters in the same period.

Bank chartering in New York became embroiled in partisan politics from the beginning. Early banks, whether in New York or elsewhere, were popularly identified by their founders' political affiliations. New York's first banks were Federalist and Hamiltonian. Although Republicans distrusted economic privilege and financial operations, they set aside their concerns when they observed how banks could be harnessed to advance a political agenda (Alexander 1906, p. 187; Wright 2002). As dispensers of credit, banks favored those to whom they loaned, and, if controlled by a

political party, a bank could insure that party supporters were disproportionately advantaged with share ownership and, perhaps, access to credit.[2]

The question is why frustrated borrowers did not just change parties.
Some undoubtedly did. But in early America, party affiliations among the
political and economic elite were publicly known long before banks came
into being, and changing parties did not erase years of built-up partisan
animosities. Even after banking became well established in the antebellum
era, party affiliation alone did not guarantee access to bank credit or ownership. Becoming a bank insider required open and dedicated service to the
party, something that opportunistic party switchers did not provide.

Because the legislature limited the number of bank charters, a charter
was valuable and prospective bankers were willing to pay potentially large
sums in return for a license. Allegations of bribery surfaced at least as early
as 1804 with the chartering of the Merchants' Bank of New York City,
when it was disclosed that one state senator had promised shares to two
other senators, along with a guarantee that they could sell the shares at a
substantial premium after the charter was passed (Knox 1903, p. 397).[3]
Bribery finally became a public issue in 1812. A charter for the Bank of
America in New York City was crafted with a proposed capital of $6 mil-
lion, or six times the size of the then largest bank in the city. Although the
petitioners were Federalists, they hired two prominent Republicans—
David Thomas of Washington, DC, and Solomon Southwick of Albany—
to lobby a Republican-dominated legislature on their behalf (Alexander
1906, p. 194). Thomas was described as crafty, unscrupulous, and ambitious, Southwick as handsome, personable, and charming. Their person-
alities complemented each other well, and together they became effective
lobbyists. But when the petitioners hired several other lobbyists, events
spun out of control.

Several charter requests were laid before the legislature in the opening
days of the 1812 session, and in his annual address to the legislature in January Governor Tompkins advised the legislature to be wary of bank promoters who used "intrigue and hollow pretenses" to "corrupt and subdue
republican notions" (Lincoln 1909, p. 697). In March Governor Tompkins
chose to exercise his constitutional privilege to suspend the Assembly and
Senate for sixty days. In his message dismissing the legislators, Tompkins
alluded to improper means used in soliciting a bank charter in the previous
legislative session and accused four Federalist members of the Assembly
and one state senator of accepting bribes from the Bank of America's lob-

2. Lamoreaux (1994) shows that banks in early New England loaned disproportionate
amounts to insiders (shareholders and officers), as well as the friends, family, and business associates of insiders. Evidence concerning the extent of insider lending among New York's
banks is mostly anecdotal but is consistent with the New England experience.

3. Wright (1997) finds that the first bribery accusations surfaced with the charter of the
New York State Bank in 1803. The accusations rose to the level of public scandal in 1812.

byists (Cole 1984, pp. 27–28). He asked the legislative members to return home, consult with their constituents, and reflect on the enormity of their actions (Lincoln 1909, p. 711). Tompkins also instructed the attorney general to investigate. Several agents for the petitioners were indicted for bribery, among them a former clergyman who was eventually sentenced to the state penitentiary. Thomas was accused of liberally spreading the petitioners' money on both sides of the aisle, and both Thomas and Southwick were indicted and tried. Both were acquitted, however, when the prosecution's star witnesses—a state senator and the speaker of the Assembly—refused to testify. Ultimately, Governor Tompkins's decision to suspend the legislature had no effect. Shortly after it reconvened, both houses approved the Bank of America's charter. Charges of bribery surfaced throughout the 1810s, but none rose to the level of the Bank of America scandal.

7.2.2   The Albany Regency, the Safety Fund System, and Chartering as Party Discipline

New York politics between 1810 and 1820 is a tangled tale of a waning Federalist Party and a Democratic-Republican Party divided into as many as a half-dozen factions, each claiming to represent the true Jeffersonian faith (Countryman 2001, p. 300). Although there were minor ideological squabbles, the party fractured mostly down sectional lines (Kass 1965, p. 110). Even at the time it was recognized that the dominant faction would be the one that provided a leader capable of quieting divisive voices, blunting sectional rivalries, and guiding members to a common purpose. Although DeWitt Clinton was a charismatic visionary who could rally popular support for specific projects, such as the Erie Canal, he was unable to organize supporters into a unified political party. Where Clinton fell short, Martin Van Buren excelled. Van Buren's gift was his ability to transform a loose coalition of sometimes cooperative but often bickering factions into a powerful, focused, and reasonably stable political machine.

Van Buren entered the state senate in 1813 with what a number of historians and biographers generously describe as a pragmatic approach to politics (Cole 1984, pp. 39–51). He rose to prominence in 1817 when, sensing a strong and growing support for the project, he reversed his outspoken opposition to the Erie Canal and delivered a powerful speech in support.[4] His speech vaulted him into the political leadership, and from this experience Van Buren learned the value of being on the popular side of an issue. He subsequently built a formidable coalition of Republicans called Bucktails

4. Miller (1962, p. 45) argues that Van Buren's decision to block passage of the Erie Canal's chartering act in 1816 was a political ploy. Van Buren asked for additional studies of the canal's routing and prospects because such a massive undertaking required careful and deliberate consideration. In the 1817 session, Van Buren could then steal Clinton's thunder by arguing that he was as supportive of the project as the others, but more cautious, scrupulous, and fiscally responsible than his political rivals.

by their friends (so named because each wore a buck's tail on his hat at party conventions) or the Albany Regency by their detractors.[5]

By 1819, Van Buren's Bucktails were already powerful enough to openly challenge Governor Clinton's nominations to the New York Council of Appointment, and his Bucktails dominated the 1820 legislative elections.[6] Clinton was reelected governor, but he was surrounded by Bucktails who controlled the Council of Appointment and swept the state's appointive offices of Clinton supporters, replacing them with Bucktail men. At this point, Van Buren favored young men on the rise, and his political appointees formed the nucleus of New York's Republican Party through the 1830s. By 1823 the Regency was a well-entrenched, well-organized, smoothly operating political machine—the pride of its supporters, the envy of its rivals, and the prototypical machine for the next century (Cole 1984, p. 86).

Policy was developed by a small group of men who debated privately but never squabbled publicly.[7] Orders from the leadership were transmitted to the legislative party caucus in Albany and disseminated through the hinterlands by the party press, including the highly influential Albany Argus, and by appointed judges as they rode their circuits (Cole 1984, pp. 86–87; Countryman 2001, pp. 300–302). At the grassroots level, the Regency controlled the appointment of thousands of justices of the peace, county judges, and examiners of chancery, who were all expected to further the party's agenda. Failure to do so resulted in the individual's dismissal from his patronage office. Although its control was never absolute, the Regency was so effective that contemporaries commented on "the perfection of Mr. Van Buren's party discipline" (Cole, p. 155).

Charges of corruption swirled around nearly every bank charter introduced between 1813 and 1821. In an attempt to mitigate corruption, the state constitution of 1821 required a two-thirds majority of both houses to incorporate a bank. Supporters of this measure argued that the supermajority requirement would lead to only truly meritorious bankers receiving corporate privileges (Seavoy 1982, p. 128). Critics argued that the supermajority requirement simply raised the stakes. If more votes were needed,

---

5. Though the Revolutionary generation had largely passed from power by this time, labeling one's political opponent a "monarchist" was still an effective political strategy. Thus, by referring to Van Buren's small circle of Republican (uppercase *R*) leaders as Regents, opponents tarred them with the brush of anti-republicanism (lowercase *r*). Eventually, the tar stuck and the electorate turned against rule by what was commonly perceived as the Regency elite.

6. Under New York's 1777 constitution, the Council of Appointment was composed of the governor and four state senators who, by 1821, appointed nearly 15,000 local and state administrative positions, including sheriffs, county clerks, city mayors, justices of the peace, and all state officers except the treasurer, who was appointed by the legislature. It was this appointive power that formed the basis of the Regency's spoils.

7. Even those Regency leaders who squabbled too much privately found themselves on the outside. Once a trusted insider, William L. Marcy was eventually pushed out of the inner circle even while he was Democratic governor of New York (Spencer 1959).

more legislators would have to be persuaded, through whatever means. Whatever its effect on bribery, the two-thirds requirement's effect on the growth of banking was clear. Only 12 new banks were chartered between 1821 and 1828, with no new banks chartered in 1822, 1826, 1827, or 1828. At the end of 1828, crisis loomed for the state's banking system. Table 7.1 reveals that with less than $9 in authorized bank capital per capita New York was less financially developed than Massachusetts (about $28 per capita) or Pennsylvania (about $12 per capita).[8] Moreover, the charters of thirty of the forty banks then operating were due to expire during the next five years (Root 1895, p. 288). If these banks' charters expired and the banks wound up without new ones to replace them, New York would be without a legitimate financial sector and the Republicans would have failed in their obligation to promote the commonweal.

The newly elected governor, Martin Van Buren, sought a solution to the banking problem that could simultaneously address three issues. First, any new banking policy needed to eliminate the chartering logjam created by the two-thirds majority mandated by the 1821 constitution for all bank charters. Second, a new policy needed to protect the public against payments system collapses. Third, chartering needed to remain under the Regency's control. Resolving the second issue would largely resolve the first. One purpose of restrictive incorporation (legislative chartering) was that the legislature owed a duty to the public to protect it from reckless, irresponsible or excessively risky projectors. But because bankers received charters more for their ability to subvert the political process than for their business acumen (though the two need not have been mutually exclusive) cautious legislators were reluctant to issue charters and set potentially bad bankers loose on an unsuspecting public. Finally, Van Buren needed to bend banking policy to his will. So long as the Bucktail Democrats could retain control of issuing charters, loyal party members would be rewarded with lucrative interests in newly chartered banks.

Van Buren's solution was the 1829 Safety Fund Act.[9] The act required all subsequently chartered banks, whether their charters were de novo or renewed, to contribute an amount equal to 6 percent of their paid-in capital to a fund that would reimburse noteholders and depositors of any failing member bank. The act also laid down common charter conditions and established one of the first banking oversight bureaucracies in the nation.

The act engendered broad support and unleashed a legislative supply

8. Table 7.1 reports authorized bank capital per capita because these data are available for the entire period. Using data for loans per capita or total bank assets per capita for 1820 and after (when these data become reasonably reliable) does not appreciably alter the main conclusions. Massachusetts remains the most financially developed state, Pennsylvania lags far behind, and New York is an intermediate case. In 1830, for instance, bank loans per capita in Massachusetts were $45.85; in New York, $18.23; and in Pennsylvania, $14.25. By 1860 the figures are Massachusetts, $96.80; New York, $51.63; and Pennsylvania, $20.41.

9. See Calomiris (1989) and Bodenhorn (2003) and sources therein for descriptions and analyses of the Safety Fund.

Table 7.1   Bank capital per capita in Massachusetts, New York, and Pennsylvania
(for selected years; current dollars)

Year	Massachusetts ($)	New York ($)	Pennsylvania ($)
1800	9.01[a]	5.81[b]	8.06[a]
1805	12.22	7.27[b]	10.04
1810	14.16	7.75[b]	7.41[c,d]
1815	23.07	15.93[b]	16.38[d]
1820	20.26	15.38[b,e]	14.02[d,f]
1825	25.74	16.04[b]	n.a.[f]
1830	31.61	12.44[b,e]	10.84[d,f]
1835	45.36	14.72[b,g]	11.65[f]
1837[h]	54.99	16.43[i]	14.86
1840	45.75	15.15	14.04
1845	36.24	15.94	7.32
1850	37.13	15.29	7.43
1855	53.05	24.19	7.67
1860	54.00	28.72	8.80

Sources: Unless otherwise noted, estimates are based on capital accounts reported in U.S. Comptroller of the Currency (1876) and U.S. Census Office (1872). Population estimates for noncensus years calculated from continuously compounded growth rates between census years.

Note: n.a. = not available.

[a]Estimates are for 1801.

[b]Bank capital from Williams (1837, p. 235). Gallatin (1831, pp. 97–103) implies slightly different figures: 1811, $7.57; 1815, $16.57; 1820, $13.83; 1830, $12.78.

[c]Estimate for 1811.

[d]Estimates from Gallatin (1831, pp. 97–103).

[e]Fenstermaker's (1965) reports for capital imply different figures: 1819, $0.84; 1830, $3.54.

[f]Fenstermaker's (1965) reports for capital yield different figures: 1820, $6.37; 1825, $7.57; 1830, $9.51; 1835, $12.39.

[g]U.S. Comptroller of the Currency's (1876, p. CIII) figure implies $14.14.

[h]Last year of legislative bank chartering in New York State.

[i]Fenstermaker's (1965) figure implies $16.21.

that would satisfy a pent-up demand for new banks. Between 1821 and 1828, New York legislators chartered just twelve banks, only ten of which opened (Fenstermaker 1965). Eleven de novo charters were issued in 1829 alone; nine more in 1830; nine more again in 1831; seven in 1832; eight in 1833; eight in 1834; and twelve in 1836. By making the banks mutually responsible for one another's debts, the act relieved concerns about the capabilities or actions of any single banker. Under the co-insurance scheme, the costs of bad banking would fall primarily on the banks rather than the public. With fewer concerns about bank quality, legislators could focus on quantity. In short, the insurance guarantee calmed legislators' fears, and they chartered more banks—sixty-four de novo charters and twenty-nine recharters between 1829 and 1836 (Root 1895, pp. 290–91). Despite the rash of new bank charters, New York remained woefully financially underdeveloped compared to its nearest commercial rivals (see table 7.1).

Because it was not meant to, the Safety Fund system did not reduce chartering corruption, a fact that invited anti-Regency protest. One contemporary contended that "lobby men" still engaged in their "mercenary employment[s]," and the *Albany Evening Journal* (hereafter *AEJ*), an anti-Regency newspaper, published numerous allegations of legislative bribery (Johnson 1850, p. 611). On 13 April, for example, the *AEJ* reported that the Chemical Bank's charter passed after a long delay and "with the loss of the reputation of a Senator." In March 1833 Alvah Bebee was indicted for bribing state assemblyman John De Mott. During a legislative hearing, Bebee's attorney argued that his client was being unfairly singled out. He had knowledge of comparable cases in which "members of the Legislature had received stock in banks, for charters on which they had voted, and there had been no concealment in those cases—no sense of impropriety" (*AEJ*, February 21, 1831). Indeed, Erastus Root, who served in the state assembly between 1798 and 1830, claimed that "no one would hesitate, from motives of delicacy, to offer a member [gratis] shares in a [proposed] bank" (Alexander 1906, p. 190). After a brief debate, the House reprimanded Bebee in a "forcible and solemn manner" and sent him on his way.[10]

Statistics reported in table 7.2 provide some appreciation for the potential scale for corruption and bribery. Between 1830 and 1837, the New York State Assembly received 535 petitions, each one "praying" for a charter from a group of would-be bankers. From those 535 petitions, Assembly committees drafted and reported 236 separate chartering bills for debate on the floor. Of those 236 bills, 134 eventually passed. Of those, only 53, or less than half, later passed the Senate. While citizens could freely petition the legislature, getting the eight members of the Assembly banking committee to take notice of a petition, turn it into a bill, and report it to the floor demanded something notable or especially meritorious on the part of the petitioners. It was common for petitions to be delivered in person by groups of "interested citizens." In most instances how those citizens' interests were expressed is left to the imagination because even contemporary critics generally did not report details of the bribes. In those few instances

10. Bebee's comments about members receiving shares in banks whose charters they had voted on stand in contrast to the *AEJ*'s recurring complaints about legislators' purposely excusing themselves from votes on some bank charters. Excusing oneself from a vote was an odd strategy for a legislator with a personal financial stake in the outcome, but there was a law prohibiting lawmakers from voting on incorporation acts in which they had a personal interest. Legislators who had been given or promised shares were under a legal obligation to excuse themselves. Of course, it does not mean that they did not influence the outcome through vote trading or other forms of log rolling. It is clear from reading the biographies of several members of the Regency that these men did not think it morally contradictory to accept shares in return for legislative influence but then scrupulously adhere to the letter of the law concerning voting rules. It was also not uncommon to draw a distinction between cash payments (bribes) and promises of shares (not bribes). It seems that the risks assumed in holding shares, compared to the certainty of taking cash, led some legislators to believe that they were fundamentally different transactions.

Table 7.2   **Petitions received, bills reported, and chartering acts passed by New York Assembly and Senate, 1830–37**

Year	Assembly			Senate			House and Senate
	Petitions received	Bills reported	Bills passed	Petitions received	Bills reported	Bills passed	Chartering acts
1830	23	22	12	37	34	13	9
1831	54	36	26	27	26	20	9
1832	91	49	19	23	19	16	7
1833	83	38	22	39	26	12	8
1834	92	31	21	33	24	13	8
1835	20	4	2	1	1	1	0
1836	118	54	32	36	28	19	12
1837	54	2	0	3	0	0	0
Totals	535	236	134	199	158	94	53

Source: Albany Evening Journal, various issues, 1830–37.

where the details became public, the most common form of a bribe was a promise of a handful of free shares in the proposed bank should the charter pass (J. Hammond 1852, p. 334; Seavoy 1982, p. 84). Given the low probability of receiving a charter, cash payments were less common. Promises of shares aligned the legislators' and the promoters' incentives.[11]

What is notable about the Regency leaders is that they channeled this corruption to the party's benefit rather than their own ends. Although the party's leaders did not line their own pockets, they made it possible for others to line theirs. The Regency's dominance, as Cole (1984, p. 95) notes, was based on the spoils system. Regency leaders understood that bending the system to their personal benefit would quickly alienate voters. But the party leadership realized that political machinery was fueled with money and jobs, and they distributed both to their friends and supporters. The Regency aligned banks and party through the distribution of equity shares in newly chartered banks to loyal party members.

11. Calculating the economic costs of the distortions engendered by this rent seeking is beyond the scope of this paper, but the potential costs of rent seeking are widely recognized (Murphy, Shleifer, and Vishny 1993). It is also notable that New York received substantially less revenue, as a percent of all state tax revenue, from bank dividends and taxes than any other state. Revenues from banks in New York exceeded 10 percent of state revenues in only one decade, whereas they made up about one-fifth of average state revenues in the antebellum era (Sylla, Legler, and Wallis 1987, pp. 400–401). New York's relatively low tax yield from banks was due to the state's relative financial underdevelopment. It may also have resulted from the policy of granting charters to party members who resisted returning those rents to the state in the form of taxes. Small distributional coalitions, as Olson (1965) shows, will be more effective lobbyists than large groups. Because banks were few and shares were closely held and managed by party favorites, the Regency-controlled legislature may have been reluctant to impose substantial taxes on banks.

Beginning in 1811, every incorporation act appointed administrators charged with distributing shares in the new bank. The issue of how shares were allocated gained popular attention in 1825 when the opposition party press publicized the distribution of the Commercial Bank of Albany's initial public offering. The men appointed to distribute the stock allocated most of the shares to themselves and a handful of friends. Political opponents contended that the administrators "had converted a matter of general interest into an affair of individual profit and speculation" (Chaddock 1910, p. 252).[12] During debate on the charter of the Bank of Herkimer County, Assemblyman Isaac Van Duzer of Orange County offered an amendment reducing the number of shares that the administrators could subscribe from 200 to 50. The amendment was soundly defeated, at which time Van Duzer exclaimed on the floor that the "Regency manifested no disposition to surrender the source of 'Spoils'" (*AEJ,* February 4, 1833).

It was 1837 before these distribution practices were changed. Twelve banks were chartered in 1836, and the distribution of stock in these banks was so partisan that even the Regency-appointed bank commissioners criticized the abuses in their annual report to the state assembly. The commissioners provided the details of the distribution of shares in the Jefferson County Bank of Watertown. Nine appointed administrators kept the subscription books open for two days, receiving more than 500 individual subscriptions for varying numbers of shares. Because the offering was oversubscribed, as nearly all new bank offerings were, the administrators had to develop a distribution scheme. Although the administrative panel was bipartisan, the Bucktails held a five to four majority, and their distribution plan was adopted. Through proxies and powers of attorney the bank's 12,000 shares were effectively divided between the nine administrators, each of whom took his legal limit of 250 shares, and seven other men who between them took 7,695 shares. At the time of the investigation, all 12,000 shares were held by just 36 men when about 500 had subscribed.[13] The re-

12. Limiting share ownership to a group of party friends and loyalists created potentially sharp distributional effects. Lamoreaux (1994) shows that many New England banks were insider affairs, wherein shareholders received the majority of their bank's loans. To the extent that New York banks were similarly insider institutions, non–party members were effectively denied access to credit (assuming that the demand for credit exceeded the supply and banks rationed credit based on party affiliation, which is consistent with even a casual reading of the contemporary and historical literature). The existence of a secondary market for shares, even if it was not particularly liquid, could mitigate this effect. If non–party members were willing to pay more for credit than party members, they could buy shares and become insiders and have preferential access to credit. In the latter instance, existing credit was (reasonably) optimally allocated, but a wealth transfer from non–party members to party members occurred. It does not, however, imply that the existing volume of available credit was socially optimal.

13. There was no formal secondary market in country bank shares so that shares traded informally and price information was not made public. Nevertheless, the market value of the Regency's share giveaway was surely substantial. City bank shares regularly traded at prices 25 to 30 percent above par.

port suggested that the Jefferson County Bank case was typical. It represented one of the many ways the Bucktails encouraged and rewarded party loyalty.

If the number of editorials appearing in the opposition press (the *Albany Evening Journal* was the most prominent) is a fair measure, by 1837 the public's tolerance for spoils, especially in connection to bank chartering, was waning. Flagrantly inequitable practices had fallen from favor and the legislature moved to correct them in response to growing public dissatisfaction. An 1837 act dictated that shares were to be sold at public auction. No individual was allowed to buy more than five shares on the first day of the auction or more than ten on the second or subsequent days. In an effort to guarantee local ownership, buyers had to be residents of the bank's home county. To head off speculation, shares could not be sold until three months after the entire capital had been raised. All transfers within the first year had to be accompanied by an oath that the seller was the bona fide owner and had not contracted to sell the shares prior to the initial auction. Ultimately, the law was a dead letter because New York's legislature never issued another bank charter.

Capitalizing on the electorate's growing frustration with Regency spoils and a financial panic in 1837, Whigs wrested control of the state legislature from the Democrats in the autumn 1837 elections. In the opening days of the 1838 legislative session, a senate committee was established to study the appropriateness of rewriting the banking laws to allow free entry of private bankers and reform the system of chartering commercial banks. The committee reported back that the time had come to replace the current chartering system, which was "utterly at war with equal rights and free government" (New York State Senate 1838, p. 4). As the end of the legislative term approached, a free banking act was hammered out and passed in April.

After more than a decade of debate, New York passed the Free Banking Act of 1838. In 1825 and 1828 special legislative commissions had studied comparable proposals but had rejected them. Indeed, the initial 1828 Safety Fund proposal (adopted in 1829) included some features of the 1838 free banking act, namely free entry and bond-secured note issue, but they were removed in favor of continued legislative chartering and regulatory oversight. By the mid-1830s, however, appeals to equal rights were commonplace and state-sanctioned economic advantages were attacked from all sides as usurpations of the true spirit of representative democracy and laissez-faire economics. New York's Free Banking Act, however, represented neither the inception nor the culmination of the electorate's backlash against state-supported economic privilege. It was not, as Redlich (1968) argued, incipient populism run amok. It was one step, albeit an important one, in New York's movement toward greater political representation and economic liberty.

7.3   Free Banking as Reform

Writing in the Regency-controlled *Albany Argus* in December 1836, New York State Comptroller Azariah Flagg announced the party's new position. "The law as it now exists," he wrote, "abridges the fair business rights of individuals, discountenances the free use of capital, and is detrimental to trade and commerce" (Flagg 1868, p. 8). To have Flagg, a high-ranking Regency official, publish such a statement in the official party newspaper represented an announcement roughly comparable to, say, Francis Perkins publicly announcing in 1936 that the Democratic leadership considered the National Labor Relations Act an unconstitutional restraint of trade. Flagg's editorial signaled widening cleavages within the electorate, the party rank and file, and the party leadership.

Indeed, abuses like those surrounding the distribution of stock in 1836 had created deep fault lines within New York's Democratic Party. Churchill C. Cambreleng, Van Buren's trusted lieutenant in the U.S. House of Representatives, wrote Van Buren condemning the Regency's banking policy (Seavoy 1982, p. 129). How and why had the Regency's leadership changed their views? Why were they willing to abandon the Safety Fund, often held up as one of their principal legislative achievements, just nine years after its enactment? Was it, as B. Hammond (1957) and Dowd (1992) contend, that the corruption involved in securing a bank charter and distributing shares had finally grown so politically indefensible or so socially costly that the entire structure was thrown over?

It turns out that the causes were more complex. While corrupt practices in the 1830s certainly played a role, free banking's origins date back a decade or more and represent not the culmination, but one leg of a long passage wrought by changing attitudes among the electorate, changes the Bucktails embraced only when they could no longer resist them and remain politically viable. A growing debate in New York over the extent of political participation and the extension of the franchise carried over into a parallel debate about the appropriate boundaries of economic freedom. Banking policy represented the ground where these concurrent struggles converged.

7.3.1   Setting the Stage for Free Banking

Free banking did not spontaneously emerge in 1838 without cause or precedent. Neither was it culmination of a simple agrarian populism. It was indicative of a broader push toward greater *political* and *economic* freedom occurring in states throughout the United States. In New York constitutional reform in 1821 extended the franchise and eliminated two principal sources of political and administrative centralization, the Councils of Revision and Appointment. The Council of Revision retained veto power over all legislation; the Council of Appointment made appointments to most municipal offices, including justices of peace, sheriffs, and mayors, and formed the basis of the Bucktails' spoils system. The constitutional reforms, resisted by the political elite for more than twenty years, conceded greater *political* determination to the electorate through greater local administrative autonomy and political self-determination.

Popular demands for greater political liberty led naturally to calls for greater freedom of economic association. In the early nineteenth century New York conceded greater freedom of association in religious, educational and charitable institutions instituting general incorporation laws for these institutions, but the state closely guarded its chartering privilege for business incorporation. As the economy developed in the northeastern United States and profitability, even in agriculture, became more dependent on access to credit and transportation, and to markets generally, the notion that incorporation could be reserved for the few became increasingly indefensible (Handlin and Handlin 1947, p. 113).

Several New England states liberalized incorporation in the early nineteenth century, but in New York the Bucktails retained control to bend incorporation to the party's will. The original 1828 Safety Fund proposal, in fact, included free incorporation and bond-secured note issue—the defining features of free banking—but Van Buren rejected these aspects of the original proposal because the party would have lost an important element of its spoils system. Even in 1838, when Governor William L. Marcy, one of Van Buren's lieutenants, signed the free banking act, he did so reluctantly mostly because the free incorporation clause stripped the party of one of its more lucrative sources of spoils. During the decade between 1828 and 1838, however, public opinion had turned strongly against the status quo. The state had long since ceded freedom of association for religious, educational, and charitable associations. It had long been asked to extend the privilege of corporate freedom of association to business corporations. It finally relented in 1838.

7.3.2   The Anti-Masons and Political Reform

The ultimate cause for banking reform can be traced to a long-simmering demand for greater economic freedom. But one of the more important proximate influences and one that brought the demand to a boil was an unlikely event—the disappearance on the night of 14 September 1826 of William Morgan, an unremarkable stonemason and disaffected Freemason of Batavia, Genesee County, New York. In the 1820s, Freemasonry was popular. From just 347 lodges and 16,000 members nationally in 1800, there were 450 lodges and more than 20,000 members in New York state alone in 1825 (Formisano and Kutolowski 1977). Bitter and nearly broke, Morgan threatened to publish Freemasonry's secrets. Local Masons, outraged by Morgan's betrayal, torched David Miller's printing shop and had both men arrested on trumped-up charges. Both were released from jail, but Morgan was kidnapped and never seen again. Rumor had it that a group of Freemasons spirited Morgan off to Fort Niagara, where he was briefly detained before being taken into to boat, thrown overboard into Lake Erie, and presumably drowned.

Investigations into Morgan's disappearance implicated a number of prominent Masons who were politically connected members of the Regency. Sheriffs initially refused to arrest them. When they were arrested, prosecutors refused to bring charges. When forced by popular outcry to bring the conspirators to trial, the tribunals quickly became theater, attracting hundreds of spectators. Newspapers published verbatim transcripts, and news spread by word of mouth. For more than four years, the public devoured the news, most of which demonstrated Freemasonry's (and, by association, the Regency's) subversion of the political and judicial systems. When most of the alleged conspirators were acquitted, a "firestorm of popular protest" was unleashed that grew into a legitimate political movement (Gunn 2001, p. 374). One contemporary book concluded that the abduction, murder, and cover-up was the work of hundreds of men, including prominent legislators, lawyers, and sheriffs. Special prosecutors appointed by the legislature reported on Masonic obstructionism and concluded that the basic charges of conspiracy, kidnapping, and murder were true.

Anti-Masonry's appeal and, therefore, its political legitimacy grew because reasonable men believed that Freemasonry disproportionately influenced the administration of justice (Vaughn 1983). Several sheriffs, prosecutors, judges, and other officials involved in the investigation and prosecution of the crime were Masons. Most discharged their duties fairly and impartially, but others manipulated the system to protect fellow Masons. Formisano and Kutolowski (1977, p. 153) conclude that a widespread conviction that there had been "a systematic corruption of justice . . . was far from fantastic." Building a platform on equality before the law, the Anti-Mason Party quickly emerged as a viable political force. The hot-button issues in the 1828 New York election were less the burning national issues of states' rights and internal improvements than the candidates' characters, Anti-Masonry, and whether it was time for special privilege to give way to the popular will. Andrew Jackson polled an unimpressive 51 percent in New York; Van Buren won the governorship, but only because two opponents, including Solomon Southwick, the Anti-Mason candidate, split the opposition vote (Benson 1961, p. 31).[14]

Anti-Masonry's consequences were profound. Between 1828 and 1835 the number of Masonic lodges in New York fell from 490 to 80, and active membership declined from 20,000 to just 3,000 (Benson 1961, p. 36). Once

14. We met Solomon Southwick before. He was one of the prominent lobbyists in the 1812 Bank of America chartering scandal.

it had crushed its principal opponent, neither the movement nor the Anti-Masonic Party petered out. An effective leadership with access to more than forty-five newspapers expanded the message. Privilege subverted more than criminal justice. Privileged and secretive organizations of all types, including politically favored corporations, subverted all forms of republican virtue. Equality before the law, equality of representation, and equality of opportunity became the party's watchwords. One speaker at the 1829 Anti-Mason convention insisted that "public opinion . . . must properly govern everything, which is properly subject to governmental power" (quoted in Benson, p. 22). The party's message appealed to a leveling impulse: universal male suffrage, universal state-supported education, anti-slavery, and better treatment of Indians, orphans, and the mentally ill (Van Deusen 1944).

Anti-Mason calls for reform quickly incorporated the era's hot-button economic issues. The party favored strict enforcement of usury laws, elimination of imprisonment for debt, expanding the transportation network, and, of course, greater sectional equality in the distribution of banking and financial services. Early histories of Anti-Masonry argued that it was motivated by rural-agrarian jealousies of urban commercial wealth and power. But Anti-Masonry was more than radical agrarian populism. It was driven more by middle-class frustrations over lack of access to banks and transportation infrastructure.

Many earlier banking historians, including B. Hammond (1957) and Redlich (1968), too readily interpreted western squawking about the shortage of banks as inflationist agrarianism. But Anti-Masonry had little to do with radical agrarianism. Instead, it was the political manifestation of a growing discontent among western merchants about lack of access to banks and bank credit. And merchants outside the traditional Bucktail strongholds had legitimate grounds for complaint. Table 7.3 reports bank capital per capita by senate district at selected dates between 1830 and 1857.[15] Not surprisingly, New York City outstripped all other regions, with Albany a distant second. But even outside the two principal urban-commercial areas, there were sharp disparities in the distribution of bank capital. The Adirondack/Lake Champlain region (IV) had just $0.45 in per capita bank capital, while the Finger Lakes region had $5.66. The eight-region Gini index for 1830 is 0.69, implying substantial inequalities. Moreover, in 1830 fully two-thirds of all New York counties, mostly in western and southern New York, were without a bank.

Passage of the Safety Fund, and the increased chartering that accompanied it, led to more equally distributed bank capital per capita. Even in the

---

15. The dates were chosen to control for broad macroeconomic events to the extent possible. The 1830s and 1850s were both periods of relative early prosperity followed by sharp financial panics in 1837 and 1857.

Table 7.3   Per capita bank capital by New York State Senate district
(current dollars)

Senate district	Bank capital per capita ($)			
	1830	1837	1850	1857
I	51.18	56.17	36.56	65.38
II	1.77	7.44	9.22	12.07
III	11.67	19.04	16.50	33.02
IV	0.45	3.43	4.91	10.94
V	2.45	8.56	11.13	16.14
VI	1.49	5.64	5.43	10.50
VII	5.66	9.37	8.75	12.41
VIII	1.25	6.64	9.04	14.44
Gini index	0.69	0.48	0.35	0.36
Counties with no banks (%)	66.1	26.8	15.5	5.2

Sources: U.S. Department of State (1832, 1841), U.S. Census Office (1853, 1864), New York State Assembly (1831, 1838, 1858), *Daily Albany Argus* (25 November 1850).

Notes: District I includes New York City and Long Island; district II, the counties just north of New York City; district III, the counties surrounding Albany; district IV, the Adirondacks; district V, the Syracuse, Oswego, Watertown areas; district VI, the Southern Tier, around Binghamton; district VII, the Finger Lakes region; and district VIII, the western counties from Rochester to Buffalo and south to the Pennsylvania border

relatively underdeveloped Adirondack/Lake Champlain region bank capital per capita increased from $0.45 to $3.43 between 1830 and 1837. The Gini index declined to 0.48, and the number of counties without a bank declined sharply. It took free banking and a long period of economic prosperity between 1845 and 1857 to bring about greater equality of per capita banking capital and to provide nearly every county with at least one commercial bank. By the mid-1850s, every senate district attained double-digit per capita bank capital, and only three counties (5.2 percent) remained without a commercial bank. By 1850, too, the Gini index declined to 0.36 and remained steady throughout the decade.

Given the disparities in the geographic allocation of bank capital in 1830, it is not surprising that Anti-Masonry cut across economic classes (Kutolowski 1984; Formisano 1993). Indeed, support for Anti-Masonry was stronger in townships with more improved acreage, higher population densities, and higher values per acre. Anti-Masonry's leaders were mostly drawn from the middling to upper classes of western and southern New York—regions where the transportation and financial revolutions had not yet fully arrived (Kutolowski 1984). The Anti-Mason challenge was elementary, if somewhat naive: should not all men living in a democratic society have equal access to the opportunities offered by a rapidly expanding economy? Was it fair that the Masonic-dominated Regency granted unfair advantages in the race for wealth and prestige? In this respect, the movement appealed most strongly to those eager to "utilize participant politics to gain further transportation improvements, banking facilities, and . . . favorable local public policy" (Kutolowski, p. 281). Anti-Masonry flourished where the market had brought some limited prosperity. Its leaders wanted greater access to wealth-generating technologies—banks, canals, railroads—controlled by the Regency.

It was some time before the egalitarian impulse was translated into specific policies, such as free banking (Benson 1961, p. 37), but the movement gained momentum in the 1830s. In 1831, imprisonment for debt was abolished. The state expanded funding for education. Feeder canals were proposed, surveys done, and construction begun. Calls for the elimination of restraining laws on private banking reemerged in 1835 and 1836. Free banking was seriously debated in both houses of the legislature in 1837, just as a movement for a new constitutional convention took shape. At the Utica Convention of 1837 delegates called for the abolition of legislative chartering in all forms, demanded the elimination of all regulations restricting entry into any profession or occupation, and proposed a constitutional amendment prohibiting future legislatures from passing laws that favored one group over another (Gunn 1988, p. 172).

By 1837, legislative debates on banking policy were unmistakably Anti-Masonic. In condemning the assembly's committee on banks' decision not to report a bill for a bank, Assemblyman John Wilkinson of Onondaga County fumed that "the citizens of New York [City] cannot, without arrogance, assume to judge the propriety of incorporating a bank at Utica" (*AEJ,* March 22, 1836). That decision was best left to the citizens of Utica. A group of citizens in Albion forwarded a petition to the legislature stating that "the people are coming. . . . The spirit of reform is awake throughout the State" (*AEJ,* March 28, 1837). Indeed, the reform spirit had grown so strong that Regency governor William L. Marcy, in his annual message to the legislature, urged reform. The current system was "unquestionably injurious," and it was "the essential characteristic of private property, that the owner should not only have the right of exclusive possession, but the liberty of free use" (*AEJ,* January 3, 1837). Marcy's position, insofar as it dealt with banking, represented a significant liberalization of Regency attitude and policy. His position was more Anti-Masonic than Democratic.

Anti-Masonry demonstrates the sometimes serendipitous nature of economic reform; namely, how it can be dependent on events seemingly far removed from the underlying issue. Could those Masons who tossed William Morgan overboard have had any idea that they would unleash a political movement that would shake Masonry and the Regency to their foundations? Could they have contemplated the notion that the events they would unleash would result in rewriting the contract between the state and the business community? Of course not. This is not to argue that free banking depended on William Morgan's unsolved disappearance. Something akin to free banking had been proposed, but rejected as politically unpalatable, in 1828, a half decade prior to the establishment of the Anti-Masonic Party.

It does argue, however, that a seemingly unrelated, random event can be a critical element in bringing a latent demand for change to the fore. In this case, it led to the formation of an opposition political party that tapped into a latent demand for change in banking policy, sharpened its focus, and made it a prominent element of the party's platform. As B. Hammond (1957) and Redlich (1968) discuss, demands for greater access to bank credit were just as strong in Ohio, Indiana, Kentucky, and elsewhere as in western New York, yet change occurred at a more measured pace outside New York. Although seventeen other states adopted free banking, there was about a fifteen-year hiatus between free banking's enactment in New York and its adoption elsewhere (Rockoff 1975, p. 3).[16] Without an event such as Morgan's disappearance to galvanize the electorate, change was slower in coming. Thus, Anti-Masonry was, perhaps, not critical to change, but it accelerated the pace of change.

7.3.3 The Confluence of Party Rhetoric and Political Change in the Mid-1830s

Regency support for free banking became official policy only when the reform impulse was so far beyond their control that support for the repeal of the Safety Fund system came from a Democratic splinter group known as the Loco-Focos (or, sometimes, the Equal Rights Party). These were mostly tradesmen and small entrepreneurs in New York City who believed that the current system threatened their economic well-being. They believed that economic independence was based on property ownership. Any government that passed laws that favored accumulation by the few, as the Safety Fund did, was bad government. "A viable urban-industrial democracy required that opportunities for business profits had to be equalized" (Seavoy 1982, p. 130). And more than anything else, equality of opportunity implied equality of access to bank credit. The elimination of chartered commercial banking and its replacement with private banking was the best means to achieve this end.

Likewise, Jacksonian Democrats were driven by a strong egalitarian impulse (Schlesinger 1945; Sellers 1991). Jefferson's Republicanism had extended equality of opportunity to the yeomanry in the newly settled West. Banking policy in the early West was both inflationary and developmental (Bodenhorn 2003). States such as Kentucky, Tennessee, and Illinois, among others, established wholly state-owned banks to provide medium-term mortgage credit to farmers wanting to buy land. As a result, migrants

---

16. Michigan passed a free banking act in 1837 that was quickly rescinded, and New York and Georgia passed free banking laws in 1838. No further acts were passed until Alabama in 1849, followed by ten states between 1851 and 1853.

flowed in, bought up land, and, in a brief period, turned a frontier into a thriving agricultural community. As the Jacksonians saw it, something similar was needed to stem the rising tide of economic inequality in the emergent urban-industrial regions of the East.[17]

Free banking aligned Anti-Masons, Jacksonians, and the Loco-Focos. Loco-Foco calls for equality of opportunity appealed to the Jacksonians' sense of fair play. The nagging issue for banking policy, however, was how to simultaneously equalize opportunity and provide a safe, redeemable currency. Two bills introduced in the 1837 session skirted the issue. One bill would have repealed most of the 1804 restraining act that prohibited unincorporated firms from engaging in any banking functions. It would have allowed for the creation of limited-liability partnerships granting unincorporated associations of individuals the right to engage in all pertinent banking functions, except the circulation of notes (*AEJ,* March 18, 1837). The second bill would have created unincorporated banks with all the privileges of banks, including note issue, but these banks would not be allowed to circulate notes of denominations under $20 (*AEJ,* March 3, 1837). Both bills protected the public from bad banking by limiting their ability to interact with the public. Deposit banking was not yet widespread except among merchants, and few people engaged in routine transactions had much use for $20 or greater notes. Neither bill passed the state senate, largely because the attorney general believed that they were both unconstitutional in that they would have created de facto corporations in violation of the constitutional two-thirds requirement. In the end, the legislature rolled back certain features of the restraining act so that brokers could engage in some limited private banking functions (Seavoy 1982, p. 150).

Before the autumn elections in 1837, panic swept the nation's financial markets. Banks suspended specie payments, and Whigs soundly defeated the Bucktails at the polls. Whigs interpreted their victory as a mandate to dismantle the Safety Fund, and many traveled to Albany intent to pass a general incorporation law. Although William L. Marcy, the Bucktail governor, publicly recommended passage of a free banking law, he remained privately opposed. He understood that a general incorporation law would undermine the party's stranglehold on an important source of patronage.

17. Such a brief description of Jacksonian policy necessarily obscures the many contradictions that permeated Jackson's Democratic Party. The charismatic Jackson assembled a coalition of pro-bank and anti-bank men, rural agrarians and urban mechanics, ardent supporters of federally supported internal improvements and those equally ardently opposed to such expansion of federal intervention, as well as former Federalists and old Republicans. Thus, a cornerstone of Jacksonian Democracy was a deep antagonism toward banks. But it was also a party supportive of entrepreneurship and enterprise. Even Jackson's veto of the Second Bank's recharter did not "clarify the party's stance and future relationship with the hundreds of other banks in the country" (Sharp 1970, p. 5). Some Jacksonians sought to make banks safer so that more could be chartered. Others sought the complete abolishment of banking. The latter contributed the lasting party rhetoric, but the former ultimately had a greater influence on policy, as free banking in New York and elsewhere testifies.

Moreover, it might threaten the stability of the Safety Fund system itself. Seavoy (1982, p. 152) contends, as well, that Van Buren's subtreasury plan at the federal level—predicated on the idea that the government should separate itself from the business of banking—discredited the Regency's long and close connection with the state's banks. Marcy was forced into a corner and had little choice but to advocate passage of what he hoped would be a carefully crafted general incorporation law.

In April 1838, New York enacted free banking. Gunn (1988, p. 229) contends that the law represented "one of the most important pieces of state legislation in the first half of the nineteenth century." It reflected a transformation in the role of the legislature in economic matters: a movement away from, but not a complete abandonment of, the commonwealth ideal. Incorporation became a purely administrative function. The legislature relinquished its power to confer privilege to a bureaucracy charged to implement a set of procedures and policies applicable to all. Free banking depoliticized the business corporation and reflected the decline of legislative authority in economic matters. The corporation lost its essentially public character and became a purely private matter. It is ironic, however, that although the franchise was substantially widened, free banking and similar measures significantly restricted the electorate's ability to influence social and economic outcomes. Shortly after the public gained a greater say in politics, the polity built firewalls between itself and the economy. It was almost as if the electorate had come to appreciate the efficiency costs of Mancur Olson's (1982) distributional coalitions and did what it could to eliminate some of the costs by taking away at least one mechanism for establishing them.

7.3.4   The Consequences of Free Banking

Much was expected of free banking. A report of the select committee of the Assembly effectively summarizes contemporary expectations for free banking. A general incorporation law would eliminate the privilege and monopoly associated with the Safety Fund system. It would eliminate one source of legislative corruption and reduce log rolling. Bank ownership would be more widely dispersed. The banks themselves would be more rationally located. Greater access to credit would encourage commercial and manufacturing businesses. And, finally, it would increase and add stability to the currency.

Two major aspects of free banking are relevant to the issues addressed in this chapter, namely, privilege and greater equality of opportunity, especially among small-scale entrepreneurs. First, free banking replaced special interest legislation with a "rule of law." Relatively inflexible administrative procedures and policies replaced highly idiosyncratic, flexible, personalized charter conditions. Regulators administering rules were less prone to corruption than legislative committees and others given a measure of discretion (Glaeser and Shleifer 2003). The administrative policy was clear and precise and less likely to be subverted by legislative or judicial corruption.

Second, free banking reflected the leveling impulse of the Jacksonian era. The 1838 act brought together many of the features of the two 1837 proposals. One would have lifted restraints on individuals and partnerships wanting to operate private banks, and it was intended to promote the establishment of relatively small institutions that could respond to and accommodate local needs. The second proposal aimed to replace the current system of chartering relatively large, incorporated commercial banks. The final 1838 act included both features in that it established one standard for larger joint-stock banks and a lesser standard for individual (effectively note-issuing private) banks. Indeed, free banking encouraged small-scale entrepreneurship fully consistent with Anti-Masonic and Jacksonian, even Jeffersonian, rhetoric. In March 1850, for example, twenty-nine of forty-seven individual banks had $20,000 or less in paid-in capital, and between 1840 and 1850 the capitalization of the average free bank declined from $263,000 to $176,000.[18]

In its encouragement of small business, free banking advocates believed they had simultaneously addressed the issues of corruption, privilege, equality of opportunity, and protection of the public against incompetent bankers through the 100 percent note-collateral provision. Some Jacksonians criticized banks because they believed that banks, and corporations generally, occupied privileged positions, exercised disproportionate economic power, and were capable of doing serious political and economic damage. Anti-bank Democrats were convinced of the economic damage that could be wrought by banks when, during the bank war, Nicholas Biddle contracted the Second Bank's credit and threw the economy into recession. If a bank hiccuped and the economy fell into recession, what might happen if one or more large banks failed? What if they aligned themselves in opposition to the commonweal? Such questions brought concerns for the safety and security of bank creditors to the forefront. Free banking, it was believed, simultaneously addressed these multiple concerns. In encouraging small banks, they would not obtain disproportionate political or economic influence, and their ability to inflict losses would be limited.

Although loss rates for failed free banks in the 1840s were substantial, by the 1850s the loss rate fell sharply and was well below that experienced by the failures of eleven of the Regency's Safety Fund banks. This reduced loss rate in tandem with a more responsive allocation of bank capital made

18. The capitalization of the average chartered bank remained constant at about $375,000. Banks chartered under the Safety Fund system or earlier were allowed to maintain their charter for the lifetime of the charter (twenty years to perpetuity) but were forced to convert to a free banking charter at expiration of their original charter. The last Safety Fund banks switched to free banking charters in the late 1850s.

free banking attractive. Eventually seventeen other states passed free banking laws modeled after New York's. Three others significantly liberalized chartering and adopted bond-secured note issue. During the U.S. Civil War, free banking went national when the national banking system adopted several features of New York's 1838 law. While Anti-Masonry was not particularly exportable, as the party never became much of a factor outside New York, free banking was eminently exportable. The reform impulse of the Jacksonian era was strong, but translating the latent impulse into specific policies differed from state to state. Investigating the political conditions under which free banking was adopted elsewhere would be a potentially fruitful line of future research.

7.4   Concluding Remarks

Free banking was neither Jacksonian laissez-faire run amok, as Redlich (1968) would have us believe, nor was it a knee-jerk reaction by newly ascendant Whigs looking to tear down a prominent component of the Regency's political machine. It resulted from parallel movements begun in the early nineteenth century that called for greater political and economic self-determination. Changes in New York's constitution in 1821 largely met the former demands, but Van Buren's Regency retained enough control over the distribution of economic privilege, through special incorporation acts for all types of businesses, to fester discontent.

An unlikely event, however, sparked the formation of a rival political party, one committed to economic equality and one with an ability equal to the Regency's to get its message out to the electorate through the partisan press. Thurlow Weed's *Albany Evening Journal* was an effective counter to the Regency's *Albany Argus.* Indeed, rarely a fortnight passed between 1830 and 1837 when there was not an editorial about banking or bank chartering in Weed's *Journal.* There were an equally small number of weeks in which the *Argus* dared to discuss the subject.[19] Apparently, the Regency's official strategy was to ignore Anti-Masonic attacks on its bank chartering policy. That, in the end, may have been one of the Regency's larger mistakes. It let the opposition define the debate and rarely responded with a defense of its policy. The Regency's silence must have appeared to many contemporaries as conceding the point—that corruption was rampant, that the Democrats were the party of "spoils," and that they had no intention to reform the system. Such sentiments, combined with a common belief that increased access to banks accelerated the rate of capital accumulation and economic growth, spurred a reform impulse to which the

---

19. This observation is based on a reading of nearly every issue of each newspaper published between 1830 and 1837.

Democrats failed to respond. Free banking—and, later, general incorporation—was but one consequence of the leveling impulse in New York.

References

Alexander, DeAlva Stanwood. 1906. *A political history of the state of New York.* Vol. I. New York: Henry Holt.

Benson, Lee. 1961. *The concept of Jacksonian democracy: New York as Test Case.* Princeton, NJ: Princeton University Press.

Bodenhorn, Howard. 2003. *State banking in early America: A new economic history.* Oxford: Oxford University Press.

Calomiris, Charles W. 1989. Deposit insurance: Lessons from the record. *Federal Reserve Bank of Chicago Economic Perspectives* 13 (May/June): 10–30.

Chaddock, Robert E. 1910. The Safety Fund Banking System in New York, 1829–1866. 61st Cong., 2nd Sess. Senate Document no. 581. National Monetary Commission. Washington, DC: Government Printing Office.

Cole, Donald B. 1984. *Martin Van Buren and the American political system.* Princeton, NJ: Princeton University Press.

Countryman, Edward. 2001. The Empire State and the Albany Regency. In *The Empire State: A history of New York,* ed. Milton M. Klein, 295–306. Ithaca, NY: Cornell University Press.

Dowd, Kevin. 1992. U.S. banking in the "free banking period." In *The experience of free banking,* ed. Kevin Dowd, 206–40. London: Routledge.

Evans, George Herberton, Jr. 1948. *Business incorporations in the United States, 1800–1943.* New York: National Bureau of Economic Research.

Fenstermaker, J. Van. 1965. *The development of American commercial banking, 1782–1837.* Kent, OH: Bureau of Economic and Business Research, Kent State University.

Flagg, Azariah C. 1868. *Banks and banking in the state of New York from the adoption of the Constitution in 1777 to 1864.* Brooklyn, NY: Rome Brothers.

Formisano, Ronald P. 1993. The new political history and the election of 1840. *Journal of Interdisciplinary History* 23 (Spring): 661–82.

Formisano, Ronald P., and Kathleen Smith Kutolowski. 1977. Antimasonry and Masonry: The genesis of protest, 1826–1827. *American Quarterly* 29 (Summer): 139–65.

Frye, Timothy, and Andrei Shleifer. 1997. The invisible hand and the grabbing hand. *American Economic Review Papers and Proceedings* 87 (May): 354–58.

Gallatin, Albert. 1831. *Considerations on the currency and banking system of the United States.* Philadelphia: Carey and Lea.

Glaeser, Edward L., and Andrei Shleifer. 2003. The rise of the regulatory state. *Journal of Economic Literature* 41 (June): 401–25.

Gunn, L. Ray. 1988. *The decline of authority: Public economic policy and political development in New York, 1800–1860.* Ithaca, NY: Cornell University Press.

———. 2001. From factions to parties: The emergence of the second party system. In *The Empire State: A history of New York,* ed. Milton M. Klein, 369–82. Ithaca, NY: Cornell University Press.

Hammond, Bray. 1957. *Banks and politics from the Revolution to the Civil War.* Princeton, NJ: Princeton University Press.

Hammond, Jabez. 1852. *The history of political parties in the state of New York.* Syracuse, NY: Hall, Mills and Company.

Handlin, Oscar, and Mary Flug Handlin. 1947. *Commonwealth: A study of the role of government in the American economy; Massachusetts, 1774–1861.* New York: New York University Press.

Johnson, A. D. 1850. The legislative history of corporations in the state of New York. *Merchants' Magazine and Commercial Review* 23 (December): 610–14.

Kass, Alvin. 1965. *Politics in New York State, 1800–1830.* Syracuse, NY: Syracuse University Press.

King, Robert. On the economics of private money. *Journal of Monetary Economics* 12:127–58.

Knox, John Jay. 1903. *A history of banking in the United States.* New York: Rhodes.

Kutolowski, Kathleen Smith. 1984. Antimasonry reexamined: Social bases of the Grass-Roots Party. *Journal of American History* 71 (September): 269–93.

Lamoreaux, Naomi R. 1994. *Insider lending: Banks, personal connections, and economic development in industrial New England.* Cambridge: Cambridge University Press.

Lincoln, Charles Z., ed. 1909. *Messages from the governors.* Vol. II. Albany: J. B. Lyon.

Mauro, Paolo. 1995. Corruption and growth. *Quarterly Journal of Economics* 110 (August): 681–712.

Miller, Nathan. 1962. *The enterprise of a free people: Aspects of economic development in New York State during the canal period, 1792–1838.* Ithaca, NY: Cornell University Press.

Murphy, Kevin M., Andrei Shleifer, and Robert W. Vishny. 1993. Why is rent-seeking so costly to growth? *American Economic Review Papers and Proceedings* 83 (May): 409–14.

New York State Assembly. 1831. Report of the bank commissioners. Assembly Document no. 59, 25 January. Albany, NY: Author.

———. 1838. Annual report of the bank commissioners. Assembly Document no. 71, 24 January. Albany, NY: Author.

———. 1858. Annual report of the superintendent of the banking department. Assembly Document no. 4, 5 January. Albany, NY: Author.

New York State Senate. 1838. Report of the Select Committee on the Bill to Repeal the Laws Restraining Private Banking. Senate Document no. 42, 20 February. Albany, NY: Author.

Olson, Mancur. 1965. *The logic of collective action: Public goods and the theory of groups.* Cambridge, MA: Harvard University Press.

———. 1982. *The rise and decline of nations: Economic growth, stagflation, and social rigidities.* New Haven, CT: Yale University Press.

Redlich, Fritz. 1968. *The molding of American banking: Men and ideas.* New York: Johnson Reprint Company.

Rockoff, Hugh. 1975. *The free banking era: A re-examination.* New York: Arno Press.

Root, L. Carroll. 1895. New York bank currency: Safety fund vs. bond security. *Sound Currency* 2 (February): 285–308.

Schlesinger, Arthur M., Jr. 1945. *The age of Jackson.* New York: Book Find Club.

Seavoy, Ronald E. 1982. *The origins of the American business corporation, 1784–1855.* Westport, CT: Greenwood Press.

Sellers, Charles. 1991. *The market revolution: Jacksonian America, 1815–1846.* New York: Oxford University Press.

Sharp, James Roger. 1970. *The Jacksonians versus the banks: Politics in the states after the panic of 1837.* New York: Columbia University Press.

Spencer, Ivor D. 1959. *The victor and the spoils: A life of William L. Marcy.* Providence, RI: Brown University Press.

Sylla, Richard, John B. Legler, and John J. Wallis. 1987. Banks and state public finance in the new republic: The United States, 1790–1860. *Journal of Economic History* 47 (June): 391–403.

U.S. Census Office. 1853. *The seventh census of the United States, 1850.* Washington, DC: Robert Armstrong.

———. 1864. *Population of the United States in 1860.* Washington, DC: Government Printing Office.

———. 1872. *A compendium of the ninth census, 1870.* Washington, DC: Government Printing Office.

U.S. Comptroller of the Currency. 1876. *Report of the comptroller of the currency.* Washington, DC: Government Printing Office.

U.S. Department of State. 1832. *Fifth census, or enumeration of the inhabitants of the United States, 1830.* Washington, DC: Duff Green.

———. 1841. *Sixth census, or enumeration of the inhabitants of the United States.* Washington, DC: Blair and Rives.

Vaughn, William Preston. 1983. *The Antimasonic Party in the United States, 1826–1843.* Lexington: University of Kentucky Press.

Van Deusen, Glyndon G. 1944. Thurlow Weed: A character study. *The American Historical Review* 49 (April): 427–40.

Williams, Edwin. 1837. *The New York annual register for the year of our lord 1837.* New York: G. and C. Carvill.

Wright, Robert E. 1997. Banking and politics in New York, 1784–1829. PhD diss., State University of New York, Buffalo.

———. 2002. *Hamilton unbound: Finance and the creation of the American republic.* Westport, CT: Greenwood Press.

Regime Change and Corruption
A History of Public
Utility Regulation

Werner Troesken

8.1 Introduction

The history of public utility regulation in the United States has an odd circular quality. During the late nineteenth century, gas and electric companies were subject to limited regulatory oversight; by the early twentieth century, they were subject to burdensome municipal regulation; and by 1940, most gas and electric companies were subject to state and federal regulation (Stigler and Friedland 1962; Troesken 1996). Yet during the 1980s and 1990s, the regulatory bodies that had built up over the previous 100 years were abrogated, and gas and electric companies began operating in regulatory environments akin to those that had existed in the 1880s and 1890s (Joskow 1989). Similarly, in the American water industry, the governance regime progressed from private provision with limited municipal oversight during the nineteenth century to widespread municipal ownership by the mid-twentieth century (Baker 1897; Troesken 1999). During the 1970s and 1980s, municipally owned water companies were privatized by the score and returned to the governance regime that had prevailed during the nineteenth century, with private provision and limited municipal oversight (Galiani, Gertler, and Schargrodsky 2003; Vitale 2001).

What explains the circularity of public utility regulation? At least three possibilities suggest themselves. The first possibility is that technological changes altered the viability of alternative governance regimes over time.

Werner Troesken is a professor of history at the University of Pittsburgh and a research associate of the National Bureau of Economic Research.

I gratefully acknowledge helpful comments from conference participants, discussants, and referees. This research has been supported by the a grant from the NIA/NIH, P01-AG10120-09A1.

The second possibility is that ideological changes altered the preferences of voters and policymakers. During the early twentieth century, these ideological changes led policymakers to favor state-oriented solutions; by the late twentieth century, these changes led policymakers to favor market-oriented solutions. The third possibility appeals to the work of Mancur Olson (1982), who argued that over time institutions tend to ossify and slow economic growth as entrenched interest groups work to secure a greater share of society's resources. Olson's work suggests that transitions in regulatory and governance regimes—whether from market-oriented to statist, or vice versa—can dramatically improve the operation markets.

I argue that technological and ideological change can only partially account for the circularity of public utility regulation. Olson's theory of institutional ossification, which suggests that occasional regime changes are desirable in public utility markets, provides a more complete explanation. In developing this line of thought I build on three observations. First, corruption is endemic to public utility industries; corruption exists, in some form, across all regulatory and ownership regimes. Second, regime change in utility industries does not eliminate corruption; it only alters the type of corruption observed. Third, for any type of governance regime (e.g., state regulation or municipal ownership) corruption grows increasingly severe over time and, at some point, becomes politically untenable.

8.2   The Evolution of Public Utility Regulation

The following sections examine public utility regulation in the gas and electric industries and the water industry.

8.2.1   The Gas and Electric Industries

Regulation in the gas and electric industries evolved in four distinct phases: the first phase (ca. 1850–99) was a period of weak municipal control, referred to here as franchise regulation; the second phase (ca. 1900–1909) was a period of aggressive municipal control, referred to here as municipal regulation; the third phase (ca. 1907–77) was a period of state regulation; and the fourth phase (ca. 1978–present) has been characterized by limited state and municipal control and competition, and in many ways it mimics the first evolutionary phase described here.

In the first phase, gas and electric companies were regulated by municipal franchises. Franchises gave utilities the power to dig up streets and operate in particular cities and, in return for these rights, imposed obligations on the utility in question. Typically franchises were written as long-term contracts running from twenty to fifty years. These contracts also established price ceilings and minimum service thresholds. Franchises often expressed price ceilings in nominal dollars. Nominal price ceilings, however, worked poorly because the general price level fell steadily over the nineteenth century and because the technology of producing gas and electricity improved rapidly. These changes drove down the profit-maximizing price for gas and electricity. Consequently, within a few years of being established, price ceilings were typically not binding, even for firms holding monopoly positions. For example, Cleveland issued a franchise to the People's Gas Light Company in 1867. The franchise prohibited the company from charging more than $3 per 1,000 cubic feet (MCF), yet by the early 1870s, the company was charging only $2 MCF (Troesken 1996, pp. 12–15; Wilcox 1910).[1]

On occasion, cities supplemented their efforts to regulate gas and electric companies by encouraging competition. In large cities it was not uncommon to have as many as six or seven companies competing with one another, and there is little question that such competition reduced utility rates. For example, in Chicago during the late 1880s, competition among multiple gas companies on the city's west side drove gas prices down from $2.25 MCF to $1.00. However, except for very large cities like Chicago and New York, most markets were not sufficiently large to support competition, and even in those places where competitive price wars erupted, effective competition was short-lived. In Chicago, within a few years of the aforementioned price wars, all of the city's competing companies had merged into a single firm, and gas rates in the city were increased by 25 percent. The pattern observed in Chicago—competitive price wars followed by merger and price increases—was also observed in Atlanta, Baltimore, Buffalo, Cleveland, New York, and other large American cities (Troesken 1996, pp. 26–34).

It is important to be clear that municipal franchises were contracts. They imposed obligations on both the city and the private utility company, and they required the consent of both parties. City authorities could not unilaterally dictate the terms of the franchise. Indeed, in most areas, state constitutions prohibited municipal governments from directly and unilaterally regulating the rates charged by gas companies and other utilities without express legislative permission. As one federal court explained, "the regulation of the prices to charge consumers by gas companies is not one of the powers essential to municipal government, and is not included in general powers conferred on cities." The same court went on to explain that unless the state legislature explicitly granted regulatory powers to city governments, only the state could regulate gas rates: "and such power cannot be exercised by a city unless it has been delegated by the state in express words, or by fair implication from a power expressly granted" (*Mills v. City of Chicago, et al.,* 127 Fed. 731 1904, p. 731).

---

1. It was worth noting that in cable television, the regulatory structures adopted by cities in the late twentieth century were identical to those described here: franchises awarded to companies who would agree to terms specified by city officials. Compare the franchises described by Wilcox (1910) to those described by Williamson (1985).

The second phase in the evolution of public utility regulation took place between 1900 and 1909. During this period, many states began to pass laws authorizing municipal governments to directly regulate the rates charged by gas and electric companies, as well as other utilities. The states that passed municipal regulation laws were Arkansas, California, Florida, Iowa, Kansas, Minnesota, Mississippi, Missouri, Nebraska, and Ohio. The new municipal regulation laws meant that once a utility company's franchise contract with the city expired, city authorities could unilaterally dictate rates; gas and electric companies did not have to consent to the rates in order for them to become legally binding. Even in those states that did not pass these general municipal regulation laws, it was not uncommon to have the state legislature authorize specific cities to regulate utility rates. For example, in 1887 Tennessee authorized the City of Memphis to regulate gas rates, subject to the provision that the city never set rates below $1.50; other cities in the state continued to use municipal franchises to regulate gas rates.[2]

State regulation, the third phase in the regulation of gas and electricity, began in earnest around 1910. However, harbingers of this phase could be observed as early as 1887, when Massachusetts created a statewide commission to regulate public utilities in the state. Other states that created state regulatory commissions before 1910 were Georgia (1907), Michigan (1909), New York (1907), Vermont (1908), and Wisconsin (1907). The years between 1910 and 1920 witnessed the most rapid growth in state public utility commissions, with the following twenty-nine states introducing such commissions: Alabama, Arizona, California, Colorado, Connecticut, Idaho, Illinois, Indiana, Kansas, Maine, Maryland, Missouri, Montana, Nevada, New Hampshire, New Jersey, North Carolina, North Dakota, Ohio, Oklahoma, Oregon, Pennsylvania, Rhode Island, Tennessee, Utah, Virginia, Washington, West Virginia, and Wyoming (Stigler and Friedland 1962; Troesken 1996, pp. 6–17).

Of the phases of regulation discussed thus far, state regulation appears to have been the most durable and longest lasting. It was not until 1978 that the fourth phase in the regulatory history of gas and electricity was reached. In 1978, Congress passed the Public Utilities Regulatory Policy Act. Ostensibly designed to promote renewable energy sources, this law encouraged entry into the gas and electric industries across the United States and according to one authority "demonstrated the viability of competitive entry into the capital-intensive power generation business" (White 1996, p. 207). The competition-promoting aspect of this law was furthered when Congress passed the Energy Policy Act of 1992. The Energy Policy Act

2. See *New Memphis Gas & Light Company v. City of Memphis,* 72 Fed. 952 (1896). See also Troesken (1997).

mandated that the operators of regional transmission networks act as common carriers and allow unaffiliated producers to transmit power over their networks. The economic logic underlying this law was that the transmission of power had the characteristics of a natural monopoly but that the production of such power did not. In the years following the Energy Policy Act, individual states began allowing power consumers to purchase gas and electricity from any number of competing producers (White 1996).

8.2.2   The Water Industry

The water industry in the United States passed through three regulatory phases. In the first phase (1800–1879) privately owned and operated water companies were governed by municipal franchises, which, as noted above, were a weak form of municipal control. The second phase (1880–1970) was marked by municipal ownership, and private water companies governed by municipal franchises were replaced by municipally owned enterprises. The rise of municipal ownership began slowly during the late nineteenth century and grew quickly during the early twentieth century. Between 1890 and 1920, the proportion of water companies that were municipally owned grew from 43 percent to 68 percent. Similarly, between 1880 and 1932 the number of municipally owned water companies grew from 293 to 7,853 (Troesken 2001).

8.3   Corruption and Other Problems

All of the contractual mechanisms described above—franchise regulation, municipal regulation, state regulatory commissions, and municipal ownership—are imperfect devices, and each is susceptible to corruption, rent seeking, and other economic distortions. Understanding how these problems vary across different regulatory regimes is essential if one is to explain the link between corruption and the circular evolution of public utility regulation.

Before discussing the problems associated with each regulatory regime, a definition is in order. For my purposes, corruption refers to the *illicit* sale of political influence. The sale of political influence can take many forms, including the following: patronage arrangements (politicians buy votes by offering plum jobs at above-market wages); political extortion (politicians can extract bribes from private utility companies by threatening to impose confiscatory regulations and taxes); and industry capture (private utilities spend resources to make friends with regulators). For these examples of the definition of corruption offered above, the word *illicit* is critical. The act of selling political influence is not, in and of itself, corrupt. For example, through franchise bidding schemes, private utility companies pay for the right to an exclusive and legally protected market. As long as the fees private utilities pay for this right are returned to voters, either directly in the form of reduced taxes or through the provision of public services, this is a completely legitimate sale of political influence. The act only becomes corrupt if politicians pocket for themselves some or all of the proceeds of the sale.

8.3.1   Municipal Franchises

Municipal franchise regulation in many ways mirrored the franchise bidding schemes advocated by Demsetz (1968). Demsetz argued that by auctioning off the exclusive right to operate in a particular market, local governments could secure the benefits of regulation with none of the costs. Ex ante competition for the franchise, not a costly and corruptible administrative agency, would govern the behavior of the utility. As long as Demsetz's bidding scheme is fair and open, the utility that won the franchise would offer rates and service such that the utility would earn zero economic profits; price would equal average total cost. This solution is, of course, second best. A first-best solution would force the utility to adopt marginal-cost pricing and offer the utility a subsidy to compensate for its losses (Telser 1969, 1971). In an exchange with Telser (1969), Demsetz (1971) argued that concerns about marginal cost pricing were relatively unimportant in the context of public utility markets. History suggests Demsetz was correct on this point; there are much bigger fish to fry, particularly those related to corruption.

Franchise bidding schemes are subject to myriad corrupt and inefficient practices. The most obvious potential source of corruption relates to the initial sale of the franchise. It is easy to imagine scenarios whereby politicians allow producers to charge rates above average cost and then split the subsequent excess rents with producers through outright bribes and political donations. Different forms of corruption can also emerge depending on the length of the utility's franchise. Consider the case of a public utility that is offered a very short franchise, say for five years. Because the utility's assets are much longer lived, when the franchise comes up for renewal there are potential holdup problems. Politicians, for example, could claim that the utility failed in some areas of performance and then deny renewal. Local politicians could then undervalue the exiting firm's capital and split the rents with the entering firm, which acquires the capital at bargain rates (Miller 1993).

8.3.2   Regulatory Commissions

State regulatory commissions are subject to two problems. The first problem is not related to corruption and stems from the mechanics of rate regulation. State commissions in the United States set utility rates high enough to allow private utilities to earn a reasonable rate of return on their capital investments, typically around 8 percent. Rate-of-return regulation creates strong incentives for private utilities to exaggerate the size of their capital stock so that they will be able to charge higher rates. Jarrell (1979) presents evidence that, during the mid-twentieth century, privately owned electric companies that were regulated by state commissions had suspiciously high levels of capital investment. But private utilities need not cook their books to get favorable treatment; simply by investing more in capital investments than would unregulated firms, private utilities are able to secure a more favorable rate base (Averch and Johnson 1962).

The second problem comports with the definition of corruption offered above and is the long-standing idea that regulatory commissions are subject to industry capture. Crudely put, industry capture occurs when regulators get too close to the industry they regulate and begin promoting the interests of the industry at the expense of broader societal interests. More formally, one might think of industry capture in the context of the well-known work by McCubbins, Noll, and Weingast (1987, 1989). In this work, administrative agencies (like regulatory commissions) embody a contract between the legislature that created them and the interest groups that originally lobbied for them. It is in the interest of the legislature that creates an administrative agency to make it difficult for subsequent legislatures to undo their legislative actions, which represent a contract with the interest groups. It is also in the interest of the creating legislature to design a set of rules so that no matter the political, ideological, or economic background of the administrators, the agency will reflect the needs and wishes of the interest groups with whom the legislature struck its bargain. When subsequent legislatures undo the original contract, it is called coalitional drift. When subsequent administrators undo the original contract, it is called bureaucratic drift (Macey 1992; Shepsle 1992).

Industry capture is a type of bureaucratic drift. As the word itself connotes, capture upsets the original contract between the legislature and the interest groups, and it does so because the regulators get cozy with the industry. The legislature that creates a regulatory commission can try to limit the amount of coziness through any number of rules. It might, for example, prohibit commissioners from working in the regulated industry for some number of years after leaving the commission. It might also prohibit commissioners from communicating with industry leaders outside of a narrow set of official channels. But no matter how many rules the legislature makes, there always exists the possibility that the ideological or economic backgrounds of future regulators will undo the legislature's original commitments.[3]

---

3. While historical studies of regulatory commissions provide numerous examples of industry capture, they also suggest that industry capture is not inevitable. Moreover, to the degree that regulatory commissions have been captured in the past, it is not always producers who capture them. There are examples of consumers capturing the regulatory apparatus. The most famous of these is Albro Martin's (1971) study of farmers and the Interstate Commerce Commission during the early twentieth century.

8.3.3   Municipal Ownership

Municipal ownership is subject to the following three types of problems, which depending upon one's perspective might be considered corrupt. First, the assets of public utilities are long-lived, with distribution systems lasting 50 to 100 years before they are fully depreciated. Yet the time horizons of local politicians and voters—that is, those who control the assets under municipal ownership—are relatively short. Politicians come up for election every few years, and most voters move once or twice in a lifetime. This means that, confronted with a choice between the long-term viability of the utility system and an immediate short-term payoff, such as reduced rates for consumers or well-paying jobs for political supporters, politicians would invariably choose the short-term payoff. Investments that pay off ten to twenty years down the road are of little use to politicians concerned with the next election, or for voters with weak ties to the municipality served by the utility system in question.

The incentive to sacrifice the long-term viability of the capital stock for short-term payoffs can be minimized by granting control over investment and finance decisions to federal authorities (while most voters move from town to town, relatively few move from country to country) or by creating an oversight agency that is immune to short-term political cycles (as are many state judiciaries). The problem with these solutions is that they are, by their construction, immune to democratic forces, even though one of the standard justifications for public ownership is that it allows for a more democratic and egalitarian distribution of resources.

A second and related concern is the idea that municipal ownership supports a giant patronage scheme. In particular, politicians might garner support by giving away jobs at the local gas and electric companies. Nobody said it better than George Washington Plunkitt, the inimitable boss of Tammany Hall (Riordon 1994, p. 78):

> Some of the reformers are sayin' that municipal ownership won't do because it would give a lot of patronage to the politicians. How those fellows mix things up when they argue! They're givin' the strongest argument in favor of municipal ownership when they say that. Who is better fitted to run the railroads and the gas plants and the ferries than the men who make a business of lookin' after the interests of the city? Who is more anxious to serve the city? Who needs the jobs more?

Progressive Era conservatives worried that as the number of municipally owned utilities grew, so too would the number of municipal employees. Eventually municipal employees would come to dominate local politics. "One day," prophesied Robert Porter, the "unconsidered trifles who cluster round the local authority" would grow into a political "Frankenstein," a collective monster "so huge" that its "creators would not be able to control" it (Porter 1907, p. 109).[4]

The third concern with municipal ownership relates to the transition from private to public ownership. Consider the case of a city trying to purchase a private water company. Because the water company's capital is fixed, the city can use its power to regulate and tax strategically to reduce the water company's asking price. This difficulty is compounded by the fact that in nearly all situations there is a bilateral monopoly problem: there is only one seller (the private utility company) and only one buyer (the city). Of course, to the degree the municipality and the water company anticipate these difficulties, they can devise their primary contracts accordingly and minimize some of the problems associated with the transition from private to public ownership. Unfortunately, in practice, it was difficult for parties to anticipate every possible contingency, and some contracts simply were not allowed by the courts. Consequently, the actual transition from private to public ownership has, at least in the United States, frequently resulted in litigation—during the early twentieth century, about one-third of all attempts by cities to municipalize private water companies in their jurisdictions culminated in litigation (Troesken and Geddes 2003).

8.4   Corruption and Municipal Franchises, 1850–1905

During the nineteenth and early twentieth centuries, cities and private utility companies contracted through municipal franchises. As stated above, this arrangement mimicked the franchise bidding scheme proposed by Demsetz (1968). In theory, franchise bidding schemes sounded great. If the private utility (city) refused to agree to the rate ceiling (limits on regulatory authority), the city (private utility) could have turned to another private company (city) that was more amenable to such promises. Their actual historical performance was much less satisfactory, however. In practice, there was a dearth of firms competing for the right to enter specific urban markets, and more seriously, the absence of even a single firm willing to enter with only the promise of competitive returns. All potential entrants seemed to realize that there were substantial risks of ex post opportunism, no matter what cities might have promised in writing. Consequently, as compensation for this risk, private firms generally refused to enter unless there was a real possibility of recouping most of their investments within a relatively short time span. This meant that to attract private

---

4. Although municipal ownership might have facilitated patronage arrangements, it was not a prerequisite for patronage. Private utility companies and local politicians could just trade favors directly: "you hire our friends and political supporters, and we'll go easy on you the next time the city sets gas rates." In describing the situation during the late nineteenth and early twentieth centuries, Yearly (1970, pp. 117–18) observes that in return for favors from local politicians, private utility companies "were obliged to respond not only with cash but also with places for those who, though deserving, could not be accommodated on the public payroll."

capital, cities typically had to permit utility companies to charge rates at or near monopoly levels (Troesken 1997; Troesken and Geddes 2003).

The promise of high profits, even it came with risks, was sufficient to attract private investors. For monopolistic franchises with few regulatory constraints, private companies were willing to pay handsomely, and it was this willingness to pay that helped finance much corruption. To highlight the connection between monopolistic franchises and corruption, consider the following examples. During the early 1900s, in Grand Rapids, Michigan, the mayor and multiple members of the city council were implicated, and eventually convicted, in a scheme to sell a lucrative franchise to a private water company. The politicians and the promoters of the water company were eventually caught, tried, and convicted. Their trials garnered nationwide attention and were front-page news in cities as far away as New York and Phoenix. At one point during the trials, at least one defendant tried to bribe jury members to vote against conviction.[5]

In Chicago in 1894, the promoters of a local railway company spent lavishly to secure passage of a valuable franchise that faced widespread voter opposition. Four members of the city council received $25,000 each for their votes in favor of the franchise, and other members of the council received $8,000 each for their votes. One particularly important Chicago politician was said to have received $100,000 for his role in securing passage of the franchise. W. J. Onahan, for two years the comptroller for the City of Chicago, believed that all of the bribery and graft associated with the sale of franchises cost the city millions of dollars that otherwise could have been used to lower taxes:[6]

> If the city . . . had received proper annual compensation for all the franchises that have been ignorantly and corruptly disposed of for nothing, Chicago would today have income enough to run its affairs without levying a dollar of taxation on real estate or personal property. . . . The street railways, the gas companies, the electric lighting companies, the telephone companies, the water privileges, the dock privileges . . . every one of these favored interests, which secured their privileges by bribing Aldermen and corrupting officials, ought to [pay] millions in annual tribute to the city.

In St. Louis in 1898, the promoter of a local railway company paid bribes between $3,000 and $17,500 to local politicians in return for securing a

---

5. See *Arizona Gazette* (Phoenix), December 1, 1903, p. 1, and December 2, 1903, p. 1; and the following issues of the *New York Times:* November 15, 1903, p. 2; November 22, 1903, p. 1; December 1, 1903, p. 1; December 2, 1903, p. 3; and December 27, 1903, p. 2. For some of the legal issues surrounding the trials of the men convicted in this scheme, see the following court cases: *People v. Albers,* 137 Mich. 678 (1904); *People v. Mol,* 137 Mich. 692 (1904); *People v. McGarry,* 136 Mich. 316 (1904); and *People v. Salsbury,* 134 Mich. 537 (1904).

6. The information and quotation in this paragraph are from Stead (1894), pp. 176–77 and 199.

franchise to operate in the city. In the end, the promoter paid about $250,000 in bribe money, none of which was returned to the city. The promoter, however, was eventually convicted and sentenced to five years in prison, as were several prominent St. Louis politicians. The same basic story obtained when St. Louis granted lighting franchises. Once, in the midst of all this graft and corruption, a newly elected member of the city council expressed concern that if voters discovered such schemes he and other politicians might be voted out of office. His colleagues "laughed" and "assured him that the political power of the boodlers was too great."[7] The histories of Chicago, St. Louis, and Grand Rapids, while perhaps exceptional in terms of the richness of the historical record and the detailed information about the amount of money that changed hands, are representative of a much larger pattern of graft and corruption associated with the granting of franchises to private utility companies.[8]

8.5 Corruption and Municipal Regulation, 1900–1915

As stated above, during the early twentieth century, many states began to pass laws authorizing municipal governments to directly regulate the rates charged by gas and electric companies, as well as other utilities (Troesken 1997). These new municipal regulation laws meant that once a utility company's franchise contract with the city expired, city authorities could unilaterally dictate rates; gas and electric companies did not have to consent to the rates in order for them to become legally binding. Although the political origins of this form of municipal rate regulation have not been studied extensively, the existing evidence seems to suggest that it was consumers and local politicians who pushed state legislatures to authorize municipal governments to regulate utility rates unilaterally (Troesken 1996, pp. 55–63). Consumers saw municipal regulation as a way to get lower utility rates while local politicians saw it is a way to extract rents from the industry more effectively. Unfettered municipal rate regulation probably helped to reduce utility rates to consumers, but it did not eliminate the presence of corruption, and might have even exacerbated it.

Describing municipal regulation of urban transit systems during the late twentieth century, Pashigian (1976, p. 1258) writes: "With some exceptions, the regulatory agencies [at a local level] have been captured not by the transit firms of the industry but by the riders." Observers of the early twentieth-century gas industry said the same thing. In a speech be-

---

7. These events are recounted in an article published by a St. Louis district attorney, Folk (1903).
8. See, for example, Brown (1905), National Civic Federation (1907), National Municipal League (1896), Rosewater (1903), Zueblin (1918), and Steffens (1964). See also Troesken (1996, pp. 45–49) for the corruption associated with the granting of gas company franchises in Chicago.

fore the Pacific Gas Association, an officer of a San Francisco gas company stated:[9]

> When the time for the regulation of rates arises, a [city] councilman or supervisor, elected on a platform that calls for a reduction in the gas and electric rates, is hardly in a proper frame of mind to listen to evidence and impartially vote thereon. No matter what the evidence is, if he does not vote for a reduction a large number of citizens, and all of the daily papers, will accuse him of being biased in favor of the corporation.

Forrest McDonald, biographer of Samuel Insull and noted historian, concurs: "At the turn of the century, public utilities were regulated by municipal governments. Such regulation was governed largely by political concerns; shrewd politicians . . . recognized . . . that voters were often inclined to respond favorably to attacks on utilities" (McDonald 1957, p. 117).

A few examples illustrate the politicized and often corrupt nature of municipal regulation. In 1905 Illinois granted the Chicago City Council the authority to regulate gas rates. A few years later, Carter Harrison ran as a Chicago mayoral candidate. Harrison, and several candidates for city council, promised that, if elected, they would reduce gas rates in the city from 85¢ to 70¢. After Harrison and his friends won they launched an investigation into the costs of manufacturing and distributing gas. The expert they hired, W. J. Hagenah of the Wisconsin Public Utilities Commission, recommended a 77¢ rate. According to Hagenah, anything lower than 77¢ would not allow producers a reasonable rate of return. Chicago authorities promptly fired Hagenah and hired Edward Bemis. After paying Bemis five times the salary they paid Hagenah, Chicago authorities got the result they wanted. Bemis recommended, and the city eventually passed, a 70¢ rate ordinance. Ironically, earlier in his political career Carter Harrison had opposed attempts by the city to regulate gas rates, arguing that the city would use the power to regulate rates only as a way of "blackmailing" Chicago gas companies—if the gas companies did not pay off the city council, the city would order them to reduce rates (Troesken 1996, pp. 67–73).

On May 4, 1891, the Cleveland City Council passed an ordinance requiring the city's two gas companies to reduce their rates from $1.00 to $0.60. The ordinance grew out of a plan launched by Cleveland's newly elected mayor. The mayor thought the city paid too much to light streets and public buildings. He directed several members of the city council to meet and devise a plan to lower the city's gas bill. At one of these meetings, one council member suggested that private consumers also paid too much for their gas. Someone else said that the price of gas for private consumers

---

9. From a speech delivered before the Pacific Gas Association at its annual convention in the fall of 1908. The speech was reprinted in the *American Gas Light Journal,* September 28, 1908, p. 527.

should be reduced to 60 cents. The other council members agreed that 60 cents was a good rate. Within a few days, and without any investigation into the costs of manufacturing gas, the council passed an ordinance setting rates at 60 cents.[10] Officials in other cities exhibited a similarly cavalier attitude.[11]

Perhaps the clearest example of outright corruption occurred in San Francisco. In 1906, fifteen of the city's sixteen supervisors took bribes from the Pacific Gas Light and Coke Company in return for reducing not to 75¢ but to 85¢ per 1,000 cubic feet. These supervisors had been elected on the Union Labor platform which during the preceding election had promised voters that rates would be reduced to 75¢ (Jacobson 2000, p. 99).

Although substantive due process[12] protected utility companies from the most egregious forms of municipal regulation, securing that protection was neither cheap nor timely. Recall the story about Chicago and the 70¢ gas ordinance. After the city enacted the ordinance, Chicago gas companies sued for injunctive relief. They claimed, among other things, that 70 cents was a confiscatory rate. Litigating in every state and federal court imaginable, the city and Chicago gas companies battled for nearly two decades before the gas companies won (Troesken 1996, pp. 71–72). Litigating substantive due process questions took so long, in part, because of the rules adopted by the courts. For example, the courts granted immediate injunctive relief only when there was overwhelming evidence that regulators had set confiscatory rates. In more ambiguous cases, the courts allowed the rates to go into effect. If after the rates went into effect the company continued to find them confiscatory, it could file another claim.[13]

10. The following issues of the *Cleveland Leader and Herald* describe the battle between the city council and the gas company: May 5, 1891, p. 8; August 11, 1891, p. 8; August 12, 1891, p. 5; August 25, 1891, p. 8; August 28, 1891, p. 8; November 14, 1891, p. 8; and June 1, 1892, p. 1.

11. One might ask if the examples from Cleveland and Memphis truly illustrate corruption. They clearly illustrate bad public policy, but this is not necessarily the same thing as corruption. What happened in Cleveland and Memphis was corrupt in the following sense. Local politicians used gas rates as a way to score short-term political points at the expense of the longer-term and broader interests of voters in both cities. One might also argue that had voters been fully aware and informed of the long-term consequences of such capricious regulatory behavior they would not have tolerated such actions.

12. Substantive due process, which grew out of the Fourteenth Amendment, protected private utility companies against confiscatory rate regulation—regulation that set rates so low that firms could not earn a reasonable rate of return. The famous *Reagan* and *Smyth v. Ames* decisions established the rule: when regulators set rates too low, they violated producers' Fourteenth Amendment rights. Reconstructionists intended the Fourteenth Amendment, adopted in 1868, to protect recently emancipated slaves from the ravages of Jim Crow. As it read, the amendment guaranteed all persons "equal protection of the laws" and forbade governments from depriving "any person of life, liberty, or property, without due process of law." Whatever its original purpose, though, by the late nineteenth century, the Fourteenth Amendment protected all industries against overzealous regulatory policies. See Hovenkamp (1991) and Troesken (1996), p. 12.

13. See *William R. Wilcox v. Consolidated Gas Company of New York,* 29 S. Crt. 192 (1908), and *Des Moines Gas Company v. City of Des Moines,* 35 S. Crt. 811 (1914).

Municipal rate regulation undermined the long-term viability of private utilities in much the same way as termites destroy a home: slowly eating away at unseen support structures. Once local politicians acquired the ability to regulate utility rates unilaterally, they abused that authority to win election or extort bribes from private utility companies. This raised the costs of operating private utilities and discouraged future investment in utility industries. As Troesken (1996, pp. 74–76) shows, the implementation of municipal regulation of gas rates in Chicago was associated with a slowdown in investments in new gas lines in the city. Other studies show that onerous municipal regulations discouraged capital formation in the gas and water industries throughout the United States (Troesken 1997; Troesken and Geddes 2003). In the case of water, underinvestment posed serious public health risks, leaving cities vulnerable to epidemics of typhoid, cholera, and diarrheal diseases (Troesken 2001).

8.6   Corruption and State Regulation, 1907–70

Between 1907 and 1922, nearly thirty states created statewide commissions to regulate public utilities (Stigler and Friedland 1962; Stotz and Jamison 1938, p. 450). Legislators created regulatory commissions largely in response to the lobbying efforts utilities. Utilities lobbied for state regulation because they saw it as a politically expedient way to undermine the periodic shakedown schemes implemented by local authorities. Testifying before the Illinois legislature, an official of the People's Gas Light and Coke Company (of Chicago) pleaded (*Chicago Tribune,* April 28, 1905, p. 6):

> By city regulation you place it in the hands of the people interested to sit in judgement of their own case. Despite their protestations of fairness they could not restrain from giving themselves the best of it. Therefore we fear city regulation. . . . [W]e do not want to be at the mercy of the city. Let there be a commission appointed, a state commission appointed by the governor. . . . Let this commission examine books and investigate accounts, let the commission fix rates.

Blackford (1970 and 1977), McDonald (1957, 1958 and 1962) and others document the same patterns in many other states.

Although utilities supported state regulation because they believed it would undermine the onerous policies of local regulators, it is important to be clear that in a perfect world they would have preferred to have been subject to no rate regulation whatsoever. Furthermore, there is evidence that consumers and municipal governments played an instrumental role in shaping the creation of state public utility commissions. Indeed, state commissions represented, at least initially, a compromise position among utility companies, local governments, and consumer groups (Troesken 1996, pp. 79–89). The nature of this compromise was highlighted by the Illinois

General Assembly (1913, p. 861) when the assembly recommended the creation of a state regulatory commission:

> If municipalities are incapable of protecting their citizens for any reason from the unjust exactions of public service corporations, it is the duty of the State to protect them in such a manner it deems right and proper. Conversely, if the citizens of a municipality, through their representatives, take such action as will destroy or confiscate public utility investments, it is likewise duty of the State to assert its paramount authority to the end that justice may be accorded to citizens interested in such concerns.

In short, state regulatory commissions were designed to protect the interests of both consumers and producers from the opportunistic behavior of competing parties (Goldberg 1976; Troesken 1996).

During the early years of state regulation, it appears that the regulatory commissions did a reasonably good job balancing the interests of consumers and producers. Existing studies of the effects of utility regulation during the period from 1915 through 1940 find that the commissions kept rates substantially below their monopoly levels but at the same time not so low that they were confiscatory (see, for example, Troesken 1996, pp. 81–93, and Twentieth Century Fund 1948).

This early optimism, however, eventually gave way to pessimism, and since the 1960s a series of studies have emerged suggesting that regulation during the late twentieth century has been much less effective. In a seminal paper, Stigler and Friedland (1962) compared electric rates in states with and without state utility commissions; their data come from the early twentieth century when regulatory regimes varied across space. Stigler and Friedland found that rates and profits were not significantly lower in states with utility commissions. From this, they concluded that state regulation allowed utility companies to charge high rates and earn monopoly profits. Similarly, Moore (1970) estimates demand and cost equations to isolate the effects of regulation. Moore uses a cross section of electric utilities operating in 1962. He finds that state regulation lowered rates from monopoly levels by only 3 percent.[14]

The evolution suggested by the extant literature is that state utility regulation grew increasingly pro-producer over time and that state commissions gradually came to be captured by the interests of private utility companies. Although the origins of the deregulation movement of the late

14. A study by Meyer and Leland (1980) is slightly more sanguine and finds that state regulation can, in some cases, have a substantial effect on utility rates. Meyer and Leland pool data from forty-eight states over the period 1969 through 1974. These data, and the estimating procedure used, allow for the possibility that the effectiveness of regulation varies over time and across space. Allowing for this possibility distinguishes Meyer and Leland's study from earlier work. They find "pervasive differences" in "regulatory impact across states." In a few states, state regulation significantly reduced utility rates; in other states it did not.

1970s and early 1980s remain puzzling to many students of political economy (e.g., Peltzman 1989), one possibility is that industry capture and corruption became too costly to be sustained and that deregulation was pursued as a means to reduce these costs. It is still too early to tell if the deregulation of private utility companies was a complete success (see Joskow 1989, 1997). Nonetheless, if history is any guide, it would seem that to the extent current governance frameworks mirror those that were tried in the past (i.e., franchise bidding schemes), they too will give way to problems of corruption.

8.7 Corruption and Municipal Ownership, 1880–1970

Largely a response to concerns about corruption (Glaeser forthcoming), the move to public ownership was, at least initially, associated with dramatic and observable improvements in the operation of utility industries. In particular, public acquisition was associated with dramatic price reductions; expansions in service to previously underserved neighborhoods; and, in the case of water, reduced disease rates especially for poor socioeconomic groups. In terms of the effect of public ownership on prices, consider the following. In 1899 the federal government conducted a survey of the rates charged by public and private water companies. Including nearly one-third of all water companies then operating in the United States, the survey found that the rates charged public water companies were, on average, 24 percent lower than the rates charged by private companies (U.S. Commissioner of Labor 1899). However, the discount offered by public companies varied with size; small public companies offered large discounts from comparably sized private companies while large public companies offered little, if any, discount from comparably sized private companies. Historical time series data suggest the same interpretation: utility prices fell sharply after public acquisition (see, for example, Thompson 1925). Formal econometric studies comparing the rates of public and private utility companies during the late twentieth century provide further corroboration: publicly owned utilities tend to charge lower rates than privately owned utilities (e.g., Peltzman 1971; Kwoka 2002).

The experiences of Billings, Montana, and New Orleans, Louisiana, illustrate the dramatic improvements in service quality and the reduction in waterborne disease rates that often followed public acquisition. Before being taken over by the city, the Billings Water Company had no purification plant and only a limited system of mains. After acquiring the company in 1915, city officials immediately began raising funds to build a purification plant and extend mains to all areas of Billings (*Engineering News,* February 18, 1915, p. 365).

In New Orleans, the New Orleans Waterworks Company began operations in 1878. A private corporation chartered by the State of Louisiana, the company was the exclusive supplier for the portion of New Orleans located on the north side of the Mississippi River. Court documents and government investigations indicate that the company distributed water from the Mississippi unfiltered. Because thousands of municipalities upstream of New Orleans dumped raw and untreated sewage into the Mississippi, failure to filter and chlorinate water generated serious outbreaks of waterborne diseases such as typhoid fever and infantile diarrhea. In addition to being tainted by disease, the water distributed by the New Orleans Waterworks Company was visibly muddy. Consequently, almost no one used the water for drinking, and instead most city residents purchased bottled water or used cisterns to collect rainwater. When the National Board of Fire Underwriters visited New Orleans at the turn of the century, they found the city's water system wholly inadequate, and recommended the city take immediate steps to extend mains and increase the number of fire hydrants.

During the 1890s, residents of New Orleans grew so dissatisfied with the high rates, poor service, and rampant political corruption associated with the New Orleans Waterworks Company that they began pushing to have the company's charter revoked. These efforts were successful, and the state supreme court appointed a receiver to liquidate the company's assets in 1901. The city initiated proceedings to acquire the New Orleans Waterworks Company in 1903 and acquired the water system in 1908.[15]

Soon after the city acquired the water company, there was an unprecedented expansion in service. Miles of water mains per 10,000 persons grew by a factor of 4.5 between 1905 and 1915. Besides extending mains to all areas of the city, local officials also installed a water filtration system immediately after acquiring the waterworks in 1908—the new filtering system employed sedimentation, coagulation, slow sand filtration, and mechanical filtration. The installation of filters and the extensions in service reduced waterborne disease rates in New Orleans. In the years before the city municipalized the water system, typhoid rates in the city rose steadily, but after the system was municipalized in 1908, the trend was reversed and typhoid rates began a permanent downward trend (Troesken 2001).

But the initial benefits of public acquisition eventually gave way to problems as politicians began using municipally owned utility systems to win short-term political payoffs and in the process allowed the associated infrastructure to deteriorate. In particular, investments in patronage and unremunerative rate structures steadily displaced investments in upkeep and new equipment. Nathan Matthews, a Boston mayor, lent credence to this hypothesis as early as 1894 when he argued that local politicians derived

15. This paragraph is based on the following sources: *State v. New Orleans Waterworks Company* 107 La. 1 (1901); New Orleans, *Water Purification;* and National Board of Fire Underwriters, *New Orleans.*

electoral benefits by setting water rates at municipal plants below those that would have prevailed at private plants: "there have been deliberate attempts in various cities . . . to reduce rates below the point of profit . . . for the mere purpose of deriving some temporary popularity for the administration that happens to be in power" (Matthews 1894, p. 3). Matthews believed that this practice would, in the long run, undermine the financial viability municipal utilities and city finances, and delay the construction of needed improvements in utility systems.

In terms of using employment at municipal utilities to garner political support, there is much historical evidence to suggest that patronage was a serious problem. Exploiting a sample of nearly 90,000 workers in turn-of-the-century America, Troesken (1999) provides evidence that in cities where patronage was widespread, state and local employees earned 40 percent more per hour, worked 16 to 17 percent fewer hours, and earned 22 percent more per week than comparable workers in the private sector. Similarly, a study conducted by the National Civic Federation—a lobbying group that strongly favored municipal ownership—claimed that municipal employees often had to pay sizable annual assessments to incumbent politicians. Such assessments were intended to defray the costs of local elections. Workers that failed to pay their assessments were fired. Data reported by the National Civic Federation suggest that the size of assessments ranged between 2 and 4 percent of a worker's annual salary depending on the worker's occupation (National Civic Federation 1907, pp. 488–92).

In addition, the federation found that employees of publicly owned utilities were often required to work in local elections. Politicians also hired more workers than needed just so that they would have more supporters come election time. Conditions at the Wheeling Gas Company, a municipally owned and operated firm, were described as follows (National Civic Federation 1907, p. 492):

> The Superintendent of the Gas Works requires his employees to assist in the primaries and the elections. It is partly on account of the political usefulness of these gas workers that the Superintendent has employed about 20 per cent more men than are needed to do the work. He makes his appointments as much as possible to conciliate the Councilmen.

Elsewhere the same gas plant was characterized as follows (National Civic Federation 1907, p. 156):

> The management is honeycombed with politics. Appointments in the gas department are parceled out and controlled by the councilmen. All employees are supposed to belong to the party in power. Should that party change, it is probably true that the whole force in the department would change. All employees are regularly assessed for campaign purposes . . . the assessment ranging from $2 to $75.

The National Civic Federation (1907, pp. 149–52) found the same level of patronage and political influence at the municipally owned and operated gas works in Philadelphia.

The cumulative effect of patronage and unprofitable rate structures was a long-term decline in service quality. By the late 1970s, municipally owned water systems in the United States were in such disrepair that many were unable to meet federal guidelines for water quality. The response to this was privatization; by privatizing these systems officials hope to inject new capital and life into urban water supplies, in much the same way that municipalization had done some fifty to seventy years earlier.

The long-term effects of patronage and low rates has been made clear in a recent paper by Paul Gertler and his coauthors. Galiani, Gertler, and Schargrodsky (2005) describe the motivation and effects for privatization of municipal water systems in Argentina. They show that municipal companies had such bloated payrolls that those companies were unable even to replace or repair existing water mains when they burst. As a result, whole urban neighborhoods were often without water service for weeks at a time. Infant mortality rates from diarrheal diseases were high until the water systems were privatized and patronage employment eliminated. Galiani, Gertler, and Schargrodsky show that infant mortality rates fell by as much as 25 percent following privatization and that these reductions were particularly large for the poorest segments of society.

8.8   Alternative Interpretations

There are at least two other plausible explanations for the circular history of public utility regulation. One possibility is that regulatory regimes changed in response to technological changes. For example, perhaps gas and electric utilities were deregulated during the 1980s and 1990s because technological changes altered the cost structure of producing these commodities. There are three problems with this interpretation. First, while one might be able to identify technological changes in the production of electricity that made the industry more competitive (Joskow 1989; White 1996), it is difficult to identify similar changes taking place in the gas and water industries. Second, there exists an historical counterexample. During the nineteenth century there were, in fact, technological innovations that lowered the fixed costs associated with manufacturing lighting gas. These technological changes induced much entry in the gas industry in the short run, but in the long run they played a central role in promoting more aggressive forms of municipal and state regulation (Troesken 1996, pp. 21–57). Third, the deregulation and privatization of gas, electricity, and water occurred at the same time as deregulation in airlines, trucking, banking, telecommunications, railroads, cable television, and brokerage services (Winston 1993, 1998). It seems unlikely that such a large and diverse group of industries simultaneously experienced technological changes that made regulation less attractive.

This third point—that simultaneous regime change was observed across a wide spectrum of industries—is strong evidence in favor of an explanation rooted in ideological change. In particular, during the late twentieth century, policymakers and voters began to prefer market-oriented solutions to problems and pushed for deregulation and privatization. By the same token, during the early twentieth century, the rise of Progressive Era politics was associated with a preference for state-centered solutions to problems. As a result, municipalization and state regulation grew increasingly common. One needs to ask, however, why ideology was changing. Was there a shift in preferences independent of some underlying economic or political pathology? While there is room for debate on this question, there is much evidence to suggest that ideological changes about the proper role of the state in regulating public utilities were driven by genuine dissatisfaction with the operation of utility markets. For example, the discussion above shows that voters began demanding state regulation of gas and electric utilities in response to real problems associated with various forms of municipal regulation. By the same token, it is clear that the deregulation and privatization waves of the 1980s were a response to a growing body of evidence showing that regulation and public ownership had failed on several important margins (Winston 1993, 1998).

8.9   Concluding Remarks

In conclusion, it is useful to contrast the findings of Galiani, Gertler, and Schargrodsky (2005) and with my own research (Troesken 2001). Galiani, Gertler, and Schargrodsky present clear and incontrovertible evidence that privatizing water systems in Latin America had a large and beneficial effect on waterborne disease rates and that these benefits were particularly large for the poor. In contrast, my research shows that municipal acquisitions in the United States some 100 years earlier had the same effect: they reduced waterborne disease rates substantially, and this was particularly true for the poor (Troesken 2001). How does one reconcile the findings of Galiani and colleagues with my earlier work? Or more precisely, why would one expect privatization to reduce waterborne disease rates in one context and municipalization (the exact opposite process) to reduce disease rates in another context?

This paper has offered one possible avenue of reconciliation. Based on the historical evidence presented above it appears that corruption, and the necessity to eliminate corruption when it gets too costly, accounts for the efficacy of regime change. In this context, the direction of regime change— from public to private, or private to public—is of second-order importance. What matters is some radical reshuffling of the institutional matrix to disrupt the underlying corrupt relationships. Unfortunately, this disruption is only temporary, and gradually new forms of corruption emerge and must again be broken down by institutional change.

References

Averch, Harvey, and Leland Johnson. 1962. Behavior of the firm under regulatory constraints. *American Economic Review* 52:1052–69.

Baker, Moses. 1897. *Manual of American water works.* New York: Engineering News.

Blackford, Mansel G. 1970. Businessmen and the regulation of railroads and public utilities in California during the Progressive Era. *Business History Review* 44: 7–19.

———. 1977. The politics of business in California, 1890–1920. Columbus: Ohio State University Press.

Brown, Wolstan R. 1905. Municipal ownership and league organization. *The Arena* 33:377–82.

Demsetz, Harold. 1968. Why regulate utilities? *Journal of Law and Economics* 11: 55–65.

———. 1971. On the regulation of industry: A reply. *Journal of Political Economy* 79:356–63.

Folk, Joseph W. 1903. Municipal corruption. *The Independent* 55:2804–6.

Galiani, Sebastian, Paul Gertler, and Ernesto Schargrodsky. 2005. Water for life: The impact of the privatization of water services on child mortality. *Journal of Political Economy* 113:83–111.

Glaeser, Edward L. Forthcoming. Public ownership in the American city. In *Urban issues and public finance: Essays in honor of Dick Netzer,* ed. A. E. Schwartz. Northampton, MA: Edward Elgar.

Goldberg, Victor. 1976. Regulation and administered contracts. *Bell Journal of Economics* 7:426–52.

Hovenkamp, Herbert. 1991. The political economy of substantive due process. *Stanford Law Review* 40:404–60.

Illinois General Assembly, Illinois Legislative Public Utilities Commission. 1913. Report of the Special Joint Committee to Investigate Public Utilities. Springfield, IL: State Printing Office, April 17.

Jacobson, Charles. 2000. *Ties that bind: Economic and political dilemmas of urban utility networks, 1800–1990.* Pittsburgh: University of Pittsburgh Press.

Jarrell, Gregg A. 1979. Pro-producer regulation and accounting for assets: The case of electric utilities. *Journal of Accounting and Economics* 1:93–116.

Joskow, Paul L. 1989. Regulatory failure, regulatory reform, and structural change in the electrical power industry. *Brookings Papers on Economic Activity, Microeconomics:* 291–327.

———. 1997. Restructuring, competition, and regulatory reform in the U.S. electricity sector. *Journal of Economic Perspectives* 11:119–38.

Kwoka, John E., Jr. 2002. Governance alternatives and pricing in the U.S. electric power industry. *Journal of Law, Economics, and Organization* 18:278–94.

Macey, Jonathan R. 1992. Organizational design and the political control of administrative agencies. *Journal of Law, Economics, and Organization* 8:93–114.

Martin, Albro. 1971. *Enterprise denied: Origins of the decline of American railroads, 1897–1917.* New York: Columbia University Press.

Matthews, Nathan. 1894. Address of welcome to thirteenth annual convention of the New England Water Works Association. *Journal of the New England Water Works Association* 9:1–8.

McCubbins, Matthew D., Roger G. Noll, and Barry R. Weingast. 1987. Administrative procedures as instruments of political control. *Journal of Law, Economics, and Organization* 3:243–72.

———. 1989. Structure and process, politics and policy: Administrative arrangements and the political control of agencies. *Virginia Law Review* 75:431–82.

McDonald, Forrest. 1957. *Let there be light: The electric utility industry in Wisconsin, 1881–1955.* Madison, WI: American History Research Center.

———. 1958. Samuel Insull and the movement for state utility regulatory commissions. *Business History Review* 32:241–54.

———. 1962. *Insull.* Chicago: University of Chicago Press.

Meyer, Rober A., and Hayne E. Leland. 1980. The effectiveness of price regulation. *Review of Economics and Statistics* 62:555–71.

Miller, Geoffrey P. 1993. Comments on Priest. *Journal of Law and Economics* 36: 325–30.

Moore, Thomas Gale. 1970. The effectiveness of regulation of electric utility prices. *Southern Economic Journal* 36:365–81.

National Civic Federation. 1907. *Municipal and private operation of public utilities.* Part I, vol. I, *General conclusions and reports.* New York: National Civic Federation.

National Municipal League. 1896. *Proceedings of the fourth annual Conference for Good City Government and second annual meeting of the National Municipal League.* Held at Baltimore, MD, May 6–8. Philadelphia: National Municipal League.

Olson, Mancur. 1982. *The rise and fall of nations: Economic growth, stagflation, and social rigidities.* New Haven, CT: Yale University Press.

Pashigian, B. Peter. 1976. Consequences and causes of public ownership of urban transit facilities. *Journal of Political Economy* 84:1239–59.

Peltzman, Sam. 1971. Pricing at public and private enterprises: Electric utilities in the United States. *Journal of Law and Economics* 14:109–47.

———. 1989. The economic theory of regulation after a decade of deregulation. *Brookings Papers on Economic Activity, Microeconomics:* 1–49.

Porter, Robert. 1907. *The dangers of municipal ownership.* New York: Century Company.

Riordon, William L. 1994. *Plunkitt of Tammany Hall: A series of very plain talks on very practical politics.* Ed. Terrence J. MacDonald. Boston: Bedford Books.

Rosewater, Victor. 1903. Municipal ownership of electric lighting. *The Independent* 55:93–96.

Shepsle, Kenneth A. 1992. Bureaucratic drift, coalitional drift, and time consistency: A comment on Macey. *Journal of Law, Economics and Organization* 8: 111–18.

Stead, William T. 1894. *If Christ came to Chicago!* Chicago: Laird and Lee. Repr., Chicago: Chicago Historical Society, 1992.

Steffens, Lincoln. 1964. *The shame of the cities.* New York: Hill and Wang.

Stigler, George J., and Claire Friedland. 1962. What can regulators regulate? The case of electricity. *Journal of Law and Economics* 5:1–16.

Stotz, Louis P., and Alexander Jamison. 1938. *History of the gas industry.* New York: Stettiner Brothers.

Telser, Lester G. 1969. On the regulation of industry: A note. *Journal of Political Economy* 77:937–52.

———. 1971. On the regulation of industry: Rejoinder. *Journal of Political Economy* 79:364–65.

Thompson, Carl D. 1925. *A survey of public enterprises, municipal, state, and federal, in the United States and elsewhere.* New York: Thomas Y. Crowell.

Troesken, Werner. 1996. *Why regulate utilities? The new institutional economics and the Chicago gas industry, 1849–1924.* Ann Arbor: University of Michigan Press.

———. 1997. The sources of public ownership: Historical evidence from the gas industry. *Journal of Law, Economics, and Organization* 13:1–27.

———. 1999. Patronage and public-sector wages in 1896. *Journal of Economic History* 59:424–46.

———. 2001. Race, disease, and the provision of water in American cities, 1889–1921. *Journal of Economic History* 61:750–76.

Troesken, Werner, and Rick Geddes. 2003. Municipalizing American waterworks, 1897–1914. *Journal of Law, Economics, and Organization* 19:373–400.

Twentieth Century Fund. Power Committee. 1948. *Electric power and government policy.* New York: Twentieth Century Fund.

U.S. Congress. House. 1899. *Fourteenth annual report of the commissioner of labor: Water, gas, and electric light plants under private and public ownership.* 56th Cong., 1st sess. House Document 107, no. 713. Washington, DC: Government Printing Office.

Vitale, Robert. 2001. Privatizing water systems: A primer. *Fordham International Law Journal* 24:1382–1404.

White, Matthew W. 1996. Power struggles: Explaining deregulatory reforms in electricity markets. *Brookings Papers on Economic Activity, Microeconomics:* 201–67.

Wilcox, Delos F. 1910. *Municipal franchises: A description of the terms and conditions upon which private corporations enjoy special privileges in the streets of American cities.* Vol. I. New York: McGraw Hill.

Williamson, Oliver. 1985. *The economic institutions of capitalism.* New York: Free Press.

Winston, Clifford. 1993. Economic deregulation: Days of reckoning for microeconomists. *Journal of Economic Literature* 30:1263–89.

———. 1998. U.S. industry adjustment to deregulation. *Journal of Economic Perspectives* 12:89–110.

Yearly, C. K. 1970. *The money machines: The breakdown and reform of governmental and party finance in the north, 1860–1920.* Albany: State University of New York Press.

Zueblin, Charles. 1918. *American municipal progress.* New York: MacMillan.

IV

Reform and Regulation

9

The Irony of Reform
Did Large Employers Subvert Workplace Safety Reform, 1869 to 1930?

Price V. Fishback

Workplace safety was a centerpiece of Progressive Era reforms. Between 1869 and the early 1900s state governments established safety regulations for mines and factories and reformed the liability for workplace accidents. In the 1910s nearly all state governments adopted workers' compensation laws that changed the employers' liability for workplace accidents from common law negligence liability to a form of strict liability. The safety reformers' stated aims were to reduce the risk faced by workers and ensure that the families of workers injured or killed in accidents received reasonable medical care and compensation for lost earnings. Yet large employers often wielded significant clout in state government during this period and likely worked to shape the legislation to aid their own interests. This paper explores the extent to which large employers, measured by average number of employees, subverted the safety reform process, including the adoption of safety legislation, its scope, and the resources devoted to enforcement of the laws.

Defining subversion is a controversial issue, and scholars have different opinions on the scope of what should be considered subversion. In their discussion of the rise of the regulatory state, Glaeser and Shleifer (2003, p. 402) suggest that "subversion" can be defined as a series of legal or illegal strategies that powerful interests might follow to weaken the impact of regulations or shape the rules to their benefit.

> The legal ones include acquiring favorable legislation and regulation (even after an accident), lobbying for an appointment of friendly law enforcers (including both judges and regulators), hiring top lawyers, or us-

Price V. Fishback is a professor of economics at the University of Arizona and a research associate of the National Bureau of Economic Research.

ing delay tactics in case of a suit. Illegal subversion strategies include intimidating and bribing judges, regulators, or juries.

Their definition covers a broad range of activity, so it is useful to divide subversion into subcategories. The pressure for favorable legislation and regulation and lobbying for friendly enforcers might well be considered lobbying or "rent-seeking" behavior that would be followed by any interest group. Success in such lobbying has been described as "capture" of the legislature or the regulator in various studies.[1] Although unions and others might capture the legislature or the regulator, most discussions of capture examine ironic situations where the target of the regulation, the employer in this case, controls the process. The hiring of top lawyers and the legal use of delay tactics in suits or administrative hearings could be more narrowly defined as "gamesmanship," while the illegal practices are pure "corruption."

The workplace safety laws were the result of the conflicts and compromises that arose from the interest group struggles between reformers and employers, and large employers played a central role in the process. Reformers sought to impose the workplace safety changes on large employers because they saw the increased mechanization in their workplaces as a source of increased risk and they feared that large firms were wielding too much power over the existing system. Large employers might have followed two different strategies that would have subverted the reformers' goals: work to shape new laws in such a way to raise their rivals' costs, or follow a defensive strategy at every turn.

I follow a two-pronged approach to examining how large employers influenced the safety laws. First, I analyze the variation across states and time to establish the relationship between the average number of employees per establishment and the extent of regulation. A finding that large employers were associated with earlier adoption of regulation, more breadth of regulation, and more resources devoted to enforcement is consistent with either reformers imposing regulations on large firms or large firms' raising rivals' costs. Had large employers followed a defensive strategy, we would expect them to be associated with slower adoption, limited breadth, and fewer resources devoted to enforcement. Second, I supplement the quantitative analysis with analytical narratives that describe in more depth the extent to which employers shaped the legislation and the actual enforcement of the laws in various states. The results show that there is no single coherent story that can be told about all industries. In coal mining large employers followed a defensive strategy, limiting the breadth of regulation, pressing for regulations that were enforced more against workers than against em-

---

1. Becker (1983), Stigler (1971), Pelzman (1976), and Buchanan, Tollison, and Tullock (1980) discuss how interest groups might capture the legislative process. Once the rules are in place we might also see both capture and corruption of the regulatory process (Kolko 1963, 1965).

ployers and managers, and weakening the enforcement of the laws. In manufacturing, on the other hand, safety regulations were introduced earlier in states with larger average establishment sizes. This finding suggests that reformers may have succeeded in imposing regulations on large manufacturing employers. However, the finding is also consistent with large firms working to raise rivals' costs. Analytical narratives suggest that manufacturing employers at times shaped the legislation to their benefit and that the regulations were often poorly enforced.

9.1   Large Firms and Regulation

Progressive Era social reformers, workers, and unions called for safety regulations as a means to resolve "market failures." They perceived that expansions in the use of machinery and increases in the pace of work, typically in large firms, increased the dangers that workers faced. They argued that employers profited by skimping on safeguards, that labor markets provided inadequate wages to compensate workers for workplace dangers, and that insurance and the legal system were designed, both in theory and even more so in practice, to limit payments to injured workers. They anticipated that the reforms they proposed would contribute to better workplace safety and increase the actual payments received by injured workers. These changes would leave workers better off because wages would not fully adjust downward.[2]

A number of Progressive leaders, including Woodrow Wilson, saw regulation as a means of curbing the worst excesses from the expansion of large firms. Using the reformers' claims as a guide, Glaeser and Shleifer (2003) built an elegant formal model that examines optimal accident prevention in a situation where amoral firms are willing to subvert the existing regulatory system when the benefits of subversion exceed the costs.[3] A set of rules that might be optimal in the absence of subversion could be suboptimal if firms have incentives to subvert the system. The rules under negligence liability in the late 1900s called for full compensation of the injured worker if the worker could show in court that the employer had not exercised due care. As employers increased the number of workers, the potential for large-scale accidents and thus the stakes for court decisions on liability rose accordingly. Even accidents with only a single accident victim could lead to high stakes for a larger firm because a negligence decision that went

---

2. Fishback and Kantor (1995, 2000) find that when workers' compensation was introduced union members actually did not experience wage cuts that offset improvements in postaccident payments, while nonunion workers experienced reductions to varying degrees. Even nonunion workers who experienced reductions saw improvements in their welfare because they were better insured against accidents.

3. For discussions of optimal design of regulation and liability, see Landes and Posner (1987), Shavell (1987), Polinsky and Shavell (2000), and Glaeser and Shleifer (2003).

against the employer might set a precedent that raised the probability that the employer would lose in later cases. The greater stakes for large employers increased the benefit to the employer of subverting the process. By introducing safety regulations, which imposed smaller penalties prior to accidents for failure to follow established procedures, and workers' compensation, which called for workers to receive two-thirds or less of their lost earnings, the stakes of regulatory decisions were lowered.[4] Large employers had less incentive to subvert the process than before, so that regulations and workers' compensation might have worked better than negligence liability with no regulation.

The relationships described by these reform hypotheses suggest that reformers in states with larger employers would have anticipated greater benefits from regulation and thus pressed harder. If reformers imposed the regulations on larger employers, states with larger firms would have adopted regulations earlier and been more likely to have had a broader set of regulations. The impact of large firms on state decisions about enforcement resources is less clear. Reformers intent on making sure that the regulations were followed by large firms typically demanded more resources per worker for enforcement. But there may have been countervailing effects that would have weakened this demand. If the cost of inspection included a substantial fixed cost for visiting an establishment plus a cost per worker in the establishment, states with larger establishments could have reached the same level of enforcement as states with smaller establishments with a smaller budget per worker. This potential lower enforcement cost per worker might have offset the reformers' greater demand for enforcement resources in states with larger employers.

Reformers, however, were not the only groups determining safety legislation. The laws were forged through the interplay of interest group struggles, coalition formation, and compromise in state governments between 1869 and 1930. Large employers, in particular, wielded significant political clout.[5] Not only did they have more funds to lobby legislators and finance

4. The stakes involved in many decisions were lower under workers' compensation than under negligence liability. Under negligence liability the stakes in each decision were high because each involved an all-or-nothing decision about fault. In contrast, most workers' compensation disputes arose over the extent of the injury and measures of the workers' wage in determining the appropriate values to plug into the state's formula for compensation. The remaining decisions, however, were all-or-nothing decisions with far-reaching consequences for workers' compensation policy. Decisions on what constituted a work-related injury and opinions on whether the employer was willfully negligent (which removed the restrictions on compensation) established the boundaries of workers' compensation and were similar in scope to the stakes in a major negligence case. Given the large number of settlements under negligence liability, the annual number of these boundary decisions may have been similar to the number of negligence cases that were actually decided by the courts.

5. For studies of the roles played by major employers during the Progressive Era, see, for example, Wiebe (1962), Weinstein (1967), Lubove (1967), Moss (1996), Graebner (1976), Aldrich (1997), and Fishback and Kantor (2000).

political campaigns, but large firms employed large proportions of workforce. In 1909 establishments with over 500 workers employed up to 58 percent of manufacturing workers in some states (24 to 28 percent nationwide) despite accounting for less than 2 percent of all establishments. To the extent that employers could influence their workers' votes, they could deliver a substantial part of the electorate. Thus, government officials faced lower political organizing costs in dealing with a few large firms than in negotiating with groupings of small firms.

As large employers sought legislation favorable to their own interests, they would have followed one of two paths consistent with the broad definition of subversion: a defensive strategy of obstructionism against the demands of reformers or attempts to adopt and design regulations to raise rivals' costs. In following the defensive strategy employers would have prevented or slowed the adoption of safety legislation by pressuring legislators to kill the bills in committee or on the legislative floor. If that failed, they would have worked to limit the scope of the legislation through amendments or compromise proposals, while removing the teeth of the regulation by providing inadequate funds for enforcement. If legislation were enacted, employers would have sought to weaken it further by controlling regulators and actively fighting fines in court. If larger employers adopted a full-scale defensive strategy, states with larger employers would have adopted the regulations later, chosen regulations with less breadth, and provided fewer resources for enforcement.

Large employers might have adopted an alternative strategy to press for regulations that raised their rivals' costs.[6] By lobbying for regulations that codified their own practices they could have raised rivals' costs and not their own by forcing other employers to switch practices. To the extent that there were economies of scale or high fixed costs to compliance, the average costs of complying were larger for smaller firms. States with larger firms therefore would have been more likely to press for earlier adoption, an expanded scope of regulations, and more resources for enforcement to insure that the other firms were forced to comply. The attempt to raise rivals' costs might have benefited only large firms at the expense of other firms and workers. On the other hand, large employers would have found the political sledding smoother if their proposals had meant an improvement in the welfare of workers at the firms that had to change to comply with the new regulations. Large employers were more likely to pay higher wages, offer better benefits, provide model housing and towns, and provide safer workplaces (Jacoby 1997, chap. 1; Fishback 1992, chap. 9; Brandes 1970). Regulations raising safety standards with only limited loss in em-

---

6. Ann Bartel and Lacy Glenn Thomas (1985) claim that the Occupational Safety and Health Administration's (OSHA) persistence despite relatively little measured impact on accident rates since 1971 is the result of lobbying by large and unionized employers.

ployment would have led reformers, workers in smaller firms, and unions to become willing members in a coalition with large firms to lobby for the new legislation.

9.2   Workplace Safety Regulation and Liability Reform, 1869–1930

Just after the Civil War the government's role in workplace safety was largely confined to adjudicating disputes over injury claims in the common law courts. Over the next several decades, the structure of common-law workplace accident compensation evolved through a series of court decisions.[7] Under the full-blown liability system in the late nineteenth century, workplace accident compensation was based on common law rules of negligence combined with the defenses of assumption of risk, fellow-servant, and contributory negligence. If a worker was injured on the job, he bore the burden of proving that his employer had failed to exercise due care in preventing the accident and that the employer's negligence was the proximate cause of the injury. Judge Learned Hand once described due care as requiring the employer to prevent accidents when his costs of accident prevention were lower than the expected costs of the accident. If an injured worker was able to show his employer's negligence, then he was theoretically entitled to compensation up to the amount of his financial losses from the accident (lost wages and medical expenses) plus remuneration for "pain and suffering." Even if the employer was found negligent he might not be liable if he could invoke any of three defenses: that the employee had assumed the risks associated with the employment (assumption of risk); that a coworker (fellow servant) had caused the accident; or that the worker himself was negligent or had not exercised due care (contributory negligence).[8] The studies of accident causes in the late 1890s and early 1900s often suggested that worker fault was the cause of a very large percentage of the accidents, so court rulings of no compensation were likely in a large number of cases.

Lawrence Friedman (1985, pp. 300–301) argues that the system developed to encourage industrial enterprise; the courts knew that imposing strict liability on industrial enterprises would have stunted the growth of industry.[9] Employers likely had a hand in the development of the system as

7. For discussions of the early evolution of the common law of workplace accident compensation cases, see Tomlins (1988 and 1993, chap. 10). The basic principles for liability would continue to evolve into the early 1900s. See Friedman (1985), Friedman and Ladinsky (1967), and Fishback and Kantor (2000, chap. 2).

8. See Posner (1972, p. 32), Landes and Posner (1987), and Fishback and Kantor (2000, pp. 30–33).

9. Gary Schwartz (1981) challenges this "industry subsidy" view with an ample number of exceptions from his analysis of cases in California and New Hampshire. Numerous economic analyses have suggested that negligence liability combined with the three defenses can be an optimal accident prevention system in theory under specific conditions. See Landes and Posner (1987), Glaeser and Shleifer (2003), Shavell (1987).

they defended themselves against negligence suits and lobbied elected officials in the selection of judges. In examining the actual operations of the system, Shawn Kantor and I (2000) found little or no documented evidence that bribery of judges and juries was a significant problem in negligence liability cases.[10]

On the other hand, the high costs of going to court might have contributed to significant gamesmanship in settlement negotiations. Empirical studies suggest that under the de facto system the legal rules provided a baseline guide as to what to expect when people went to court. The compensation in settlements was loosely correlated with the de jure rules, but there was a great deal of noise in the system. The fear of delay, of gamesmanship by the employer or the insurer, and the workers' own high costs of going to court (25 to 40 percent of the compensation in contingency fees plus emotional costs) might have prevented some workers with legitimate claims from receiving compensation. In the samples of settlements collected by various state employer liability commissions, few families received payments that might match the present value of a lifetime stream of earnings. On the other hand, some workers with more generous employers, with employers seeking to avoid the nuisance of a suit, or with better access to legal advice might well have fared better than the expected payments under the highly restrictive de jure rules (Fishback and Kantor 2000). The views of accident causation evolved away from blaming the worker in the early 1900s with the publication of Crystal Eastman's *Work Accidents and the Law*. Had workers' compensation not been adopted, it is probable that more workers would have received compensation after Eastman's findings had become widespread.

If there was gamesmanship and subversion of the negligence liability system, it might well have been practiced more by the middlemen than by the employer. In nearly every state liability commission report, employers and workers complained of the large transactions costs in the system. Lawrence Friedman (1985, p. 484) summarizes these claims: the system "siphoned millions of dollars into the hands of lawyers, court systems, administrators, insurers, claims adjusters. Companies spent and spent, yet not enough of the dollars flowed to injured workmen." We have no way of knowing how much of the transactions costs were devoted to gamesmanship, but the primary beneficiaries of the negligence system may well have been the trial attorneys, an interest group that opposed workers' compensation in some states.

---

10. To develop a sense of the publicity of judicial bribery just prior to the introduction of workers' compensation I created a sample of corrupt events using the ProQuest search engine on the *New York Times* index for the period 1900 to 1910 using the word combination "judge" and "bribe." The search unearthed five episodes where judges had reported to the press on attempts to bribe them but there was no evidence that they had accepted the bribe. In seven cases the judges were charged with and sometimes convicted of bribery or corruption, but only two could be related to workplaces.

9.2.1   Coal Safety Regulations

As the negligence system evolved, states began to supplement it with direct regulation soon after the Civil War. The first industry to be widely regulated was coal mining, among the most dangerous industries of the era. Pennsylvania led the way in adopting coal mining regulations in 1869 for anthracite mines. The states with significant bituminous coal production introduced regulations between 1872 and 1912 in the order presented in Table 9.1.[11] Federal involvement began with the formation of the Bureau of Mines in 1911, but the agency was informational and did not obtain coercive powers until 1941 (Graebner 1976).

As a rough guide to some of the correlates of the adoption of the law, table 9.1 includes information on workers per mine, the number of coal workers, and the number of coal union chapters as of 1880. Simple correlations suggest that states with larger mines tended to adopt earlier. The correlation between average mine size in 1880 and the year of adoption is −0.4. The simple correlation seems to be inconsistent with the defensive hypothesis, while being consistent with the reform and raising-rivals'-costs views of large firms. However, there were other important factors influencing the timing of adoption. For example, unionization and the overall size of industry in 1880 were also negatively correlated with the year of adoption; the simple correlations are −0.55 and −0.49, respectively. The multivariate analysis that follows isolates the impact of each, holding the other factors constant.

The early regulations were rudimentary and were focused on mapping the mines, providing appropriate ventilation, and preventing explosions. Often they were targeted at smaller operations where the operators' knowledge of customary safety practices was likely to be more limited. As the technology of mining improved with the introduction of cutting machines, electricity, and mechanical motors, the regulations expanded, particularly after 1900. To capture the major changes after 1900, I develop a mine regulation index that counts the number of regulations that the states had adopted from the following list: the mine must be sprinkled or rock dusted, a fire boss must examine the mine for gas daily in gaseous mines, mine management must provide adequate timbers to prop the roof, underground electric wires must be

---

11. Although this paper focuses on industry, railroad regulation and liability also went through a series of transformations. The dangers in the railroad industry were a driving force in the development of the common law liability regime (Tomlins 1993, chap. 10). State railroad commissions between 1840 and 1890 imposed some rudimentary safety regulations. Federal safety regulations began in 1892 with the Railroad Safety Appliance Act. The safety laws for railroads were targeted specifically at railroading at the state and federal levels. Accidents for interstate railroad workers are still handled under a negligence liability system, although the fellow-servant defense and assumption-of-risk defenses have been eliminated and contributory negligence has been replaced with comparative negligence. See Clark (1891), Aldrich (1997), and Kim and Fishback (1993).

Table 9.1   Year of adoption of state coal mining law, early coal production and inspection budgets per coal worker in early 1900s

State	Year of adoption	1880 information			Coal law index		Inspection budget per worker (1967$)		UMWA share, 1902–23
		Coal workers	Workers per mine	Coal union chapters	1902	1930	1902	1930	
Pennsylvania Anthracite	1869	70,069	255	33.5	n.a.	n.a.	n.a.	n.a.	0.90
Illinois	1872	16,301	28	15	6	9	1.02	0.81	0.94
Iowa	1873	5,024	22	9	4	6	1.39	2.28	0.87
Ohio	1874	16,331	26	32	1	8	1.03	3.07	0.80
Maryland	1876	3,677	115	0	2	9	0.99	6.06	0.13
Pennsylvania Bituminous	1877	33,248	50	33.5	8	10	1.39	2.27	0.37
Indiana	1879	4,496	21	0	6	9	1.05	2.23	0.82
Missouri	1881	2,599	18	4	3	4	0.59	2.04	0.74
Tennessee	1881	1,092	55	0	0	6	0.63	2.17	0.19
Kansas	1883	3,617	19	2	4	5	1.95	4.08	0.69
West Virginia	1883	4,497	35	0	3	8	0.85	1.93	0.1
Colorado	1883	1,434	57	0	4	9	1.50	4.04	0.10
Washington	1883	261	65	0	2	9	1.31	8.14	0.61
Kentucky	1884	2,826	43	0	1	6	0.67	0.55	0.19
Wyoming	1886	1,009	168	0	4	8	1.47	4.37	0.66
Michigan	1887	412	69	1	4	5	1.80	2.78	0.79
Arkansas	1889	130	9	0	1	4	1.60	1.30	0.72
Montana	1889	3	3	0	3	8	3.97	2.40	0.97
Alabama	1891	1,513	80	0	3	8	0.91	2.54	0.13
Oklahoma	1891	0	0	0	2	9	1.38	3.10	0.72
New Mexico	1891	0	0	0	2	4	4.16	1.65	0.10

(continued)

Table 9.1 (continued)

| State | Year of adoption | 1880 information | | | Coal law index | | Inspection budget per worker (1967$) | | UMWA share, 1902–23 |
		Coal workers	Workers per mine	Coal union chapters	1902	1930	1902	1930	
Utah	1896	91	15	0	5	5	4.21	n.a.	0.65
North Dakota	1905	0	0	0	0	8	0.00	3.97	n.a.
Texas	1907	0	0	0	0	3	0.00	3.07	0.72
Virginia	1912	4,497	35	0	0	7	0.00	1.32	0.19

Notes and sources: Information that was not available is marked as n.a. Year of law adoption is from Aldrich (1997, p. 70). Information on production, number of mines, and employees in 1880 is from the U.S. Bureau of the Census (1886, pp. 681–87). The number of coal union chapters is the number of local unions and chapters of national unions associated with coal mining from the Weeks Report (Weeks, 1886, pp. 14–19). The regulation index is the number of coal safety regulations enacted in the state by that date from the following list: the mine must be sprinkled or rock dusted, a fire boss must examine the mine for gas daily in gaseous mines, mine management must provide adequate timbers to prop the roof, underground electric wires must be insulated, miners must not ride on coal cars underground, permissible explosives must be used, state inspectors must pass a qualifying exam, inspectors can close the mine immediately for some violations, inspectors have the power to make arrests for safety violations, mine foremen must be licensed by a state board, all miners must be licensed by a state board, foremen must ensure that all men have training, and the foreman must make a minimum number of visits to the workplace each day. A table showing the dates of enactment of each regulation for each state can be found in Fishback (1986, pp. 284–85, and 1992, pp. 114–15). The inspection budget per miner divides the appropriations for coal mining inspection by the number of miners in the state and adjusts for inflation using the Consumer Price Index (1967 = 1) from U.S. Bureau of the Census (1975, series E-135, p. 211). Information on the laws and inspection budgets came from various issues produced by the U.S. Commissioner of Labor (1892, 1896, 1904, 1908) and the U.S. Bureau of Labor Statistics (1914, 1925) with titles similar to "Labor Laws in the United States" and the legislative statute volumes for each state. The number of miners in 1902 and 1930 are from U.S. Geological Survey (1902) and U.S. Bureau of Mines (1930). See Fishback (1992, pp. 238–40) for a lengthy description of the sources and methods used. Membership in the United Mine Workers of America (UMWA) as a share of employment is from the U.S. Coal Commission (1925, pp. 1052).

insulated, miners must not ride on coal cars underground, permissible explosives must be used, state inspectors must pass a qualifying exam, inspectors can close the mine immediately for some violations, inspectors have the power to make arrests for safety violations, mine foremen must be licensed by a state board, all miners must be licensed by a state board, foremen must ensure that all men have training, and the foreman must make a minimum number of visits to the workplace each day. As seen in table 9.1, the number of clauses varied between zero in some states without mining laws to eight in Pennsylvania. By 1930 most states had expanded coverage, and the number ranged from three in Texas to ten in Pennsylvania.

A key to effective laws is their enforcement. Table 9.1 contains the inspection budget in 1967 dollars per coal worker, which is based on the salaries and the number of inspectors listed in the mining law or in appropriations bills for each state. Most inspection budgets in 1902 were less than \$2 per worker, although New Mexico and Utah were spending over \$4 per worker. Generally, the budgets had expanded along with the breadth of the laws by 1930.

9.2.2   Manufacturing Safety Regulations

The states' interest in regulating safety in factories also developed soon after the Civil War. Massachusetts led the way in 1869 in establishing a bureau to collect information on wages and working conditions for factory workers, and roughly half of the states had followed suit by 1890 (see table 9.2). Massachusetts was the first state to add teeth to the law by establishing factory inspectors in 1879. Roughly 40 percent of the states added a factory inspector within five to fifteen years after creating a labor bureau or department (see table 9.2). Some states like West Virginia and Tennessee provided for an inspector without actually appointing one. Table 9.2 also contains information on average establishment size, total manufacturing workers, and the number of chapters of trade unions in 1880. As was the case for the coal regulations, simple correlations show that all three were associated with earlier adoption (–0.43, –0.51, and –0.40, respectively, with the initial laws and –0.51, –0.56, and –0.35, respectively, with the factory inspector laws). The factory safety laws were amended during the Progressive Era in response to new technologies as well as to the grisly lessons learned from horrible accidents like the Triangle Shirtwaist Factory fire in New York in 1910.

9.2.3   Liability Law Changes

The increasing use of factory and mine inspectors coincided with the states' experimentation with employer liability laws that limited one or more of the three defenses in the 1890s and 1910s.[12] Unions and workers

---

12. See Fishback and Kantor (2000, appendix G) for categorizations of the state laws.

Table 9.2   Year of introduction of labor commission, factory inspectors, departments of labor, and industrial commissions

State	First labor bureau	Factory inspection adopted	1880 information for manufacturing			Industrial commission introduced	Extent of code writing by industrial commission	Permanent workers' compensation law
			Mean workers per establishment	Total workers	Union chapters			
Alabama	1907[a]	1907[a]	4.8	10,019	22			1919
Arizona	1925[b]	[b]	3.3	220	0	1925	Few	1913
Arkansas	1913	[c]	3.8	4,557	1			1939
California	1883	1885	7.4	43,693	18	1913	Extensive	1911
Colorado	1887	1911	8.5	5,074	24	1915	No codes	1915
Connecticut	1887	1887	25.2	112,915	44			1913
Delaware	1893	1893	16.9	12,638	9			1917
Florida	1893[d]	[e]	12.9	5,504	0			1935
Georgia	1911	1916	6.9	24,875	5			1920
Idaho	1890[f]	[g]	2.4	388	0	1917	No codes	1917
Illinois	1879	1893	9.9	144,727	179			1911
Indiana	1879	1899	6.2	69,508	61			1915
Iowa	1884	1897	4.1	28,372	21			1913
Kansas	1885	1901	4.3	12,062	20			1911
Kentucky	1892[h]	1903	7.0	37,391	53			1914
Louisiana	1900	1908	7.8	12,167	11			1914
Maine	1887	1887	11.8	52,954	14			1915
Maryland	1888[i]	1898	11.0	74,945	40	1928	No codes	1912
Massachusetts	1869	1879	24.5	352,255	105	1913	Extensive	1911
Michigan	1883	1893	8.7	77,591	45			1912
Minnesota	1887[j]	1891	6.1	21,247	12			1913
Mississippi	1914	1914	3.9	5,827	3			1948
Missouri	1879	1891[k]	7.4	63,995	127			1926
Montana	1893[l]	[l,m]	2.9	578	0	1915	No codes	1915
Nebraska	1887[n]	1895[n]	3.4	4,793	5	1929	No codes	1913
Nevada	1915	1915	3.1	577	4	1919	Few	1913
New Hampshire	1893	1917	15.4	48,831	2	1917	No codes	1911
New Jersey	1877	1878	17.7	126,038	2			1911
New Mexico	[o]	[o]	3.9	557	112			1917
New York	1882	1883	12.4	531,533	187	1913	Extensive	1913
North Carolina	1887	[e]	4.8	18,109	1	1931		1929
North Dakota	1899	1905			0.5	1919	No codes	1919
Ohio	1877	1884	8.9	183,609	199	1913	Extensive	1911
Oklahoma	1907	1910			0			1915

Pennsylvania	1872	1889	12.4	58,072	5.6	1915 for mines only	Extensive	1912
Rhode Island	1887	1894	28.5	62,878	8		Extensive	1912
South Carolina	1912	1912	7.6	15,828	2			1935
South Dakota	1890	[p]			0.5			1917
Tennessee	1881–84[q]	1897[r]	5.2	22,445	9	1923	Few	1919
Texas	1911	1911	4.1	12,159	5			1913
Utah	1892[s]	1917	3.9	2,495	1	1917	Extensive	1917
Vermont	1912	1912	6.1	17,540	2			1915
Virginia	1897	1919	7.0	40,184	9			1918
Washington	1903	1910	4.4	1,147	8	1919	Few	1911
West Virginia	1890[t]	1899[u]	6.0	14,311	81			1913
Wisconsin	1883	1883	7.4	57,109	14	1911	Extensive	1911
Wyoming	1917	1917	6.9	391	0			1915

Notes and sources: "First labor bureau" refers to the introduction of either a commissioner of labor, a bureau of labor statistics, or a factory inspector. "Factory inspection adopted" refers to the first statutory provision for a factory inspector. For dates of adoption of inspectors and departments of labor I started with evidence from Brandeis (1935, pp. 628–45), Holmes (2003), and the U.S. Commissioner of Labor (1896). When the precise date of introduction was unknown, the microfiche for the State Session Laws of American States and Territories was searched until the original act was found. The earliest commissioner of labor was in Massachusetts in 1869, and the earliest factory inspector was in Massachusetts in 1879. Information on workers and establishments for 1880 is from the Report on Manufacturing for the Eleventh Census (U.S. Bureau of the Census 1895, pp. 67–69). Information on Industrial Commissions is from Brandeis (1935, p. 654), who was citing work of John Andrews of the American Association of Labor Legislation. The information on the adoption of workers' compensation is from Fishback and Kantor (2000, pp. 103–4).

[a] Alabama had a mine inspector and later a board of arbitration but no official department of labor.

[b] Arizona had a mine inspector as of 1908.

[c] Arkansas had an inspector of mines in 1894 or earlier.

[d] The Florida agriculture department was given the responsibility to collect statistics on manufactures.

[e] No law as of 1924.

[f] Idaho established commission in constitution. No record of laws passed between 1879 and 1890.

[g] Idaho had an inspector of mines in 1893 or earlier.

[h] The Kentucky commissioner was to devote efforts to collect statistics on agriculture, manufacturing, and mining.

[i] The initial Maryland law in 1868 was for agriculture and industry, with most of the focus on agriculture. The code of 1888 with amendments in 1892 is more specific to industry.

[j] The Minnesota law included language about enforcing laws and prosecuting violations by the commissioner, but only funds for the commissioner were provided.

[k] Missouri statute for inspector in 1891. Not found in earlier years.

[l] The Montana act established a bureau of agriculture, labor, and industry.

[m] Montana had a mine inspector as of 1908.

[n] Nebraska gave the commissioner the power to inspect workplaces.

[o] New Mexico had a mine inspector as of 1908.

[p] South Dakota had a mine inspector as of 1903.

[q] The Tennessee Law called for the Bureau of Agriculture, Mining, and Statistics to collect information on labor. The original Bureau of Agriculture was established in 1871 and became the Bureau of Agriculture, Mining, and Statistics in 1875 but appears to have obtained the role of collecting labor statistics sometime between 1881 and 1884. We have had trouble pinning down the date.

[r] In Tennessee and West Virginia there were no regular inspectors. Commissioner merely had the power to inspect.

[s] The Utah legislature had authorized a bureau of labor statistics or labor department earlier.

[t] West Virginia gave the commissioner the power to inspect workplaces but only to report on findings there.

quickly became dissatisfied with the inadequacy of employer liability laws. In addition, employers sought relief from increasing uncertainty about the three defenses and a seeming increase in "jackpot" awards. Insurers, furthermore, sought ways to resolve problems with moral hazard and adverse selection in insuring workers. The solution for all was workers' compensation.

The move to workers' compensation in most states in the 1910s altered the liability rules in mining and manufacturing from negligence liability to strict liability. The laws established that all workers injured in the course of employment or in activities arising out of employment were expected to receive compensation from employers. Unlike negligence liability, which was supposed to fully compensate workers for their loss, workers' compensation imposed limits so that injured workers were to be paid a maximum of two-thirds or less of their income loss. Maximums on weekly payments meant that many workers received substantially less than two-thirds of their income while injured.

Ultimately, large employers strongly influenced the adoption of workers' compensation legislation. Fishback and Kantor (2000) find that the majority of people in each of the major interest groups—employers, workers, and insurers—gained from its passage. Employers saw a reduction in uncertainty about large jury awards and managed to pass much of their increased insurance premiums back to their workers in the form of higher wages. Workers on average received higher accident payments than under negligence liability and were better insured even if their wages adjusted downward. Insurers saw an expansion in their business, despite the introduction of state insurance in a number of states.

Most states developed some form of administrative body to replace the courts in administering workers' compensation. A handful of states, led by Wisconsin in 1911, carried the process a step further and created industrial safety commissions that not only administered workers' compensation but expanded into a rule-making body that wrote an extensive safety code for Wisconsin industry. As seen in table 9.2, eighteen states had established industrial commissions by 1930. However, only California, Massachusetts, New York, Ohio, Pennsylvania, and Utah had made substantial use of their rule-making ability.

9.3 The Role of Average Employer Size in the Development of Safety Regulations

The simple correlations between the year of adoption and average size from 1880 using the data from tables 9.1 and 9.2 suggest that safety legislation was adopted earlier in states with larger employers. Yet we also know that earlier adoption was related to more unionization and the overall number of workers to be regulated, so a multivariate analysis is needed to

Table 9.3   **Predicted signs of the relationship between average workers per establishment (mine) and safety regulations**

Motives	Probability of adoption	Enforcement budget	Breadth of laws
Reform	Positive	Uncertain	Positive
Large employers' defensive strategy	Negative	Negative	Negative
Large employers raise rivals' costs	Positive	Positive	Positive

isolate the impact of larger employers. The adoption of legislation was a dynamic process that took place over at least thirty years, so it is also important not only to capture the differences in key variables in cross-section in 1880 but also to take into account the changes in the key variables over time. Finally, the models of the relationship between large employers and regulation predict relationships that extend beyond the adoption of the laws to their scope and the resources devoted to enforcement. Therefore, I developed a state-level panel data set to examine the relationship between the average size of employers and the timing of adoption of safety legislation, the breadth of coverage of regulations, and the resources devoted to enforcing the rules.

Table 9.3 shows the predictions from the various models for the relationship between large employers and changes in safety regulations. It is important to consider how well the measure of employer size fits the theoretical concepts of employer size in the models. The measure of size used is the average number of workers per establishment (or per mine) because it is the only measure of size that is consistently available for the years 1870 through 1912, when the leading mining and manufacturing safety regulations were first adopted.[13] Average establishment size might differ in two states because the entire distribution of establishments in one state has shifted upward or because the distribution in one state is more skewed toward larger establishments.

In the hypothesis that reformers imposed regulation on large employers, both general increases in size and skewness toward very large firms might be considered important. Reformers worried about general increases in size across the entire distribution because larger establishment size was typically associated with increased mechanization that might have contributed to greater accident risk. Meanwhile, Glaeser and Shleifer (2003)

---

13. Information was not available on the size of multi-establishment firms. The average establishment size understates the average size of firms because it does not take into account firms that had multiple establishments. My impression is that multi-establishment firms more commonly ran large establishments so that the measurement error might not be a serious problem. Further, multiestablishment firms tended to own establishments in multiple states. Their political influence in those states was likely to be influenced by the size of their establishments in those states.

emphasize the importance of very large firms in their descriptions of reform in the face of potential subversion. In the employer defense hypothesis both a skewed distribution with a few very large firms or a general increase in the size of all firms would have made it easier for employers to resist reform efforts. In the skewed distribution a few large firms with many employees faced low costs of organizing and would have greater resources with which to mount their defenses. This result would hold even if larger average firm size represents larger size across the entire distribution of firms. The increase in size meant that each firm might have more resources to devote to lobbying, while successful employer lobbies would face lower costs of organizing because fewer firms would be necessary to reach critical mass. The raising-rivals'-costs hypothesis depends primarily on skewness toward large firms in the distribution because one set of employers is seeking to impose regulations that would be costly to another set of employers. In that case one might expect that large firms would have more success in raising rivals' costs when the share of very large establishments is higher either as a share of the number of establishments or as the share of employment in those firms.

When the data are available to make comparisons after 1900, it appears that the measure of average establishment size used here likely captures some of the differences in skewness toward large establishments. The correlation between average number of workers per establishment and the percentage of establishments with more than 500 workers in manufacturing in the states is 0.887 in 1904, 0.928 in 1909, and 0.928 in 1914. The correlation between average workers per establishment and the share of workers in establishments employing over 500 workers is 0.68 in 1909 and 0.65 in 1914.

In estimating the impact of large employers, the analyses control for interest group pressure from unions, who wielded influence in the states where they had a strong presence, as well as the number of workers involved in the activity to be regulated. Mulligan and Shleifer (2004) suggest that there may be substantial fixed costs to regulation; efficiency concerns imply that regulations will not be established until the population to be regulated is large enough that the benefits of regulation overcome these fixed costs. Larger populations might also be associated with more regulation in the raising-rivals'-cost model. The returns to large firms from using regulation to keep rivals out would rise significantly as the overall size of the industry increased. In several empirical tests Mulligan and Shleifer (2004) find regulatory populations to be associated with expanded regulations in a series of settings. In the analysis that follows, larger regulatory populations also contributed to earlier adoption of the initial manufacturing and coal regulations. Finally, regional differences in attitudes toward regulation are controlled with a dummy for the southern states in the adoption regressions and state fixed effects when examining coal inspection budgets and the breadth of coal regulations. The analysis that follows suggests that southern states were slower to adopt factory inspection regulation and coal mining regulations.[14]

9.3.1 Establishment Size and the Introduction of Manufacturing Regulations

Analysis of the correlates related to the adoption of manufacturing regulations and workers' compensation show that states with more workers per establishment tended to adopt the new policies earlier. Using the panel information in manufacturing, I estimated a proportional hazard model with time-varying covariates for the introduction of the two types of manufacturing regulations: first, the initial introduction of some form of labor administrative body with or without coercive power; second, the introduction of factory inspectors to enforce regulations. Since most states had their own mine inspection departments, most of the bureaus and factory inspectors specialized in manufacturing; therefore, the correlates in the adoption analysis are focused on measures of manufacturing activity. In the underlying panel of data, states who have not yet adopted are observed at the end of each decade and matched with information on average size and the number of manufacturing workers from the beginning of the decade. The state's final year in the panel is its year of adoption, which is matched with information from the prior census. See the notes to table 9.4 for a more detailed description.

The results in table 9.4 show that larger establishments were associated with earlier adoption of both factory administrations and factory inspectors. Hazard ratios greater than one imply increased probability of adoption in any year given no prior adoption (consistent with earlier adoption), and ratios less than one imply decreased probability of adoption in any year (consistent with later adoption). At the margin an increase of one worker per establishment was associated with a 5.8 percent higher probability of adoption of some form of labor administration, and 5.3 percent higher probability of adopting a factory inspector law. Both are statistically significant at the 10 percent level. It is relatively common to see differences in correlates across states of 1 standard deviation in either direction. A one standard deviation increase in average firm size of 5.3 workers per establishment was associated with roughly a one-third increase in the

---

14. In the regressions, I have experimented with other control variables, but none were found to be statistically significant in the analysis. I tried several measures of political activity in all of the adoption and coal regulation equations, including shares of votes for populist presidential candidates in the 1890s, voting for Republicans and Socialists for president in the 1900s, and Poole and Rosenthal's (1993) spatial coordinates for the location of U.S. senators along conservative/liberal spectrums and rural/urban spectrums at various times. The measures generally had small and statistically insignificant effects. Since Mark Aldrich (1997) and William Graebner (1976) suggest that large explosions contributed to expanded regulations, I developed a measure of large-scale accidents for the study in table 9.6, but its impact was always small and statistically insignificant.

Table 9.4   **Hazard ratios for factors influencing the introduction of state labor administrations and factory inspectors, 1869–1930**

			(1)		(2)	
Variable	Mean	SD	Hazard ratio	1 SD effect	Hazard ratio	1 SD effect
A. Introduction of some form of labor administration						
Manufacturing workers per establishment	7.57	5.34	1.058 (3.24)	0.31	1.056 (2.83)	0.30
Manufacturing workers (000s)	33.82	63.92	1.005 (2.48)	0.32	1.006 (4.03)	0.38
Manufacturing union chapters, 1880	30.91	68.86	1.003 (0.71)	0.21		
Union index	6.11	3.05			1.019 (0.55)	0.06
Southern state	0.29		0.734 (−1.06)		0.725 (−1.14)	
p			2.811		2.736	
Wald chi-square			47.30		45.82	

			(3)		(4)	
Variable	Mean	SD	Hazard ratio	1 SD effect	Hazard ratio	1 SD effect
B. Introduction of factory inspector						
Manufacturing workers per establishment	7.90	5.26	1.053 (1.74)	0.28	1.054 (1.65)	0.28
Manufacturing workers (000s)	41.66	68.32	1.009 (5.91)	0.61	1.008 (7.51)	0.55
Manufacturing union chapters, 1880	32.36	73.18	0.998 (−1.49)	−0.15		
Union index	6.67	3.35			0.973 (−0.62)	−0.09
Southern state	0.29		0.419 (−2.06)		0.429 (−1.99)	
p			3.254		3.420	
Wald chi-square			110.63		110.29	

Notes and sources: The 1 standard deviation (SD) effect is the change in the probability of adoption in a specific year given that the state had not yet adopted associated with a one standard deviation increase in the variable. The values are hazard ratios from a Weibull hazard estimation with time-varying covariates. The z-scores in parentheses below the hazard ratios are based on robust standard errors and the null hypothesis that the hazard ratios are equal to one. If $h(t) = h_0(t)\, e^{X(t)\beta}$, then each hazard ratio reported above equals e^b, where b is an element of β. Time zero ($t = 0$) is 1860 in the model. The Weibull model assumes that the hazard takes the form $h(t) = p\, t^{p-1} e^{X(t)\beta}$. Time zero ($t = 0$) is 1860 in the model. Estimates for p in all of the models are statistically different from one in Wald chi-square tests with four degrees of freedom, implying that the probability of adoption rose substantially over time.

Information on the timing of adoption is in table 9.2. Observations in the data set were constructed the following way. States were observed in the last year of the decade with information on workers and workers per establishment from the beginning of the decade. In the year the state adopted, the year for that observation is the year of adoption. For example, Maine adopted its first labor administrative law in 1887. The first Maine observation is for the end of the 1860s, the year is recorded as 1869, the adoption indicator is zero, and values for average workers per establishment and total workers are from 1860.

Table 9.4   (continued)

The second Maine observation records the year as 1879, the adoption indicator is zero, and the census values are from the 1870 census. Since Maine adopted in 1887, the final Maine observation shows the year as 1887, the adoption indicator as one, and the values for workers per establishment and total workers are from the 1880 census. For Massachusetts, which adopted in 1869, I included a value for 1865 with census information from 1860 attached; the 1869 observation uses 1870 census information. There were 179 observations for the analysis of the introduction of any labor administration, with three of the forty-eight states not adopting by 1930. In the factory inspector analysis there were 229 observations, with eight of the forty-eight states not adopting by 1930. Information on workers and establishments from the censuses for 1860, 1870, 1880, and 1890 is from U.S. Bureau of the Census (1895, pp. 67–69). Data on workers and establishments from the 1900, 1910, and 1920 censuses are from U.S. Bureau of the Census (1933, pp. 43–600, and 1902, pp. 58–61). In the 1904 manufacturing census, the Census Bureau focused the survey on factories and eliminated the hand trades. I spliced the data for total workers and workers per establishment after 1900 with the earlier series by multiplying by the ratio in 1900 of workers in factories and hand trades to workers in factories. The same procedure was followed for workers per establishment. Information on unionization at the state level is sparse, and two measures of unionization were tried. Neither fully covers the period. The union index is described by Fishback and Kantor (2000, p. 263), who developed it for 1899, 1909, 1919, and 1929 for their workers' compensation study. High values of the index imply that the state has a higher share of workers in industries that at the national level were more unionized. For observations prior to 1899, the 1899 values of the index were used to approximate the union index for observations. In the other version of the estimation, the number of manufacturing union chapters is the number of local unions and chapters of national unions associated with manufacturing in the state as of 1880 from the Weeks Report (Weeks, 1886, pp. 14–19). States were given the same value in each year observed. Southern states included Maryland, Virginia, Kentucky, Arkansas, Oklahoma, Texas, and all states south and east of those states.

conditional probability of adopting some form of labor administration in any year and a one-fourth increase in the probability of introducing a factor inspector.

The findings are inconsistent with the view that large firms were successful at obstructing the introduction of legislation. The adoption of the early labor administrations without inspection might have been a situation where both large firms and unions anticipated benefits, or where unions succeeded in imposing the legislation on larger employers. The union hazard ratios are all greater than one, consistent with unions contributing to earlier adoption. Although we cannot reject the hypothesis of no effect in the statistical model, extra qualitative evidence from Elizabeth Brandeis (1935) suggests that these early labor bureaus were often created in response to pressures from the National Labor Union and the Knights of Labor.

The adoption of factory inspection is more consistent with the raising-rivals'-costs model in a situation where reformers and reformers were not anticipating much gain. While large firms were associated with earlier adoption, unions were not. The hazard ratios for the union measures were both less than one, and increases of 1 standard deviation in the union measures reduced the probability of adoption in any one year by 9 to 15 percent. The effects are not statistically significant, so it is too strong at this point to say that unions were categorically opposed to the introduction of the factory inspectors. Yet there is evidence that union leaders circa 1900 were skeptical of the benefits of regulation on the grounds that business interests wielded significant clout in the legislatures and were likely to strongly influence the writing of the regulations. Instead, they focused on organizing drives in which they argued that workers would benefit more through the collective bargaining process than they would by relying on legislatures (Weinstein 1967, p. 159; Skocpol 1992, pp. 205–47; Asher 1969, p. 457).

The adoption of workers' compensation in the 1910s, on the other hand, was a win-win situation for large firms, unions, and reform groups. In statistical work on the timing of adoption of workers' compensation Shawn Kantor and I (Fishback and Kantor 1998, 2000, pp. 106–11, 256–57) found that large firms, unions, and reform groups all were associated with earlier adoption of the laws. These relationships showed up in comparisons of means for groups of states who adopted earlier, as well as in multivariate analysis with a wide range of controls. In addition, there was ample qualitative evidence that all three groups after 1909 lobbied for the general concept of workers' compensation although in some states there were intense struggles over the choice of benefit levels and the state's role in insuring workplace accident risk.

9.3.2   Average Mine Size and Coal Regulations

The results are quite different for the relationship between average mine size and the adoption of coal mining regulations from 1869 to the mid-1890s. I estimated a similar proportional hazards model for a panel of data for the twenty-four states that produced more than 500,000 tons of bituminous coal consistently by 1925. An additional cross-sectional observation has been added for Pennsylvania anthracite coal because Pennsylvania adopted separate regulations and inspection departments at different times for the two types of coal. More details on this panel are found in the notes of table 9.5. Larger coal mines were not associated with earlier adoption of the coal safety legislation, whether large mines are measured in terms of workers per mine or output per mine. The hazard ratios in table 9.5 are not statistically significantly different from one, and the effects of changes of 1 standard deviation are very small. The absence of a relationship between adoption and mine size suggests that either large firms were indifferent to the coal regulations or they were unsuccessful at staving off the efforts of reformers. The impact of unionization suggests that it might have been the latter. An increase of 1 standard deviation in the number of coal union chapters in the state raised the probability of adoption in a specific state by 40 to 47 percent.

More insight into the role played by large firms can be gained by examining their impact on the breadth of regulation and the resources devoted to enforcement. I created a panel data set for the years 1902, 1910, 1920, and 1930 for the twenty-three leading bituminous coal mining states with

Table 9.5   **Factors influencing the introduction of coal mine safety laws, 1869–1912**

	Mean	SD	(1) Hazard ratio	(1) OSD effect	(2) Hazard ratio	(2) OSD effect
Coal workers per mine	42.41	51.34	1.001 (0.38)	0.05		
Coal workers in state (000s)	2.28	6.85	1.047 (2.11)	0.32		
Tons per mine (000s)	18.67	27.41			0.999 (−0.08)	−0.03
Total tons in state (millions)	0.89	2.29			1.164 (2.09)	0.38
Coal union chapters	3.38	8.99	1.052 (2.50)	0.47	1.044 (1.72)	0.40
Southern state	0.28		0.400 (−1.74)		0.398 (−1.80)	
p			3.417		3.271	
Wald chi-square (4)			86.19		62.24	

Notes and sources: A 1 standard deviation (OSD) effect is the change in the probability of adoption in a specific year, given that the state had not yet adopted, associated with a 1 standard deviation increase in the variable. The values are hazard ratios from a Weibull hazard estimation with time-varying covariates. The z-scores in parentheses below the hazard ratios are based on robust standard errors and the null hypothesis that the hazard ratios are equal to one. For notes on the Weibull hazard model see table 9.4. Time zero is 1860. Estimates for p in all of the models are statistically different from one in Wald chi-square tests with four degrees of freedom, implying that the probability of adoption rose substantially over time. Observations in the data set were constructed the following way. States were observed in the last year of the decade and were matched with information on miners, miners per mine, tons produced, and tons per mine from the beginning of the decade. In the decade when the state adopted, the year of the observation was the year of adoption. For example, West Virginia adopted its mine safety law in 1883. The first West Virginia observation is for the end of the 1860s, the year is recorded as 1869, the adoption indicator is zero, and values for miners et al. are from 1860. The second West Virginia observation records the year as 1879, the adoption indicator is zero, and the census values are from the 1870 census. Since West Virginia adopted in 1883, the final West Virginia observation shows the year as 1883 and the adoption indicator as one, and the values for workers per establishment and total workers are from the 1880 census. For Pennsylvania anthracite, which adopted in 1869, I included a value for 1865 with census information from 1860 attached; the 1869 observation uses 1870 census information. States were not included in the sample unless they consistently produced more than 100,000 tons of coal by the 1920s. Anthracite and bituminous coal in Pennsylvania are treated as two separate state observations because Pennsylvania had separate regulatory codes and inspection staffs for the different types of coal. Southern states were Alabama, Arkansas, Kentucky, Maryland, Oklahoma, Tennessee, Texas, and Virginia. The twenty-five states led to seventy-nine observations, and all states adopted the law during the period under study. Information on production, number of mines, and employees is from the following U.S. mining censuses: U.S. Bureau of the Census (1865, pp. clxxiii–clxxiv) for 1860; (1872, pp. 760–67) for 1870; (1886, pp. 681–87) for 1880; (1892, pp. 347–48) for 1890; and (1905, 709–17) for 1902. Information for 1910 came from U.S. Geological Survey (various years). The coal union chapters figure is the number of local unions and chapters of national unions associated with coal mining from the Weeks Report (Weeks, 1886, pp. 14–19). The number of chapters in Pennsylvania were split evenly between the anthracite and bituminous observation. The number of chapters was the same for each state for all years that they were observed.

evidence on the breadth of coal mining regulations and the appropriations for coal mining inspection per coal worker in the state measured in 1967 dollars (see table 9.1).[15] The information on regulations and inspection budgets was then matched in the panel with evidence on the average number of employees per mine in the state, the United Mine Workers of America (UMWA) membership as a percentage of the coal workforce in the state, and the number of miners in the state. Estimations are also performed with firm size and industry scale measured as production per mine and total production.

The model is estimated both without and with state and year fixed effects. The fixed-effects estimation controls for some types of unmeasured heterogeneity across states and time. The year effects are incorporated to control for shocks to the national economy and technological shocks to mining technology common to the entire mining industry in each year that would have influenced the choice of safety regulations and the level of inspection at particular points in time. The state effects are included to capture geological differences in mining deposits that influenced mining practices as well as long-term attitudes toward political reform that were invariant across time within the states.

The panel regression results in table 9.6 are consistent with the view that large coal employers worked to limit breadth of the legislation, possibly offsetting efforts by coal unions to expand the regulations. The law index displays a negative relationship with average mine size that is stronger with controls for state and time effects. The coefficients are statistically significant at confidence levels of roughly 15 percent in two-tailed tests. Increases of 1 standard deviation in average mine size led to reductions in the law index of close to half of a law. The large employers' efforts to restrict the breadth of laws appear to have been counteracting lobbying by the UMWA. In the estimation without state and year effects, increases of 1 standard deviation in the percentage of miners in the UMWA were associated with a more than half a law increase in the regulatory index. The UMWA's efforts appear to have been correlated with time-invariant features in the states, because the inclusion of fixed effects in the model reduces the size and statistical significance of the UMWA coefficient.

Even after limiting the breadth of legislation, larger mines were also associated with reduced resources for enforcement. Average mine size displays a negative relationship with the inspection budget per coal worker that increases in size and in statistical significance with the inclusion of state and year effects. The fixed effects estimates in panel A in table 9.6 suggest that a 1 standard deviation increase of 35.7 workers per mine is associated with a reduction in the inspection budget of 64¢ per worker in 1967

15. North Dakota was in the adoption sample, but missing data forced its elimination from the study of inspection budgets and coverage of the laws.

Table 9.6   Ordinary least squares and fixed effects estimates for inspection budgets per coal worker (1967$) and coal regulation index, 1902, 1910, 1920, 1930

	Mean	Standard deviation	Inspection budget per coal worker (1967$)				Coal mining law index			
			(1)		(2)		(1)		(2)	
			Coefficient	OSD effect	Coefficient	OSD effect	Coefficient	OSD effect	Coefficient	OSD effect
A. Correlates based on number of workers										
Constant			2.408		2.574		3.938		3.984	
			(4.62)		(4.46)		(4.96)		(4.18)	
Workers per mine	70.9	35.7	−0.005	−0.18	−0.018	−0.64	−0.005	−0.17	−0.010	−0.37
			(−1.49)		(−2.98)		(−0.69)		(−1.42)	
Number of workers	20.5	33.96	−0.006	−0.20	0.005	0.16	0.036	1.23	0.013	0.45
			(−2.12)		(0.73)		(7.05)		(0.99)	
Percent UMWA	49.5	32.3	−0.004	−0.14	−0.003	−0.11	0.016	0.53	0.004	0.14
			(−0.95)		(−0.48)		(2.11)		(0.41)	
Year 1910					0.518				1.373	
					(1.56)				(2.62)	
Year 1920					−0.383				3.373	
					(−1.30)				(7.40)	
Year 1930					1.594				3.938	
					(4.26)				(8.60)	
State effects					Included				Included	
R²			0.134		0.658		0.239		0.796	
No. of observations			90		90		92		92	
B. Correlates based on tons of coal produced										
Constant			2.243		2.030		3.505		3.839	
			(4.77)		(4.90)		(4.86)		(4.79)	
Tons per mine (000)	56.6	36.1	−0.004	−0.15	−0.015	−0.55	0.002	0.06	−0.012	−0.42
			(−1.09)		(−2.66)		(0.23)		(−1.50)	

(*continued*)

Table 9.6   (continued)

	Mean	Standard deviation	Inspection budget per coal worker (1967$)				Coal mining law index			
			(1)		(2)		(1)		(2)	
			Coefficient	OSD effect	Coefficient	OSD effect	Coefficient	OSD effect	Coefficient	OSD effect
Tons produced (millions)	17.8	32.5	−0.005	−0.16	0.003	0.11	0.037	1.21	0.014	0.44
			(−1.80)		(0.47)		(7.63)		(1.03)	
Percent UMWA	49.5	32.3	−0.005	−0.15	−0.004	−0.13	0.018	0.58	0.005	0.15
			(−1.05)		(−0.52)		(2.25)		(0.41)	
Year 1910					0.178				1.244	
					(−0.690)				(2.70)	
Year 1920					−0.353				3.404	
					(−1.25)				(7.70)	
Year 1930					1.553				4.007	
					(3.96)				(8.59)	
State effects					Included				Included	
R^2			0.043		0.635		0.243		0.800	
No. of observations			89		89		91		91	

Notes and sources: A 1 standard deviation (OSD) effect is the change in the probability of adoption in a specific year given that the state had not yet adopted as-sociated with a 1 standard deviation increase in the variable. The *t*-statistics in parentheses are based on robust standard errors and on the null hypothesis that the coefficients are equal to zero. The data set is a panel for the twenty-three leading bituminous coal mining states for the years 1902, 1910, 1920, 1930. North Dakota appeared in the adoption regressions in table 9.5 but is absent here due to missing data. The regulation index is the number of coal safety regulations enacted in the state by that date from the list described in the notes to table 9.1. A table showing the dates of enactment of each regulation for each state can be found in Fishback (1986, pp. 284–85, and 1992, pp. 114–15). The inspection budget per miner divides the appropriations for coal mining in-spection by the number of miners in the state and adjusts for inflation using the Consumer Price Index (1967 = 1) from U.S. Bureau of the Census (1975, series E-135, p. 211). Information on the laws and inspection budgets came from various issues produced by the U.S. Commissioner of Labor (1892, 1896, 1904, 1908) and the U.S. Bureau of Labor Statistics with titles similar to "Labor Laws in the United States" and the legislative statute volumes for each state. See Fishback (1992, pp. 238–40) for a lengthy description of the sources and methods used. The number of mines in 1902 is from U.S. Bureau of the Census (1905, pp. 709–17). Information on total employment and tons produced for all years and on the number of mines for 1910, 1920, and 1930 come from various issues of the annual report Mineral Resources of the United States, Nonmetals, issued by the U.S. Geological Survey (various years) through 1922 and by the U.S. Bureau of Mines (various years) after 1922. Specific page numbers for each year are reported in Fishback (1992, pp. 234–36). Information on membership in the United Mine Workers of America is from the U.S. Coal Commission (1925, p. 1052). The source did not provide information for 1930, so the 1923 values, the latest available, were assumed for that year.

dollars. Similarly, a 1 standard deviation increase in tons produced per mine in panel B in table 9.6 was associated with 55¢ per worker less in the inspection budget. There may be other explanations for the negative relationship between average mine size and inspection budgets. If there were substantial economies of scale in inspecting each mine, a smaller inspection budget per mine worker might have achieved the same results as the average mine increases in size. However, there was plenty of evidence that reformers were pressing for large budgets per worker to enhance enforcement and reduce accident rates. They were right to do so, as empirical studies show that increased inspection budgets inspection per worker (or per ton) were associated with lower accident rates (see Aldrich 1997, pp. 337–38, and Fishback 1986 and 1992).

Meanwhile, the UMWA share of employment had no positive relationship with the size of mine inspection budgets. Problems with inadequate inspections and the emphasis on prosecutions of miners in some of the states documented later in the paper might have led the UMWA to shift their efforts away from pressing for stronger government enforcement of the laws. Instead, they relied on their own negotiations with employers to press for compliance with the aspects of the code that the union was interested in enforcing.

9.4   Narrative Evidence on Employer Influence in Coal Mining

The quantitative analysis suggests that larger coal employers adopted a defensive strategy against coal mining regulations rather than one of raising rivals' costs. Large firms were not associated with later adoption of the early coal regulations, but they were negatively related with the breadth of coal regulations and the size of the inspection budget. The view that large employers were following a defensive strategy receives ample support from narrative evidence from various states at various times.

The leading studies of coal mining legislation all suggest that employers significantly influenced the writing of coal regulations.[16] Mark Aldrich (1997, pp. 69–71), for example, finds that most of the early laws were "incomplete, poorly written, and hard to enforce" and often bore "the strong imprint of operator influence." In Colorado, mine inspectors considered the original 1883 law to be "very incomplete" and "wholly inadequate." When the law was revised in 1913, it was "the product of a committee dominated by large operators . . . and it largely codified their practices."

William Graebner's (1976, pp. 72–87) description of the evolution of West Virginia mining law suggests that through 1907 the law had little or no bite. Mine operators and even the mine inspectors were opposed to new legislation. In cases where proposed laws limited their mining methods, the

---

16. See Aldrich (1997), Fishback (1992), and Graebner (1976).

workers themselves actively opposed change. In response to a series of large mine explosions, the legislature passed a revision in 1907 in which mine operators played a major role. Two additional explosions led the chief mine inspector to become more of an activist in proposing legislation, yet an investigative committee that studied many of the explosions published a report that concluded that changes in the law would do no good. The legislature, in response to the demands of mine operators, rejected all of the chief mine inspector's recommendations for new regulations.

One sign that the mining laws were influenced by employers is that a number of them restricted the behavior of miners in ways that employers had had trouble enforcing within their mines. These restrictions often promoted safety but required extra effort for no obvious gain in pay on the part of the miners. For example, both Illinois and West Virginia banned the practice of "shooting off the solid," in which miners blasted without making an undercut at the base of the seam. The practice required more explosives, produced smaller, less valuable chunks of coal, and generally was considered more dangerous. It was popular with miners because it was much less strenuous than lying on one's side and hacking away at a wall of coal and rock for several hours before blasting the coal. The miners' response was to routinely disregard these and other restrictions that they found onerous.[17] When I estimated the impact of coal mining laws on accident rates (Fishback 1986, 1992, pp. 115–20) there were only three regulations that passed statistical significance tests in reducing accident rates: requirements that foremen visit workplaces more often, that miners use permissible explosives, and that miners not ride on coal cars. All of these are devoted at least in part to monitoring and changing the behavior of miners, which is consistent with a view that employers used regulations to help them enforce their own desired limits on the miners' behavior.

Lobbyists who are trying to take the teeth out of legislation often seek to limit the funds available for enforcement. In a number of states, there were not enough inspectors budgeted to meet the minimum number of visits of mines required in the mining statutes.[18] Low salaries led to high turnover of inspectors and limited the department's ability to attract talented inspectors. Inspectors earned only about 50 percent more than the average salaried worker in manufacturing in 1910 and less than 10 percent more in 1920.[19] West Virginia Governor John Cornwell in 1919 described their rate of pay as "less than that of men who drive mules" (quoted in Graebner 1976, p. 90). With larger budgets, the mine departments likely would have

17. See Aldrich (1997, pp. 58–73) and Graebner (1976, pp. 94–95).
18. See Fishback (1992, p. 113) and Graebner (1976).
19. Comparisons are based on mine inspector salaries in state mining laws and average annual earnings of coal miners (Fishback 1992, pp. 80–81) and average annual earnings for salaried workers in manufacturing from the manufacturing census (U.S. Bureau of the Census 1933, vol. 3, pp. 43–600).

had an impact on accident rates, as econometric studies by Fishback (1986, 1992) and Aldrich (1997, pp. 337–38) find that expansions in resources for inspection were associated with lower accident rates.[20]

Although much of Graebner's (1976) work on mine safety implies that many mine inspectors were honest advocates for safer mines, there were still worries about a revolving door between mine management and the inspection service. There were few opportunities to move up within the inspection bureaucracies, so some state mine inspectors accepted positions with coal companies at 50 to 100 percent pay increases. Many state inspectors were already sympathetic to the problems mine owners faced in running mines because they had moved to the job from posts as mining managers or superintendents. Union leaders were livid when the coal mine operators in 1908 "engineered" the appointment to West Virginia chief mine inspector of John Laing, himself the owner of several mining properties. After leaving office, Laing became the head of the Kanawha County Coal Operators' Association.[21]

Mine owners were not shy about pressuring the inspectors. In 1908 a West Virginia inspector stated "there are coal operators who will endeavor to have a district inspector removed from office rather than obey the mining laws, or carry out the recommendations made by an inspector." As a general rule, the mine owners appear to have had the advantage in the interest group struggle over inspector appointments, even in highly unionized states. In Illinois, where the UMWA was strong and the inspection staff had a reputation for being somewhat radical, a frustrated miner claimed: "There is not an inspector in the state who is not holding his job through the influences of some coal operator" (Graebner 1976, p. 91).

Most mining laws contained fines and potential jail sentences for offenders, but the inspectors could not impose these unilaterally. Instead, they disclosed their findings to a state or local government prosecutor who decided whether to take the offenders to court. The courts determined whether there was a violation and set the size of the fine.[22] There is little evidence of prosecutions of employers for mining violations in Pennsylvania, Ohio, and West Virginia prior to 1904. The number of prosecutions then rose to a peak at 395 in 1910 and 312 in 1911 (compared with approximately 3,200 mines and 250,000 employees) before trailing off to zero after 1912. Nearly all of these prosecutions were targeted at miners and not supervisors or mine owners. Miners accounted for 159 of the 163 prosecu-

---

20. Spending on factory inspection may have been less effective than spending on mine inspection. Estimates of the impact of state inspection budgets by David Buffum (1992) and James Chelius (1977) on measures of fatal accidents in industry do not find statistically significant reductions in accident risk.

21. See Graebner (1976, pp. 90–91) and Corbin (1981, p. 17).

22. In a handful of states the coal mine inspector had the power to close a mine considered unsafe, but even here the inspector had to secure an injunction through the proper court (Graebner 1976, pp. 97–100).

tions in West Virginia in 1910. Of 489 prosecutions between 1908 and 1911 in Pennsylvania, 392 were directed at mine workers, only 27 at superintendents, and 70 at foreman and fire bosses (Graebner 1976, pp. 97–100). Further, the probability of paying penalties was even lower. In Ohio in 1911 the total amount collected in fines under a new mining law came to $400, and this was a law described as having strong penalty provisions.

One reason for the lack of prosecutions may have been the intransigence of the courts. According to Graebner (1976, p. 99), when coal inspectors closed mines, which they did infrequently, they "received as much opposition as aid from local courts":

> West Virginia inspectors, moreover, evidently ceased prosecuting operators and managers when it became clear that they could not be convicted. . . . A district inspector reported that workers had 'completely lost all confidence in the local courts . . . [and were] thoroughly convinced that justice could not be obtained towards the enforcement of the mining laws.'

9.5   Employer Influence of Legislation and Enforcement in Manufacturing

Earlier adoption of the initial manufacturing regulations in states with larger establishments is consistent with both the reform and raising-rivals'-costs hypotheses. A completed data set on the factory inspection resources and the breadth of the specific manufacturing safety regulations is not yet available, so I cannot do the same tests that I did for coal mining. Qualitative evidence, however, suggests that at least in some states manufacturers wielded the same types of influence as coal employers did over the type of laws adopted. Problems with enforcement of regulations also carried over into manufacturing.

The introduction of factory safety legislation in Washington State in 1903 offers an example of how manufacturing employers influenced the writing of safety legislation. Safety regulations often served as focal points in negligence cases for issues related to "due care" and "assumption of risk." Employer violation of regulations eased the burden for workers in demonstrating employer negligence, while the absence of a violation could prevent recovery. When workers violated regulations targeted at their activities, employers were better able to invoke the contributory negligence defense.

Washington employers pressed for factory safety legislation in reaction to a series of court decisions related to the negligence liability system. One aspect of the assumption of risk defense had always been a major irritant to workers and reformers. In a number of cases workers reported malfunctions or lack of safeguards that increased their risk of injury, were told to return to work, and then were injured. Compensation had been denied on the basis that the workers had known the risk in the now more dangerous setting and assumed it when they returned to work. In *Green v. Western American Company* (1902) the Washington Supreme Court eliminated the assumption of risk defense in these situations. Fearing the complete elimination of the assumption of risk defense, employers played a significant role in the passage of Washington's Factory Inspection Act in 1903. Under the new act employers were to be considered negligent for accidents in settings where they violated the inspection acts. However, the law also provided for certifications that the employers' workplace was "safe." A number of lower courts then invoked the assumption of risk defense to prevent recovery by injured workers in several cases involving mines so certified. The Washington State Supreme Court disagreed and reaffirmed that lack of safeguards on machines was negligence whether the mine was certified or not. In 1905 the employers went back to the legislature and succeeded in altering the language of the Inspection Act so that employers had only to provide a "reasonable" safeguard (as opposed to a "proper" one). This change in language may have worked for a while but ultimately proved to be of little help to the employers, because the Supreme Court finally eliminated the assumption of risk defense by arguing that a machine lacked necessary safeguards by virtue of being the cause an accident (Tripp 1976, p. 535).

Inadequacy of inspection resources might have been an even more severe problem for the factory inspectors than for coal inspectors. There were far more factories than mines, and Brandeis (1935, pp. 632–33) notes that inspectors typically investigated only upon complaint. Rarely were the factory inspectors in a position to routinely and randomly inspect a significant share of the factories. Problems with enforcement likely contributed to the conditions that led to the deaths of 146 garment workers in the horrendous Triangle Shirtwaist Fire in New York City in 1911.[23] On the day of the fire, many workers reported that a key door to a stairway was locked, a violation of the factory regulations.

Just prior to the fire a State Labor Department inspector had reported an inadequate fire escape (Stein 1962, pp. 181–89), but jurisdictions over fire escapes were not well established. The factory inspection laws gave the inspector the power to demand a proper fire escape, but the factory inspectors claimed that the courts had ruled that fire escapes were outside the labor department's jurisdiction. Building safety therefore came under the jurisdiction of the New York City superintendent of buildings, to whom a report had been forwarded by the labor inspector. When the Asch building, where the fire broke out, was planned in 1900, the building inspector had agreed to allow the architects to forgo a required staircase because they promised that the fire escape they planned would act as a third staircase all the way to the ground. When the building was erected, the

---

23. These accounts are largely based on Stein (1962) and McEvoy (1995).

agreement was violated and the fire escape only reached the second floor. When this was pointed out in 1911, Building Department officials defended themselves by saying that their resources were inadequate. The department had only forty-seven inspectors to inspect 50,000 buildings. They claimed: "We do not hear of violations of the law in the old buildings unless they are particularly called to our attention." In that year the Fire Department had designated over 13,000 buildings as dangerous, but the department could only inspect 2,051. Once they found a violation, the building inspectors argued, they still faced significant obstacles in punishing the violators. "We must enforce all our rulings through the civil courts. When we bring an action, there is invariably a long fight. The record will show the owner is usually the victor." In other cases they hesitated to call for changes because "It would work a great hardship on the owners of buildings to require changes. This is especially true of fire escapes."[24]

In the aftermath of the Triangle Fire the State Labor Department was overhauled and New York State adopted a series of new fire-related regulations. Appropriations for labor issues in New York quadrupled between 1911 and 1915 to over a million dollars, but this coincided with expansions of duties in other areas and the development of workers' compensation. Although this is described as the golden era of labor regulations in New York, the inspection budgets per manufacturing worker were lower there than inspection budgets per miner in most coal mining states.[25] The increase in budgets still did not resolve the enforcement issue. A February 1916 editorial in the *New York Times* claimed that of 3,711 violations by factories of the new stairway regulations, "only 246 owners complied with the law, and two prosecutions were begun!" (The Industrial Commission," *New York Times,* February 23, 1916, p. 12).[26]

9.6 Summary

Did large employers subvert workplace safety reform? I found few examples of documented bribery or other illegal corruption, but there was considerable evidence that a number of actions by large employers met the broader definition of subversion in the introduction. The quantitative analysis of the relationship between average establishment size and regula-

24. Quoted in Stein (1962, p. 116).
25. The new million-dollar budget in New York came to only about 69¢ per manufacturing worker. Probably no more than half of the budget was devoted to inspections. Thus, 35¢ per worker in 1914, which translates into $1.16 in 1967 dollars, was below many of the figures for mining inspection in 1902 in table 9.1.
26. Problems with inadequate inspections remain today, but the sanctions when such problems are caught are much greater. See McEvoy (1995, pp. 648–50).

tions in the states and the analytical narratives suggest that we cannot tell one coherent story about the influence of large employers. Rather, we must tell one story for coal mining and another for manufacturing. In the coal industry, large employers practiced a defensive strategy, limiting the breadth of mining regulation and inspection resources per miner. Large employers in manufacturing, on the other hand, were associated with earlier adoption of safety regulations and workers' compensation.

A question remains as to why large employers adopted a defensive strategy in coal mining and less so in manufacturing. My sense is that there were two key factors, the focus on one industry in the coal regulations and the lack of women working in the mines. Coal regulations were targeted narrowly at a specific industry, while manufacturing regulations and workers' compensation often covered a broad range of industries. Labor relations in mining were more fractious than in most industries, and the reform proposals that employers opposed were often made by unions. The organization of opposition to objectionable laws was made easier by the narrowly defined interests of the large coal employers, who were already organized into coal associations to deal with labor relations and other issues specific to the industry. Since mines were often in isolated areas, coal employers wielded much greater political clout locally and thus likely had more influence over the enforcement of the laws in the courts (Fishback 1992, 1995). Manufacturing safety regulations, on the other hand, covered a broader range of industries, and the regulations might have left many industries only mildly constrained. Large employers interested in fighting the laws therefore found it more difficult than in coal mining to organize the fight across a set of employers in different industries.

Another key factor explaining the difference in strategies was the gender of the workers involved. Coal mines employed no women. Reformers found protective labor legislation of all kinds easier to sell for women and children, while employers found such legislation harder to obstruct. A number of the manufacturing safety regulations were designed to improve safety and workplace conditions for women and children in textiles and other industries. Thus, large employers who had moved away from employing women and children found it fruitful to join with reformers in pressing for regulations that raised the costs to employers who still relied on them. The protection of women and children likely played an important role in the introduction of workers' compensation, as well. Workers' compensation received so much support in part because it insured that the share of women and children receiving compensation when their breadwinners were injured or killed rose to 100 percent from less than 50 percent under negligence liability. This move dovetailed with Progressive Era mothers' pension programs that provided benefits to widows and children.

References

Aldrich, Mark. 1997. *Safety first: Technology, labor, and business in the building of American work safety, 1870–1939.* Baltimore: Johns Hopkins University Press.

Asher, Robert. 1969. Business and workers' welfare in the Progressive Era: Workmen's compensation reform in Massachusetts, 1880–1911. *Business History Review* 43 (Winter): 452–75.

Bartel, Ann P., and Lacy Glenn Thomas. 1985. Direct and indirect effects of regulation: A new look at OSHA's impact. *Journal of Law and Economics* 28 (April): 1–25.

Becker, Gary S. 1983. A theory of competition among pressure groups for political influence. *Quarterly Journal of Economics* 98 (August): 371–400.

Brandeis, Elizabeth. 1935. Labor legislation. In *History of labor in the United States,* vol. III, ed. John R. Commons and associates, 399–697. Repr. New York: Augustus Kelley Publishers, 1966.

Brandes, Stuart D. 1970. *American welfare capitalism, 1880–1940.* Chicago: University of Chicago Press.

Buchanan, James, Robert Tollison, and Gordon Tullock. 1980. *Toward a theory of the rent seeking society.* College Station: Texas A&M University Press.

Buffum, David. 1992. Workmen's compensation: Passage and impact. PhD diss., University of Pennsylvania.

Chelius, James R. 1977. *Workplace safety and health: The role of workers' compensation.* Washington, DC: American Enterprise Institute.

Clark, Frederick C. 1891. State railroad commissions and how they may be made effective. *Publications of the American Economic Association* 6 (6): 11–110.

Corbin, David Alan. 1981. *Life, work, and rebellion in the coal fields: The southern West Virginia Miners, 1880–1922.* Urbana: University of Illinois Press.

Fishback, Price V. 1986. Workplace safety during the Progressive Era: Fatal accidents in bituminous coal mining, 1912–1923. *Explorations in Economic History* 23 (July): 269–98.

———. 1992. *Soft coal, hard choices: The economic welfare of bituminous coal miners, 1890 to 1930.* New York: Oxford University Press.

———. 1995. An alternative view of violence in labor disputes in the early 1900s: The bituminous coal industry, 1900–1930. *Labor History* 36 (Summer): 426–56.

Fishback, Price V., and Shawn Everett Kantor. 1995. Did workers gain from the passage of workers' compensation laws? *Quarterly Journal of Economics* 110 (August): 713–42.

———. 1998. The adoption of workers' compensation in the United States, 1890–1930. *Journal of Law and Economics* 41 (October): 305–42.

———. 2000. *A prelude to the welfare state: The origins of workers' compensation.* Chicago: University of Chicago Press.

Friedman, Lawrence. 1985. *A history of American law.* 2nd ed. New York: Simon and Schuster.

Friedman, Lawrence, and Jack Ladinsky. 1967. Social change and the law of industrial accidents. *Columbia Law Review* 67 (January): 50–82.

Glaeser, Edward L., and Andrei Shleifer. 2003. The rise of the regulatory state. *Journal of Economic Literature* 41 (June): 401–25.

Graebner, William. 1976. *Coal-mining safety in the Progressive Era.* Lexington: University of Kentucky Press.

Holmes, Rebecca. 2003. The impact of state labor regulations on manufacturing input demand during the Progressive Era. PhD diss., University of Arizona.

Jacoby, Sanford. 1997. *Modern manors: Welfare capitalism since the New Deal.* Princeton, NJ: Princeton University Press.

Kim, Seung-Wook, and Price V. Fishback. 1993. Institutional change, compensating differentials and accident risk in American railroading, 1892–1945. *Journal of Economic History* 53 (December): 796–823.

Kolko, Gabriel. 1963. *The triumph of conservatism: A reinterpretation of American history, 1900–1916.* New York: Free Press of Glencoe.

Kolko, Gabriel. 1965. *Railroads and regulation, 1877–1916.* New York: W. W. Norton.

Landes, William M., and Richard A. Posner. 1987. *The economic structure of tort law.* Cambridge, MA: Harvard University Press.

Lubove, Roy. 1967. Workmen's compensation and the prerogatives of voluntarism. *Labor History* 8 (Fall): 254–27.

McEvoy, Arthur. 1995. The Triangle Shirtwaist fire of 1911: Social change, industrial accidents, and the evolution of common-sense causality. *Law and Social Inquiry* 20 (Spring): 621–51.

Moss, David. 1996. *Socializing security: Progressive-Era economists and the origins of American social policy.* Cambridge, MA: Harvard University Press.

Mulligan, Casey B., and Andrei Shleifer. 2004. Population and regulation. NBER Working Paper no. 10234. Cambridge, MA: National Bureau of Economic Research, January.

Pelzman, Samuel. 1976. Toward a more general theory of regulation. *Journal of Law and Economics* 19 (August): 211–48.

Polinsky, A. Mitchell, and Steven Shavell. 2000. The economic theory of public enforcement of law. *Journal of Economic Literature* 38 (March): 45–76.

Poole, Keith T., and Howard Rosenthal. 1993. The enduring battle for economic regulation: The Interstate Commerce Act revisited. *Journal of Law and Economics* 36 (October): 837–60.

Posner, Richard A. 1972. A theory of negligence. *Journal of Legal Studies* 1 (January): 29–96.

Schwartz, Gary T. 1981. Tort law and the economy in nineteenth century America: A reinterpretation. *Yale Law Journal* 90 (July): 1717–75.

Shavell, Steven. 1987. *Economic analysis of accident law.* Cambridge, MA: Harvard University Press.

Skocpol, Theda. 1992. *Protecting soldiers and mothers: The political origins of social policy in the United States.* Cambridge, MA: Harvard University Press.

Stein, Leon. 1962. *The Triangle fire.* New York: J. B. Lippincott.

Stigler, George. 1971. The theory of economic regulation. *Bell Journal of Economics and Management Science* 2 (Spring): 3–21.

Tomlins, Christopher. 1988. A mysterious power: Industrial accidents and the legal construction of employment relations in Massachusetts, 1800–1850. *Law and History Review* 6 (Fall): 375–438.

———. 1993. *Law, labor and ideology in the early American republic.* New York: Cambridge University Press.

Tripp, Joseph. 1976. An instance of labor and business cooperation: Workmen's compensation in Washington state, 1911. *Labor History* 17 (Fall): 530–50.

U.S. Bureau of the Census. 1865. *Manufactures of the United States in 1860; compiled from the original returns of the eighth census.* Washington, DC: Government Printing Office.

———. 1872. *Ninth census.* Volume III, *The statistics of the wealth and industry of the United States.* Washington, DC: Government Printing Office.

———. 1886. *Report of the mining industries of the United States.* Washington, DC: Government Printing Office.

———. 1892. *Report on mineral industries in the United States at the eleventh census: 1890.* Washington, DC: Government Printing Office.

———. 1895. *Report on manufacturing industries in the United States at the eleventh census: 1890.* Part I, *Totals for states and industries.* Washington, DC: Government Printing Office.

———. 1902. *Twelfth census of the United States: 1900.* Vol. 7, *Manufactures.* Washington, DC: Government Printing Office.

———. 1905. *Special reports: Mines and quarries, 1902.* Washington, DC: Government Printing Office.

———. 1913. *Thirteenth census of the United States: 1910.* Vol. 1, *Population;* vol. 4, *Occupations;* vols. 8 and 9, *Manufactures.* Washington, DC: Government Printing Office.

———. 1933. *Fifteenth census of the United States: 1930.* Vols. 1 and 3, *Manufactures.* Washington, DC: Government Printing Office.

———. 1975. *Historical statistics of the United States, 1790–1970.* Washington, DC: Government Printing Office.

U.S. Bureau of Labor Statistics. 1914. Labor laws of the United States, with decisions of courts relating thereto. 2 parts. *Bulletin of the United States Bureau of Labor Statistics* no. 148. Washington, DC: Government Printing Office.

———. 1925. Labor laws of the United States, with decisions of courts relating thereto. *Bulletin of the United States Bureau of Labor Statistics* no. 370. Washington, DC: Government Printing Office.

U.S. Bureau of Mines. Various years. *Mineral resources of the United States: Nonmetals.* Washington, DC: Government Printing Office.

U.S. Coal Commission. 1925. *Report,* part III. Washington, DC: Government Printing Office.

U.S. Commissioner of Labor. 1892. *Labor laws of the various states and territories and the District of Columbia, second special report of the U.S. commissioner of labor.* House of Representatives Report no. 1960. 52nd Cong., 1st sess. Washington, DC: Government Printing Office.

———. 1896. *Labor laws of the United States, second special report of the commissioner of labor.* Washington, DC: Government Printing Office.

———. 1904. *Labor laws of the United States with decisions of courts relating thereto, tenth special report of the commissioner of labor.* Washington, DC: Government Printing Office.

———. 1908. *Labor laws of the United States with decisions of courts relating thereto, 1907, twenty-second annual report of the commissioner of labor.* Washington, DC: Government Printing Office.

U.S. Geological Survey. Various years. *Mineral resources of the United States: Nonmetals.* Washington, DC: Government Printing Office.

Weeks, Jos. D. 1886. Report on trade societies in the United States. *Report on the statistics of wages in manufacturing industries with supplementary reports on the average retails prices of necessaries of life and on trade societies, and strikes and lockouts.* Washington, DC: Government Printing Office.

Weinstein, James. 1967. Big business and the origins of workmens' compensation. *Labor History* 8 (Spring): 156–74.

Wiebe, Robert. 1962. *Businessmen and reform: A study of the progressive movement.* Cambridge, MA: Harvard University Press.

The Determinants of Progressive Era Reform
The Pure Food and Drugs Act of 1906

Marc T. Law and Gary D. Libecap

10.1   Introduction

The late nineteenth and early twentieth centuries witnessed the birth of the American regulatory state. During the Progressive Era, federal authority over banking, insurance, transportation, competition, and interstate trade in food and drug products greatly expanded. Indeed, it is during this period that the federal government began to displace state and local governments as the primary source of regulation in the economy. Government regulation became not only more federal, but more intrusive. The question is why.

Broadly speaking, there are three views of the emergence of the federal regulatory state.[1] One is a *public interest* view that argues that federal regulation arose to solve market failures that state and local governments could not address, and that Progressive Era reformers interested in improving consumer welfare lobbied in favor of these regulations. While this account is supported by a large historical literature, it fails to explain why regulation, as opposed to the court system, was needed to safeguard consumer welfare (Glaeser and Schleifer 2003). A second view is that regulation was adopted to give a competitive advantage to business groups. This *regulatory capture* argument is intuitively appealing, but it cannot account

Marc T. Law is an assistant professor of economics at the University of Vermont. Gary D. Libecap is the Anheuser Busch Professor and professor of economics and law at the University of Arizona, Tucson, and a research associate of the National Bureau of Economic Research.

We thank Dan Carpenter, Ed Glaeser, Claudia Goldin, and participants of the NBER Corruption and Reform Conference for their helpful comments. Tomas Nonenmacher and Lee Alston graciously provided data on reform interest groups.

1. For an overview and synthesis of some of these views see Levine and Forrence (1990).

for why there was so much contemporaneous popular support for regulation. A third view emphasizes the role played by the *muckraking press and entrepreneurial bureaucrats* in galvanizing public support for regulation. The exact mechanisms by which these interests influenced the adoption of regulation, however, have not been explored. While the first view emphasizes the efficiency-improving role of regulation, the latter two suggest that regulation may have had dubious effects on consumer welfare.

In this chapter, we examine these three explanations for the adoption of Progressive Era regulation through the lens of federal food and drug legislation. In 1906 the federal government enacted the Pure Food and Drugs Act, the first federal law that gave regulators unprecedented authority over interstate trade in food and drug products. The central issues we investigate are the timing and nature of support for the food and drugs act. We also explore the early enforcement of this law and its effects on consumer welfare. The passage of this act can reveal much about the entire Progressive agenda and the establishment of the Food and Drug Administration (FDA).[2]

We find that aspects of all three views of regulation explain the adoption of the Pure Food and Drugs Act, that producer, consumer, and bureaucratic interests maneuvered to mold the law to their benefit, and that the muckraking press influenced the timing of adoption. Both the legislative history and statistical analysis underscore the desires of various producer groups to tilt the competitive playing field, of federal bureaucrats to expand their regulatory mandates, and of Progressive reform interests to ensure that consumers were not deceived about the quality of food and drugs they purchased. Even so, while several pure food and drug bills were considered during the 1890s and early 1900s, none were passed. Conflict among these competing interests made it impossible to form an enacting political coalition. In 1905–6, however, with the publication of Upton Sinclair's *The Jungle* along with sensational muckraking articles in leading magazines and newspapers, popular opinion in favor of food and drug regulation was electrified, and this in turn facilitated the formation of an effective coalition in favor of final passage of the law.

We also find that because the interests behind the legislation were unable to entirely shape the enforcing agency or the legal environment in which enforcement took place, these groups did not ultimately benefit from regulation as initially anticipated. Accordingly, while a combination of the three views of regulation furnishes an explanation for why regulation arose at the time that it did, it does not provide a complete account of the ultimate effect of policy. A more eclectic approach that takes into account the

2. Until the late 1920s, the organization that we know today as the FDA was the Bureau of Chemistry, an agency within the federal Department of Agriculture. In 1927 the regulatory portion of this agency was renamed the Food, Drug and Insecticide Administration. In 1930 its name was shortened to the Food and Drug Administration.

abilities of interest groups to influence the institutional environment is needed to fully understand the causes and consequences of Progressive Era regulation.

10.2 Market Changes and a Conceptual Framework for Analysis of Reform

Three important developments characterized the market for food and drugs in the late nineteenth and early twentieth centuries. The first was the introduction of new and cheaper food and drug products that threatened to erode the dominant position enjoyed by older products. These competitive changes gave rise to trade wars among rival firms. The second was scientific advances that increased the complexity of many products. This situation created opportunities for cost-saving deception by some firms through alteration or adulteration of their products in ways that consumers could not easily perceive. Uncertainty about product quality, in turn, placed consumers at risk of being cheated about quality or, more ominously, of being poisoned. The third was the creation of national markets that affected consumers, producers, and government agencies. Increasingly, consumers purchased food and drugs that were made in other states, often outside the jurisdiction of local or state courts and regulatory bodies. In disputes over product quality, individual state regulations and tort actions were ineffective as remedies. Additionally, firms producing for the national market were faced with different and often conflicting regulatory environments that made compliance and product standardization difficult. Growing interstate trade and general concerns about product safety therefore created new opportunities for federal regulators to extend their mandates. In contrast, state regulatory officials were often jealous of their prerogatives and suspicious of any expansion of federal authority. All in all, these developments in the market for food and drugs meant that the demand for federal regulation during the Progressive Era could come from three different sources, described below.

10.2.1 Regulation as a Solution to Market Failure

Asymmetric information about product ingredients and product quality created concerns that there was a "lemons" problem in the market for many food and drug items (Akerlof 1970). Because consumers could not detect many forms of food and drug adulteration, markets could not always guarantee the delivery of quality food and drug products (Darby and Karni 1973; McCluskey 2000). Hence, there was a productive role for product quality regulation by scientific experts, who had a comparative advantage in judging the quality of food and drug items. Since national markets were involved, federal politicians could improve consumer welfare and also garner votes by adopting federal regulatory legislation. Under this view there was a market failure to be corrected, and the Pure Food and Drugs Act and its administering agency were a means of solving the problem; regulation was consumer driven and aimed at solving real economic problems.

10.2.2   Rent Seeking through Regulatory Capture

An alternative view based on the work of Kolko (1963), Stigler (1971), and Peltzman (1976) highlights the role of regulation in advancing specific producer interests rather than the efficiency gains from regulation. Firms captured the regulatory process in order to raise the costs of their rivals through constraints on entry or other production restrictions (Wood 1986). This action benefited firms that sought to mitigate any advantages their rivals gained from the adoption of new production technologies. Politicians responded because these groups could offer votes and campaign contributions in exchange. At the state level, some laws were designed to strategically advantage local and regional producers who faced new interstate competitive pressures. More national producers and interest groups, in contrast, sought federal legislation to create uniform regulatory standards, thwart more aggressive state regulation, and to disadvantage other producers. If the regulations were effective, successful producer groups could secure monopoly rents through higher prices and reduced output. Hence, under this view, the principal advocates of the legislation were industry groups seeking competitive advantages relative to their rivals. The Pure Food and Drugs Act was an example of the capture of government by business interests, and the Bureau of Chemistry and FDA were agents of that capture. The distributional gains secured by business offered no consumer benefits. Indeed, by restricting entry, the law may have harmed consumers.

10.2.3   Rent Seeking by Enterprising Federal Bureaucrats and the Press

A final possibility emphasizes the roles played by entrepreneurial federal bureaucrats seeking to expand their jurisdictions and agency budgets (Niskanen 1971) and by muckraking journalists seeking to sell newspapers, magazines, and books. These two parties formed a natural alliance in favor of regulation because the press could publicize the self-serving "scientific" concerns of federal regulators about food and drug safety. Muckraking publications could galvanize public support for regulation through grisly tales about consumers being defrauded and even poisoned. Additionally, sensational muckraking disclosures attracted readers. These claims were credible because new production technologies and products were not well understood by consumers and their quality and health effects could not be easily assessed. If regulation were adopted by taking advantage of limited consumer and voter information, it too would provide little or no welfare gain for consumers. Accordingly, under this view, consumers were manipulated by an aggressive press and federal bureaucracy seeking to exploit their ignorance of the content of new products and processes. Enactment of the Pure Food and Drugs Act was a response less to real economic problems than to rising consumer concerns fueled by a newly effective, sensational media. The major proponents of the law then were consumer groups, the muckraking press, and federal bureaucrats.

To see how each of these views performs in explaining the adoption of federal regulation we turn to an examination of the market for food and drugs in the late 1800s and the legislative history of federal food and drug regulation.

10.3   Market Changes and the Legislative History of Federal Regulation

Regulation may have had multiple advocates with different objectives. The key constituencies potentially involved in food and drug regulation include ideologically motivated Progressive reformers, state regulators, federal regulators, incumbent firms producing "old" goods, entrant firms producing "new" goods, the muckraking press, and consumers. These parties had conflicting incentives for federal regulation of product quality. These differences shaped political constituencies as well as the nature of the conflict surrounding proposed pure food and drug bills.

10.3.1   The Changing Market and Producers' Incentives to Lobby for Regulation

Expanding markets combined with advances in food processing gave rise to new products that better met the needs of certain market segments and were cheaper than those produced by older firms. These older firms thus had an incentive to organize to obtain government support in blocking or limiting the spread of these new products.

Consider the following products and their impacts on the market. Oleomargarine, the first viable butter substitute, was introduced to the American market in the early 1870s. Invented in 1869 by the French chemist Mège-Mouries, oleomargarine (margarine) quickly became popular among working-class households because it was considerably cheaper than butter (Dupré 1999). Similarly, declining transportation costs and the development of the refrigerated rail car made it possible for large meat packinghouses located in Chicago, St. Louis, and other midwestern cities to slaughter cattle centrally and ship prepared beef carcasses (known as "dressed beef") to eastern markets. By the 1880s, sales of dressed beef rivaled sales of locally slaughtered meat in New York, Boston, and other cities on the east coast (Yeager 1981; Libecap 1992). Advances in chemistry gave rise to a new form of baking powder—alum-based baking powder—that was cheaper than traditional cream of tartar baking powders. Additionally, other improvements in canning and preserving technology made it possible to expand both the geographical and temporal distances between the production and consumption of fruits, vegetables, meats, and seafood.

As a consequence of these developments, conflicts among competing factions of the food trade became common. Dairy producers, threatened by the growing popularity of oleomargarine, slandered oleomargarine as "the greasy counterfeit" and, importantly, sought regulations at the state and federal level to stem the growth of the oleomargarine trade. Local butchers, in concert with disgruntled cattlemen, charged that dressed beef was unsafe and lobbied for meat inspection and antitrust to disadvantage the large Chicago packinghouses. A long and protracted battle emerged between the cream of tartar baking powder interests and the alum-based baking powder interests, each of whom charged that the other product was dangerous to health and attempted to obtain regulation that disadvantaged the other product. Similar conflicts also arose between "straight" and "blended" whiskey producers, each claiming that the other product was impure and unsafe for consumers. The arrival of newer, cheaper substitute products clearly stimulated a demand for regulation on the part of certain producer groups who desired regulation as a way of shifting demand away from competing products (Wood 1986, pp. 152–80).

Indeed, some of the laws regulating the food industry were closely tied to the efforts of industry groups to weaken their rivals. For instance, regulations enacted by state governments that required oleomargarine to be colored differently from butter, that prohibited the use of oleomargarine in boarding houses, prisons, or in restaurants, or that tightly regulated or even prohibited its sale were enacted primarily to benefit dairy farmers. Further, the 1886 Oleomargarine Tax enacted by Congress required oleomargarine producers to mark and stamp their product in various ways, imposed an internal revenue tax of $0.02 per pound on oleomargarine, and levied a fee of $600 per year on oleomargarine producers, $480 per year on oleomargarine wholesalers, and $48 per year on oleomargarine retailers (U.S. Senate 1900–1901; Lee 1973; Dupré 1999).

Correspondingly, the 1891 Meat Inspection Act was enacted in part to satisfy a coalition of cattlemen and local butchers in eastern markets, who wanted regulation that would stem the growth of the dressed meat trade and disadvantage the large Chicago packers. The large packers, however, also supported the law because it helped to create foreign markets for their meats by requiring inspection of cattle and hogs destined for interstate and foreign commerce (Libecap 1992).

10.3.2   The Changing Market and Consumers' Incentives to Secure Regulation

Consumers also had reasons to be worried about changes in the market for food and drugs. As food production moved out of households and into impersonal markets, and as foods became more sophisticated as a result of advances in manufacturing and processing, it became increasingly difficult for ordinary consumers to discern product quality and composition. Fears about the quality of food products—specifically about the ingredients contained in foods, as well as in the nutritional value of foods containing chemicals, preservatives, and other manufactured components—began to be expressed by chemists, home economists, public health officials, and other reform-minded individuals. These parties expressed their concern for consumer welfare by highlighting the potential problems and by calling for a more active role for government.

For instance, there was a burgeoning literature on how food was "adulterated" (i.e., cheapened through the addition of impurities) by manufacturers and distributors in an effort to obtain dear prices for cheap items, and on the consequences of food adulteration for health and longevity. "We buy everything, and have no idea of the processes by which articles are produced, and have no means of knowing beforehand what the quality may be," wrote Ellen Richards, one of the leaders of the home economics movement, in her 1885 book entitled *Food Materials and Their Adulteration.* "Relatively we are in a state of barbarous innocence, as compared to our grandmothers, about the common articles of daily use" (quoted in Strasser 1989, p. 255). Asymmetric information about food ingredients thus gave rise to the perception that there was a lemons problem in the markets for many food and drug items.

State and federal agencies were attracted to the issue, and studies conducted by analytical chemists employed in state and federal public health and agricultural departments revealed extensive food adulteration. According to a 1902 Senate Report that surveyed the findings of several adulteration studies conducted during the prior two decades, food adulteration was reasonably common (U.S. Senate 1902). Numerous independent studies found that milk was watered down or skimmed without warning. Others found butter to be cheapened by the addition of oleomargarine. Cottonseed oil was often added to lard that was marketed as "pure leaf lard." Glucose and chemical preservatives were frequently added to canned and prepared goods without indication on product labels. Many of these actions were documented in 1887 in *Food Adulteration and Its Detection* by J. P. Battershall, a chemist employed by the U.S. Public Health Department.

Claims were also made by advocates of regulation that adulterated food posed health risks, but the available evidence was more mixed, perhaps because understanding about the basics of human nutrition was very primitive at the time, even among leading physicians and public health officials. In testimony to congressional hearings on food adulteration in the late 1890s and early 1900s, physicians and scientists disagreed about the nutritional value of preservatives like borax and salicylic acid, about the effects on human digestion of alum-based as opposed to cream of tartar–based baking powders, and about the health risks associated with the consumption of artificial sweeteners like glucose (U.S. Senate 1899–1900; Young 1989, pp. 140–45).

Charges that particular food products were poisonous and could lead to death were largely unsupported, since there was little evidence of widespread poisonings resulting from the consumption of dressed beef, canned fruits, vegetables, and meats, or other manufactured and processed food items.[3] Much of the scientific debate involved government officials, and it centered on the more subtle consequences of food consumption on digestion and nutrition.

Reputation mechanisms may have been a market solution for reducing consumer uncertainty about food quality. Product branding proliferated as producers of canned and processed foods like Swift, the National Biscuit Company, and H. J. Heinz worked to establish reputations for providing high-quality products (Strasser 1989). Retail grocery chains like A&P and Kroger also emerged in the late 1800s, partly in response to the need to assure consumers of the quality of foodstuffs (Kim 2001).

In general, however, it was difficult for consumers to know if the foods they ate were harmful or healthful, or if chemical preservatives or low-quality ingredients had been added to their food. Hence, market-based solutions to the asymmetric information problem, which relied on ex post verifiability of product quality, likely were insufficient to guarantee the delivery of those dimensions of quality that had "credence" characteristics (Darby and Karni 1973; McCluskey 2000). This sentiment was expressed by a member of the Forty-Ninth Congress (1885), who made the following argument in a speech to the House on the need for pure food regulation:

> In ordinary cases the consumer may be left to his own intelligence to protect himself against impositions. By the exercise of a reasonable degree of caution, he can protect himself from frauds in under-weight and in under-measure. If he can not detect a paper-soled shoe on inspection, he detects it in the wearing of it, and in one way or another he can impose a penalty upon the fraudulent vendor. As a general rule the doctrine of *laissez faire* can be applied. Not so with many of the adulterations of food. Scientific inspection is needed to detect the fraud, and scientific inspection is beyond the reach of the ordinary consumer. In such cases the Government should intervene. (*Congressional Record* 1885, pp. 5040–41)

Concerns about food quality generated demand for food regulation among advocates for consumers. Progressive reform groups—most notably women's groups like the General Federation of Women's Clubs (GFWC), the Women's Christian Temperance Union (WCTU), as well as

---

3. Olmstead and Rhode (2004) report a more direct growing human health threat through bovine tuberculosis. Federal regulatory responses began in 1913.

leaders of the home economics movement and public health officials—lobbied for regulations that banned the sale of adulterated and misbranded food products.

Accordingly, some of the food regulations enacted during the Progressive Era appear to have had clear public interest motivations. In particular, the general pure food and dairy laws enacted by state governments during the last two decades of the nineteenth century were aimed at improving the accuracy of product labels. While the content and form of these laws varied somewhat from state to state, in general the goal of these regulations was to ensure that mixtures and impurities that were added to products be indicated clearly on product labels. In so doing, these state pure food laws helped solve a lemons problem in the market for many food products. This action benefited certain consumers, who desired better information about product quality, as well as higher-quality producers, who felt that regulation would help them segment the market for their wares (Law 2003).

10.3.3   Market Changes and Government Officials' Incentives to Secure Regulation

Efforts to expand regulation provided opportunities for state and federal bureaucracies to increase their budgets, staffing, and authority. Regulation by "experts" made sense to advocates because chemists and other scientists employed in government agencies had a definite comparative advantage over consumers in detecting food adulteration. Indeed, during the 1880s and 1890s, most state governments enacted "pure food" and "pure dairy" laws that outlawed the sale of adulterated foods and that gave officials employed in state pure food agencies the authority to seize adulterated and misbranded products and prosecute manufacturers and dealers who violated these regulations (U.S. Senate 1900–1901).

By the 1890s, however, it became clear that state governments were not optimally positioned to systematically regulate the content of food labels. This was for three reasons. First, the expansion of interstate trade in food products made it increasingly difficult for state governments to regulate goods produced out of state or even enforce their own pure food laws. Although state governments had the authority to regulate goods produced and sold within their borders, they had no authority over the production of goods in other states and could not control the sale of out-of-state goods sold within their boundaries. By shipping goods in an "original and unbroken package," out-of-state manufacturers and distributors could circumvent a state's pure food regulations (U.S. Senate 1899–1900, pp. 529–30).

Second, the pure food laws enacted in many states were often not enforced. Although nearly every state enacted a pure food law between 1880 and 1900, only half of these state laws entrusted enforcement to a particular state agency (Law 2003). The pure food laws enacted by the remaining states were essentially window-dressing laws that had little bite. Narrative evidence presented by Goodwin (1999, pp. 68–70) suggests that enforcement was limited or even nonexistent in those states that did not have an enforcement agency. While there is some evidence that lax enforcement in some states may have been in response to pressure from particular food manufacturers (Okun 1986), a close examination of congressional testimony on proposed food and drug bills and other contemporary sources does not suggest that "corruption" of state regulators by industry interests played a systematic role in undermining state efforts. Regulation was lax in many states not because manufacturers deliberately made it so but rather because government in general was small and budgets were limited. As a result, pure food regulations in many states did little to solve the asymmetric information problem regarding product ingredients.

Finally, in testimony to Congress, manufacturers and distributors engaged in interstate trade in foodstuffs also complained that compliance with several different state regulations was costly. These manufacturers and distributors desired a uniform federal pure food law because they felt that it would reduce compliance costs and because a national law might preempt more onerous state regulation. For instance, according to the director of a large Chicago wholesaler,

> The various states throughout this country . . . have passed pure-food laws, and in the distribution of merchandise—some kinds of merchandise—I find that at times errors are very likely to crop up in the shipping of goods in these states on account of the lack of uniformity, as the law of one State differs from the law of another, so that for the last ten years the merchants and manufacturers of Chicago have been clamoring for a national pure-food law, in the same manner that we clamored for a national bankruptcy act. It requires a lawyer for each State to know what the requirements are in each state in order to know the rules that prevail in them. (U.S. Senate 1899–1900, p. 73)

As the push for federal regulation intensified, however, conflict arose among bureaucrats at the federal and state level regarding who should enforce a federal pure food law and who should have authority to set food standards. Beginning in 1887, the Bureau of Chemistry, an agency within the Department of Agriculture, began to publish several high-profile studies documenting the nature and extent of food adulteration in the United States. Under the leadership of Dr. Harvey Wiley, the Bureau of Chemistry began to develop a reputation for its analysis of food adulteration in America. By the mid-1890s it became clear that the Bureau of Chemistry would become the agency responsible for enforcing a federal pure food and drugs law.

Federal officials within the Bureau of Chemistry faced a strong incentive to lobby for federal pure food regulation since they would capture the benefits of regulation through an expansion of their regulatory mandate. Regulators from some states opposed federal regulation, partly because it had the potential to make them redundant, but also because they were suspicious that federal regulators (specifically, Harvey Wiley) would not be independent of certain manufacturing interests with whom Wiley had ties. On the other hand, the Association of Official Agricultural Chemists (AOAC) as well as regulators from other states were solidly behind Harvey Wiley and the Bureau of Chemistry. Jockeying among bureaucratic interest groups thus also contributed to political stalemate over regulatory reform (Coppin and High 1999).

10.3.4   Political Stalemate and the Muckraking Press in the Timing of Regulation

The conflicting objectives of business, consumer, and state and federal government interests created a political stalemate and blocked action at the federal level for food and drug regulation. Consider for example, the Paddock Bill, introduced in 1890 by Senator Paddock of Nebraska to protect producers and consumers against commercial fraud in food products (adulteration) and to improve the reputation of American food products abroad and thereby promote exports. Despite claims of widespread support for the bill from citizens, state legislatures, wholesale grocery and drug associations, boards of trade, and farm organizations, no action was taken in 1890 or 1891. Corn and hog producers, who were waging a trade war against adulterated lard that had cottonseed oil added to it, were strong advocates, and in 1892 the bill was reintroduced to the Senate in a weakened form. It passed the Senate, but in the House cottonseed oil producers, through their congressional representatives, were able to prevent it from becoming law (Anderson 1958, pp. 78–80; Young 1989, pp. 97–99).

Similarly, competing baking powder interests stalled other federal pure food bills. In these cases, producers of cream of tartar baking powders wanted the regulations to be written in a way that put alum-based baking powders at a competitive disadvantage. Naturally, producers of alum-based baking powders wanted assurances that the regulations would not be enforced in a way that discriminated against their product. Hence, according to Anderson (1958, p. 135), by 1900 "the situation had reached a point where, no matter how the bill was phrased, it would encounter opposition from either of the two great camps of baking powder producers."

Additionally, conflict among straight and blended whiskey producers contributed to political gridlock over efforts to secure a pure food law in the early 1900s. Straight (distilled) whiskeys, produced in Kentucky, Maryland, Virginia, and Pennsylvania, competed with cheaper "blended" (rectified) whiskeys, produced in Illinois, Indiana, and Ohio. Straight whiskey interests, who were the incumbent producers, viewed blended whiskeys as impure products and sought regulation that would disadvantage blended whiskies, which were rapidly gaining market share. Pure food bills were drafted to require that "mixtures, compounds, combinations, imitations or blends" (blended whiskey) be "labeled, branded, or tagged, so as to show the character and constituents thereof."[4] Concerned that this clause would force blended whiskey manufacturers to disclose valuable trade secrets, the National Wholesale Liquor Dealers' Association, the trade organization of blended whiskey producers, organized successfully to fight these bills (Young 1989, pp. 165–68).

Finally, disagreement over whether pure food regulation should include medicines—in particular, drugs that were not listed in the *United States Pharmacopoeia* (*USP*) or the *National Formulary* (*NF*)—also generated political opposition to federal regulation. Selected progressive reform groups, in particular women from the WCTU, wanted patent medicines and proprietary nostrums to be regulated because of their alcohol content. Organized medicine, represented by the American Medical Association (AMA), also desired regulations that limited the availability of "quack" drugs (Anderson 1958, pp. 169–71). The AMA was motivated in part because of the health risks posed by patent medicines, but also because, by functioning as a substitute for physicians' services, patent medicines were a competitive threat to physicians.

The trade organizations for patent medicines, the Proprietary Association, and other drug producers, as well as newspapers that were dependent on patent medicine advertising as a source of revenues, lobbied against proposed pure food and drug regulations that would include drugs not listed in either the *USP* or the *NF*.[5] They feared that the federal government would begin to regulate the therapeutic claims made about their products. According to the Proprietary Association's Committee on Legislation, regulation that defined drugs more broadly "would practically destroy the sale of proprietary remedies in the United States" (quoted in Young 1989, p. 169).

These legislative conflicts might have effectively prevented adoption of any federal law had it not been for the rise of muckraking journalism and its sensational claims that raised the political costs of opposing regulation. Indeed, muckraking journalism, by making the issue of food and drug adulteration emotionally salient, served as a coordinating device through which diffuse consumer interests were harnessed.

Several factors contributed to the appearance of muckraking journalism in the late 1800s, and these factors were closely tied to the undercurrents of Progressive reform more broadly and to food and drug regulation more specifically. Many Progressive reformers were writers and journalists, who

---

4. According to Young (1989, p. 167), Wiley "abominated" blended whiskey and "leagued with the distillers to plot ways of checkmating the blenders' stratagems."

5. Patent medicines were in fact among the most important sources of newspaper and magazine advertising revenues during this period. See Young (1967).

believed in the "power of the pen" to inform readers of social and economic problems and to persuade ordinary citizens of the need for reform (Hays 1957). Further, technological and organizational developments made it possible for these writers and journalists to reach a larger audience than ever before. The adoption of high-speed presses and the perfection of halftone photoengraving reduced production costs and improved the quality of illustrations. Declining postal rates during the 1880s and 1890s lowered the cost of distributing periodicals throughout the nation. The growth of a national market for consumer products and the sale of magazine and periodical space to national advertising companies made it possible for periodicals to be sold to consumers at extremely low prices (often less than ten cents per copy). Owners of periodicals like *McClure's, Cosmopolitan, Colliers Weekly, Everybody's,* and *Munsey's* soon discovered a profitable combination in the marriage of low-cost, high-distribution, advertising-intensive magazines with sensational journalism that exposed readers to important social and economic problems (Chalmers 1974; Filler 1976). Hence, muckraking journalists like Samuel Hopkins Adams, Ray Stannard Baker, Henry Demarest Lloyd, Upton Sinclair, Lincoln Steffens, Charles Edward Russell, and Ida Tarbell were hired by these periodicals to write articles exposing unscrupulous business practices, slum urban conditions, and political corruption.

Two major muckraking episodes appear to have been especially critical in the enactment of the Pure Food and Drugs Act (Anderson 1958; Young 1989; Carpenter 2001). One was the publication in 1906 of Upton Sinclair's *The Jungle,* which exposed unsanitary conditions in Chicago meat-packing plants and generated public outrage over the quality of meat.[6] First published as a serial in the muckraking journal *Appeal to Reason,* Sinclair's novel revealed how the large meat packers deceived consumers about the quality of their products. Sinclair described how "potted chicken" contained no chicken at all; how meat that had turned sour was rubbed with soda to remove the smell; how moldy sausage rejected from Europe found its way back into the American market; and how meat was contaminated on the slaughterhouse floor. The direct result of Upton Sinclair's muckraking was the 1906 Meat Inspection Act, which significantly expanded the U.S. Department of Agriculture's (USDA) inspection of the slaughtering, packing, and canning of meats (Young 1989, pp. 221–50).

The second muckraking episode was a set of articles published in *Colliers* that revealed how patent medicine manufacturers were using their power over the press to defeat state regulation, but, more important, it

---

6. Sinclair's main objective in writing *The Jungle* was to provoke outrage over industrial working conditions of immigrants rather than to reveal deception on the part of the meat packers regarding product quality. See Young (1989, p. 252).

alerted the public to the dangers associated with the use of patent medicines. In a November 4, 1905, article, "The Patent Medicine Conspiracy against the Freedom of the Press," Mark Sullivan exposed the influence of the patent medicine industry over the press and state efforts to regulate proprietary remedies. This attack on the nostrum industry was accompanied by a series of articles by Samuel Hopkins Adams, also published in the autumn of 1905, which pointed to the dangers associated with the indiscriminate use of patent medicines and the widespread presence of alcohol and opiates in these drugs. "Gullible America," wrote Adams, "will spend this year some seventy-five million dollars in the purchase of patent medicines. In consideration of this sum it will swallow huge quantities of alcohol, an appalling amount of opiates and narcotics, a wide assortment of varied drugs ranging from powerful and dangerous heart depressants to insidious liver stimulants; and, far in excess of all other ingredients, undiluted fraud" (quoted in Carpenter 2001, p. 269).

The effect of Adams's muckraking about patent medicines on the progress of regulatory reform was dramatic. By making the public aware of the dangers of patent medicines, Adams informed citizens of the possible public benefits of regulation and therefore provided consumers with a stronger incentive to lobby actively for food and drug regulation. Congress was thus inundated with petitions from women's groups and other consumers throughout the country who demanded regulation of patent medicines. Harvey Wiley and the Bureau of Chemistry supplied chemical analyses of patent medicines to advocate groups who desired more evidence of their dangers. Adams's articles were reprinted in the *Journal of the American Medical Association* and distributed to physicians throughout the country, who in turn lobbied Congress for regulation (Anderson 1958, pp. 172–80; Carpenter 2001, pp. 269–70).

Muckraking journalists clearly benefited from the increased sales and prestige generated by their revelations. However, since the Bureau of Chemistry was the organization that would be empowered to enforce a federal food and drug law, it is not surprising that Wiley, more than any other individual in the federal bureaucracy, tirelessly strove to drum up political support for a federal food and drug law. For instance, during the early 1900s, Wiley conducted a series of high-profile experiments on USDA employees (who became popularly known as the "poison-squad") on the effects of preservatives on human digestion. Wiley also spoke regularly at women's club events about the extent of food and drug adulteration and its consequences for human health (Carpenter 2001, pp. 263–66). Additionally, a close relationship between Adams and Wiley was forged as the former gathered materials for his *Colliers* articles (Young 1989, p. 203). The alliance between the Bureau of Chemistry and a muckraking press was vital in forging an enabling political coalition to enact a federal food and drug law.

10.4   Econometric Analysis of the Theories of Progressive Era Reform

The legislative history of the Pure Food and Drugs Act suggests that each of the three views of Progressive Era reform contributed to the adoption of federal food and drug regulation. We now turn to an econometric analysis of congressional voting on two key food and drug bills to provide an additional empirical test of these three hypotheses. By correlating congressional voting on proposed pure food bills with variables that capture the influence of different groups, we can illustrate how competing interests aligned themselves over regulation. Evidence that proxies for key producer and consumer interests influenced congressional voting provides support for the regulatory capture and public interest views of regulation. Additionally, by comparing votes on food and drug legislation before and after the muckraking episodes of 1905, we can determine the effect that the muckraking press and its bureaucratic allies had on the enactment of legislation, which provides a partial test of the third hypothesis for regulation.

Unfortunately, roll call data on congressional votes on the various pure food and drug bills introduced prior to 1905 are scarce. Bills never reached a vote, or if they did, no roll call was tabulated. Prior to the February 21, 1906, Senate vote on the bill that became the Pure Food and Drugs Act, we were only able to find one recorded roll call vote of interest to us: the March 3, 1903, Senate vote on whether or not to consider the Hepburn-Hansborough bill. This bill was very similar to the 1906 law. It called for federal regulation of patent drugs not listed in the *USP* or the *NF,* and it required disclosure of ingredients aimed particularly at blended whiskeys and food manufacturers who used preservatives in their products.

Hence, for our empirical analysis, we examine how different interest groups with a stake in the legislation shaped Senate voting on March 3, 1903, and February 21, 1906.

10.4.1   Econometric Analysis of Senate Voting in 1903

By 1903 the main interests that were engaged in the debate over pure food and drug regulation were (a) patent medicine manufacturers and organized medicine, who opposed or supported the Hepburn-Hansborough bill because of its patent drug regulation; (b) food manufacturers who used preservatives and glucose, who feared that regulators would target their items unfairly; (c) straight and blended whiskey manufacturers, who took opposing sides on the pure food issue; (d) large food manufacturing firms engaged in interstate trade, who desired federal regulation in order to reduce regulatory compliance costs; and (e) consumer-oriented progressive reform groups who desired regulation in order to improve the informational accuracy of product labels. In our regression framework, we include variables that capture the influence of these interest groups in each state. We also control for party membership and include first-dimension D-

Table 10.1   Descriptive statistics by state

Variable	Mean	Standard deviation
Dependent variable		
Vote in 1903 (Yes = 1)	0.32	0.46
Vote in 1906 (Yes = 1)	0.71	0.46
Producer interest variables		
Value of patent medicine production per capita ($)	0.67	0.84
Number of physicians per 1,000 in 1900	1.63	0.53
Number of NFMA firms per 100,000	0.13	0.22
Blended whiskey indicator (0, 1)	0.07	0.25
Straight whiskey indicator (0, 1)	0.09	0.30
Large food manufacturing indicator (0, 1)	0.48	0.50
Consumer interest variables		
WCTU dues per 1,000	0.32	0.20
Protestant index	0.24	0.13
Other controls		
Republican indicator (in 1903)	0.64	0.48
Republican indicator (in 1905)	0.63	0.48
First dimension D-Nominate score (in 1903)	0.18	0.65
First dimension D-Nominate score (in 1905)	0.21	0.64

Notes and sources: Voting data as well as information on the number of National Food Manufacturers Association (NFMA) firms in each state are from the *Congressional Record* (1903, 1906). The value of patent medicine production is in dollars and is taken from U.S. Bureau of the Census (1905). The number of physicians in 1900 is from U.S. Bureau of the Census (1900). The large food manufacturing indicator variable is a binary variable that equals 1 in states that have food manufacturing firms that produce in excess of $1,000,000 of output and 0 otherwise. Data on food manufacturing production are taken from the U.S. Bureau of the Census (1905). Blended and straight whiskey indicators are included to measure the influence of blended and straight whiskey manufacturers. Blended whiskey and straight whiskey were produced in different states. The blended whiskey indicator is a binary that equals 1 for IL, IN, and OH and 0 otherwise. The straight whiskey indicator equals 1 for KT, MD, VA, and PA, and 0 otherwise. First-dimension D-Nominate scores are from VOTEVIEW (http://voteview.uh.edu). Lower scores indicate a more "liberal" ideology toward economic issues. The Republican indicator is a binary variable that equals 1 if a senator was Republican and 0 otherwise. Information on party membership was also taken from VOTEVIEW. WCTU dues per capita and the Protestant index were supplied by Tomas Nonenmacher and Lee Alston.

Nominate scores to hold constant a senator's ideology.[7] Descriptive statistics for the regression variables are shown in table 10.1.

Column (1) of table 10.2 displays probit regression estimates of the factors shaping Senate voting on whether or not to consider the 1903 Hepburn-Hansborough Bill. The marginal effects of each of the explanatory variables (evaluated at their means) on Senate voting are shown in the first column of table 10.3. Overall, the regression results are consistent with the

7. First-dimension D-Nominate scores are widely used to measure a legislator's ideological position on economic issues. D-Nominate scores use Congressional roll call votes as the basis for the estimation of the spatial (ideological) position of individual legislators. See Poole and Rosenthal (1997) for a more detailed discussion of how D-Nominate scores are constructed.

Table 10.2   **Probit regression estimates of the factors shaping Senate voting on pure food and drug regulation in 1903 and 1906**

	Vote in 1903 (Yes = 1) (1)	Vote in 1906 (Yes = 1) (2)
Constant	−1.00	−0.18
	(0.68)	(0.76)
Value of patent medicine production per capita	−0.73**	−0.20
	(0.31)	(0.22)
Number of physicians per 1,000 persons in 1900	0.14	0.63*
	(0.39)	(0.37)
Number of NFMA firms per 100,000 persons	0.001	0.09
	(0.08)	(0.09)
Blended whiskey indicator	−6.76***	−0.26
	(0.43)	(0.71)
Straight whiskey indicator	2.23***	1.94***
	(0.62)	(0.71)
Large food manufacturing firm indicator	0.24	0.96
	(0.45)	(0.76)
WCTU dues per 1,000	1.30	3.87***
	(0.95)	(1.34)
Protestant index	0.06	0.79
	(1.70)	(1.95)
Republican indicator	0.51	1.89*
	(0.76)	(1.01)
First dimension D-Nominate score	−1.38**	−0.83
	(0.76)	(0.81)
McFadden R^2 statistic	0.32	0.30
Likelihood ratio statistic	34.47***	30.37***

Notes: Regressions were estimated by a probit model. Heteroskedasticity-robust standard errors are in parentheses.
*Statistically significant at the 10 percent level.
**Statistically significant at the 5 percent level.
***Statistically significant at the 1 percent level.

qualitative evidence on the configuration of producer and consumer interest over food and drug regulation. The results also are supportive of the capture view of regulation but provide more limited support for the public interest view. Other things being equal, an increase in the size of the patent medicine industry in a state had a negative and statistically significant effect on the probability that a senator from that state would vote in favor of the bill. Additionally, an increase in the number of physicians per capita in a state, a measure of the established medical industry, had a positive but not significant effect on the likelihood a state's senator would vote in favor of the bill. In states where blended whiskeys were produced, senators were less likely to vote for regulation, whereas in states where straight whiskeys were manufactured senators were more likely to vote for regulation. An in-

Table 10.3   Marginal effects of explanatory variables on Senate voting in pure food and drug regulation in 1903 and 1906

	Vote in 1903 (1)	Vote in 1906 (2)
Value of patent medicine production per capita	–0.14	–0.04
Number of physicians per 1,000 persons in 1900	0.02	–0.04
Number of NFMA firms per 100,000 persons	0.002	0.13
Blended whiskey indicator	–0.13	–0.02
Straight whiskey indicator	0.42	0.39
Large food manufacturing firm indicator	0.04	0.20
WCTU dues per 1,000	0.25	0.77
Protestant index	0.01	0.16
Republican indicator	0.10	0.38
First dimension D-Nominate score	–0.26	–0.16

Note: These values are based on the probit regression estimates reported in table 10.2 and are calculated at their mean values.

crease in the number of food manufacturers in a state who used preservatives (proxied by membership in the National Food Manufacturers Association, or NFMA) had a positive but statistically not significant influence over the likelihood that a state's senator would vote in favor of pure food regulation. Reform interests (proxied by WCTU dues per capita and the Protestant index) had a positive but statistically insignificant impact on the probability that a senator would vote in favor of regulation.[8]

The coefficient estimates suggest that those producer interests who perceived that regulation would disadvantage their products (patent medicine makers and blended whiskey producers) opposed regulation, whereas those who felt that regulation would place them at a competitive advantage and who played a role in shaping the features of the proposed food and drug bill (organized medicine, straight whiskey makers) supported it. The fact that senators representing organized medicine and straight whiskey interests were more likely to vote for regulation is consistent with the regulatory capture argument since both of these groups sought regulation to disadvantage their lower-cost rivals. While the coefficients on the reform interest variables are both positive, they are not significant, which furnishes weak evidence consistent with the public interest hypothesis. That these reform interest variables are not significant is perhaps unsurprising,

8. Qualitatively similar results were obtained when we used WCTU membership per capita (instead of WCTU dues per capita) to proxy for reform interests. Additionally, the inclusion of income per capita does not materially affect the results. The Protestant index measures the presence of evangelical Protestant groups in each state. This is a reasonable proxy for Progressive reform interests, since membership in Progressive reform groups was heavily dominated by evangelical Protestants.

since consumers, being a large and heterogeneous group, faced high collective action costs (Olson 1965).

Among the political control variables, Republican Party membership does not play a significant role in voting in 1903, but the D-Nominate score has a significant and negative coefficient. More positive D-Nominate scores indicate a more conservative ideology, and such ideologically motivated senators were more likely to vote against an extension of federal regulation.

10.4.2   Econometric Analysis of Senate Voting in 1906

We can empirically evaluate the role that muckraking journalism played in breaking the political deadlock over pure food and drug regulation by examining the factors that shaped Senate voting in 1906 on the bill that became the Pure Food and Drugs Act. In our analysis of Senate voting in 1903 (the premuckraking period) we found that patent medicine and blended whiskey interests had a negative and statistically significant influence on the probability that senators would vote in favor of considering the Hepburn-Hansborough bill, while reform interests had a positive but statistically insignificant influence on Senate voting. If muckraking journalism about patent medicines (which began around October 1905 with the publication of Samuel Hopkins Adams's articles in *Colliers*) provoked widespread consumer interest in favor of regulation, it would have helped to break the political deadlock over food and drug regulation. Accordingly, in an examination of Senate voting in the postmuckraking period (after October 1905), antiregulation producer interests should be less likely to have a negative and significant influence over Senate voting, and Progressive reform interests should have a positive and significant influence over Senate voting. Antiregulation producer interests should be less significant because muckraking should have made it more costly for politicians representing these groups to continue to oppose regulation. Reform interests should become significant factors influencing Senate voting if muckraking, by increasing the perceived benefits of food and drug regulation, galvanized consumer-oriented groups to actively pressure politicians to back reform.

Column (2) of table 10.2 presents probit regression estimates of the factors shaping Senate voting on February 21, 1906; the corresponding marginal effects are shown in the second column of table 10.3. The coefficients representing blended whiskey and patent medicine interests are no longer statistically significant, whereas one of the coefficients representing reform interests (WCTU dues per capita) is positive and significant. These postmuckraking regression results conform to our predictions regarding the role that muckraking journalism played in breaking the political deadlock over regulatory reform. By making the issue of food and drug quality emotionally salient, muckraking provoked proconsumer interests to lobby for regulation and made it more costly for politicians representing antiregulation business groups to continue to block regulation. In our regression framework, this is suggested by the fact that one of our proxies for reform interests is now positive and significant, while our proxies for patent medicine interests and blended whiskey interests are no longer significant.[9]

The Republican Party variable becomes positive and significant in 1906, reflecting President Theodore Roosevelt's efforts to push his party in Congress to support food and drug regulation in the wake of the publication of Upton Sinclair's *The Jungle* (Anderson 1958, p. 181; Young 1989, p. 254). Prior to 1905–6, food and drug regulation was not a particularly partisan issue. The D-Nominate variable no longer has a significant effect on Senate voting. With consumer/voter reaction to muckraking revelations, it became more costly for conservative senators to continue to oppose regulation, making ideology less important.

Overall, these regression results provide evidence supporting each of the three views of regulation. The straight whiskey variable and the number of physicians per capita are positive and significant, which supports the regulatory capture hypothesis for regulation. Per capita WCTU dues also have a positive and significant effect on the probability that a senator voted for regulation. This suggests the importance of organized consumers as a pro-regulation constituency, which is consistent with the public interest view. However, the fact that this variable is positive and significant in 1906 (postmuckraking) but not in 1903 (premuckraking) suggests that the muckraking press and its bureaucratic supporters also played an important role in generating broad consumer interest in regulation. Hence, taken together, the evidence is also consistent with the possibility that consumers were manipulated by a muckraking press.

10.5   Enforcement of the Pure Food and Drugs Act and the Long-Term Benefits of Regulation

Given that a mixture of consumer, industry, and bureaucratic interests were involved in the struggle for federal food and drug regulation, it is worth investigating the welfare implications of this law. Was federal regulation, once enacted, enforced in a way that benefited specific industry groups at the expense of competitors and overall economic efficiency? Or did enforcement of the Pure Food and Drugs Act ultimately produce benefits for consumers and improve the efficiency of food and drug markets?

It is difficult to address these issues because few scholars have systematically analyzed the impact of the Pure Food and Drugs Act on the markets

---

9. As before, we find that using WCTU membership per capita yields qualitatively similar results. Additionally, the coefficient estimates are robust to the inclusion of other variables like income per capita.

for food and drugs. Nevertheless, what we know about enforcement of the law suggests that no view on its own is satisfactory. The evidence on early enforcement of the act (under the stewardship of Dr. Wiley) suggests that certain industry groups were favored, which would be consistent with the regulatory capture view. According to Coppin and High (1999), Wiley attempted to enforce the law in ways that favored straight whiskey makers and that advantaged manufacturers that did not use preservatives in their foods. Controversy surrounding Wiley's enforcement efforts and his resignation from the Bureau of Chemistry in 1911, however, prevented these groups from obtaining longer-run benefits. While certain industry interests may have "captured" Wiley, their influence did not extend to his successors or to the bureau more generally. Indeed, the personnel of the bureau and its leadership in the post-Wiley period consisted primarily of professional bureaucrats, whose interests were not closely aligned with industry. Hence, because those pro-regulation industry groups who stood to gain most from regulation did not ultimately control the administering agency, they did not realize the expected long-term benefits from reduced competition from substitute products. This outcome weakens the argument in favor of a regulatory capture view of regulation.

Did consumers then capture the benefits of regulation? The evidence from the post-Wiley period suggests that although the Bureau of Chemistry attempted to enforce the Pure Food and Drugs Act in ways that improved the quality of food and drugs and that reduced asymmetric information about food and drug quality, the bureau was not always successful in achieving these objectives. Because the bureau was small with limited resources, and because the Pure Food and Drugs Act was difficult to enforce in the courts, the agency relied upon rewards to firms that complied with the law. For instance, as one way to promote compliance with the law, it provided quality certification and direct technical advice on how to improve product quality (Law 2004). Effective enforcement, when it happened, generally yielded socially beneficial outcomes; the bureau's product certification efforts reduced asymmetric information about the quality of foodstuffs, and as a consequence of its offering technical assistance to firms, the quality of many foods improved (Robinson 1990; Young 1992).

These efficiency-enhancing outcomes are more consistent with the public interest view than the regulatory capture view. Certain producers benefited from these enforcement efforts because they were assisted by the bureau's expertise, but there were few restrictions on entry, the classic capture objective. Nevertheless, it is notable that enforcement successes could only be achieved when industry also stood to gain from the bureau's expertise.[10]

10. It is also noteworthy that those industry groups that benefited from the bureau's expertise were different from those groups that anticipated that the Pure Food and Drug Act would tilt the competitive playing field to their advantage. See Law (2004).

When industry could not benefit from the bureau's actions, effective enforcement was unlikely since it was difficult for the agency to prosecute manufacturers in court. For instance, the 1912 Sherley Amendment to the law required the agency to prove fraud in order to obtain a conviction (Young 1967, pp. 49–51). As a result, the patent medicine and proprietary nostrum industry—the industry whose products provoked widespread consumer interest in favor of food and drug regulation in the first place—was never successfully regulated. The fly-by-night nature of much of the nostrum industry, combined with the fact that it was extremely difficult for the bureau to uphold its rulings in court, meant that the agency was generally ineffective in controlling misleading therapeutic claims (Young 1967, pp. 60–65; Temin 1980, pp. 27–37). Accordingly, while consumers benefited from enforcement of the Pure Food and Drugs Act, they did not benefit in the way that they had originally anticipated—through improved information about drug quality and safety.

10.6 Conclusion

We explored the origins and effects of the Pure Food and Drugs Act of 1906. Both the narrative and statistical evidence suggest that a nuanced combination of the three main views of Progressive Era reform (regulatory capture, public interest, rent seeking by bureaucrats and the press) explains the adoption of the law. Regulation was sought by specific producer, consumer, and bureaucratic interests to advance their private goals. Because their objectives conflicted a political stalemate ensued. The muckraking press eventually galvanized widespread consumer interest in food and drug regulation and broke the impasse, allowing the law to be finally enacted.

Even so, without examination of enforcement, it is impossible to know whether these interest groups obtained the benefits of regulation that they anticipated. If not, the impact of regulation may fail to conform neatly to the predictions of any of the three theories of regulation. Because those producer interests who initially sought regulation for private gain did not shape the composition of the Bureau of Chemistry and the incentives it faced, enforcement of the Pure Food and Drugs Act did not dramatically change competitive conditions to their advantage. Similarly, because those consumer groups who lobbied for regulation did not anticipate that the Pure Food and Drugs Act would be so difficult to enforce in the courts, regulation also failed to significantly improve the quality of information about patent medicines. Hence, the "public interest" was not advanced in the market that mattered most to these consumers. Perhaps the one group that obtained lasting benefits from regulation was the Bureau of Chemistry. By successfully lobbying for legislation, Wiley secured the future of his agency. This was only a partial success, however, since the bureau's authority was very limited and the agency remained relatively small until the late 1930s.

The bureau's enforcement efforts produced some gains for consumers and certain food producers, but the margins along which these gains were realized were not anticipated by those interest groups that lobbied actively on behalf of regulation in the first place. Accordingly, the history of the Pure Food and Drugs Act suggests that understanding the origins and impact of Progressive Era regulation requires analysis not only of interest group motivation but also of the organizational and institutional constraints that limit the benefits that such groups are ultimately able to obtain.

References

Akerlof, George A. 1970. The market for "lemons": Quality uncertainty and the market mechanism. *Quarterly Journal of Economics* 84 (August): 488–500.

Anderson, Oscar E., Jr. 1958. *The health of a nation: Harvey W. Wiley and the fight for pure food.* Chicago: University of Chicago Press.

Carpenter, Daniel P. 2001. *The forging of bureaucratic autonomy: Reputation, networks, and policy innovation in executive agencies, 1862–1928.* Princeton, NJ: Princeton University Press.

Chalmers, David M. 1974. *The muckrake years.* New York: Van Nostrand.

Congressional Record. 1885. Washington, DC: Government Printing Office.

———. 1903. Washington, DC: Government Printing Office.

———. 1906. Washington, DC: Government Printing Office.

Coppin, Clayton, and Jack High. 1999. *The politics of purity: Harvey Washington Wiley and the origins of federal food policy.* Ann Arbor: University of Michigan Press.

Darby, Michael R., and Edi Karni. 1973. Free competition and the optimal amount of fraud. *Journal of Law and Economics* 16 (April): 67–88.

Dupré, Ruth. 1999. If it's yellow, it must be butter: Margarine regulation in North America since 1886. *Journal of Economic History* 59 (June): 353–71.

Filler, Louis. 1976. *Progressivism and muckraking.* New York: R. R. Bowker.

Glaeser, Edward L., and Andrei Shleifer. 2003. The rise of the regulatory state. *Journal of Economic Literature* 41 (June): 401–25.

Goodwin, Lorine S. 1999. *The pure food, drink, and drug crusaders, 1879–1914.* Jefferson, NC: McFarland.

Hays, Samuel P. 1957. *The response to industrialism, 1885–1914.* Chicago: University of Chicago Press.

Kim, Sukkoo. 2001. Markets and multiunit firms from an American historical perspective. *Advances in Strategic Management* 18:305–26.

Kolko, Gabriel. 1963. *The triumph of conservatism: A reinterpretation of American history.* New York: Macmillan.

Law, Marc T. 2003. The origins of state pure food regulation. *Journal of Economic History* 63 (December): 1103–30.

———. 2004. How do regulators regulate? Enforcement of the Pure Food and Drug Act, 1907–38. University of Vermont, Department of Economics. Unpublished manuscript.

Lee, R. Alton. 1973. *A history of regulatory taxation.* Lexington: University of Kentucky Press.

Levine, Michael E., and Jennifer L. Forrence. 1990. Regulatory capture, public interest, and the public agenda: Toward a synthesis. Special issue, *Journal of Law, Economics, and Organization* 6:167–98.

Libecap, Gary D. 1992. The rise of the Chicago packers and the origins of meat inspection and antitrust. *Economic Inquiry* 30 (April): 242–62.

McCluskey, Jill J. 2000. A game theoretic approach to organic foods: An analysis of asymmetric information and policy. *Agricultural and Resource Economics Review* 29 (April): 1–9.

Niskanen, William A. 1971. *Bureaucracy and representative government.* Chicago: Aldine-Atherton.

Okun, Mitchell. 1986. *Fair play in the marketplace.* Dekalb: Northern Illinois University Press.

Olmstead, Alan L., and Paul W. Rhode. 2004. The "Tuberculosis Cattle Trust": Disease contagion in an era of regulatory uncertainty. *Journal of Economic History* 64 (December): 929–63.

Olson, Mancur. 1965. *The logic of collective action: Public goods and the theory of groups.* Cambridge, MA: Harvard University Press.

Peltzman, Sam. 1976. Toward a more general theory of regulation. *Journal of Law and Economics* 19 (August): 211–40.

Poole, Keith, and Howard Rosenthal. 1997. *Congress: A political-economic history of roll-call voting.* New York: Oxford University Press.

Reiger, Cornelius. 1932. *The era of the muckrakers.* Chapel Hill: University of North Carolina Press.

Robinson, Lisa M. 1990. Regulating what we eat: Mary Engle Pennington and the Food Research Laboratory. *Agricultural History* 64 (April): 143–53.

Stigler, George J. 1971. The theory of economic regulation. *Bell Journal of Economics and Management Science* 2 (Spring): 3–21.

Strasser, Susan. 1989. *Satisfaction guaranteed: The making of the American mass market.* New York: Pantheon Books.

Temin, Peter. 1980. *Taking your medicine: Drug regulation in the United States.* Cambridge, MA: Harvard University Press.

U.S. Bureau of the Census. 1900. *Census of population.* Washington, DC: Government Printing Office.

U.S. Bureau of the Census. 1905. *Census of manufactures.* Washington, DC: Government Printing Office.

U.S. Senate. 1899–1900. Adulteration of food products. 56th Cong., 1st sess. Senate Report no. 516, v. 3888.

———. 1900–1901. Adulteration of food products. 56th Cong., 2nd sess. Senate Report no. 141, v. 4038.

———. 1902. Adulteration of articles of food: A tabulated statement prepared by the agriculture department for the Senate Committee on Manufactures Showing the Adulteration of the Most Common Articles of Food Consumed in the United States. 57th Cong., 1st sess. Senate Document no. 181, v. 4234.

Wood, Donna J. 1986. *The strategic uses of public policy: Business and government in the Progressive Era.* Marshfield, MA: Pitman.

Yeager, Mary A. 1981. *Competition and regulation: The development of oligopoly in the meat packing industry.* Greenwich, CT: JAI Press.

Young, James H. 1967. *The medical messiahs: A social history of quackery in twentieth century America.* Princeton, NJ: Princeton University Press.

———. 1989. *Pure food: Securing the Federal Food and Drugs Act of 1906.* Princeton, NJ: Princeton University Press.

———. 1992. Food and drug enforcers in the 1920s: Restraining and educating business. *Business and Economic History* 21 (June): 119–28.

11

Politics, Relief, and Reform
Roosevelt's Efforts to Control Corruption and Political Manipulation during the New Deal

John Joseph Wallis, Price V. Fishback, and
Shawn Kantor

Prior to the New Deal almost all public social welfare spending, or what contemporaries called "relief," was provided by local governments. The administration of local public relief had long been associated with patronage, political manipulation, and corruption. Between 1933 and 1940, federal, state, and local governments combined to spend $2 billion per year to provide relief to at least 2 million cases (families) per month. In 1933, when unemployment reached 25 percent, the federal government introduced a relief program redistributing 4 percent of gross national product (GNP) to a quarter of all the nation's families. The possibility of providing cash payments to a quarter of the nation's families offered an opportunity for corruption unique in the nation's history. Surprisingly, however, while the administration of public relief was widely regarded as corrupt before 1933, the modern federal/state public welfare system that developed out of the New Deal reforms is often castigated as bureaucratic, but rarely corrupt. What changed? How did the country enter the Depression with a public welfare system riddled with political manipulation and emerge with one that was not?

Our answer is straightforward. The president, Franklin Roosevelt, and other members of the executive branch gained little or nothing from the kinds of local corruption involved in public relief. But they stood to incur

John Joseph Wallis is a professor of economics at the University of Maryland and a research associate of the National Bureau of Economic Research. Price V. Fishback is a professor of economics at the University of Arizona and a research associate of the National Bureau of Economic Research. Shawn Kantor is a professor of economics at the University of California, Merced, and a research associate of the National Bureau of Economic Research.

We would like to thank Claudia Goldin, Edward Glaeser, Robert Margo, Paul Rhode, Kenneth Sokoloff, and the conference participants for helpful comments.

enormous losses if the New Deal relief program was perceived as politically manipulative and corrupt by the voting public. Roosevelt and the Democrats brought relief to millions of families every month, and the gratitude of relief recipients was Roosevelt's political payoff. Other politicians—senators, representatives, governors, and mayors—wanted to control relief and use it for political gain. Both houses of Congress, the states, and local governments maneuvered, manipulated, and cajoled to get their hands on a share of the billions spent each year on relief. Although Roosevelt made substantial concessions to Congress and to state and local governments in the administration of relief, he sought to curb corruption at the state and local level by his influence over the discretionary allocation of relief funds, by establishing offices to investigate complaints of corruption, and, in the long run, by bureaucratizing the administration of public welfare. During the New Deal, when the relief programs were reorganized to give the Roosevelt administration more control over the distribution of funds within states, it used that control to limit state and local political manipulation and increased the responsiveness of the allocation of funds within states to the high-minded goals of relief, recovery, and reform. Politics was paramount in the structure of New Deal relief programs; it just turned out that the best political outcome meant a reduction in corruption at the state and local level. This does not mean that Roosevelt did not use the administration of relief for his own political ends. There is ample evidence that presidential politics mattered in the distribution of relief funds. Corruption by others was curbed because it was in Roosevelt's political interest to see it curbed.

We begin by discussing the types of corruption involved with relief during the New Deal. We present a brief overview of the New Deal programs, followed by a more detailed history. We then trace how political influences shaped the administration of relief programs and document how relief administered by the national government differed from relief administered by states.

11.1 Defining Corruption and Political Manipulation

Corruption has many dimensions. During the Great Depression the New Deal Democrats were often accused of "playing politics with relief." This dimension might be considered corruption by some observers or political business as usual by others. Whatever we called it, the way relief could be used for personal or political gain clearly differed by level of government. Roosevelt explicitly stated the goals of the New Deal as "relief, recovery, and reform." A growing political economy literature has tried to evaluate whether Roosevelt pursued those goals or whether he used New Deal policies, particularly the allocation of federal grants among the states, to pursue political goals.[1] For example, if the level of unemployment in states did not affect the allocation of relief spending across states, but the margin of Roosevelt's victory in the 1930s presidential election did affect allocations, this is evidence that Roosevelt was playing politics with relief. At the state level, governors occasionally required administrative employees to make contributions to political parties. At the local level, political machines were often accused of selecting from potential relief recipients on the basis of party or requiring recipients to vote for machine candidates. These are all examples of politicians using the administration of relief to further their political ambitions, in the large and in the small.

Clear examples of corruption occurred through time-honored methods of fraud and featherbedding. For example, relief workers could be assigned to work on projects that benefited private landowners rather than the public;[2] suppliers could overbill for materials and make kickbacks to project supervisors;[3] or workers could pad their hours and receive benefits for work they never performed.[4] At their margins, these criminal types of corruption may be indistinguishable from playing politics. But they are substantively different enough that reducing political manipulation requires different policies than reducing criminal corruption. It appears that the

---

1. The literature begins with Arrington (1969, 1970), Reading (1973), and Wright (1974) and continues in Wallis (1984, 1987, 1991). Anderson and Tollison (1991) criticized Wright and Wallis for not including congressional information, which led to the response by Wallis (1998) and the exchange between Fleck (2001) and Wallis (2001). Couch and Shugart (1998 and 2000) examined New Deal spending as well. Investigation of the determinants of county allocations and a summary of the entire literature can be found in Fishback, Kantor, and Wallis (2003). The overall fiscal implications of the New Deal for national, state, and local governments is discussed in Wallis and Oates (1998).

2. A restriction on the "extension or improvement of streets and utilities in relatively underdeveloped areas . . . was the direct result of cases developed by the Division [of Investigation], some of which were prosecuted in Federal courts, showing that, at times and through subterfuge, real estate firms or developing companies, for example, sought to divert relief funds to their own benefit in constructing streets and private utilities in undeveloped areas to the enhancement of the value of the real estate owned by them" (WPA Division of Investigation 1943, p. 7).

3. "This type of case involved the submission of false time claims to the government in the rental of equipment; the short delivery of materials to WPA projects by venders, at times in collusion with WPA supervisory employees; or the furnishing of equipment or material below the specifications of the contract which resulted in loss to the Government. Cases of this character frequently involved considerable amounts of money. . . . In this connection, it should be remembered that the Works Projects Administration operated a program consisting of projects which ranged from the building of two miles of farm-to-market road in Texas, to the construction of LaGuardia Airport at New York City" (WPA Division on Investigation 1943, p. 23).

4. "Due to the fact that the program employed large numbers of people, frequently in rather small units, an operation involving the preparation of a vast number of payrolls, irregularities in connection with these payrolls were the most common type of complaint. These irregularities in general consisted of normal and routine "padding" operations in which persons were paid for time when they were absent from their WPA duties or were dually employed" (WPA Division of Investigation 1943, p. 21).

New Deal was successful at reducing some forms of political corruption in the administration of welfare. Fraud, however, will always be with us, and its reduction requires eternal vigilance.[5]

The administrative structure of a government program limits the methods available to combat corruption. In general, corruption depends on administrative discretion. Officials can be corrupt only if they have some leeway to make decisions. The creation of rules and procedures is one way to limit corruption. For example, Roosevelt could only play politics with the allocation of relief funds between the states if the executive branch possessed the power to allocate funds at their discretion. If funds are allocated by a formula or a rule—for example, equal per capita grants or matching grants—the federal administrator does not possess the option of playing politics along this dimension. Similarly, if a local case worker has the discretion to set the monthly relief benefit for each case, he or she has much more opportunity to be corrupt than if relief benefits per case are fixed.

While discretion and rules are, to a certain extent, substitutes as governing devices, it is rarely possible to construct an administrative mechanism without some discretion. In the hectic days of 1933 it was extremely difficult to come up with sensible rules. As a result, the key aspect of administrative structure was who had administrative discretion. Was it lodged with the national government, with the president, or with the state and local governments? Our central hypothesis maintains that political manipulation at the state and local level in the administration of federal relief funds was reduced when administrative discretion lay with the executive branch of the national government. Criminal corruption was reduced by the promulgation of rules and vigorous prosecution of offenders. The tests of this proposition developed in the empirical section depend, of course, on identifying political manipulation or criminal corruption, and then distinguishing whether corruption was addressed by creating rules or changing the location of administrative discretion.

11.2   A Brief History

The history of the New Deal relief programs falls into two eras: from May 1933 to the summer of 1935, and after the summer of 1935. The periods are distinguished by the amount of administrative discretion exercised by the national government and the discretion remaining in the hands of state and local officials. Table 11.1 provides a list of the major New Deal relief programs. The first columns of the table give the beginning and ending

---

5. The evidence for the New Deal's success at eliminating political corruption is the virtual absence of complaints, for example, that party orientation of a recipient has any impact on the probability of getting a Social Security check or an Aid for Families with Dependent Children (AFDC) payment. Evidence that political corruption was important before the New Deal is presented in the historical section.

Table 11.1   **Major relief programs, dates, and administrative character**

Started	Ended	Agency	Administration
May 1933	Fall 1935[a]	Federal Emergency Relief Administration (FERA)	Federal
April 1933	July 1942	Civilian Conservation Corp (CCC)	National
November 1933	March 1934	Civil Works Administration (CWA)	National
Spring 1935	1942	Works Progress/Projects Administration (WPA)	National/federal
1935	1994[b]	Rural Electrification Administration (REA)	National
1937	1946[c]	Farm Security Administration (FSA)	National
Summer 1935	Present	Old Age and Survivors Insurance (OASI)	National
Summer 1935	Present	Unemployment insurance	Federal
Summer 1935	1974[d]	Old Age Assistance (OAA)[c]	Federal
Summer 1935	1974[d]	Aid to the Blind[c]	Federal
Summer 1935	1996[e]	Aid to Dependent Children (ADC)[d]	Federal

Sources: National Resources Planning Board (1942, pp. 26–97); Fishback and Thomasson (forthcoming); Alston and Ferrie (1999, pp. 91–98); Columbia University Press (2005).

Notes: "Federal administration" refers to joint administration by the state and national governments. "National administration" refers to programs administered by the national government. General relief was provided by local governments throughout the period.

[a]Some FERA projects were phased out over a period lasting through March 1937.

[b]The Rural Electrification Administration in 1949 was authorized to make loans for telephone improvements and in 1988 was permitted to give interest-free loans for job creation and rural electric systems. Its duties were assumed by the Rural Utilities Service when it was abolished in 1994.

[c]The Farm Security Administration took over the role played by the Resettlement Administration begun in 1935. Some of its programs were eventually taken over by the Farmers Home Administration in 1947.

[d]Old age assistance and aid to the blind were almost entirely superseded by the Supplemental Security Income Program in 1974.

[e]Aid to Dependent Children was renamed Aid to Families with Dependent Children in 1962, and the program was replaced by Temporary Aid for Needy Families in 1996.

dates for each program (several Social Security programs are still in force). The last column classifies programs by their administrative character: that is, how discretion was allocated within the program. In "national" programs the national government exerted a preponderance of administrative influence. In "federal" programs state and local governments shared administrative discretion with the national government and in many programs possessed the preponderance of influence. Table 11.2 lists the average monthly number of cases receiving relief for the nation as a whole and for each of the major relief programs.

In the spring of 1933 the Federal Emergency Relief Act created the Federal Emergency Relief Administration, known as FERA, the largest and most important relief program up to 1935. Roosevelt chose Harry Hopkins as the FERA administrator. The original act appropriated $500 million to be allocated among the states, half on a matching basis and half at the discretion of the administrator. Once funds were granted, however, FERA funds legally became the property of the states. Hopkins attempted to raise the standards of relief administration, but his ability to do so was limited

Table 11.2 Average monthly case loads by major programs (000s of cases)

Year	Total	Federal Emergency Relief Administration	Civil Works Administration	Works Progress Administration	Old age assistance	Local relief	Unemployment insurance
1933	5,022	3,836	2,565		109	1,990	
1934	6,593	4,474	2,970		142		
1935	6,320	4,655		1,156	303		
1936	5,758			2,544	737	1,667	
1937	5,202			1,793	1,369	1,445	
1938	5,995			2,611	1,559	1,543	698
1939	6,285			2,407	1,852	1,661	718
1940	5,943			2,102	1,941	1,547	1,065
Months reported	1/33–6/40	6/33–12/35	11/33–4/34	8/35–6/40	1/33–6/40	1/33–5/33, 1/36–6/40	1/38–6/40

Source: Social Security Administration (1941, table 9, pp. 68–70).

Notes: All figures are the average of monthly caseloads for the months reported in each year in the original source. For example, the FERA listing in 1933 is the average monthly caseload for the months June through December of that year. The UI listing in 1940 is the average monthly caseload for the months January through June of 1940. The CWA listing in 1934 includes a peak of 4.311 million cases in January 1934, down to 1.1 million cases in April after the program was ended and was winding down.

by the relative independence of state relief administrations. Hopkins could, and did, threaten to withhold federal grants for relief to states with corrupt, politically manipulative, or inefficient relief administrations. Withholding funds, however, was a blunt policy tool that worked to the direct disadvantage of the unemployed in the state, in contradiction to FERA's mandate.

In 1935, Roosevelt submitted an "economic security act" to Congress. As passed, the act provided a permanent, nationally administered program of old age insurance, which we call Social Security today. It also provided for a national payroll tax for unemployment insurance programs run by the individual states; 90 percent of the payroll taxes paid in each state were held in trust for that state. Finally, the act provided relief for three categories of persons: old age assistance, aid to the blind, and aid to dependent children. The categorical programs were financed from general revenues and allocated among the state by strict matching grants. Federal grants to states were determined solely by state expenditures. As a result, it was the states, and not the federal government, that controlled spending on the categorical programs.

The second element of the 1935 reforms was the creation of an "emergency" relief program, funded by a series of ongoing emergency relief appropriation acts. Under the act of 1935, Roosevelt created the Works Progress Administration (WPA) and a number of smaller relief programs: the National Youth Administration (NYA), the Rural Electrification Administration (REA), the Farm Security Administration (FSA), and others. The WPA, also headed by Hopkins, was structured so that Roosevelt could make discretionary allocations between the states, and, importantly, WPA officials retained the right to approve individual projects within states. Over time, Congress required a larger degree of state and local participation. This moved the WPA closer to a matching program, but matching was never complete. The WPA also financed a number of nationally administered programs in the arts—theater, literature, and history—that did not have state or local sponsors. After the summer of 1935, the WPA was the largest single relief program.

Our hypothesis is that Roosevelt found it in his interest to reduce corruption and political manipulation, particularly at the state and local levels, while Congress and state and local governments continued to press for a relief structure that allowed them to use relief to their own political advantage. The key element, therefore, was the allocation of administrative discretion. If the president possessed administrative and fiscal discretion, he and Hopkins could reduce corruption and political manipulation at the state and local levels. Likewise, if state and local relief administrators possessed administrative and fiscal discretion, they could pursue their own political ends. Accordingly, our empirical approach considers the development of administrative policy. We examine the specific role that administrative discretion played in the difference between Senate and House versions of bills, differences that correspond directly to the interests of state and local governments. We also compare the allocation of funds within the states under FERA and the WPA. Hopkins possessed a much wider range of policy instruments to control the distribution of federal funds within states under the WPA, and we expect and find that the allocation of WPA spending differed significantly from the FERA allocations. When Roosevelt and Hopkins gained more discretion over the distribution of funds within the states, they paid more attention to promoting relief, recovery, and reform and to reducing fraud and other forms of illegal corruption.

11.3 Early Relief: 1933 to 1935

Early twentieth-century American social welfare policy had its roots in the English Poor Law. Relief was administered locally through a complex network of public and private agencies, ranging from the poorhouse to the Community Chest, that assessed need and distributed benefits. The intellectual high ground in the emerging field of social work was dominated by private, rather than public, organizations. The centuries-old debate over using relief to care for the truly needy as opposed to providing a dole for the idle, shiftless, and worthless produced a philosophy of social welfare focused on the individual case. Social workers identified the deserving poor, and relief was tailored to meet the needs of the needy and to discourage the dissolute. Independent private social agencies could make these distinctions without bias. The preference for private rather than public relief was further strengthened by the general low regard for the capacity of local governments, which were run by local machine politicians and staffed by untrained politicos as rewards for political service.[6] Public relief agencies were tainted by the possibility of the using relief for political purposes. Patronage and political influence—political manipulation—rather than the interests of the poor were believed to motivate public relief.[7]

---

6. On the general low opinion in which local government was held by public administration experts and political scientists in the early years of the twentieth century see Brock (1988, pp. 50–83). "When Americans used the word 'politician' in a derogatory sense (as they often did), they had most in mind the local official in city wards, townships, or counties seeking patronage and spoils, favoring friends, juggling contracts, and acknowledging some obligation to their party but none to the community. Civic reformers, students of public administration, and almost every issue of the *American Political Science Review* produced abundant evidence of local incompetence" (p. 51).

7. "There was ample evidence in the reports of the studies already mentioned that this system [pre–New Deal local relief] encouraged petty graft as well as the use of relief for political power. Merchants sometimes failed to report the death of customers who were on the relief lists and continued to collect for their private tills the pittances of the dead from the relief funds of the town or county. Legal restrictions on pauper voting were usually not enforced in the states where they existed. Hence men and women on relief built up a solid vote for officials from whom they got relief" (Brown 1940, p. 16).

The sharp division between the proponents of private and public relief is clear evidence of the deep-rooted concern over competence, political manipulation, and corruption in the administration of public relief.[8] It is very difficult to credibly measure the extent of corruption in the administration of relief before, during, or after the New Deal. It is, however, a matter of historical record that a significant share of relief was administered by private social welfare agencies before 1933, and that private administration was preferred to public administration largely on grounds of competence, political manipulation, and corruption. These fears did not miraculously disappear in 1933. As we discuss, private social workers continued to argue that public relief was potentially corrupt well into the mid-1930s. By the 1950s, when social welfare advocates continued to complain about the inadequacy of relief in the state-administered categorical programs, charges of political manipulation were much less common.[9] This is clear historical evidence of a reduction in its prevalence in the administration of relief over the course of the New Deal.

Because of the dominance of the private relief administration in the 1920s, it came as a surprise when the newly formed Committee on Social Statistics reported in 1929 that, in fifteen large cities, 71.6 percent of all relief funds, whether disbursed by public or private agencies, came from local governments.[10] Relief, it turned out, was often publicly financed even where it was privately administered. As the depression deepened, both public and private sources of funds were called upon. The growing burden of relieving the unemployed was well beyond the ability of private agencies, and relief spending by local, and eventually state, governments rose

8. "Most relief workers on either the private or public side were chiefly bent on destructive criticism and critical comment regarding the opposition" (Brown 1940, p. 45). "The community of interests in public welfare shared by both the voluntary social agency and the political authority have not always prevented the private agency from viewing the government as an inimical and antagonistic body opposed to the constituents of the private agency, instead of being their political creature and the medium of their democratic expression of their ideals and purposes" (Joseph Logan, quoted in Brown 1940, p. 53). Brown's first chapter is a discussion of the national, state, and local responsibility for relief and the conflict between private and public relief advocates.

9. Brock (1988), Brown (1940), and Katz (1986, pp. 36–57) talk extensively about the problem of politics, corruption, and relief prior to the 1930s. Historical studies of the post–New Deal programs spend almost no time discussing corruption. Harsh critics of the welfare system, such as Piven and Cloward (1993) and Katz (1986), argue that relief has become an instrument of social control but concede that relief has become more professionally administered. There is little discussion of corruption in the distribution of relief funds after the New Deal. Patterson (1967, 1986) discusses the problem of corruption prior to the New Deal and the political debates between Congress and Roosevelt during the New Deal.

10. See Brown (1940, p. 55). "The amazement with which this information was received and the significance attached to it are shown by the extent to which the figures are cited in the literature of the period. They appear like a refrain, in conference papers and reports, magazine articles, statements of policy and recommendations for programs put out by national and local agencies, both public and private. They are quoted with satisfaction and triumph by proponents of public welfare and with some consternation and trepidation by private agency executives" (Brown, p. 56).

steadily.[11] Public relief officials, who had taken a backseat to professional private social workers for decades, began exerting a larger influence in planning for a larger relief effort. But the leaders of the social work movement had their roots in private social agencies, and these leaders assumed important positions in the national government after 1933. They brought with them the idea that local public relief administration was inefficient and subservient to politics.

Those ideas posed problems for Roosevelt and Hopkins when they began operations under FERA. The dominant philosophy of private social work in the 1920s was to determine what was best for each relief recipient on a case-by-case basis, allowing the local relief agency the maximum degree of flexibility and discretion in spending money. The prospect of distributing $500 million in federal government funds through the existing system of local public relief agencies presented a nightmare of accountability for Hopkins. Giving control of the funds to state and local public relief agencies seemed guaranteed to exacerbate the use of relief for political and corrupt purposes. Giving control of the funds to private agencies seemed guaranteed to insure that millions of decisions about who would receive how much relief would be made by social workers in the best interest of the needy, with no possibility of consistently explaining why one person received relief and another did not.

Roosevelt and Hopkins were in a hurry, however, and their initial decisions about FERA reflected the need to start quickly. In the summer of 1933 they had to figure out how to get hundreds of millions of dollars in relief to millions of families throughout the country. FERA required Hopkins to distribute the money to the states, even though most states had no formal structure for administering relief. The understanding was that most of the money would be distributed by local relief agencies. Hopkins and FERA were given some discretion in passing out money between the states (in the initial $500 million appropriation, half the money allocated by matching state and local contributions and the other half as allocated at the discretion of the administrator on the basis of need). By November 1933 the rule-based matching features of the allocation were dispensed with and Hopkins was given full discretion to pass out the funds to the states while taking into account need and state and local contributions to the effort. Hopkins could use this discretionary fiscal power to influence the standards of relief administration within individual states. The original appropriation seriously underestimated the nation's relief needs. The FERA spent roughly $4,000 million between the summer of 1933 and

11. New York was the first state to establish an unemployment relief agency, the Temporary Emergency Relief Administration (TERA) in May 1931. Roosevelt was governor, and Harry Hopkins was appointed the first TERA administrator. By May of 1933, twenty-two states had provided some money for unemployment relief, but not all states had a functioning state relief administration.

the summer of 1935, under a series of emergency Congressional appropriations.

Hopkins made three key administrative decisions in 1933: (a) all relief funds would be spent by public agencies; (b) relief benefits would be set on a case by case basis using a need based standard;[12] (c) FERA would enforce the highest standards of relief administration possible, would use the threat of withholding funds to enforce and persuade state and local relief administrations to meet those standards, and would vigorously prosecute state and local relief officials who used relief for their own political purposes.

With the establishment of these rules, Hopkins began to implement procedures to insure the efficient administration of relief. The FERA initiated a program requiring each state to file monthly financial and administrative reports, detailing case loads, benefit payments, and administrative costs in each county. Hopkins continually pressed states to increase the amount of funding they provided for relief, to raise the standards of relief administration, and to reduce corruption and the political use of relief. But Hopkins was continually frustrated in these efforts. A FERA monthly grant was legally the property of the state it was granted to. Hopkins could only threaten to withhold funds from a state, severely constraining his ability to affect the administration of relief within a state. Eventually, FERA established a division of investigation that looked into over a thousand complaints (ranging from the trivial to the felonious). Yet even here Hopkins became frustrated because FERA's decentralized structure meant that the states were responsible for the investigations and the attention paid to rooting out fraud and corruption varied significantly across states.

The goal of FERA was getting the maximum amount of relief to the largest number of people, quickly, and with a minimum of administrative costs.[13] The state and local share of relief expenditures varied from a high

12. Local relief agencies investigated each case, determined the amount of resources available to each family or individual in need, and then determined the benefits to be paid each month as the difference between the families' available resources and the relief "standard" for families of a given size. This reflected the philosophy of private social work that each case should be treated individually. This opened the door to wrangling about the determination of benefits. On the other hand, it was popular with the social workers who staffed local relief agencies and it gave the entire relief structure an inherent fiscal flexibility. Since benefits were determined case by case on the basis of need, it was relatively easy, when budgets got tight, to reduce all benefits slightly. Had benefits been flat and fixed, adjustments to budget fluctuations would have had to come in the number of cases rather than the generosity of benefits, which was something everyone wanted to avoid. Budget flexibility turned out to be important: the initial FERA appropriation was intended to last two years but was exhausted by the fall of 1933. The FERA received new appropriations roughly every six months. The flow of national, state, and local funds to local relief agencies was never steady.

13. During the winter of 1933–34, Roosevelt established the Civil Works Administration (CWA), which was a temporary program designed to provide jobs for 4 million unemployed. The CWA was a "national" program, in the sense that the federal government issued checks to individual recipients, and CWA administrators nominally worked for the federal government. In effect, the CWA was largely administered by FERA personnel. Most were state and local employees temporarily transferred to the federal government's payroll during the winter.

of 62 percent in Rhode Island to a low of 5.4 percent in Alabama. There was constant friction between FERA and state governments over the administration and financing of relief. Hopkins threatened to withhold FERA grants to several states that refused to increase state contributions. The disputes were significant in twelve states. He made good on his threat to withhold funds in Colorado and Missouri. Dissatisfaction with the way relief was administered led Hopkins to take over, or "federalize," the administration of relief in six states.[14] In North Dakota, Governor Langer was indicted and convicted for extorting kickbacks from federal government employees, although he wiggled out of serving jail time. In Ohio, Governor Davey had a feud with Hopkins over the administration of relief. When Roosevelt finally authorized the federalization of relief in Ohio, his letter began "My Dear Mr. Hopkins: I have examined the evidence concerning corrupt political influence with relief in the State of Ohio. Such interference cannot be tolerated for a moment. I wish you to pursue these investigations diligently and let the chips fall where they may. This administration will not permit the relief population of Ohio to become the innocent victims of either corruption or political chicanery."[15]

Roosevelt reaped enormous political gains from the relief programs: he was seen as the source of relief for millions of American families. At the same time, garnering the credit for relief obligated Roosevelt to bear the political costs of corruption and political manipulation when it was exposed.[16] Roosevelt might be willing to risk appearing to be playing politics in distributing relief funds if he received the benefits. Roosevelt, however, received no direct benefits from corruption and political manipulation by others in the system. Thus, Roosevelt's interest in a system that would not be corrupted or manipulated at the state and local levels were at odds with the interests of individual Democratic senators, congressmen, governors,

14. The six states were Oklahoma, North Dakota, Massachusetts, Ohio, Georgia, and Louisiana. Federal officials federalized relief in Oklahoma on 2/23/34 when the governor announced that he would not apply for relief unless he had control over the distribution; in North Dakota on 3/1/34 as the result of charges that employees of the state relief administration were being assessed for political contributions; for work relief in Massachusetts on 3/7/34 because the state had a statute that all grants from the state had to be distributed on a population basis, not on a need basis; in Ohio on 3/16/35 in a dispute over whether Ohio had supplied a fair share of relief funds; and in Louisiana (4/8/35) and Georgia (4/19/35) due to long-running disputes between the governors and federal administrators over the use of the funds. Hopkins withheld funds from Colorado in December 1933 and from Missouri in April 1935 until the state legislatures produced funds to help pay for relief. Threats to withhold funds went out to Alabama and Kentucky in 1933 and to Illinois in 1934. See E. A. Williams (1939, pp. 170–78, 203–5).

15. As quoted in Brown (1940), p. 210.

16. The "political economy of New Deal spending" literature provides a thorough, but somewhat inconclusive, picture of the overall use of federal allocation of grants between the states for political purposes. See the citations in footnote 1. There is evidence that Hopkins was in direct contact with relief administrations in large cities, including important and influential Democratic machine politicians. See Dorsett (1977).

mayors, and state legislators who benefited much less from relief if they could not use it for their own political purposes.

The decision to make FERA a joint effort of national, state, and local governments was mandated by the national emergency in 1933. There was no other way to spend several billion dollars on relief on short notice without using the existing relief bureaucracy. The decisions made by Harry Hopkins about how relief would be administered inevitably involved setting the interests of the federal government at odds with state and local governments and, critically, involved conflicts between the president and Congress over how the relief program should be structured. Out of the resolution of these conflicts emerged the modern welfare state.

11.4   Relief after 1935

Planning for a more permanent relief system began in 1933. From FERA's beginning its loose administrative structure embroiled Hopkins in arguments with governors and state relief systems across the country about how much financial support state governments would provide, how relief benefits were to be determined, what constituted adequate relief, whether relief was to be given in cash or in kind, and over state and local efforts to bend the administration of relief to serve political ends. Characteristically, Republicans accused Hopkins of playing politics with relief while Democrats accused Hopkins of appointing Republicans to important relief posts. There was no happy medium for Hopkins. His only certain solution to corruption was to create a national relief agency, staffed by civil servants answerable only to Hopkins; that solution was not acceptable to Congress or state and local governments. The compromise reached in 1935 enabled Hopkins and the federal government to put some bounds on the agency problem they faced in allocating federal relief at the local level.[17]

The second stage of New Deal relief administration was marked by the passage of the Emergency Relief Appropriation Act of 1935 (ERAA) and the Social Security Act of 1935 (SSA). The two bills embodied the compromise between the president and the Congress. Both bills were introduced in January; the ERAA was passed in March and the SSA in August. Two distinctions were critical: between employable and unemployable persons and between the emergency and the permanent relief programs. The ERAA appropriated $4.8 billion for the relief of the unemployed, to be spent at the discretion of the president, through agencies unnamed in the bill but to be created under its authority (these ultimately included the WPA, REA, FSA, and NYA). This was emergency legislation: a one-time, temporary appropriation of funds for the relief of employable persons

---

17. The compromise between Congress and Roosevelt in 1935 is studied in detail in Wallis (1991).

(people who would have been employed had it not been for the Depression).[18] The emergency appropriation was intended to tide the country over until the "permanent" relief structure could be put in place.

The SSA created the permanent program. Congress placed old age insurance under the administration of the national Social Security Board. Administration of the categorical relief programs was lodged with state governments and financed by matching national grants. Unemployment insurance was funded by a nationally administered payroll tax. Unemployment insurance (UI) programs were administered by state governments, which could draw on their individual state funds. Because states had a right to draw on their UI funds and the rules in categorical programs called for federal matching of qualified state expenditures, the national government had virtually no control over spending in this part of the welfare system.[19] Although the Social Security Board was responsible for approving the initial design of state programs, actual administration of the programs was left up to the states. Significantly, the board was explicitly prohibited from interfering with personnel policies of the state administration or withholding matching funds because of personnel policies. Control over patronage in unemployment insurance and categorical relief programs was firmly located at the state and local level. The board did have some ability to enforce standards of relief administration, a power that became important later. During the FERA administration, Hopkins had used the threat of withholding funds and federalizing relief to pressure state relief administrations. Those tools were taken away from the national administration in the SSA.

The elements of the compromise were clear. Roosevelt was given a free hand in the administration of emergency relief for the remainder of the Depression. The emergency programs created under the ERAA, of which the WPA was the most important, provided the lion's share of relief for the rest of the 1930s. How Roosevelt used his authority was up to him, subject to Congress's power to approve further appropriations. Congressional Democrats lost the immediate advantage of controlling relief. But their position as the majority party was strengthened by the prospect of Roosevelt's reelection, and they could reasonably expect to share in some of the benefits of administering relief through the normal political process. Roosevelt and Hopkins could not afford to alienate powerful congressional interests. And in the permanent program almost all of the discretionary powers over relief administration had been reserved for the states. There the national government's hands were tied, fiscally and administratively.

Private social welfare professionals were incensed at what they perceived

18. There were also Emergency Relief Appropriation Acts in 1936, 1937, 1938, and 1939.
19. The Social Security Board could exercise fiscal influence in times of crisis. For example, when states exhausted their unemployment insurance trust funds, the board could impose administrative changes on states in return for providing funds.

to be a betrayal of their basic principles. Control over the permanent relief program was given back to the states. National support and administration of relief were abandoned. Responsibility for general relief, relief for those who did not fit into a category of relief supported under the Social Security program, was returned to local governments. Only the needy who were unemployed, aged, blind, or dependent children came under the protection of the federal system. The social welfare professionals feared that the compromise of 1935 cast relief back into the realm of politics: "One of the greatest difficulties in the way of sound organization [after 1935] was political interference with legislation and standards of personnel. . . . The fact remains that much of the confusion and many of the backward steps taken in state and local administration were due to political pressures" (Brown 1940, p. 321).

11.5   Congress and the Politics of Relief: Geography and Jurisdiction

Political institutions that endure must provide political actors with incentives to maintain the system. Prior to 1933, local governments dominated the provision of public relief and the financing of private relief. Accepted wisdom was that local public relief could be used more effectively for political purposes than private relief: relief was more likely to go to the politically connected needy, or at least to those in need willing to pledge their vote; that relief expenditures were likely to line the pockets of patrons; that funds were likely to go to wards or counties where votes mattered; and that administrative jobs went not to those with professional training but those enjoying political patronage. If the New Deal relief programs challenged these local prerogatives, why did politicians elected from state and local constituencies support the New Deal reforms? Or, as many have argued, did elected politicians support New Deal relief programs because they believed that they perpetuated, rather than reformed, the local political abuses of relief?

In this section, we examine the passage of New Deal legislation to determine whether Congress played politics with relief. Did the House and Senate design the rules and administrative authority in the relief bills in ways that enhanced their own gains from the relief programs? First, differences between House and Senate versions of the same bill are examined to see if the two branches of Congress designed the rules for allocating funds between large and small states in a predictable way. Large states are better represented in the House and small states in the Senate. These differences provide a simple and clean test of whether politics mattered in the political economy of New Deal spending. Second, differences between House and Senate versions of the same bill are scrutinized to see if the House was more likely to create administrative discretion and authority at the local level and if the Senate was more likely to create administrative discretion and

Table 11.3   Regressions for the 48 states of the difference in predicted spending between the House and Senate versions of bills on the voting share in House

Act title	Bill number	Constant	Votes	R^2	Critical vote
Emergency Relief and Construction Act of 1932	HR 12445	−0.601 (−1.75)	14.39 (−1.22)	0.03	15.2
Federal Emergency Relief Act of 1933	HR 4606	−0.03 (−0.72)	3.89 (−2.60)	0.13	2.8
Emergency Appropriation Act of 1935	HR 9830	−11.38 (−2.99)	277.51 (−2.71)	0.14	15
Emergency Relief Appropriation Act of 1935	HJR 117	−6.49 (−5.07)	157.26 (−3.59)	0.22	15.1
Emergency Relief Appropriation Act of 1936	HR 12624	−1.38 (−8.22)	33.71 (−5.86)	0.42	14.9
Emergency Relief Appropriation Act of 1938	HJR 361	−0.82 (−2.90)	19.81 (−2.04)	0.08	15.1
Emergency Relief Appropriation Act of 1939	HJR 679	0.18 (−0.27)	−4.13 (−0.18)	0.0007	15.9

Notes and sources: The dependent variable in all regressions is the difference in per capita spending between the House and Senate versions of the bill in each state. The independent variable in each regression is the state's share of total votes in the House of Representatives. There are forty-eight state observations, and all regressions have forty-six degrees of freedom. The *t*-statistics are in parentheses below the coefficients. Allocations in House and Senate bills taken from copies of the bills in the Law Library, Library of Congress, as described in Wallis (1981).

authority at the state level. Since using relief for political ends required administrative discretion, these results give us an indirect indication of what politicians hoped to accomplish by structuring the relief programs in particular ways. The ten important pieces of relief legislation during the New Deal are listed in tables 11.3 and 11.4.

Congress influenced the geographical allocation of relief spending in two ways. First, within a given program legislation could specify that funds be spent in a particular way or according to a given formula. For example, in the Federal Emergency Relief Act, HR 4606 72nd Congress, the Senate bill appropriated $500 million to be divided between a $300 million matching fund ($3 state to $1 national matching rate) and a $200 million discretionary fund to be allocated by the relief administrator. The House bill allocated $250 million to each fund. The Act was ultimately passed with the House allocation. We can compare how the $50 million would have been allocated under the House and Senate versions, using the actual allocation of funds in the discretionary and matching funds to guide the counterfactual. Alternatively, Congress could have distributed funds between programs with different patterns of allocation. In the ERAA of 1935, HR 9830 73rd Congress, the Senate proposed a transfer of $100 million in FERA funds to the Public Works Administration (PWA); the House version did not transfer the funds. Since FERA and the PWA expenditures across

Table 11.4   **Features of relief bills where the Senate version favored state interests over local interests**

		Senate bill favored state over local interests?			
Bill title	Bill number	Money	Patronage	Project selection	Recipient selection
Emergency Relief and Construction Act of 1932	HR 12445	Yes			
Emergency Relief Act of 1933	HR 4606	No	Yes		
Act of February 15, 1934	HR 7527		Yes	Yes	
Emergency Appropriation Act of 1935	HR 9830	Yes			
Emergency Relief Appropriation Act of 1935	HJR 117	Yes	Yes	Yes	
Emergency Relief Appropriation Act of 1936	HJR 12624	Yes	Yes		
Emergency Relief Appropriation Act of 1937	HJR 326		Yes		Yes
Emergency Relief Appropriation Act of 1938	HJR 361	Yes			Yes
Emergency Relief Appropriation Act of 1939	HJR 679	Yes		Yes	Yes

Notes and sources: Entries correspond to differences in the House and Senate versions of each bill, where Yes means that the Senate version favored state over local interests; No means that the Senate version did not favor state over local interests; and blank cells mean that there was no difference in this aspect of the House and Senate versions of the programs. House and Senate bills taken from copies of the bills in the Law Library, Library of Congress, as described in Wallis (1981).

states were different, we can compare the House and Senate allocations by examining how the $100 million would have been spent under the two proposals.

The difference between the House and Senate allocation of funds to state i is

(1) DF_i = House allocation$_i$ − Senate allocation$_i$.

The proposition that the House will allocate more funds to large states better represented in the House than in the Senate can be tested using the regression

(2) $DF_i = a + b \cdot$ Voting Share$_i$,

where the independent variable is the voting share of state i in the House.

The House and Senate differed over the allocation of funds in seven of the ten pieces of New Deal relief legislation. Estimates of equation (2) for those seven bills are shown in table 11.3. The dollar differences ranged between $50 million and $200 million, significant amounts of money but fairly small portions of the overall appropriations. In five of those cases the differences between the House and Senate versions were positively and statistically significantly related to a state's voting share in the House. In the other two cases the coefficients were statistically insignificant, one positive and the other negative. Geographical interests in most cases were an important determinant of differences between the House and Senate.

A curiosity of the regression results lends additional support to the geographic story. We can solve for the voting share in the House that results in no difference between the House and Senate versions (that is, $x = -a/b$ from equation [2]). The last column in table 11.3 lists the implied "critical size" for each regression estimate. In six of the seven cases, states with fifteen votes in the House received more money from the House bill than the Senate bill. Only nine states had 14 or more votes in the House, but the total vote of those states was 217, one vote shy of a majority of the 435 House votes. The nine states that, on average, benefited more from the House version than the Senate version were the minimum number of states required to pass legislation in the House.

The House and Senate allocations differ in systematic and understandable ways. Unemployment, and therefore relief spending at the state level, was concentrated in the large industrial states of the northeast and upper Midwest. These states were much better represented in the House, and the House pursued programs that allocated relative large amounts of money to large states. An important way of doing that was through matching grants, since the more wealthy, industrial, and hard-hit states spent more of their own state and local funds on relief and therefore qualified for larger matching grants. The Senate, on the other hand, tended to prefer (relative to the House) programs and methods of allocation that favored the geographically large, sparsely populated states of the west and Midwest. They preferred allocation formulas, like population or land size, that funneled more money into the west. They also showed a strong preference for large public works projects, like the type conducted by Harold Ickes and the PWA, located primarily in western states with an abundance of public land, over the small, often urban work relief projects conducted by Harry Hopkins and the WPA.[20]

Jurisdictional differences between the House and Senate were more marked and more important than geographic differences. Jurisdictional matters determined which level of government possessed elements of administrative discretion. Geographical differences usually arose over substantial amounts of money but were minor in relation to the whole relief package, and they never proved to be a significant impediment to the passage of legislation. Jurisdictional disputes, however, were fought over central issues of administrative control and, on at least one occasion, were ca-

---

20. The importance of land area in the literature on the political economy of New Deal spending reflects the geographic differences between the east and west. See Wallis (1998) and the ensuing exchange between Fleck (2001) and Wallis (2001).

pable of bringing the whole legislative process to a halt.[21] There were four dimensions of administrative discretion: decisions about money, patronage, project selection, and recipient selection. In general, we expect the House to locate administrative control over these functions at the local level and the Senate to locate control at the state level. table 11.4 lists the ten relief bills, whether there was a difference in one of these four areas, and whether the difference was as expected. An example from each category follows.

Money: The very first relief bill, HR 12445 72nd Congress, authorized the Reconstruction Finance Corporation (RFC) to make loans to the states for relief purposes. The Senate version of the bill restricted RFC loans to the states. Local governments could not apply. The House version of the bill allowed cities to apply directly to the RFC for loans, rather than going through the state government. In this case the House version was adopted.

Patronage: In the ERAA of 1935, the House proposed that any county relief agency be required to hire its administrative employees from the residents of that county, which would have given local relief authorities and congressmen strong control over patronage. The Senate version stipulated that administrative employees within a state had to live within the state, but employees from one county could be hired in another county. Neither restrictive residency requirement survived in the final bill.

Project selection: Under the WPA, a class of projects called "federal projects" were financed and administered directly by the WPA with no state or local sponsorship. The most prominent of these were the art and theater projects. In the Emergency Relief Appropriation Act of 1939, both versions of the bill eliminated all federal theater projects, and the House version of the bill required that any new federal projects have a local spon-

---

21. The case where a jurisdictional dispute prevented any legislation from passing was, interestingly, a relief bill proposed in the last Hoover Congress. The jurisdiction at issue was national versus state. In January of 1932 a bill sponsored by Senators LaFollette and Costigan, 72nd Congress S. 3045, proposed the creation of a Federal Emergency Relief Board that would be given $375 million to allocate between the states for relief purposes and an equal amount for highway construction. Forty percent of the $375 million would be divided between the states on the basis of population, the remainder to be allocated at the discretion of the relief board. The bill failed to pass the Senate, but not because of lack of support for relief. A substitute bill was proposed by Senators Black, Walsh, and Bulkley, which differed in only two ways. The substitute bill provided loans rather than grants and allocated all of the $375 million on the basis of population, thereby eliminating the need for a federal board of any kind. The substitute bill failed by a vote of 48 to 31, and the original bill failed the next day, after extensive debate, by a vote of 48 to 35. Only fifteen senators voted for both bills—in all eighty-one senators had expressed voting support for some kind of relief program. The bill failed to pass because of differences over how the program should be administered, specifically whether the states should answer to a national relief board or be completely free to administer relief on their own. Since only a handful of states had any existing relief program, the struggle in the Senate was over administrative arrangements that might be created, not interests that already existed.

sor. The Senate bill had no provision for local sponsorship. The local sponsorship provision stayed in the final bill.

Recipient selection: There was never a hard and fast legislative decision on who should select the recipients for the WPA. In practice, local relief agencies "referred" potential recipients to the WPA, and it was usually impossible to receive a WPA relief job without the referral.[22] Local relief agencies were not paid, at least not directly, for this task and so effectively remained independent of the WPA. Hopkins and the WPA several times requested funds from Congress to pay local relief agencies for providing referral services, and a provision for payment was included in several Senate bills. In every case the provision was eliminated from the bill by the House. Hopkins was unable to exert even indirect control on local recipient selection by providing money for the referral service, money that could have been withheld or reduced.

These examples are indicative of House and Senate concerns in relief legislation. As table 11.4 shows, differences in the kind of administrative arrangements preferred by the House and Senate were frequent, persistent, and systematic. In seventeen of the eighteen cases where the House and Senate differed over administrative procedures, the differences are as predicted.[23] Both senators and congressmen were interested in locating administrative control of the relief program at the level of government where they exercised the most control.

11.6   Roosevelt's Interests: Comparing the Intrastate Allocation of FERA and WPA Funds

Dividing administrative control over relief between national, state, and local governments was the key element in the compromise of 1935. Congress located administrative control over the permanent categorical relief programs, unemployment insurance, and general relief at the state level. The national government was given control of the emergency relief programs and the permanent social insurance program. Roosevelt and Hopkins were given a blank check for $4.8 billion in the ERAA of 1935. The magnitude of the change in New Deal relief administration cannot be un-

---

22. It was possible to get a nonrelief WPA job without a referral. These jobs were either supervisory or administrative. See Howard (1943, pp. 356–65) for a discussion of referral policy.

23. The one anomaly is a special case. In the original Federal Emergency Relief Act the Senate inserted a provision enabling the federal government to take over the administration of relief in a state. This was called "federalizing" relief, and it clearly weakened state independence, which we would not expect the Senate to do. Later, in 1934, Senator McAdoo from California asked Hopkins to federalize relief in California, because he was in a political battle with the faction of the party controlling the relief administration. It appears that the anomaly in table 11.5 was the result of the anticipated political gains that would come to Senators from "federalization." Those gains, it turns out, never materialized.

derestimated. Although control of the permanent welfare program remained largely with the states, the permanent program took time to implement. For the remainder of the 1930s and the depression, the national government would be the largest provider of relief in the country, and the ERAA of 1935 gave Roosevelt and Hopkins wide latitude and discretion in how they administered that relief.

The WPA succeeded FERA as the primary national program for the relief of the unemployed. Like FERA, the WPA under Hopkins provided work relief to over 2 million cases each month. Under the FERA structure, Hopkins had not possessed the discretion to allocate funds within states. When a state strayed from the administration's goals, the public was likely to blame the Roosevelt administration as much as or more than they blamed the state and local politicians. To guide the state back to the proper path, Hopkins could try friendly persuasion or go to the extreme of withdrawing funds or federalizing relief. But he had no intermediate punishments. This was not a problem under the centralized structure of the WPA. The WPA's administrative employees worked directly for the federal government, and the WPA administrators controlled the intrastate allocations of WPA funds.[24]

The next section examines the WPA rules and procedures adopted by Hopkins to control illegal corruption in the distribution of relief. This section examines how centralization limited political manipulation in the distribution of funds. Roosevelt's critics argued that greater federal control under the WPA allowed Roosevelt and Hopkins to better manipulate relief allocations for political purposes. If we are correct that Hopkins and Roosevelt sought to limit political manipulation by state and local officials within the states, we should see that the distribution of relief within states more closely matched the stated goals of relief, recovery, and reform under the WPA than under FERA and that political considerations had less influence on intrastate allocations under the WPA than under FERA. Information on the allocation of WPA and FERA spending from over 3,000 counties is used to examine the differences in the intrastate distribution of WPA and FERA funds. In order to compare allocation policies directly, the values for every variable (dependent and independent) for each county are normalized by subtracting the state mean for that variable and then by dividing the difference by the standard deviation within the same state. As a result every variable has a mean of zero and a standard deviation of 1 within each state. This facilitates comparison of the coefficients determining spending for FERA, the WPA, and the difference between the two pro-

---

24. There is one caveat. The WPA's grants were not distributed in the absence of state and local activity. States and local jurisdictions lobbied for and spent resources to obtain funds from both FERA and the WPA. Some of the difference in the distribution within states under the WPA and the FERA may reflect differences in state and local behavior, as well as differences in Hopkins's administrative policy.

grams.[25] We include key variables that influence the distribution of relief grants, as discussed in the literature on the allocation of New Deal funds.

One group of variables measures economic conditions across counties that reflect the New Deal's stated goals of relieving financial distress, promoting recovery, and redistributing income. Relief spending should have been positively related to a measure of unemployment (measured in the 1930 census), negatively related to economic growth from 1929 to 1933 (measured as the change in log retail sales per capita between 1929 and 1933), negatively related to a measure of the share of high-income people (the percent of the population paying income taxes in 1929), and negatively related to a measure of average consumption in 1929 (retail sales per capita in 1929). Unemployment relief programs were targeted at urban areas, so the coefficient on percent urban should be positive.

The second group of variables reflects political factors. The Roosevelt administration may have used the allocation of funds to promote their prospects for reelection by rewarding long-term loyal Democrats (measured by the mean percent voting Democrat in presidential elections from 1896 through 1928), by trying to attract voters who were relatively fickle in their support of the Democrats (measured by the standard deviation of the percent voting Democrat from 1896 through 1928), by rewarding voters who swung to Roosevelt in 1932 (the percent voting for Roosevelt in 1932 minus the mean percent voting Democrat from 1896 through 1928), or by spending more in areas with higher turnout (the number of presidential votes in 1932 relative to the population in 1930).[26]

The first two specifications in table 11.5 show the results for the WPA and FERA separately. With regard to the economic variables, both programs provided more funds per capita in urban areas, provided more funds in counties with higher unemployment, and provided fewer funds to higher-income counties as measured by retail sales per capita. The FERA provided more funds, while the WPA provided fewer funds, to counties with higher tax returns per capita. On the political side, both FERA and WPA gave less money to counties that traditionally voted Democratic and more money to counties that swung to Roosevelt in 1932 and that had higher voter turnout. The FERA gave more funds to counties with higher variance in their party voting, while the WPA gave less to these counties.

---

25. We have also explored using the ratio of the county observation to the state mean and had the same general results. We have also run the analysis by demeaning the variable but not normalizing. Demeaning the variables does not completely eliminate the scale differences between the WPA and the FERA. The WPA spent more money, so that the variance in spending was likely to be higher. In such a situation the WPA and FERA could have responded to the same differences in unemployment by raising spending by 5 percent in that county, but because the WPA spent more on average, the 5 percent will generate a larger coefficient for the WPA than for the FERA.

26. See Wright (1974); Fleck (1994, 1999, 2001); Wallis (1998, 2001); and Fishback, Kantor, and Wallis (2003) for empirical analysis of relief spending using these variables.

Table 11.5   Comparison of regression coefficients for factors determining the intrastate allocation of FERA and WPA funds across counties

Variable	WPA (1)	FERA (2)	WPA minus FERA (3)
% urban, 1930	0.216	0.125	0.091
	(7.54)	(4.29)	(3.27)
Tax returns per capita, 1929	–0.005	0.076	–0.081
	(–0.15)	(2.52)	(–2.79)
Retail sales per capita, 1929	–0.208	–0.153	–0.055
	(–6.74)	(–4.87)	(–1.84)
Retail sales per capita growth, 29–33	–0.016	–0.13	0.114
	(–0.87)	(–7.03)	(6.44)
% unemployed, 1930	0.282	0.227	0.055
	(13.9)	(11.04)	(2.77)
Democratic loyalty, 1896–1928	–0.061	–0.069	0.008
	(–3.28)	(–3.64)	(0.43)
Swing, 1896–1932	–0.034	0.03	–0.064
	(–1.74)	(1.48)	(–3.33)
Turnout, 1932	0.048	0.078	–0.03
	(2.63)	(4.21)	(–1.69)
Roosevelt swing, 1932	0.048	0.056	–0.008
	(2.25)	(2.60)	(–0.4)
R^2	0.127	0.099	0.037
Adjusted R^2	0.124	0.097	0.034
No. of observations	3061	3061	3061

Notes and sources: *t*-statistics in parentheses. The unit of observation is the county. The values for the county for each variable have been normalized by subtracting the state mean and dividing by the state standard deviation. WPA and FERA spending information is from the U.S. Office of Government Reports (1940). It was converted to per capita spending by dividing by the population in 1930. Retail sales information from 1933 is from U.S. Department of Commerce, Bureau of Foreign and Domestic Commerce (1936). The 1929 retail sales information, percent urban in 1930, population in 1930 and 1940, and the ratio of unemployed to gainfully employed in 1930 are from the update of historical, demographic, economic, and social data for the United States from 1790 by Michael Haines and ICPSR (2005). The population figures used to create our per capita estimates for 1929 and 1933 retail spending were calculated using linear interpolations of the 1930 and 1940 populations. The tax return information comes from U.S. Department of Commerce, Bureau of Foreign and Domestic Commerce (1932). The mean Democratic share of the presidential vote from 1896 to 1928, the percent voting for Roosevelt in 1932 minus the mean Democratic share from 1896 to 1928, the standard deviation of the Democratic share of the presidential vote from 1896 to 1932, and the percent of adults voting in 1932 were all calculated using information from ICPSR's (1999, no. 1) U.S. Historical Election Returns, 1824–1968. The data set consists of 3,061 counties and county-city combinations in the United States. The New Deal program information was reported for some combined counties. For a list see Fishback, Kantor, and Wallis (2003, pp. 304–5).

Our specific interest, however, is in the differences between the responses of the FERA and the WPA to key variables; therefore, we focus on the third specification in table 11.5 where the dependent variable is per capita WPA spending minus per capita FERA spending. The results of the comparison are consistent with our view that when Hopkins gained more control of the intrastate allocations he reduced state and local political manipulation by focusing spending more on relief, recovery, and reform.

The WPA distributed relatively more funds within states to areas with greater unemployment, lower economic activity, and a higher urban share of the population. Because of the way the variables were scaled, a one-unit change in a variable represents a change of 1 standard deviation in each variable. A 1 standard deviation increase in the unemployment rate produced an increase in WPA funds that was 0.055 standard deviations larger than the response by FERA. A similar increase in retail sales per capita in 1929, our measure of economic activity, was associated with a reduction in WPA spending that was .08 standard deviations greater than for FERA spending. A 1 standard deviation increase in percent urban led to a response by the WPA that was .09 standard deviations larger. All three differences are statistically significant. The differential response in WPA and FERA spending in urban areas is particularly telling. Representation in state legislatures was skewed in favor of rural areas. The national government was already distributing large amounts of aid to farmers through agricultural programs. Hopkins wanted FERA and the WPA to focus on relief of unemployed workers, not low-income farmers. Thus, when Hopkins gained control under the WPA he managed to shift funds back to urban areas. There is one exception in our findings. The FERA was more responsive to the depths of the crash between 1929 and 1933, as measured by the growth (or reduction) in retail sales per capita in those years.

The results in table 11.5 for the political variables suggest that Hopkins and Roosevelt resisted the temptation to take advantage of greater discretion by more vigorously pursuing political goals when they gained more control under the WPA. The effects of long-term swing voters and voter turnout on intrastate allocations were statistically significantly lower by 0.06 and 0.03 for the WPA than for FERA, respectively. The response to the Roosevelt swing voters was also lower under the WPA but not in a statistically significant way.

The major bone of contention in the political economy of New Deal spending debate is whether economic or political factors influenced the allocation of federal spending. These results clearly show that when control over the intrastate allocation of relief funds shifted from state and local politicians to Hopkins the political influence on intrastate allocations was reduced and intrastate allocations were more responsive to economic conditions.

11.7   Rules and Procedures

The switch from the FERA to the WPA offered Hopkins more than greater discretion over how relief funds were allocated within states. It also gave him more central authority over the monitoring of relief administration. The WPA continued FERA's efforts to collect financial information from state and local agencies in a timely manner. Because WPA funds were federal funds, the WPA was better able to audit the finances on individual projects whether the projects were carried out by state or local governments or by the WPA itself. Administrative discretion was reduced in several areas. The WPA introduced a "security wage" policy that set the wages of WPA employees according to a formula that took into account the employees' skill, the size of the locality in which the work was performed, and the prevailing wage for work in the area. Hours of work and standards of construction on WPA projects were more closely controlled.

The move from the FERA to the WPA allowed Hopkins to reorganize and strengthen the investigations of complaints concerning improper administration of relief and corruption. Under FERA such investigations were carried out by small staffs at the federal or state level. The administration of relief "was a new problem and a new field of investigative work," and the approaches taken were as "variable as the number of states themselves" (WPA Division of Investigation 1943, p. 1). The FERA established a Division of Special Inquiry in October 1934 that operated out of the Washington, D.C. office. Investigative efforts often were uncoordinated and were hampered at times by the transfer of legal ownership of relief funds to the state on reception of the grant. States, as a result, were the primary investigators when charges were raised.

Roosevelt's executive order creating the WPA established a "division of progress investigation" designed "to coordinate the pertinent work of existing investigating agencies of the government so as to insure the honest execution of the relief programs" (WPA 1943, p. 4). The division had its own director and field organization directly responsible to the administrator. The functions of the division

> covered the investigation of all complaints alleging fraud or loss to the government or violations of Federal statutes as they applied to the expenditure of relief funds. More specifically these functions included the handling of complaints that funds were being diverted to private rather than public benefit; that false statements had been made in obtaining allocations or benefits from relief money; that pay rolls for either personal services or the rental of equipment by WPA were being padded; complaints of extortion or kickbacks, of theft or embezzlement, or bribery or the collection of illegal fees; that false compensation claims had been filed by WPA employees or that fraud existed in competitive bidding on government contracts; that vendors to the government were not delivering in line with their contracts; that forgery had been committed in work assignments, time reports, or other official documents, and other less common types of fraud in the handling of federal funds. (WPA 1943, p. 5)

The division later investigated violations of the Hatch Act, prohibiting "pernicious political activity" and provisions passed by Congress in 1939 preventing aliens from receiving WPA employment.

A staff of fifty was based in Washington, supplemented by field offices in fifteen cities, originally, and later in the regional offices. The number of field agents peaked in number at seventy-three, supplemented by "resident agents" throughout the country.[27] There were plenty of complaints. The records of the investigative division take up 415 cubic feet plus numerous rolls of microfilm in the national archives. In 1937 alone, the division conducted 3,280 investigations.

The division evaluated complaints, investigated them if necessary, and then, if a problem was found, turned cases over to the attorney general's office for prosecution. The division investigated and reported on 17,352 cases. In 8,811 of these the charges were substantiated. A total of 2,215 were referred to the attorney general for criminal prosecution. Of the remaining 6,596 substantiated cases, 4,496 persons were dismissed, demoted, suspended, reprimanded, or debarred. When a subcommittee of the Committee on Appropriations of the House investigated the WPA in 1940 they could not uncover a single serious irregularity that had not previously been investigated by the division.

The switch from the FERA to the WPA gave Hopkins a great deal more authority over the activities of state and local WPA projects. It is clear that he took this opportunity to establish better monitoring of the programs. He and Roosevelt were concerned that charges of corruption left to fester and later be uncovered by congressional investigations would significantly damage the success of the program and ultimately the administration. Therefore, they established a more centralized investigative division that routinely investigated complaints and pressed for the prosecution of political manipulation and criminal corruption.

11.8   Concluding Remarks

The modern American welfare state was created during the New Deal. Prior to 1933, the burden of caring for the needy and unemployed fell on local governments. By late 1935, a system of nationally funded and administered old age insurance was in place; federally funded and state-administered programs providing old age assistance, aid to dependent children, aid to the blind, and UI were in place; and a substantial emergency relief structure with both national and state components was working to see the nation through the last years of the Depression. Before 1932, the administration of public relief was widely regarded as politically corrupt, a concern so prevalent that a significant portion of the nation's relief systems were administered by private social welfare agencies. Although political opponents of the New Deal often complained about the use of relief for po-

---

27. Agents were often young, and 85 percent had professional or college training as lawyers, accountants, and engineers. A number had been investigators for the Federal Bureau of Investigation (FBI) or in other settings.

litical purposes, by 1940, charges of corruption and political manipulation had diminished considerably. Corruption and political manipulation within the relief programs were reduced. How this contributed to the overall level of corruption and political manipulation in the political system within the New Deal is not clear. The importance of political machines is often claimed to have declined over the course of the New Deal, partly because the provision of national relief undercut the provision of local relief by the machines. But as we have documented, part of the relief system remained in the administrative hands of the local governments, albeit with more supervision from the Social Security Board.[28]

The transformation of public relief in the United States occurred because of the political interests of President Roosevelt and his administration. Local officials, state politicians, and members of Congress were in a position to use relief for political purposes: getting politically connected people on relief, letting contracts for materials and supplies to political allies, and using administrative jobs to reward loyal followers. Roosevelt, on the other hand, had little use for this type of political machination. The gratitude of millions of relief recipients and the general public impression that the administration was moving decisively to relieve the worst victims of the Depression garnered votes for Roosevelt. That support would have evaporated if relief had been administered in a visibly corrupt manner.

The Federal Emergency Relief Administration, the first New Deal relief program, was created in the spring of 1933 to rapidly distribute millions of dollars to families in immediate need of financial assistance. It was impossible for Roosevelt and Hopkins to solve the agency problem they faced. The crisis forced them to distribute relief money through the established local public relief administrations; it was the only existing structure capable of administering relief to over 4 million families each month. Inevitably, some of the $4 billion distributed to states between 1933 and 1935 was used to further the political ends of state and local politicians. The FERA's loose administrative structure did not give Roosevelt and Hopkins the administrative tools to limit local politicians from capturing some of the rents for themselves. As we have seen, Congress was complicit in the political maneuvering. The Senate persistently sought to allocate more money to small states well represented in the Senate, while the House worked to allocate more money to large states better represented in the House. The Senate tried to locate administrative control of relief at the state level, and the House tried to locate control at the local level. Both

---

28. Dorsett concludes his study of the New Deal and the machines this way: "The second wrong assumption is that the federal government, by assuming responsibility for welfare programs, thereby destroyed the machine's useful role as a service institution. Actually, the distribution function was not preempted by the federal government: under the New Deal many welfare programs were financed in Washington, but they were *directed* at the local level" (p. 113).

were generally hostile to locating administrative control at the national level.

The deal struck in 1935 with the passage of the Emergency Relief Appropriations Act and the Social Security Act gave the Roosevelt administration authority over the distribution of emergency relief. Congress ensured, however, that states retained control over important elements of the permanent relief program—unemployment insurance, aid to the blind, old age assistance, and aid to dependent children—but were subject to federal oversight. Although we stress the difference in the interests of Congress and the executive branch, this should not obscure the importance that all Democrats placed on reelecting Roosevelt. Giving Roosevelt control over the emergency relief program allowed him to claim credit for providing relief and employment to millions of families every month. Voters responded by supporting Roosevelt. When Roosevelt and Hopkins obtained more control over the intrastate allocation of WPA relief funds, they targeted the allocation of funds within states more at the high-minded goals of relief, recovery, and reform and resisted increasing the role of presidential politics.

The other side of the bargain gave states more control over the administration of categorical relief and unemployment insurance, as well as complete fiscal autonomy. But state independence came with a catch. The Social Security Board could not force states to spend more or less on relief, nor could it decide who would staff administrative positions, but it could and did require that relief be administered in a fair and impartial manner. The development of welfare entitlements and the evolution of higher standards of welfare administration in the states under the watchful eye of the Social Security Board are a subject beyond our current story.

Our explanation for why the New Deal relief policies sought to reduce corruption and political manipulation does not imply that Roosevelt did not play politics with relief. It was in Roosevelt's political interest to reduce political manipulation and corruption in the administration of relief at the state and local level. It was political interest, and not only enlightened social policy, that contributed to the reduction in corruption.

References

Alston, Lee, and Joseph Ferrie. 1999. *Southern paternalism and the American welfare state: Economics, politics, and institutions in the South, 1865–1965.* New York: Cambridge University Press.

Anderson, G. M., and R. D. Tollison. 1991. Congressional influence and patterns of New Deal spending, 1933–1939. *Journal of Law and Economics* 34 (April): 161–75.

Arrington, L. 1969. The New Deal in the West: A preliminary statistical inquiry. *Pacific Historical Review* 38 (August): 311–16.

————. 1970. Western agriculture and the New Deal. *Agricultural History* 49 (October): 337–51.

Brock, William R. 1988. *Welfare, democracy, and the New Deal.* New York: Cambridge University Press.

Brown, Josephine C. 1940. *Public relief 1929–1939.* New York. Henry Holt.

Columbia University Press. 2005. Rural electrification administration. *The Columbia electronic encyclopedia,* 6th ed. New York. http://www.infoplease.com/ce6/history/A0842689.html.

Couch, Jim F., and William F. Shugart. 1998. *The political economy of the New Deal.* Cheltenham, UK: Edward Elgar.

————. 2000. New Deal spending and the states: The politics of public works. In *Public choice interpretations of American economic history,* ed. J. Heckelman, J. Moorhouse, and R. Whaples, 105–22. Boston: Kluwer Academic.

Dorsett, Lyle W. 1977. *Franklin Roosevelt and the city bosses.* Port Washington, NY: Kennikat Press.

Fishback, Price, Shawn Kantor, and John Joseph Wallis. 2003. Can the New Deal's three R's be rehabilitated? A program-by-program, county-by-county analysis. *Explorations in Economic History* 40 (July): 278–307.

Fishback, Price and, Melissa Thomasson. Forthcoming. Social welfare spending. In *The millennial edition of the historical statistics of the United States,* ed. Susan Carter, Scott S. Gartner, Michael R. Haines, Alan L. Olmstead, Richard Sutch, and Gavin Wright. New York: Cambridge University Press.

Fleck, Robert K. 1994. Essays on the political economy of the New Deal. PhD diss., Stanford University.

Fleck, Robert K. 1999. The value of the vote: A model and test of the effects of turnout on distributive policy. *Economic Inquiry* 37 (October): 609–23.

————. 2001. Population, land, economic conditions and the allocation of New Deal spending. *Explorations in Economic History* 38 (April): 296–304.

Haines, Michael R., and the Inter-university Consortium for Political and Social Research (ICPSR). 2005. Historical, demographic, economic, and social data: The United States, 1790–2000 [computer file]. ICPSR version no. 2896. Hamilton, NY: Colgate University and Ann Arbor, MI: ICPSR [producers], 2004. Ann Arbor, MI: ICPSR [distributor].

Howard, Donald S. 1943. *The WPA and federal relief policy.* New York: Russell Sage Foundation.

Inter-university Consortium for Political and Social Research (ICPSR). 1999. *United States historical election returns, 1824–1968* [computer file]. Number 1. 2nd ICPSR ed. Ann Arbor, MI: ICPSR.

Katz, Michael B. 1986. *In the shadow of the poor house: A social history of welfare in America.* New York: Basic Books.

Leuchtenberg, W. E. 1963. *Franklin D. Roosevelt and the New Deal, 1932–1940.* New York: Harper and Row.

National Resources Planning Board. 1942. *Security, work, and relief policies.* Washington, DC: Government Printing Office.

Patterson, James T. 1967. *Congressional conservatism and the New Deal.* Lexington: University of Kentucky Press.

————. 1986. *America's struggle against poverty, 1900–1985.* Cambridge, MA: Harvard University Press.

Piven, Frances Fox, and Richard Cloward. 1993. *Regulating the poor: The function of public welfare.* 2nd ed. New York: Vintage.

Reading, D. C. 1973. New Deal activity and the states. *Journal of Economic History* 36 (December): 792–810.

Social Security Administration. 1941. *Social Security Bulletin* 4 (February).

U.S. Department of Commerce, Bureau of Foreign and Domestic Commerce. 1936. *Consumer market data handbook.* Washington, DC: Government Printing Office.

U.S. Office of Government Reports, Statistical Section. 1940. Report No. 10, Vol. II. Washington, DC. Mimeograph.

Wallis, John Joseph. 1981. Work relief and unemployment in the 1930s. PhD diss., University of Washington.

———. 1984. The birth of the old federalism: Financing the New Deal. *Journal of Economic History* 44 (March): 139–59.

———. 1987. Employment, politics, and economic recovery during the Great Depression. *Review of Economics and Statistics* 59 (August): 516–20.

———. 1989. Employment in the Great Depression: New data and hypotheses. *Explorations in Economic History* 26 (January): 45–72.

———. 1991. The political economy of New Deal fiscal federalism. *Economic Inquiry* 29 (July): 510–24.

———. 1998. The political economy of New Deal spending, revisited, with and without Nevada. *Explorations in Economic History* 35 (April): 140–70.

———. 2001. The political economy of New Deal spending, yet again: A reply to Fleck. *Explorations in Economic History* 38 (April): 305–14.

Wallis, John Joseph, and W. E. Oates. 1998. The impact of the New Deal on American federalism. In *The defining moment: The Great Depression and the American economy in the twentieth century,* ed. M. Bordo, C. Goldin, and E. White, 155–80. Chicago: University of Chicago Press.

Williams, E. A. 1939. *Federal aid for relief.* New York: Columbia University Press.

Works Progress Administration (WPA) Division of Investigation. 1943. The division of investigation of the Work Projects Administration. Unpublished mimeograph. WPA Records of Division of Investigation, 1934–1943, Record Group 69, General Records, box 13.

Wright, G. 1974. The political economy of New Deal spending. *Review of Economics and Statistics* 59 (February): 30–38.

Contributors

Howard Bodenhorn
Department of Economics
110 Williams Simon Center
Lafayette College
Easton, PA 18042-1776

David Cutler
Department of Economics
Harvard University
Cambridge, MA 02138

Stanley L. Engerman
Department of Economics
University of Rochester
Rochester, NY 14627

Price V. Fishback
Department of Economics
University of Arizona
Tucson, AZ 85721

Matthew Gentzkow
Graduate School of Business
University of Chicago
5807 South Woodlawn Avenue
Chicago, IL 60637

Edward L. Glaeser
Department of Economics
315A Littauer Center
Harvard University
Cambridge, MA 02138

Claudia Goldin
Department of Economics
Harvard University
Cambridge, MA 02138

Shawn Kantor
School of Social Sciences, Humanities,
   and Arts
University of California, Merced
P.O. Box 2039
Merced, CA 95344

Naomi R. Lamoreaux
Department of Economics
University of California,
   Los Angeles
405 Hilgard Avenue
Los Angeles, CA 90095-1477

Marc T. Law
Department of Economics
Old Mill Building
94 University Place
University of Vermont
Burlington, VT 05405-0114

Gary D. Libecap
Karl Eller Center, College
   of Business
McClelland Hall 202
University of Arizona
Tucson, AZ 85721-0108

Rebecca Menes
Department of Economics
George Mason University
4400 University Drive, MSN 3G4
Fairfax, VA 22030-4444

Grant Miller
National Bureau of Economic
    Research
1050 Massachusetts Avenue
Cambridge, MA 02138

Jean-Laurent Rosenthal
Bunche Hall 9262
Department of Economics
University of California,
    Los Angeles
Box 951477
Los Angeles, CA 90095-1477

Kenneth L. Sokoloff
Department of Economics
University of California,
    Los Angeles
Los Angeles, CA 90095-1477

Werner Troesken
Department of History
University of Pittsburgh
Pittsburgh, PA 15260

John Joseph Wallis
Department of Economics
University of Maryland
College Park, MD 20742

Author Index

Subject Index